HOSPITALITY MANAGEMENT

A human resources approach

SECOND EDITION

Laurie J Mullins

Principal Lecturer
University of Portsmouth

PITMAN
PUBLISHING

PITMAN PUBLISHING
128 Long Acre, London WC2E 9AN

A Division of Longman Group Limited

© Laurie J Mullins 1992, 1995
© Chapter 11 T. McEwan 1992, 1995

First published in 1992
Second Edition 1995

British Library Cataloguing in Publication Data
A catalogue record for this book can be obtained from the British Library.

ISBN 0-273-60502-X

10 9 8 7 6 5 4 3 2 1

Typeset by M Rules
Printed and bound by Clays Ltd, St Ives plc

The Publishers' policy is to use paper from sustainable forests.

To my wife, Pamela.
With a special mention for Kelvin,
and also for Brigitte in America.

CONTENTS

LIST OF FIGURES

IN ACKNOWLEDGEMENT AND APPRECIATION

A very special tribute is due to my wife Pamela, my children, my father and my family. Also to the loving memory of my mother. I am deeply appreciative of their constant interest, encouragement and moral support.

I wish also to record my gratitude and thanks to the following.

- Colleagues at the University of Portsmouth Business School. A particular acknowledgement and thank you to Tom McEwan who has written Chapter 11 on Communication in Organisations, and to Linda Hicks for her contribution to the section on sex stereotyping and gender in Chapter 2.
- Colleagues Gerry Banks, Martin Brunner, Karen Meudell and Freddie Watts for their assistance with the preparation of case material.
- Members of the Management Department, University of Wisconsin-Whitewater, USA, for their friendship and support to myself and my wife during an academic exchange and at the time of preparing this second edition. Also to my daughter Tracey Voller for maintaining the British link and her invaluable assistance with permissions.
- Christine Clements, Hospitality and Tourism Services, New Mexico State University, and Bharath Josiam, Hospitality and Tourism, University of Wisconsin-Stout for their contribution of the section on service management in Chapter 1.
- Senior publisher Penelope Woolf and colleagues at Pitman Publishing.
- Those managers who have kindly given permission to reproduce information from their organisations.
- Stella and Paul Silver, proprietors of Luccombe Chine House Country Hotel, Isle of Wight, for providing such an excellent example of hospitality management and personal service delivery (including the 'special' menus).

LAURIE J MULLINS

ABOUT THIS BOOK

The central theme of this book is improved organisational performance through the effective management of human resources – that is, the management of people.

Although the title of 'hospitality' is at present increasingly popular as a generic term to cover a wide range of different sectors within the hotel and catering industry, the use of terminology varies and headings are subject to different interpretation. But whatever the headings, no one book of manageable size could hope to cover adequately all sectors of the industry or all aspects of such a wide area of study.

The broad and variable nature of hotel operations means that they can be seen to embrace, to a greater or lesser extent, elements of associated sectors of the hospitality industry, and to exhibit a wider and more diverse range of organisational and staffing characteristics.

For this reason, and in order to obtain a reasonable level of depth and analysis, the book focuses primarily on the mainstream sector of hotel management. However, for the purposes of context and comparison, reference is made also to the hospitality industry in its generic sense.

Aims of the book

The aims of this book are to:

- indicate ways in which performance may be improved through the better use of human resources;
- examine the relevance and applications of general management theory and principles;
- present an integrated view embracing both theory and practice;
- balance academic rigour with a pragmatic approach to the subject area.

Within the scope of this book it is clearly not possible to provide detailed coverage of all aspects influencing human resource management. Rather, the intention is to enhance understanding and appreciation of the subject area, and to suggest to the reader an analytical framework in which you may think about what has been read and explore specific applications within the industry.

The book concentrates on the nature and structure of work organisations, the process of management and styles of managerial behaviour, and achieving results through the efforts of other people. Certain organisational processes, for example delegation and recruitment and selection, require managers to give attention to basic principles and procedures. Accordingly the objective analysis of hospitality operations is supported, where appropriate, by a more prescriptive stance to the execution of work.

It is intended that this book will appeal to students at undergraduate, professional or post-experience level who are aspiring to a managerial position. It is also hoped that the book will appeal to practising managers and supervisors who wish to extend their knowledge of the subject area.

The book provides a basis for the critical appraisal of organisational and managerial processes which influence the behaviour and performance of people in the hospitality industry. Hopefully this will encourage the reader to be more aware of, and sensitive to, the importance of the effective management of human resources – that is, the management of people.

PLAN OF THE BOOK

CHAPTER 1
The nature of the hospitality industry

CHAPTER 2
Working with people

| **CHAPTER 3** Organisational design and structure | **CHAPTER 4** The nature of managerial work | **CHAPTER 5** Manager– subordinate relationship | **CHAPTER 6** The personnel function |

CHAPTER 7
The execution of work

| **CHAPTER 8** Motivating the workforce | **CHAPTER 9** Group behaviour and performance | **CHAPTER 10** Managerial leadership | **CHAPTER 11** Communication in organisations |

CHAPTER 12
Improving organisational performance

GUIDE TO YOUR STUDY OF THIS BOOK

This book adopts an applied approach to the analysis of general concepts and principles of organisation and management, and their relevance to hospitality operations.

The format of the book is clearly structured and written with a minimum of technical terminology. Each chapter is fully supported with diagrams and contains:

- a short introduction and synopsis of contents;
- a summary of key points;
- review and discussion questions;
- practical assignments and/or case studies; and
- comprehensive notes and references.

There is a logical flow to the sequence of topic areas with appropriate cross-referencing between chapters. However, each chapter is self-contained, and the selection and order of chapters can be varied to suit personal preferences or the demands of your particular course of study.

The review and discussion questions provide a basis for revision, and a test of your understanding and knowledge of the chapter contents. The questions, assignments and case studies provide an opportunity to think about the major issues of each chapter, and to discuss and compare views with colleagues.

The notes and references at the end of each chapter should help you to pursue further any issues of particular interest. In order to provide more detailed and specific referencing, and to keep the main text uncluttered, a simple numbering system has been chosen. This system appears to be favoured by most readers. The thoughts and ideas of other people are not always distinguishable clearly from one's own. Whilst I have made every effort to give references to the work of other writers, I apologise to any concerned if acknowledgement has inadvertently not been recorded.

You are encouraged to complement your reading of the book by drawing upon your own practical experience. Search for good and bad strategies and examples of human resource management within the hospitality industry, and consider reasons for their apparent success or failure.

TACKLING CASE STUDIES

The case studies in this book provide you with an opportunity to demonstrate analytical ability, logical thinking, judgement and persuasiveness in the presentation of answers. Where the case study is undertaken as a group exercise, it also provides a means of assessing the ability of individuals to work effectively as members of the group and the performance of the group as a whole.

Guidelines for tackling case studies

The level and depth of analysis, and the type of answer required, will depend upon the particular case study. It is possible, however, to suggest general guidelines to help you in tackling case studies.

(i) Read through the whole of the case study in order to get a 'feel' for what it is about. Where appropriate, check what the question(s) ask you to do and whether you are to assume a specific role, for example the general manager of a hotel.

(ii) Now read the case study a second time. Look at the material carefully and attempt to identify with the particular situations and the characters involved.

(iii) Approach your analysis of the case study with an open mind. Avoid any predispositions which may influence your perception of the case material. Do not formulate hard opinions until you have collated all the available evidence. And do not jump to hasty or unfounded conclusions.

(iv) Adopt a brainstorming approach and take the case apart by exploring all reasonably possible considerations. You may need to search for hidden meanings and issues which are not at first readily apparent. Remember there may be a number of separate or related matters and a number of alternative courses of action.

(v) A particular feature of case study work is that you are likely to have only limited information. You should, therefore, make a point of studying all the details in order, firstly to make certain of the facts, and secondly to identify what deductions or inferences can be drawn from these facts. It will probably be necessary to make certain assumptions which should follow *reasonably* from the case material and serve to clarify the situation. **Make clear any necessary, reasonable assumptions as part of your answer.**

(vi) The case study may set out deliberately to present a tangle of information, events or situations which need to be unravelled. Attempt to clarify links and relationships, and to distinguish causes from effects. Concentrate on what you see to be the most important matters.

(vii) Where appropriate, relate your analysis of the case material to your studies and reading, general points of principle and relevant practical experience.

(viii) Consider how the use of visual displays such as diagrams, charts or tables may enhance the presentation of your answer. But do not be tempted to use visual displays just for their own sake, and make sure they are meaningful, accurate and clear.

(ix) Draw up a plan of key points as the basis for your answer. Identify clearly existing or potential difficulties or problem areas. Where you have identified a number of possible courses of action, indicate where you see the need for most urgent action and your recommended priorities. Bear in mind practical considerations such as priorities and timing, costs, existing personalities and likely effects on staff.

(x) Where appropriate, include a list of references and/or a bibliography.

1
THE NATURE OF THE HOSPITALITY INDUSTRY

INTRODUCTION

The hospitality industry does have a number of characteristic features, but it also shares important common features with other business industries and faces the same general problems of organisation and management. Attention should be given to ways in which ideas drawn from general management theory and practice can be applied with advantage to the industry.[1]

This chapter looks at:
- General management theory
- The organisational setting
- The hospitality industry
- The hotel industry
- Organisational and staffing characteristics
- The nature of hotel services
- Service management
- The open systems model of analysis
- Applications to hospitality management
- Environmental influences
- The analysis of hotel operations
- Organisational goals, objectives and policy
- The profit motive and performance objectives
- Social responsibilities of management
- Strategic planning

GENERAL MANAGEMENT THEORY

Managers in hotels and catering tend to view the industry as unique, to regard it as somehow special and unlike any other industry. But to what extent is such a view justified? According to Fearn, writing in 1971, management in the hotel and catering industry has not developed at the same pace as in other industries:

> . . . little progress has been made in terms of management attitudes, knowledge and thinking. When one considers the astounding management progress in industries which have been created during this century it is difficult to account for the lack of progress and change in the hotel and catering industry.[2]

Developments have clearly been made in the past 20 years and increasing emphasis is being placed on ways in which ideas drawn from general management theory may be applied to the industry.[3] There is, however, still a long way to go. For example, Medlik makes the point that 'only limited progress has been made in the translation of business management theory from manufacturing to service industries generally and to hotels in particular.'[4]

What then are the reasons for lack of management progress and change? Is it because the hospitality industry is significantly different from other industries and therefore defies meaningful comparison?

Is the hospitality industry unique?

Every industry is of course unique in the strict sense of the word. The point is that all industries share important common features but also differ in many important respects.

Accordingly the questions to be examined are:

(i) What are the common features that the hospitality industry shares with other industries?

(ii) To what extent is the industry different in significant respects from other industries? and

(iii) Are these differences sufficient to mark the hospitality industry as unique, and to restrict the application of general management theory and practice?

In order to examine these questions we need some perspective in which to attempt a meaningful comparison of hospitality operations with those in other industries. We need to consider the nature of the organisational setting.

THE ORGANISATIONAL SETTING

The process of management does not take place in a vacuum but within the context of an organisational setting. Organisations are diverse and come in all forms, shapes and sizes. The structure, management and functioning of organisations will vary because of differences in their nature and type, goals and objectives, external environment, goods and/or services supplied, customers, and the behaviour of people who work in them.

By way of an extreme example let us consider just two types of organisation towards the opposite ends of a possible continuum – say a maximum security prison and a university largely concerned with research – as a framework within which to focus our attention. We can appreciate readily that although both types of organisation will be concerned with the basic activities of management, their actual procedures and methods of operation, structure, systems and styles of management, and orientation and behaviour of members will differ considerably.

Common factors in organisations

Despite the differences among various organisations there are, however, at least four common factors in any organisation:

- people;
- objectives;

- structure; and
- management.

It is the interaction of **people** in order to achieve **objectives** which forms the basis of an organisation. Some form of **structure** is needed by which people's interactions and efforts are channelled and co-ordinated. It is through the process of **management** that the activities of the organisation and the efforts of its members are directed towards the pursuit of objectives.

The effectiveness of the organisation will depend upon the quality of its people, its objectives and structure, and the resources available to it. There are two broad categories of resources:

- **non-human** – physical assets, materials, equipment and facilities; and
- **human** – members' abilities and influence, and their management.

The interrelationship of people, objectives, structure and management, together with the efficient use of resources, will determine the success or failure of the organisation and the extent of its effectiveness (Figure 1.1).

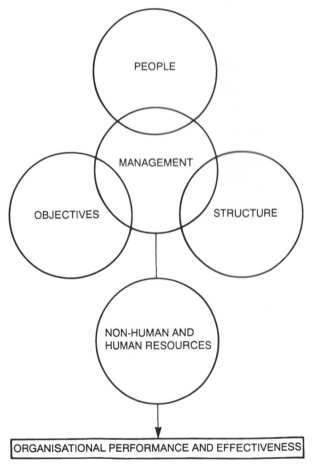

Fig 1.1 Common factors in business organisations

THE HOSPITALITY INDUSTRY

In recent years the term 'hospitality' has become increasingly popular as an all-embracing nomenclature for a larger grouping of organisations including hotels. As a collective term 'the hospitality industry' can be taken to *include* hotels, motels, guesthouses, bed and breakfast; farm houses; holiday parks; restaurants, fast food outlets, cafés, departmental store catering; public houses, clubs; industrial catering; institutional catering; and the related area of tourism and leisure.

The (then) HCITB provided the following major sector headings for the structure of the industry:

Commercial
- Accommodation;
- Meals;
- Licensed trade; and
- Tourism and travel.

Industrial and Public Services
- Industrial;
- Public services; and
- Hospitals and Residential Homes.[5]

An alternative way of dividing the industry is suggested by Hornsey and Dann who 'for the sake of convenience' use four headings:

- The hotel sector (hotels, restaurants, pubs and clubs);
- Industrial catering;
- Institutional catering and domestic services; and
- Fast food.[6]

Although there are some common factors among the different divisions, and some movement of staff from one division to another, the hospitality industry comprises separate and distinct sectors. The hotel sector and the catering sector, for example, are in many respects entirely different businesses and each is worthy of separate study.

THE HOTEL INDUSTRY

The broad and variable nature of hotel operations means that they can be seen to embrace, to a greater or lesser extent, elements of associated sectors of the hospitality industry such as the licensed trade, catering and leisure activities. In general terms then the hotel sector is also likely to exhibit a wider and more diverse range of organisational and staffing characteristics than other sectors of the hospitality industry. In this book, therefore, we are concerned primarily with the management of human resources in the hotel industry.

Types of hotels

There are, however, many different types of hotels, and many different ways of attempting to distinguish between them and to categorise them. Medlik, for example, adopts the following criteria for classifying the main types of hotels.[7]

- The **location**, for example cities, towns, coastal resorts or country; and **position** within its location, for example city or town centre, along the beach or a highway.
- The relationship with a particular **means of transport**, for example motels, railway hotels or airport hotels.
- The **purpose of visit** and main reason for the guests' stay, for example business hotels, convention hotels, holiday hotels.
- A pronounced tendency to a **short or long duration** of guests' stay, for example a transit or a residential hotel.
- The **range of facilities and services**, for example open to residents and non-residents, provision of overnight accommodation and breakfast only, or an apartment hotel.
- The distinction between **licensed and unlicensed** hotels.
- The **size** of hotel, for example by number of rooms or beds – a large hotel would have several hundred beds or bedrooms.
- The **class or grade** of hotel as in hotel guides and classification and grading systems, for example a five-star luxury or quality hotel, or a one-star basic standard hotel.
- The **ownership and management** of the hotel, for example chain or group hotels, or individually owned independent hotels.

ORGANISATIONAL AND STAFFING CHARACTERISTICS

Hotels, then, are not an homogeneous grouping. It is, however, possible to summarise a number of important organisational and staffing features which are characteristic of hotels in general, for example:

- large numbers of individual units of varying size and many different types are located throughout the whole of the country and internationally;
- many units operate for 24 hours a day, seven days a week;
- there are high fixed costs, a fixed rate of supply but a fluctuating, seasonal and often unpredictable demand;
- it is both a production and service industry;
- production and sales are combined on the same premises;
- there is a diverse range of customers seeking to satisfy a variety of needs and expectations;
- services are supplied direct to the customer on the premises and the customer leaves with no tangible product;
- a wide range of operations are combined, many of which are provided simultaneously;
- a high degree of co-ordination is required, often measured over very short time scales;
- managers are expected to demonstrate proficiency in technical and craft skills as well as in management areas;
- staff may live on the premises;
- many different skills are required but there are also high numbers of unskilled staff;

- the majority of staff receive low pay;
- staff are often expected to work long and 'unsocial' hours;
- there is a large proportion of young, female, part-time and casual staff;
- there is also a high proportion of staff from other countries;
- there are many trade unions but generally trade union membership is low;
- there is high mobility of labour within the industry, and a high turnover of staff joining and leaving the industry.

Distinctive nature of the industry

It is these characteristics which collectively determine the distinctive nature of the hotel industry, which shape organisational design and structure, and largely determine managerial policies, procedures and behaviour. It is the combination of these organisational and staffing characteristics which determines the process of management and which has a distinctive effect on the behaviour of staff and on employee relations.[8]

Clearly, however, not all of these characteristics will apply, necessarily, to every hotel. It is important to remind ourselves of the importance of the organisational setting, of the diverse nature of the industry, and to repeat that **hotels are not a homogeneous grouping**. For example, large city-centre hotels are likely to have a wider range of operations, more bureaucratic procedures, narrower and more specialised areas of responsibilities, and a proportionally higher level of mobility and staff turnover than smaller country hotels. And particular types of hotel will exhibit more specific characteristics; for example, retirement hotels will have a narrower range of customer, and provide a range of facilities and services directed specifically to their particular needs and expectations.

Small-size units

Major hotel groups provide a significant number of rooms but the industry is also characterised by a large proportion of independent hotels. Although much of the 'theory' of hotel management is rooted in the study of large-scale organisations it should be remembered that a predominant number of independent hotels are small-sized units which often may be managed and run by the owners. As an example, the Appendix to this chapter provides an original commentary on some of the characteristic features associated with the ownership and management of a six-bedroom country house hotel.

Image of the hospitality industry

In 1980, the HCITB undertook a project to investigate the image of jobs in the hospitality industry and identified three main target groups: the general public, active jobseekers and school leavers.[9] The image of the industry as an employer was found to be generally favourable in the eyes of the general public and school leavers. However, the industry was characterised to most people by jobs in cooking and waiting, whilst other jobs such as housekeeping and that of cashier tended to be forgotten. Sex stereotyping was well established and played an important part in people's evaluation of jobs.

Among the most disliked features of the work were long and awkward hours and unpleasant working environment. Although low wages featured among the criticisms of the industry, they did not emerge as such an important factor as might have been expected. High pay did not appear a priority for most people, provided other requirements of the work were satisfied.

THE NATURE OF HOTEL SERVICES

Hotel operations combine both a productive and a service element. However, although hotels are not pure service organisations, they exhibit many of the basic characteristics common to other service industries.[10]

Services may be viewed as displaying seven main characteristic features:

- the consumer as a participant in the process;
- simultaneous production and consumption;
- perishable capacity;
- site selection determined by customer demands;
- labour intensive;
- intangibility; and
- difficulty in measuring performance.[11]

The consumer as a participant in the process

Unlike physical production, where the environment of the 'factory' does not concern the eventual purchaser, the presence of the consumer requires attention to the surroundings and characteristics of the service facility. Customer satisfaction will be influenced by the location, furnishing and decoration of the hotel, and the environment in which the delivery of services takes place. The customer is part of the service process and can influence its operations. For example, hotel guests may make use of tea/coffee facilities in their own rooms and thus reduce the demand for room service.

Simultaneous production and consumption

Services are created and consumed simultaneously. Unlike manufacturing there can be no inventory of the service itself. For example, a receptionist giving assistance to a guest cannot be stored for future use. Services cannot be stockpiled to meet fluctuating demand. For the delivery of services to take place there must be direct, personal interaction with customers. In a hotel the lack of an inventory can result in customers having to wait for attention or delivery of service.

Perishable capacity

Services cannot be stored and if they are not used they are likely to be wasted. Unlike manufacturing, services are time-perishable. High fixed costs will still occur during periods of low demand. The income lost from a hotel room unsold on one day cannot be recouped later: it is lost forever. Additional hotel rooms may not be available to satisfy a higher-than-expected demand, resulting in a lost opportunity to generate additional income.

Site selection determined by customer demands

Unlike manufacturing, services do not move through distinct channels of distribution. The delivery of services and the customer must be brought together. Services cannot be provided at a single, centralised location for different geographical markets and it may not be possible to achieve economies of scale. Experience of hotel services is dependent upon personal contact. As services are provided direct to the customer this may result in smaller-scale operations and limited geographical locations.

Labour intensive

In service operations work, activity is people-oriented and labour is the important resource in determining organisational effectiveness. The personal nature of hotel services places emphasis on the importance of direct interaction between employees and customers. The effective delivery of services is dependent upon the attention and attitudes of staff as well as their performance. The increased use of technology and automation may well lead to a demand for a higher level of personal attention and service.

Intangibility

Compared with physical products, the particular features of services are more difficult to explain or communicate. Promotion requires an understanding of consumer behaviour and needs to focus attention on the actual delivery of the service. Benefits derived from services are associated with feelings and emotions. The quality of service in a hotel is usually identified with its general culture and ambience, the disposition and attitudes of staff, and the nature of other customers.

Difficulty in measuring performance

The measurement of output is difficult because there is unlikely to be a single, important criterion on which to evaluate effective performance. For example, profitability or the number of customers staying at a hotel is not necessarily a measure of the quality of service. The intangible nature of services, coupled with the heterogeneous nature of customers, means that the actual delivery of services will differ widely. It is difficult, therefore, to establish or to monitor objective standards of performance. Even within the same hotel the actual delivery of services to individual customers is likely to vary noticeably according to, for example, the reasons for the customers' presence and their particular requirements, together with the personalities and behaviour of both customers and members of staff.

Lack of ownership

Another feature of service operations is that, unlike manufacturers or suppliers of products, the purchase of services does not bestow ownership upon the customer. In a hotel all the physical features remain in the ownership of the hotelier, and customers are only hirers of facilities for the duration of their stay.[12]

ARE SERVICE INDUSTRIES DIFFERENT FROM OTHER INDUSTRIES?

Hotels, then, exhibit many of the basic characteristics of service industries and share many common features such as high fixed costs, labour-intensiveness, low wages and unsocial working hours. But is a service industry any different from other industries? Not according to leading writers such as Levitt:

> Purveyors of service, for their part, think that they and their problems are fundamentally different from other businesses and their problems. They feel that service is people-intensive, while the rest of the economy is capital-intensive. But these distinctions are largely spurious. There are no such things as service industries. There are only industries whose service components are greater or less than those of other industries. Everybody is in service.[13]

The nature of management

In addressing the question 'What is the nature of management in service industries?' Jones suggests that implicit in the question is the fundamental assumption that managers of services face different problems and act differently from other managers. However, Jones acknowledges that this assumption is contentious. And even where there is agreement that services are in some way different, there is no agreement on the cause or importance of this difference.[14]

A major characteristic of the hotel industry is of course the role of people and the direct contact and interactions between staff and customers. The majority of hotel managers of the author's acquaintance stress the need for a high level of commitment to the job and the ability to be all things to all people. (The attributes of a hotel manager are discussed further in Chapter 5.)

But whatever one's view of service industries, they still have some functions and purpose to fulfil as part of their role within society. Service industries are in need of management in order to operate effectively in the same way as any other industry.

SERVICE MANAGEMENT

Hospitality organisations, while created to provide both service and hospitality, have not always effectively managed service. Today, other service organisations as well as the hospitality industry must recognise the need to manage service effectively and deliver high-quality products. Increased emphasis on quality also means an increased focus on customer service. As this refocusing takes place, management strategies referred to as 'service management' are being developed. Service management takes a market-oriented approach to service delivery, with an emphasis on long-term customer relationships. Albrecht defines service management as 'a total organisational approach that makes quality of service, as perceived by the customer, the number one driving force for the operation of the business.'[15]

While traditional management approaches emphasise internal consequences and structure, service management emphasises external consequences and process. This change in focus requires changes in the work culture. The entire organisation needs to understand the emphasis on service and that the organisation can survive only if it meets the needs of the customer. The mission statement, along with company goals and objectives, emphasise the focus on customers. These statements clearly delineate the direction the company is taking. Employee goals are customer oriented and reward systems are based on customer satisfaction.

Service strategy

The service strategy is the formal organisational link that delineates the focus on customer satisfaction. The strategy outlines what will be done for a certain customer segment, how this should be achieved, and with what kinds of resources. The service strategy reinforces the mission strategy of the organisation. Without a clear service strategy, inconsistent behaviour is evident. Strong service strategies not only aid in strengthening customer relationships, but they also aid in retention of employees. Service strategies can be a powerful management tool to sustain a competitive advantage in the marketplace.

The priorities of the organisation are changed and the organisation pyramid is turned upside down.[16] The customers are at the top, followed by front-line employees, that is those interacting with the customers. Top management is at the bottom of the hierarchy. This also reflects the movement of operational decision-making from top management to those involved in the buyer–seller interactions.

Management focus

The focus of an organisation that utilises service management is different from that of a traditional organisation. The organisation will be structured so that it supports front-line workers and provides the resources that are necessary for them to effectively serve the customers. Decision-making, supervisory focus, reward systems and feedback mechanisms are also different. Decision-making is decentralised so that employees who are involved in the customer interaction are empowered to take action and do what is necessary to satisfy the customer. For example, if guest service representatives have an unhappy guest at the front desk, they have the authority to take care of the problem. Representatives have the authority to give a discount, offer a free meal or make arrangements with outside entities to satisfy the customer. However, long-term strategic decisions remain centralised.

Managers and supervisors focus on the encouragement and support of employees. Services by nature cannot be standardised, therefore the organisation needs to be flexible. Also, for employees to deliver quality service, some flexibility is needed to meet the special needs of every customer. The role of managers changes from that of 'order giver' and controller to 'facilitator', coach and team leader. The role of workers changes from merely being an 'order taker' to becoming an active participant in the creation of guest-satisfying values. Reward systems are based on customer satisfaction. Frequently, managers utilising a service management approach use moments of truth as evaluation points. These moments of truth are the critical points of interaction between the customer and the service provider. Performance is measured against expectations at the critical moments. Customer feedback plays an instrumental role in this type of evaluation.

Service culture

Service management strategies are successful only when they are accompanied by a corporate culture that can be labelled a service culture. The culture can be described as 'a culture where an appreciation for good service exists, and where giving good service to internal as well as ultimate external customers is considered a natural way of life and one of the most important norms by everyone.'[17] Management, top executives and front-line employees all need to live the service culture. A service culture enhances the ability to truly meet the needs of the customers.

THE OPEN SYSTEMS MODEL OF ANALYSIS

Riley suggests that the managerial task of running a hotel and catering unit can be seen as a set of systems and processes common to managing anything but that this does not contradict the case for uniqueness.[18] The important questions, however, are:

- to what extent do the particular characteristics of the hospitality industry distinguish it from other industries? and
- to what extent do general principles of management theory and practice apply to hospitality organisations as work organisations?

The open systems model provides us with a useful basis of analysis.

All business organisations can be seen as open systems which take inputs such as people, finance, materials, and information from the external environment. Through a series of activities these inputs are transformed or converted and returned to the environment in various forms of outputs such as goods produced, services provided and completed processes or procedures. Outputs are intended to achieve certain goals such as profit, market standing, level of sales or consumer satisfaction (Figure 1.2).

The following sections discuss the application of the open systems model of analysis to the hotel industry. However, the same basis of analysis applies equally to all hospitality organisations.

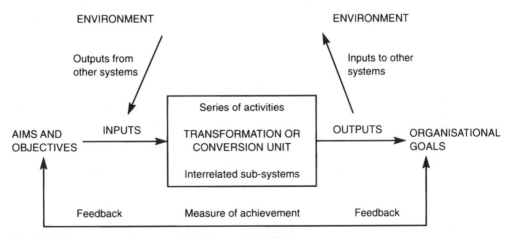

Fig 1.2 The open systems model of organisations
Source Mullins L J, *Management and Organisational Behaviour*, Third edition, Pitman (1993), p. 79

The customer as the major throughput

Hotels are 'people-moulding' organisations and they are concerned with human beings as the basis of the nature of work carried out.[19] The major input is the customer seeking satisfaction of certain needs. The desired output is a satisfied customer. In order to achieve this output the transformation or conversion process will entail the customer being suitably rested/refreshed/entertained or undergoing a rewarding experience in a comfortable and safe environment. The customer is therefore also the major throughput of the hotel system. It is the demands of the customer which will have the greatest influence on the series of activities involved in the transformation process.

Compared with most business organisations, the hotel is unusual in that customers as the main throughput are provided with and consume services within the hotel, and leave with no tangible product.[20] However, in terms of the open systems model, the hotel is no different from any other business organisation (Figure 1.3). It is subject to the same basic processes of:

- aims and objectives;
- inputs;
- series of activities as the transformation or conversion process;
- outputs;
- realisation of goals.

APPLICATIONS TO HOSPITALITY MANAGEMENT

Reservations about the application of management practices and techniques developed in other sectors of industry prompted Nailon to propose a model specifically related to elements of hospitality management.[21] This model was criticised heavily by Wood, however. The reasoning behind the attempt to create a model of management specifically suited to hospitality organisations was spurious considering the criticisms levelled at the 'blinkered' approaches of previous management theorists.[22]

Wood argues that Nailon's model could describe adequately the factors affecting the management of any organisation and follows closely the structure of the more general open systems theories which are themselves based on previous studies of manufacturing firms.

> ... there is nothing special about either management or hospitality management. A 'theoretical' understanding of 'management' can only be obtained through an appreciation of how management practices are produced within a framework of social and economic constraints, and how such practices inter-relate at the societal level in respect of *all* social and economic institutions.[23]

Comparison with management elsewhere

Viewing the hotel industry as unique, or as somehow special and different from other industries, will not improve the level of organisational performance. On the other hand it may help to account for lack of progress and change in the industry. For example, although based on a small and limited study, Dodrill and Riley were unable to find any

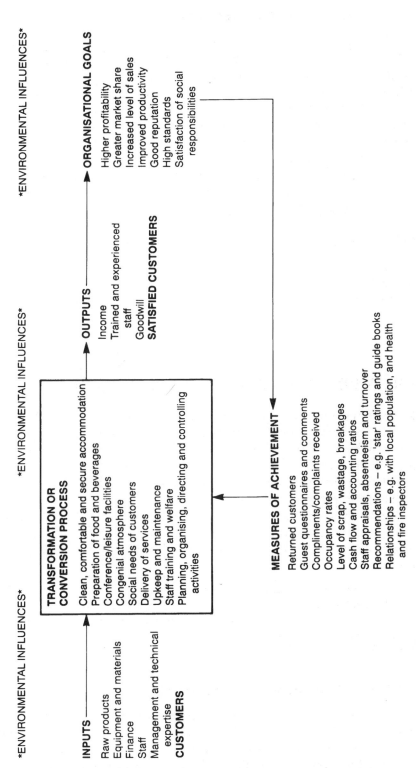

Fig 1.3 The hotel as an open system

ENVIRONMENTAL INFLUENCES

INPUTS

Raw products
Equipment and materials
Finance
Staff
Management and technical
   expertise
CUSTOMERS

**TRANSFORMATION OR
CONVERSION PROCESS**

Clean, comfortable and secure accommodation
Preparation of food and beverages
Conference/leisure facilities
Congenial atmosphere
Social needs of customers
Delivery of services
Upkeep and maintenance
Staff training and welfare
Planning, organising, directing and controlling
   activities

OUTPUTS

Income
Trained and experienced
   staff
Goodwill
SATISFIED CUSTOMERS

ORGANISATIONAL GOALS

Higher profitability
Greater market share
Increased level of sales
Improved productivity
Good reputation
High standards
Satisfaction of social
   responsibilities

MEASURES OF ACHIEVEMENT

Returned customers
Guest questionnaires and comments
Compliments/complaints received
Occupancy rates
Level of scrap, wastage, breakages
Cash flow and accounting ratios
Staff appraisals, absenteeism and turnover
Recommendations – e.g. 'star' ratings and guide books
Relationships – e.g. with local population, and health
   and fire inspectors

distinctive attitudes towards work by hotel workers.[24] (This study is discussed further in Chapter 2.) From his practical experience of hotel management, Venison comments on the striking similiarity between the hotel industry and the retail industry. Venison believes hotel management students would benefit from a study of retailing.[25] Wood also challenges the myth of uniqueness in the hotel and catering industry which provides:

> . . . for employers, managers and some workers a self-serving device for justifying the unjustifiable in terms of inadequate basic rewards, feudal management practices and the maintenance of a culture that discourages intervention in the affairs of the industry by others.[26]

We have seen, then, that the hotel industry does differ in important respects from other industries. But this should not be seen as a convenient reason for disguising comparison with management procedures and practices elsewhere.

Common point of reference

A series of activities by which inputs are transformed into outputs is a common feature of any industry, and makes possible the application of general principles of organisation and management within the hotel industry. A suitable form of structure must be designed. Essential administrative functions must be carried out. Legal requirements must be observed (for example in respect of employment legislation). The common activities of management – clarification of objectives, planning, organising, directing and control – apply to a greater or lesser extent.

It is important to emphasise these common features. There are of course differences in the activities and methods of operation of organisations even of the same type, for example in relation to the nature, size and scale of activities of different hotels. The open systems approach provides not only for the critical analysis of the operations of a particular hotel but also a basis for comparison with other hospitality organisations, for example in highlighting similarities or variations in the nature of inputs, the series of activities in organisational processes and execution of work, environmental influences, organisational goals and measures of achievement.[27]

Such an approach will remind us yet again of the diverse nature of the industry but also that differences in the application and implementation of the common features are largely a matter only of degree and emphasis. Using the open systems model provides a common point of reference and enables us to take a general approach to the study of hotels, to analyse them, and to review applications of general management theory.[28]

ENVIRONMENTAL INFLUENCES

The hotel is in continual interaction with the external environment of which it is part. In order to be effective and maintain survival and development, the hotel must respond to the opportunities and challenges, and risks and limitations, presented by changing circumstances. The open systems approach views the hotel within its total environment and emphasises the importance of multiple channels of interaction.

The increasing rate of change in major environmental factors (technical, economic, social and governmental) has highlighted the need to study the hotel as a total organisation and to adopt a systems approach. In addition to these major areas of change, the hotel faces a multiplicity of constantly changing environmental factors which affect its operations and performance (Figure 1.4).

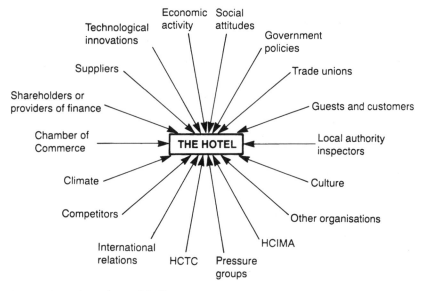

Fig 1.4 External environmental influences

Beyond the control of the hotel manager

Environmental influences are generally beyond the control of the hotel manager. Consider how the functioning and operation of a hotel might be affected by such external environment influences as, for example:

- government actions on the rate of VAT, transport policies, health and safety regulations, drink-driving laws;
- inflation, interest rates, levels of unemployment;
- international situations and foreign exchange rates;
- technological advances;
- activities of competitors;
- local business trade, or tourism or leisure attractions;
- a major trend towards eating organically grown produce;
- increased leisure time for a wider range of the population;
- bankruptcy of, or a major strike at, an important supplier;
- a large increase in trade union activities and membership;
- the opening or closure of a local catering college;
- a long spell of particularly good or inclement weather.

The effectiveness of hotel operations will be determined not only by internal considerations and choices, but also by the successful management of the opportunities, challenges and risks presented by the external environment. Hotels must therefore be readily adaptable to changes in the environment and the demands which are placed upon them.

THE ANALYSIS OF HOTEL OPERATIONS

By itself, the open systems model reveals little about the detailed activities undertaken within the hotel. To benefit from such an approach the hotel system needs to be analysed in such a way that the total operations of the hotel as a unified whole can be reviewed and amended as necessary. Within the hotel system as a whole each of the main transformation or conversion processes can be seen as separate sub-systems interacting with other sub-systems.

The analysis of the hotel system could be based upon the traditional organisation structure with different departments or sections as sub-systems – for example, front office, accommodation, food and beverage, conferences, accounting, personnel, security and maintenance. However, this form of analysis could lead to an investigation concentrating on blinkered, sectional interests rather than on the need to adopt a unified, corporate approach.

Interrelationships and interactions

Each department or section of the hotel might perhaps be operating efficiently in its own right. But what is equally important is the interrelationships and interactions with other departments or sections, and the attitudes and behaviour of staff.

For example, food preparation and food service should not be considered separately but as integrated sub-systems. The preparation of food in the kitchen and the equipment used need to be related to the method of service in the restaurant, and the training and skills of the waiting staff.[29] It is the integration of preparation and service, together with other sub-systems, which determines overall effectiveness of the hotel.

It is more beneficial, therefore, to analyse major elements or functions within the hotel system and to recognise the importance of the interdependence of sub-systems in terms of the effectiveness of hotel operations as an integrated whole.

The socio-technical system

The interrelationship of different parts of the system raises the question of identification of sub-systems. These may be identified in a number of different ways although there is a degree of similarity among alternative models.[30]

For example, following their study of changing technology in British coal mines, Trist and others drew attention to the importance of the socio-technical system.[31] This is concerned with the transformation or conversion process itself and the importance of the relationships between technical efficiency, social considerations and the effect on people.

The researchers suggested that there are three sub-systems common to any organisation:

- the **technological** sub-system;
- the sub-system of **formal role structure**;
- the sub-system of **individual members' feelings or sentiments**.

Interrelated sub-systems

Developing the idea of a socio-technical system we can analyse hotel operations in terms of five main interrelated sub-systems – task, technology, structure, people, and management (Figure 1.5).

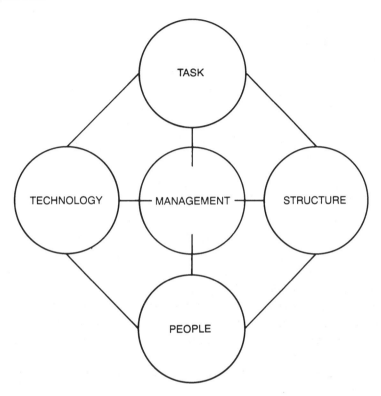

Fig 1.5 Interrelated sub-systems of hotel operations

- **Task** – the goals and objectives of the hotel and the work to be carried out. This is the scale and nature of activities, and the range and quality of services provided, for example: the type of customers and their needs; family, conference or leisure facilities; nature of accommodation; speciality menus; standards of meals and service in the restaurant; opening hours of bars; porterage and room service.
- **Technology** – the manner in which the activities of the hotel are carried out and the nature of work performance. The meaning of 'technology' is interpreted broadly and includes the physical aspects of equipment, machines, materials and work layout, and the methods, systems and procedures used in the transformation or conversion process, for example: the use of computers, microwaves and cook/chill; methods of food preparation; booking and reservation systems; procedures and methods for cleaning bedrooms. The technology of production in the kitchen is related to table d'hôte, à la carte or banquet service.
- **Structure** – patterns of organisation, lines of authority, and channels of communication among members of the hotel. This is the division of work and co-ordination of tasks by which the series of activities are carried out, for example: whether mechanistic or

organic; the extent of centralisation; management and supervisory roles; the responsibilities of departmental managers; the informal organisation.

- **People** – the nature of the hotel staff undertaking the series of activities, for example, training and qualifications; skills and abilities; loyalty; attitudes and interpersonal relationships; cultural influences; needs and expectations; group functioning and behaviour; styles of leadership.
- **Management** – co-ordination of task, technology, structure and people, and policies and procedures for the execution of the work of the hotel, for example: corporate strategy; decision-making; planning, organisation, direction and control of activities; systems and styles of management; interactions with the external environment; social responsibilities.

ORGANISATIONAL GOALS

All organisations need clear aims and objectives which will determine the nature of inputs, the series of activities to achieve outputs and the realisation of goals. A goal is a future expectation. It is something the organisation is striving to achieve. The goals of an organisation are the reason for its existence.

The meaning of a goal is, however, subject to different interpretations. It can be used in a very broad sense to refer to the overall purpose of a hotel, for example to make a profit. A goal may also refer to more specific desired achievements, for example to provide a given level of facilities and standard of service to its customers.

Integration of goals

Organisational goals are established by people, either individually or, more usually, by a number of individuals co-operating together. Strictly, hotels do not have goals; only people do.

Members and customers of the hotel have different and often conflicting goals. Owners may have a particular concern with high profits and the return on their investments, customers with prices and the standard of facilities and services, employees with security of employment, high wages and good working conditions. Members and customers will also have their own perception of the goals of the hotel, and their own personal goals which they expect to fulfil by participating in the activities of the hotel – for example responsibility to the community, social satisfaction, recognition and status.

If organisational goals and personal goals are pulling in different directions conflict will arise and performance is likely to suffer. It is the responsibility of hotel management to clarify organisational goals and to reconcile conflicting interests. This demands the formulation of clear lines of direction for the hotel as a whole and its subsequent activities and operations. To be effective, goals should be emphasised, stated clearly and communicated openly to all members of the hotel.

One important attempt at integrating organisational goals with the needs of individual members of the organisation is the approach of Management by Objectives, which is discussed in Chapter 5.

OBJECTIVES AND POLICY

Goals are translated into objectives and policy in order to provide corporate guidelines for the operations of the hotel. Objectives and policy provide a focus for management decisions and actions. Terminology varies in the literature but objectives can be seen as the 'what', and policies as the 'how', 'where' and 'when', the means that follow the objectives.

- Objectives set out more specifically the goals of the organisation, the aims to be achieved and desired end-results.
- Policy is developed within the framework of objectives. It provides the basis for decision-making and courses of action to follow in order to achieve objectives.

Objectives and policy are an essential part of the decision-making process and form a basis for the process of management.

Company philosophy

Objectives and policy may be formulated within the framework of an underlying philosophy of sets of beliefs, attitudes and conventions. These may not always be incorporated into formal policies but still influence the overall conduct of the hotel, and the behaviour and performance of staff. Company philosophy determines the common doctrine or codes of behaviour which guide the hotel in its dealings with others and the conduct of its operations. As an example, the company philosophy of Trust House Forte is given in Figure 1.6.

The Company Philosophy

To increase profitability and earnings per share each year in order to encourage investment and to improve and expand the business.

To give complete customer satisfaction by efficient and courteous service, with value for money.

To support managers and their staff in using personal initiative to improve the profit and quality of their operations whilst observing the company's policies.

To provide good working conditions and to maintain effective communications at all levels to develop better understanding and assist decision making.

To ensure no discrimination against sex, race, colour or creed and to train, develop and encourage promotion within the company based on merit and ability.

To act with integrity at all times and to maintain a proper sense of responsibility towards the public .

To recognise the importance of each and every employee who contributes towards these aims.

Fig 1.6 Company philosophy of Trust House Forte
Source Forte C (Lord), *Forte: The Autobiography of Charles Forte*, Sidgwick & Jackson (1986), p. 191

Company philosophy can be based on both an ethical foundation and an operational foundation.[32]

- The **ethical foundation** embodies basic principles which govern the external and internal relations of the hotel and concern standards of behaviour in all dealings with, for example, customers, suppliers, competitors, representatives, health or fire inspectors. educational establishments, staff and union representatives.
- The **operational foundation** relates to the nature, operation and conduct of hotel activities, for example methods of production, use of equipment, hygiene and cleanliness, dress and appearance, systems and styles of management and supervision.

The underlying philosophy of the hotel will also have a bearing on the nature of the psychological contract which is discussed in the following chapter.

Statement of objectives

Objectives may be just implicit but the formal, explicit definition of objectives will help to highlight the activities which the hotel needs to undertake and the comparative importance of its various functions. Objectives should not be stated in such a way that they detract from the recognition of possible new opportunities, potential danger areas, the initiative of staff, or the need for innovation or change. However, a clear, explicit statement of objectives may assist communications, reduce misunderstandings and provide meaningful criteria for evaluating performance.

General and sectional policy

Policy is translated into rules, directives, plans and procedures; it relates to all activities of the hotel and to all levels in the hotel. General policy is determined by top management (directors, owners or senior managers) and provides broad guidelines for the operations of the hotel as a whole.

Certain aspects of a hotel's general policy may be so dominant that they become the overriding image or 'hallmark' of the hotel and place constraints on other policy areas. An example could be a country and golf hotel that wants to see itself as a high-class establishment and goes out of its way to show that it is not a family hotel and does not provide for children under five years of age.

Sectional policy flows from general policy and provides, in more specific operational terms, guiding principles for particular aspects and activities of hotel operations. Specific policies have more defined areas of application and time limits.

For example, specific policy relating to **customer relations** could include areas of decision-making and delegation relating to types of customers, facilities provided, pricing and discounts, customer care and standards of service, attitudes and behaviour of staff, and handling of grievances and complaints.

Specific policies may also be formulated for other areas of relationships such as employees and suppliers, for main areas of activity such as accommodation, and food and beverages, and areas of functional support such as accounting and marketing.

THE PROFIT MOTIVE

The hospitality industry involves an economic activity and its aims and objectives are of a commercial nature. To be successful the primary objectives of the hotel may be seen as: to survive as a business and continue in existence, to maintain growth and development, and to make a profit. If we accept survival as the ultimate objective of the hotel, this involves the need for a steady and continuous profit. The hotel must be prepared to accept the possibility of a reduction in short-term profitability in order to provide for future investments.

The importance of profit as a means of business survival has been suggested by Lord (then Sir Charles) Forte.

> The policy which binds all our business together is the simple axiom that we are in it to make a profit and we base our policies on a strict analysis of the potential in each area we enter. We are convinced that making profit is the surest way of guaranteeing the livelihood of our workforce. It follows from this philosophy of business that there is no room, if growth is to be maintained, for lame ducks.[33]

Other considerations and motivations

Although the objective of profit maximisation is undoubtedly of great importance it is not, by itself, a sufficient criterion for the effective day-to-day management of hotel operations. This view is supported by Fearn, who suggests a somewhat different interpretation of the role of profit in the objectives of hospitality management.

> 'Why are we in business?' The favourite answer to this question, and one often thought to be the correct one, is 'to make a profit'. This is indeed important, but it is hardly an adequate basic approach to the administration of a business. To consider profit as the sole reason for the existence of a company is certainly an attractive idea, but it is more logical to consider profit as the reward for serving others well. It is therefore the things that are done to obtain profit which are the subject of objectives.[34]

In practice, there are many other considerations and motivations which affect the desire for the greatest profit or maximum economic efficiency. Attention needs to be given to multiple areas of objective setting, including the importance of social responsibilities.

MULTIPLE PERFORMANCE OBJECTIVES

Any business organisation has a number of important areas of performance and results which require the setting of objectives. Drucker has referred to the 'fallacy of the single objective' of a business. The search for the one, right objective is not only unlikely to be productive, but is certain to harm and misdirect the business enterprise.

> To emphasise only profit, for instance, misdirects managers to the point where they may endanger the survival of the business. To obtain profit today they tend to undermine the future . . . To manage a business is to balance a variety of needs and goals . . . the very nature of business enterprise requires multiple objectives which are needed in every area where performance and results directly and vitally affect the survival and prosperity of the business.[35]

Drucker lists eight key areas in which objectives should be set in terms of performance and results. This list provides a useful framework in which to review objectives of hospitality organisation.[36]

- **Market standing** – for example: type of customers and their requirements as the principal source of business, nature of facilities and services offered, distinctions from main competitors.
- **Innovation** – for example: need for flexibility in a dynamic environment, opportunities to reach new customers, developments arising from technological advances, new processes and procedures.
- **Productivity** – higher productivity distinguished from higher production or output, for example: more advanced equipment, optimum use of resources, decision-making techniques, improved methods, systems and procedures.
- **Physical and financial resources** – for example: location, size and nature of premises; equipment and facilities; supply of capital and budgeting; financial planning; provision of supplies.
- **Profitability** – for example: capital investment policy, profitability forecasts and planning, sales objectives such as for accommodation, food and beverages, measurements of profitability such as return on capital employed and food costs to sales.
- **Manager performance and development** – for example: the direction of managers' work, areas of responsibility, results achieved by subordinate staff, achievement of objectives, staff relationships, strengthening the management team, management succession planning.
- **Worker performance and attitudes** – for example: organisation and execution of work, standards of performance, control systems, staff appraisals, customer relations, personnel policies, employee relations, respect for authority, loyalty.
- **Public responsibility** (commonly referred to as social responsibilities) – demands made upon the organisation internally and by the external environment, for example by customers and staff, by law or public opinion, or by responsibilities to society and the public interest. The importance of the social responsibilities of management is considered more fully in a separate section below.

Constraints and limitations

We can see, therefore, that although the profit objective is clearly of importance it is not, by itself, a sufficient criterion for the effective management of hotel operations. Individuals in the hotel are not necessarily guided at all times by the profit objective. This is only one of a number of constraints.

> Profit may not enter directly into the decision-making of most members of a business organisation. Again, this does not mean that it is improper or meaningless to regard profit as a principal goal of a business. It simply means that the decision-making mechanism is a loosely coupled system in which the profit constraint is only one among a number of constraints and enters into most sub-systems only in indirect ways.[37]

The key areas of performance and results draw attention to the many constraints which may affect the satisfactory attainment of objectives, for example the failure to innovate, low productivity, lack of physical and financial resources, poor management development or staff training. Other limiting factors may arise as a result of general policy decisions or environmental pressures.

Realistic level of objectives

It is important, therefore, to take account of constraints and to set limitations and objectives at a realistically attainable level. Objectives set at too low a level do not stretch staff, or provide a sufficient challenge or sense of achievement. This can result in a lost opportunity for higher performance and results.

However, if objectives are set at too high a level this will be counter-productive. Staff may feel that undue pressure is put upon them and will again fail to gain a sense of achievement or personal satisfaction. If objectives are not seen to be in reasonable reach this is likely to result in the loss of positive motivation and a lower-than-possible level of performance. (See also the discussion on achievement motivation in Chapter 8.)

SOCIAL RESPONSIBILITIES OF MANAGEMENT

In striving to satisfy their goals and achieve their objectives hospitality organisations cannot operate in isolation from the environment of which they are part. Such organisations require the use of factors of production and other facilities of society. Economic efficiency is affected by governmental, social, technical and cultural variables. In return, society is in need of the products and services supplied by the organisation, including the creation and distribution of wealth.

Economic survival and performance are dependent upon a series of activities between the hospitality organisation and its environment. These exchanges and the continual interaction with the environment give rise to a number of broader obligations to society in general. These broader obligations are both internal and external and are usually referred to as social responsibilities.

Broad range of responsibilities

The potential range of social responsibilities is very broad and concerns different groups of people. Social responsibilities may be considered under a number of different headings such as, for example, employees, shareholders, customers, community, the government, and suppliers, business associates and competitors.

- **Employees** – responsibilities extend beyond formal terms and conditions of employment and include, for example, justice in treatment, consultation and participation, effective personnel and employee relations policies, equal opportunities employment, working conditions and live-in accommodation, training in new skills and technologies, job satisfaction.
- **Shareholders or other providers of capital** – shareholders are drawn from a wide range of the population, including private individuals. Many people also subscribe indirectly as shareholders through pension funds and insurance companies. Responsibilities to shareholders extend beyond a purely financial reward for risk-taking and include the safeguarding of investments, the opportunity to exercise rights as owners, participation in policy decisions, the opportunity to question top

management on the affairs of the company, the provision of full information in a clearly understood format.

- **Customers** – responsibilities to customers may arguably be seen as no more than a natural outcome of good business. There are, however, broader social responsibilities including fair standards of advertising and promotions, good value for money, a positive approach to customer satisfaction, honesty and full information on all costs and charges, prompt and courteous attention to queries or complaints, safety and security.
- **Community** – it is in the area of concern for the community at large that social responsibilities can usually be seen most clearly. The hospitality organisation has a responsibility to society, to respect environmental considerations and take care of amenities. Examples under this heading include: the effects and potential nuisance of the siting and appearance of new buildings, noise, pollution and disposal of waste, the use of biodegradable materials and aerosol sprays which do not contain chlorofluorocarbons (CFCs), concern for the welfare of the local community. Some larger organisations extend the range of social responsibilities further, for example by donations to, or sponsorship of, the arts, educational or sporting organisations, or charities.
- **Government** – hospitality management should, of course, respect and obey the law relating to the conduct of business operations even if it is not regarded as in their best interests. What is debatable is the extent to which top management should also co-operate voluntarily with actions requested by the government, for example: attempts to avoid inflation, acceptance of controls over imports, employment of staff under government training schemes, control of potential social problems such as the sale of tobacco or accidents at work.
- **Suppliers, business associates and competitors** – examples under this heading include: fair standards of trading, honouring terms and conditions of purchase and settlement dates for payment of accounts, assistance to small organisations, engaging in only fair competition and not to disparage competitors.

A question of balance

The distinction between the exercise of social responsibilities for genuine philanthropic reasons and actions taken in pursuit of what is seen as no more than good business practice and enlightened self-interest is not always easy to determine. In practice it is a question of degree and balance, of combining sound economic operations with an appropriate concern for broader responsibilities to society.

The recognition of social responsibilities should form part of strategic planning, and the formulation of objectives and policy. It is up to top management to determine the extent to which, and the manner in which, the hospitality organisation will attempt to satisfy its social responsibilities.

STRATEGIC PLANNING

Objectives and policy are formulated within the framework of a corporate strategy. Some form of corporate strategy is necessary for all organisations but particularly for large ones – and this includes service organisations.[38] Organisational performance is dependent upon the process of matching hotel structure, strategy and the environment.[39]

A series of stages

Strategic planning can be approached in a number of ways. Keiser, for example, suggests the following seven specific steps to accomplish strategic planning in the hospitality industry.[40]

- **Assess the current position of the organisation** – what are the present strengths and weaknesses, competition and market, challenges and opportunities?
- **Assess the current and future environments** – what is happening in the external and internal environment, what changes will affect present business or create possible new opportunities?
- **Assess the impact of projected changes** – what impact will the changes be likely to have on present operations, will they provide threats or opportunities?
- **Identify possible opportunities and evaluate possible risks** – identify possible opportunities from changes in the environment, and estimate the risks including cost, different markets and effects on present business.
- **Select feasible goals or objectives** – expanding current business or developing into new opportunities.
- **Establish priorities and allocate resources** – decide on selection of objectives and ensure supply of necessary resources.
- Provide operational guidelines – implement detailed operational and tactical plans.

SWOT analysis

An important aspect of strategic planning and change is the analysis of the internal strengths and weaknesses of the hotel following the formulation of objectives, and the opportunities and threats presented by its external environment.[41] SWOT is an acronym for the analysis of these Strengths, Weaknesses, Opportunities and Threats. The use of SWOT analysis can also assist the evaluation of hospitality operations and performance.

- **Strengths** are the distinctive attributes and positive aspects which provide a significant market advantage, or upon which the hospitality organisation can build and develop, for example: present market position, size and structure of operations, physical and financial resources, managerial expertise, staffing, image and reputation.
- **Weaknesses** are those deficiences in the present skills and expertise or resources of the hospitality organisation, or its image or reputation, which need to be corrected and for which action needs to be taken to minimise their effect. Weaknesses may stand in the way of achieving particular goals or objectives. Examples of weaknesses could include a high cost structure compared with competitors or a high level of customer complaints.
- **Opportunities** are favourable situations which arise from the nature of environmental change. The hospitality organisation needs to be responsive to changes which will provide an opportunity to offer new, or develop existing, facilities and services. Opportunities may arise from, for example, improved economic factors, greater leisure time, failure of competitors, new markets or products, or technological advances.
- **Threats** are the converse of opportunities. Threats refer to unfavourable situations which arise from environmental change and which are likely to endanger the

operations of the organisation. Examples could include government legislation, new competitors, or demographic changes.

(For other examples of potential opportunities or threats look back at the section on Environmental Influences above.)

SUMMARY

- Managers in hotels and catering tend to view the industry as unique. The hospitality industry has a number of distinctive features but also shares important features with other business industries. The process of management takes place within the context of an organisational setting. The interrelationship of people, objectives, structure and management determine the effectiveness of hospitality operations.
- The nature of hotel operations means that they are likely to embrace to a greater or lesser extent elements of associated sectors of the hospitality industry. Hotels are not an homogeneous grouping but in general will exhibit a number of important organisational and staffing characteristics. Hospitality organisations need to give attention to the effective management of service.
- Hotels display many of the basic characteristics of service industries and share many common features. Applying the open systems model provides a common point of reference and a perspective for a meaningful comparison with other industries. It enables a general approach to the study of hotels, the analysis of their operations and the applications of general management theory and practice.
- All organisations need clear goals, objectives and policy which provide a focus for management decisions and actions. Objectives and policy may be formulated within the framework of an underlying company philosophy which influences the overall conduct of the hospitality organisation, and the behaviour and performance of staff.
- Although undoubtedly of great importance the profit motive is not by itself a sufficient criterion for the effective management of hospitality operations. Attention needs to be given to multiple areas of objective and performance setting including social responsibilities. Organisational performance is dependent upon the process of matching organisational structure, strategy and the environment.

APPENDIX

The following original commentary has been provided by the owners/managers of a six-bedroom country house hotel.

> In the running of a small establishment as opposed to a larger organisation one of the first points to consider is what type of guest you wish to attract. This is not so narrow minded as it might appear. There are many people with like tastes and interests across the population no matter what class or creed and in a small establishment you need an easy mix of characters to create a comfortable atmosphere. This means therefore giving careful thought as to where and how you will advertise. For instance, we accentuate the aspect of wildlife, and peace and quiet with adults only. Once you have decided to stipulate any limitation, such as, for example, no children or pets, it is essential not to waver for many guests will often choose your establishment because of that stipulation.

Most small hotels are run by the owners who probably do most of the work involved, if not all of it. This means you have to be well organised, able to turn your hands to all tasks and trades, and most importantly of all not panic if things go wrong as they are bound to from time to time. When people choose a small family-run hotel they expect to receive personal attention which means you have to be around and in view for most of the day and evening with a pleasant expression, and prepared to spend time with your guests, not just the passing hello or pleasantry.

The job, which it is really, requires an abnormally high degree of dedication and input but can be most rewarding. If you are successful at putting yourself and your establishment across, your return rate of guests takes a lot of hard work from you because they will usually chat among themselves therefore setting the stage for a relaxed and happy atmosphere. Small additions to the furnishings and surroundings can add greatly to the well-being of your guests without being costly, for instance small ornaments, pictures or even photographs or personal portraits.

Finance and profitability are of course very important and require a lot of thought. Small establishments are not normally vastly profitable and most owners are happy if they can make a reasonable living from the business. Do not neglect the bookkeeping side of the business. If your accounts are in a mess then very likely your finances will be also. Try to keep on top of your bills and remember to put aside any VAT that will be due. We find it helpful to put this into a separate account and try to forget it is there until payment is due. Always look after and pay the small local traders you deal with. They are probably struggling too and you are more likely to get excellent service if you remember this.

Food is obviously very important and probably a high proportion of your outgoing commitments. We found that we could give a good, varied choice by displaying our menu each morning and asking guests that, if they were dining with us, could they possibly let us know and choose their meal at least an hour before dinner time. It is amazing how obliging people can be and often we know in the morning what to prepare as guests have already made their choice. This method not only cuts down on waste enormously but also ensures the dishes are freshly cooked and appetising.

Another important point is flexibility. If guests would like a slight variation from the menu this should be available and can easily be achieved in a small establishment. Whilst it is understandable that there is the need to be cost-effective do not be meagre in proportioning the meals. For example, a good cheeseboard always receives favourable comment. You will have far happier customers if they leave the table fully satisfied rather than still feeling peckish.

If you are fortunate enough to be able to employ staff make it clear what you require of them and then trust them to get on with the job. Nobody likes to be continually monitored and it can cause bad feeling if you are always looking over their shoulders. This does not mean that you do not check their work. This can be done quite surreptitiously and if found to be lacking then a quiet word is often sufficient to rectify any shortcomings.

Should your staff at any time seem to be struggling with a task (perhaps, for example, they may not feel well) then you should be able to muck in and help. This will gain you respect apart from showing that you can do the job as well as give orders. Often this can work as a bonus as when you are pushed for time the help will be reciprocated. Build up a trust with your staff and be prepared to back them unless you know them to be in the wrong. Contrary to popular belief the customer is not always right and good staff can be hard to get.

Honesty is of the utmost importance. It will only cause dissatisfaction if your establishment is not as advertised. Do not over-embellish or state things that are not accurate. This is the surest way of inviting complaints, and one dissatisfied customer can destroy the atmosphere for all the other guests. Should you still get a guest who is unhappy then it is best to refund the deposit if applicable and let the person find somewhere else. Even if you feel that you are in the right and the complaint is unjustified this is still the best course open to you. As the saying goes 'one bad apple in the barrel . . .'

In conclusion, it is really worthwhile to establish a successful hotel business, however small, and the sense of pride and achievement outweighs the work and worry involved.

(I am grateful to Stella and Paul Silver, proprietors of Luccombe Chine House Country Hotel, Isle of Wight, for providing the above commentary.)

REVIEW AND DISCUSSION QUESTIONS

1 Explain what is meant by the organisational setting. What are the common factors that hospitality organisations share with other work organisations?

2 Summarise, with supporting practical examples, the important organisational and staffing characteristics of hotels in general.

3 Identify clearly the main characteristic features of hotel services. To what extent are service industries different from other industries?

4 Hospitality organisations were developed on the basis of service delivery. Does this mean that hospitality organisations by nature utilise service management? Provide examples to justify your answer.

5 Explain the hotel or other hospitality organisation as an open system. How does the open systems model help in providing a basis for the analysis of hotel operations?

6 Assess the importance of organisational goals and company philosophy. Identify examples of objectives and policy from a hotel and catering organisation of your choice and comment on the effectiveness of their implementation.

7 Discuss the extent to which profit maximisation is, by itself, a sufficient criterion for the effective management of hotel operations. In what other areas should objectives be set in terms of organisational performance and results?

8 Justify the extent to which you accept the concept of the social responsibilities of management. Give practical examples of how a hospitality organisation has attempted to satisfy (and/or has failed to satisfy) its social responsibilities or obligations.

9 Explain the specific steps needed to accomplish strategic planning in the hospitality industry. Assess the practical value of SWOT analysis as part of the process of strategic planning and change.

ASSIGNMENT 1

According to Venison[42] there is a striking similarity between the hotel industry and the retail industry.

(i) Investigate: (a) a hotel organisation; (b) a retail organisation; and (c) a different type of organisation.
(ii) Develop a comparative profile of the key characteristic features of each of your chosen organisations, together with a description of what is involved in their management.
(iii) Highlight common factors, similarities and significant differences across the three organisations.
(iv) What conclusions do you draw from your analysis?

ASSIGNMENT 2

With the aid of a diagram, depict an actual hotel or other hospitality organisation of your choice in terms of the open systems model.

(i)   Explain the type and nature of the organisation including its size and location, and main characteristic features.

(ii) Give specific examples of how the functioning and operation of the organisation are affected by external environmental influences. How effective is the organisation in adapting to changes in its external environment?

(iii) Analyse, with supporting examples, the nature of the organisation's operations in terms of main interrelated sub-systems: task, technology, structure, people and management. How effective are the interrelationships and interactions among these sub-systems?

(iv) Discuss critically the effectiveness of management in co-ordinating the sub-systems and directing the activities of the organisation as a unified whole towards the accomplishment of its goals and objectives.

CASE STUDY 1

The New Jamaica Hotel

The New Jamaica is one of the smaller hotels owned by the Pearmain Group. Situated in a well-known South Coast resort the hotel has a 2-star rating which has been given largely on the strength of the cuisine. The chef is an Italian, Alberto Ciccetti, who would be able to choose a more highly paid job in almost any of the group's hotels in Britain or the rest of Europe, but Alberto's daughter has married an Englishman and they are living within a few miles of the New Jamaica, and this accounts for his presence in this particular hotel.

Another distinctive member of the staff is Jane Garner. Jane is the assistant manager. She is the first female appointed by the group to a top management post. They are watching her carefully to see whether the experiment is a success.

Jane was appointed 10 weeks ago and until now she has been understudying the manager, but he has started a fortnight's holiday. During the first week of the holiday Jane is confronted with the following problems:

1. Alberto Ciccetti comes to her office. He is distraught. His daughter has started divorce proceedings against her English husband. He says he has decided to take his daughter and grandchildren (2 boys aged 6 and 10) back to Italy at the earliest possible moment.

2. Jane has discovered that the manager has been charging the hotel more than he has been paying the suppliers, in some instances. In one particular case the invoice presented regularly for poultry and game shows £90, while the cheques paid out each week are for £96. Only two invoices are available (for the most recent payments), but both appear to have been altered from £90 to £96.

3. A young couple on honeymoon have taken possession of Room 29, one of the best rooms in the hotel, with sea views, bath en suite and balcony. No other room in the hotel has all these features. Another guest has now arrived and claims he booked the

room two months ago. It becomes obvious that a mistake was made when the receptionist made the booking. Although this guest is shown as having booked Room 30 the amount of the deposit paid obviously relates to Room 29. The guest is very upset.

4. In the course of a few days two different guests have complained of the loss of personal belongings. One has lost a roll of colour film from a bedside table. The other has lost a nearly-full phial of Chanel No. 5. There has been no suggestion of involving the police by either of the parties, but they are in no doubt that these items have been stolen.

5. Passing through the restaurant at lunch-time – it was crowded – she heard one of the customers complaining about an overcooked steak. The harassed waitress retorted, 'Don't blame me. That's the way they cooked it.' Her manner was decidedly off-hand, and the customer and his companion were obviously displeased with her manner.

(a) Discuss the main issues which are raised by each of these matters.
(b) Explain how you think Jane should deal with each of these situations.

Reprinted with permission from Chilver J, *People, Communication and Organisation*, Pergamon Press Ltd (1984).

CASE STUDY 2

The King's Restaurant

John Hill is the restaurant manager who has been employed at ABC Hotel for the last three years. He is quite good at his job, even though he only attended one catering course at the beginning of his management career. He has tried to convey an image of an experienced restaurant manager.

Mario Tazzi is an Italian waiter who is working under Hill's guidance. He has been involved with restaurants all his life, being the son of a restaurant owner. Tazzi lives in England with his attractive wife, who also works at the hotel as a silver service waitress.

Mrs Tazzi speaks very little English but she is a very charming person and many customers have told Hill how pleased they were with the way she served them at table.

A few weeks before Mr and Mrs Tazzi were employed in the King's Restaurant, Mr Hill introduced a young woman from his home town to the hotel general manager, Mr Fulbright, and this woman – Susan Green – was employed as a waitress.

Up to the time of the Tazzis' arrival Hill used to see a lot of Miss Green, and as he was in charge of allotting the shifts he always made sure that Susan worked on the same shift as he did so that they could leave the restaurant together.

Mr Fulbright received some complaints from a number of customers eating in the restaurant who said that Hill was stuck up and that Susan did not know her job at all.

Mr Fulbright called Hill to his office and told him that he had some complaints about the service in the restaurant but he did not mention that people had complained about Mr Hill's attitude, nor had Hill ever told Fulbright of the way that some customers praised Mrs Tazzi.

During the meeting they could not pinpoint the cause of the trouble, but they decided that Mrs Tazzi should change her shift with Susan so that Mr and Mrs Tazzi would not be on the same shift.

A week after this change Susan went up to Mario who had been working on her shift and told him that John Hill was having an affair with his wife.

Reproduced, with amendments, from *BACIE Case Studies for Practical Training*, 1976, with the permission of the British Association for Commercial and Industrial Education.

agerial Behaviour and Development in the Hospitality Industry',
iation of Hotel Management Schools Symposium, Leeds Polytechnic,

agement: Catering Applications, Macdonald (1971), p. 1.
rs in Hospitality: A Review of Current Research', in Cooper C (ed),
itality Management, vol. 2, Bellhaven Press, May 1990, pp. 151-167.
d edition, Heinemann (1989) p. xiv.
ng Industry, HCITB and MMD Consultants, May 1984.
nagement in the Hotel and Catering Industry, Batsford (1984).
d edition, Heinemann (1989).
d Mitchell P, Manpower Problems in the Hotel and Catering Industry,

Vork, HCITB Research Report (1981).
ustries, Pitman (1989).
ice Operations Management, McGraw-Hill (1982).
ient of Hotel Operations, Cassell (1989).
Service', Harvard Business Review, September-October 1972, p. 41.
istries, Pitman (1989).
nes-Irwin (1988), p. 20.
rvice Industry . . . Turn the Organization Chart Upside Down',
pp. 13–16.
rketing, Lexington Books (1990) p. 244.
A guide to personnel practice in the hotel and catering industries,

gy of Organizations, Second edition, Wiley (1978).
ting or Sales? Some Confusion in the Hospitality Industry',
ment, vol. 3, no. 1, 1984, pp. 38–40.
ment', International Journal of Hospitality Management, vol. 1, no.

22. Wood R C, 'Theory, Management and Hospitality: A Response to Philip Nailon', *International Journal of Hospitality Management*, vol. 2, no. 2, 1983, pp. 103–104.
23. *Ibid.*, p. 104
24. Dodrill K and Riley M, 'Hotel Workers' Orientations to Work: The Question of Autonomy and Scope', *International Journal of Contemporary Hospitality Management*, vol. 4, no. 1, 1992, pp. 23–25.
25. Venison P, *Managing Hotels*, Heinemann (1983).
26. Wood R C, *Working in Hotels and Catering*, Routledge (1992), p. 60.
27. Mullins L J, 'Is the Hotel and Catering Industry Unique?', *Hospitality*, no. 21, September 1981, pp. 30–33.
28. Mullins L J, 'The Hotel and the Open Systems Model of Organisational Analysis', *The Service Industries Journal*, vol. 13, no. 1 , January 1993, pp. 1–16.
29. See, for example, Keiser J R, *Principles and Practices of Management in the Hospitality Industry*, Second edition, Van Nostrand Reinhold (1989).
30. See, for example, Mullins L J, *Management and Organisational Behaviour*, Third edition, Pitman (1993).
31. Trist E L *et al.*, *Organizational Choice*, Tavistock (1963).
32. Brech E F L (ed), *The Principles and Practice of Management*, Third edition, Longman (1975).

33. Forte, Sir Charles, 'Catering for Everyone', *Professional Administration*, vol. 9, no. 9, October 1979, p. 24.

34. Fearn D A, *The Practice of General Management: Catering Applications*, Macdonald (1971) p. 17.

35. Drucker P F, *The Practice of Management*, Pan Books (1968) pp. 82–83.

36. For a more detailed account see Gullen H V and Rhodes G E, *Management in the Hotel and Catering Industry*, Batsford (1983).

37. Simon H A, 'On the Concept of Organisational Goal', *Administrative Science Quarterly*, vol. 10, June 1984, p. 21.

38. Jones P (ed), *Management in Service Industries*, Pitman (1989).

39. Schaffer J D, 'Structure and Strategy: Two Sides of Success' in Rutherford D G (ed), *Hotel Management and Operations*, Van Nostrand Reinhold (1990).

40. Keiser J R, Principles and *Practices of Management in the Hospitality Industry*, Second edition, Van Nostrand Reinhold (1989).

41. Ansoff H 1, *Corporate Strategy*, Revised edition, Penguin (1987).

42. Venison P, *Managing Hotels*, Heinemann (1983) p. 48.

2
WORKING WITH PEOPLE

INTRODUCTION

People are the central focus of management. It is the interaction of people in order to achieve objectives which forms the basis of an organisation. Without people the hospitality industry cannot function. If managers are to improve performance, they need a knowledge and understanding of what influences the behaviour of people at work.[1]

This chapter looks at:
- The behaviour of people
- The meaning of work
- Applications of behavioural science
- The importance of cultural influences
- The role of social science
- The people-organisation relationship
- The psychological contract

- The informal organisation
- The process of perception
- Interpersonal perception
- Sex stereotyping and gender
- Transactional analysis
- Perception of 'self'
- Frustrated-induced behaviour

THE BEHAVIOUR OF PEOPLE

We saw in Chapter 1 that a major characteristic of the hospitality industry is the role of people. Experience of hotel services is dependent upon personal interaction between staff and customers. Effective management is therefore about working with people. Unlike physical resources, people are not owned by the organisation. And of course people differ as individuals.

> People are not all made the same way. They are not all rounded. Some are angular, some are difficult, and you have to fit in with them and their personality.[2]

Members of staff will have their own perceptions of the hospitality organisation as a work organisation, and hold their own views on the systems and style of management. People bring their own feelings and attitudes towards their duties and responsibilities, and the conditions under which they are working.

Human behaviour is capricious and results from a multiplicity of influences which are difficult to identify or explain. Scientific methods or principles of behaviour cannot be applied with reliability. Tensions, conflicts and stress are almost inevitable, as are informal structures of organisation and unofficial working methods.

The study of behaviour at work

The systematic study of the behaviour of people at work is a comparatively recent development and terminology is not always consistent. The wording 'organisational behaviour' has, however, become increasingly accepted as a means of referring to the study of the behaviour of people within an organisational setting. It involves the understanding, prediction and control of human behaviour and the factors which influence the performance of people as members of an organisation.[3]

Strictly, organisational behaviour is a misnomer because rarely do all members of a hotel (or any other work organisation) behave collectively in such a way as to represent the behaviour of the hotel as a whole. In practice we are usually referring to the behaviour and actions of individuals or a small group of people. However, the wording 'organisational behaviour' is a convenient form of shorthand to refer to the multiplicity of interrelated influences on the behaviour of people within formal organisations.

THE MEANING OF WORK

Work holds a number of different meanings and values for people, and plays a variety of roles in their lives. Work helps to fulfil a range of diverse needs and expectations relating to, for example, economic rewards, intrinsic satisfaction and social relationships. (These sets of needs and expectations are discussed further in Chapter 8.) People differ, therefore, in the extent and manner of their involvement with work. Goldthorpe, for example, has identified three general sets of attitudes, or orientations, to work.[4]

- Some individuals may have only a calculative or economic involvement with work. This suggests an **instrumental orientation** with an attitude to work not as a central life issue but simply as a means to an end.
- For other individuals work may be seen more as a central life issue. There is a sense of obligation to the work of the organisation and a strong positive involvement in terms of a career structure. This suggests a **bureaucratic orientation**.
- Yet other individuals may view work primarily in terms of group activities and an ego involvement with work groups rather than the work of the organisation itself. This suggests a **solidaristic orientation** with a close link between work-related and social activities.

These different orientations will shape the individuals' attitudes towards work, and influence the importance attached to those factors which influence their motivation and job satisfaction. Some people may have a set orientation to work whatever the nature of the work environment, while for other people different work situations may influence their orientation to work.

Hotel workers' orientations to work

To what extent, then, does the nature of work in service industries and features such as low pay, poor working conditions, and the often routine and mundane nature of tasks give rise to a particular orientation or set of attitudes towards work? For example, Dodrill and Riley undertook a small research project in order to investigate the theme that hotel workers value variety and scope in their work.[5] The questionnaire project was expected to show that hotel workers display a positive attitude towards five characteristic factors – ambition, the desire for scope in the job, mobility, security and autonomy. However, the findings from 88 hotel workers of various ages and occupations, plus the control sample, did not support this contention. Only ambition and scope in the job were found as strong positive attitudes with the control sample following a similar pattern. From this, admittedly small and limited, study Dodrill and Riley conclude that hotel workers do not hold any unique orientation or distinctive attitudes towards work.

INFLUENCES ON BEHAVIOUR

The behaviour of people at work cannot be studied in isolation. The hospitality organisation as a work organisation is a constantly changing network of interrelated activities. Using the open systems model discussed in Chapter 1 we can see that effective performance will be dependent upon interactions among people and the nature of the tasks to be undertaken, the technology employed and methods of carrying out work, patterns of organisation structure, the process of management, and the external environment.

These variables provide parameters which enable us to formulate a simple four-fold framework in which to view influences on behaviour: the individual, the group, the organisation and the environment.[6]

- **The individual** – for example the personality, skills and attributes, values and attitudes, needs and expectations of individual members. The individual is the central feature of organisational behaviour, whether acting in isolation or as part of a group, in response to demands of the hotel or as a result of environmental influences.
- **The group** – for example the structure and functioning of work groups, the informal organisation, role relationships. Groups are essential to effective working and everyone will be a member of one or more groups. People in groups influence each other in many ways, and groups may develop their own hierarchies and leaders. Group pressures can have a major influence on the behaviour and performance of individual members.
- **The organisation** – for example objectives and policy, technology and methods of work, styles of leadership, methods of supervision and control. Individuals and groups interact within the formal organisation. The design of structure, patterns of management and organisational processes for the execution of work will impact on the behaviour of people.
- **The environment** – for example technical and scientific developments, economic activity, social and cultural influences, governmental actions. The hospitality organisation functions as part of the wider environment of which it is part and must be responsive to the external demands placed upon it. Environmental factors are reflected in terms of the management of opportunities and risks, the operations of the hotel and the behaviour of people.

APPLICATIONS OF BEHAVIOURAL SCIENCE

Within the framework of individual, group, organisation and environment we can identify a number of interrelated dimensions which collectively influence the behaviour of people in the work situation. The framework presents a number of alternative approaches to the study of human behaviour which give rise to frequent debate and discussion.

It is possible, for example, to adopt a psychological approach with the main emphasis on the individual, or to adopt a sociological approach with the main emphasis on human behaviour in society. It is also possible to adopt an anthropological approach with emphasis on the study of culture and customs of human behaviour as a whole.

An interdisciplinary approach

All three areas are important, as are other related areas of the social sciences such as economics and political science. But our main concern here is not with finer details of specific academic disciplines, *per se*, but with the behaviour and management of people as human resources of the hospitality industry.

An understanding of people's behaviour at work cannot be achieved in terms of the study of a single discipline. It is more appropriate therefore to take an interdisciplinary, behavioural science approach by drawing upon relevant aspects of psychology, sociology and anthropology (see Figure 2.1).

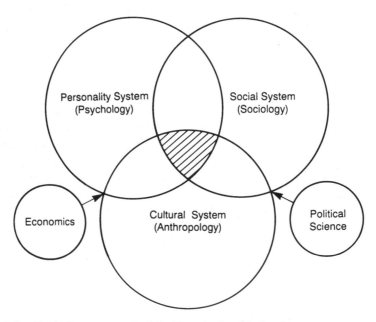

Fig 2.1 An interdisciplinary approach to the study of behaviour

● **Psychology** is concerned broadly with the study of human behaviour, with traits of the individual and membership of small social groups. The main focus of attention is on the 'personality system' and individual traits and properties such as perception, attitudes, motives and feelings.

- **Sociology** is concerned more with the study of social behaviour, and relationships among social groups and society. The main focus of attention is the 'social system' and the analysis of social structures and positions, for example the relationships between the behaviour of leaders and followers.
- **Anthropology** is concerned with the science of mankind and the study of human behaviour as a whole. A main focus of attention is on the 'cultural system' and the beliefs, customs, ideas and values within a society which affect the emphasis that individuals place on certain aspects of behaviour.

Meaning of behavioural science

Once again, terminology is not always consistent and the wording 'behavioural science' has no strict scientific definition. It may be used in a generic sense for all the social sciences concerned with the study of human behaviour. But the term is now frequently applied in a more narrow and selective way to problems of organisation and management in the work environment. Some applications of behavioural science to the hospitality industry are given by, for example, Mercer[7] and Atkinson[8].

THE IMPORTANCE OF CULTURAL INFLUENCES

The hospitality industry is very cosmopolitan and it is therefore particularly important to recognise the significance of different cultural and ethnic values, and associated traditions, religious beliefs and customs. Understanding other people's views of the world will not only make for better customer and staff relations, but may also help to prevent possible allegations of discrimination.

Account must clearly be taken of differences in language, gestures and mannerisms. There are many instances of different cultural gestures and mannerisms. For example, when the Dutch point a forefinger at their temples this is likely to be a sign of congratulations for a good idea. Elsewhere, the gesture has a less complimentary implication. In many European countries it is customary to give three or four kisses on the cheek and pulling the head away may be taken as a sign of impoliteness. A multi-cultural environment is a feature of the hotel industry. An understanding of cultural characteristics will help in understanding the behaviour of both staff and customers, and should therefore form part of induction and training programmes.

Managers also need to be aware of how cultural differences can influence the attitudes and motivations of staff, and their pace of work. This demands effective systems of communication and attention to interpersonal relationships.[9]

Effects of cultural differences

An example may be found in people who follow the Islamic faith. Under Islam the status of women is subordinate and polygamy is allowed. If they have a large number of Muslim customers some hotels may remove alcoholic beverages from the mini-bars in their bedrooms. During Ramadan, Muslim members of staff may fast through the daylight hours, eat meals only at certain times and not be prepared to work on certain days for religious reasons. The manager may therefore arrange holidays and shift working accordingly.

A number of London hotels now provide special meals for the growing number of Japanese customers and some hotels even provide separate menus and dining facilities. If there is a large number of Jewish customers some restaurant managers will not put pork on the meat trolley. Airport hotels which receive many Jewish customers may even make special arrangements for the preparation and service of kosher food.

Differences in culture may also help to explain the attitude of certain customers. Japanese businessmen who are accompanied by their wives may expect the best seats at the dining table. Americans often have a reputation for being particularly demanding and expecting a high level of personal attention. Such expectations might be better understood if managers and staff are aware of cultural differences and, as the author can testify, the high standards of customer service and concern for individual requirements which is customary in many parts of America.[10]

Culture will also influence appearance and dress. There are many examples of this: saris worn by Hindu women; long flowing robes worn by Arabs; Sikhs wearing their hair uncut and by tradition carrying a steel comb and bangle. Because of their culture many Moslem women will not wear clothes that show their legs, and will cover their heads and sometimes much of their faces with scarves. A further example is the dreadlocks hair style of Rastafarians.

THE ROLE OF SOCIAL SCIENCE

The nature of the hospitality industry as a people industry and the importance of the study of social science is widely recognised. For example, Slattery argues that the social sciences alone are able to offer theoretically grounded interpretations of people and social events in hospitality. The success of these interpretations depend upon:

- the selection of relevant theories;
- developing hospitality versions of the theories; and
- an evaluation of flaws and limitations, and value to the hospitality industry.[11]

Slattery suggests that although not all of the social sciences are useful or relevant, the range of theories which are useful is still vast. The selection of a theory depends upon the problems or issues in which we are interested. Theories of motivation, commitment and organisation are necessary bases.

The need for vocational relevance

In a critique of the role of social science subjects in hospitality management education, Wood suggests the need for a substantial reappraisal of social science education.[12] He questions the need to ensure vocational relevance and argues that such an approach could lead to dilution of the tenability of the subject matter. An alternative would be the grounding of specific components of social sciences – principally economics and sociology – with a theoretical and empirical base. However, as Wood himself states, 'whilst this approach *may* encourage intellectual integrity, it can promise nothing else.'

Such an approach as suggested by Wood would seem unlikely to gain much favour with either students or practitioners. The use of the social sciences should be seen as part of the tool kit of management, to be drawn upon and used as particular circumstances demand. The overriding objective must surely be how an understanding of the practical application of relevant aspects of social science can improve the people-organisation relationship.

A 'learning to manage organisations' approach

In a study of the teaching of sociological subjects on vocational degree courses in hotel and catering management, Lennon and Wood also report on the claimed intellectual dilution of sociology and social scientific knowledge. Such dilution is seen as a result of a number of institutional pressures including the views of industrialists, and is characterised by a multi-disciplinary approach related to the criteria of relevance to the job of a manager and a 'learning to manage organisations' approach to social studies. Lennon and Wood conclude that 'there seems little danger of contradiction in asserting that (hotel and catering) management and business studies education is, in social scientific terms at least, intellectually weak and of dubious practical value.'[13]

Although one can perhaps understand Lennon and Wood's scepticism about the idea that the social sciences represent a unified body of knowledge, this should not detract from the advantages of an interdisciplinary, behavioural science approach to an understanding of the behaviour of people at work.

Problems of organisation and management

Sociological aspects clearly can be important but much of the argument tends to be presented in the abstract and is lacking in constructive ideas on how, in practical terms, action could be taken to improve organisational performance. A requirement for intellectual rigour is of course a commendable aim. But this should not be allowed to disguise the fact that an integral part of hotel and catering management and business studies education should rightly involve an emphasis on vocational relevance and attention to learning to manage organisations.

Our knowledge of human behaviour stems from different sources. In attempting to solve problems of organisation and management in the work environment it is necessary to cut across traditional academic disciplines.[14] It is for this reason that behavioural science has developed as a body of knowledge. There is now strong support for the belief that:

> a knowledge and understanding of behavioural science, and the application of some of the key ideas about behaviour, can help improve both managerial and organisational performance.[15]

THE PEOPLE-ORGANISATION RELATIONSHIP

At the heart of successful management is the ability to relate to other people. Managers spend much of their time in meeting and talking with people,[16] and this is especially the case in the hospitality industry.[17] A high level of interpersonal skills is clearly important therefore for effective work performance. And harmonious interpersonal relationships are also likely to enhance job satisfaction and the quality of work.

Attention should be focused therefore on improving the people–organisation relationship and creating a climate in which people work willingly and effectively. The objective is to create the optimum working environment, and to reconcile the demands of the hospitality organisation for effective performance and productivity with the needs and expectations of people at work (Figure 2.2).

The manager should attempt to mould elements of individual and group behaviour in order to avoid conflict and the frustration of striving to achieve goals. This is where the application of behavioural science can assist the manager.

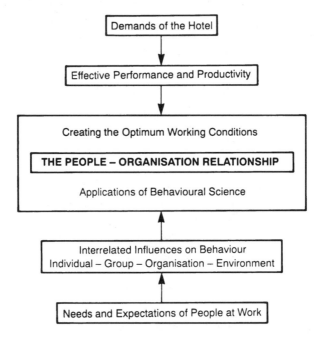

Fig 2.2 The people–organisation relationship

People as the main throughput

In Chapter 1 we saw that the main throughput of the hospitality organisation is people. The series of activities which comprise the transformation process are related to the output of a satisfied customer. Understanding the needs and expectations of people – both as staff and as customers – is therefore especially important in the hospitality industry.

The hotel student or practitioner should as part of his training consider in more depth the findings and research of behavioural scientists since they will help him to understand more fully the nature of the guest and the nature of the servers of the guest.[18]

Influences on the people–organisation relationship

Two major influences on the people-organisation relationship which also affect the behaviour of people at work are: (a) the psychological contract; and (b) the informal organisation.

THE PSYCHOLOGICAL CONTRACT

An important aspect of the people–organisation relationship is the concept of the psychological contract. This is not a written document but implies a series of mutual expectations and satisfaction of needs between the individual and the hotel (or other hospitality organisation). The psychological contract covers a range of rights, privileges, behaviour, duties and obligations which are not part of a formal agreement but still have an important influence on the behaviour of people.[19]

Expectations of the individual

Expectations of the individual vary widely and may change over time but could include that the organisation will, for example:

- pay overtime rates or allow time off for additional hours worked in excess of the contract of employment;
- adopt equitable personnel policies and procedures;
- provide a reasonable standard of live-in accommodation;
- respect the privacy of staff when not on duty;
- provide reasonable working conditions and staff facilities;
- treat members of staff with consideration and respect;
- show an understanding attitude towards any personal problems;
- provide opportunities for training in new skills and career progression.

Expectations of the hospitality organisation

Expectations of the hospitality organisation arise from the implicit attitudes and behaviour of its members. These expectations may include that members will, for example:

- accept the philosophy of the organisation and uphold its image;
- make every reasonable effort to satisfy customers' requirements;
- be prepared to work additional hours or undertake extra jobs, with appropriate recompense, when the need arises;
- show loyalty and honesty, and not betray positions of trust;
- work diligently in pursuit of objectives and accept the authority of managers;
- not abuse goodwill shown by customers or management;
- accept the approach that the customer is always right.

Bargaining and balancing

The hospitality organisation's side of the psychological contract may place emphasis on expectations, requirements and constraints which often differ from, and conflict with, the expectations of the individual. It is unlikely that all expectations of either side will be met fully. The nature of these expectations is not defined formally and there is a constant process of bargaining and balancing.

Understanding the nature of the psychological contract is an important aspect of the socialisation of members of staff new to the organisation. The informal expectations serve as important determinants of behaviour and may have a major influence on an individual's subsequent attitudes, job satisfaction and work performance, and on the level of staff turnover.

Failure to honour the psychological contract

Unfortunately the hotel industry in general does not have a good reputation for honouring the psychological contract towards its members. A prime example of this can be seen in respect of students on placement. Although not always the case, the following views expressed by college HND students appear all too typical of their experiences:

> We go on placements and see staff being treated badly which is why I would not go into the hotel industry, unless things change. It's slave labour.

> . . . I was working six days a week for 14 or 15 hours every day, receiving no training . . . When I went for my interview I was given a wonderful presentation about the training I would receive – but I was training others. I signed a contract to work 40 hours a week but when I raised the subject of overtime I was laughed at.

Situations such as these are clearly one reason why many degree and HND students turn their backs on the industry only to be snapped up by large retailing groups.[20]

THE INFORMAL ORGANISATION

The hospitality establishment is not only a work organisation, it is also a social organisation. Members of staff will establish their own social groupings and relationships, irrespective of those defined within the formal structure. The informal organisation arises from the interactions of people, their psychological and social needs, and the development of groups with their own relationships and norms of behaviour. The informal organisation is flexible and loosely structured. Relationships may be left undefined. Membership is spontaneous and with varying degrees of involvement.[21]

The style of management, the personality of members and the informal organisation will influence the operation of the establishment and actual working arrangements. What happens in practice may differ from the formal structure. According to Stewart there is a reciprocal relationship between people and the organisation.

> People modify the working of the formal organisation, but their behaviour is also influenced by it. The method of work organisation can determine how people relate to one another, which may affect both their productivity and morale. Managers, therefore, need to be conscious of the ways in which methods of work organisation may influence people's attitudes and action.[22]

Importance of the informal organisation

The informal organisation can serve a number of important functions.

- The satisfaction of members' social needs at work, and a sense of personal identity and belonging.
- A means of motivation, for example through status, social interaction, variety in routine or tedious jobs, and informal methods of work.
- Additional channels of communication. For example, through the 'grapevine' information of importance to members is communicated directly and quickly.
- A feeling of stability and security. Through informal 'norms' of behaviour a form of control is exercised over members.
- A means of highlighting deficiences or weaknesses in the formal organisation, for example areas of responsibilities not covered in job descriptions, or outdated systems and procedures. The informal organisation may also be used when formal procedures would not be appropriate to deal with an unusual or unforeseen situation.

The informal organisation, therefore, has an important influence on the behaviour of people. It affects morale, motivation, job satisfaction and work performance. The informal organisation can provide members with greater opportunity to use their initiative and creativity in both personal and organisational development. People will view the hospitality organisation through the values and attitudes of their colleagues.

The importance and nature of informal groups is discussed in more detail in Chapter 9.

Managing through the informal organisation

It is necessary for managers to recognise the existence, and importance, of the informal organisation. They should attempt to manage through the informal organisation and where appropriate use it to their advantage. Attempting to ignore the existence of the informal organisation is likely to lead only to frustration and potential conflict.

THE PROCESS OF PERCEPTION

A major determinant of behaviour, which influences the people–organisation relationship and is of particular importance within the hospitality industry, is the process of perception.

People all 'see' things differently. Owners, managers, staff, union representatives, customers, guests, visitors, suppliers, health inspectors and local residents will all have their own perception of the functioning and operations of the particular establishment. And so will each person as an individual. All people have their own, unique picture or image of how they arbitrarily view what is to them the 'real' world.

Consider the following example. The general manager is preparing a manpower plan for the hotel and wishes to gather information which may help to improve future staffing levels. The manager requests section heads to provide details of agency and temporary staff employed within their section during the past six months and projections for the next six months.

- One section head may perceive the request as an unreasonable demand, intended only to enable management to exercise closer supervision and control over the activities of the section.
- Another section head may see the request only as increased bureaucracy and more paperwork, and believe that nothing positive will come of it anyway.
- A further section head may welcome the request and perceive this as a hopeful sign of an increase in permanent staffing levels for the section.
- But yet another section head is concerned that the manager is intending to put pressure on permanent staff to work harder and longer hours.

Stimuli from the environment

Why is it that the same request can provide such mixed reactions and why do people perceive things differently? We are faced constantly with a vast amount of information (stimuli) from the environment such as shapes, colours, movement, taste, sounds, touch, smells, pain, pressures and feelings. **Perception is the process by which stimuli are screened and selected to provide meaning and significance to the individual.** The manner in which stimuli are selected and organised gives rise to individual behavioural responses (Figure 2.3).

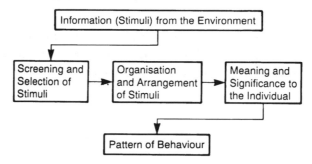

Fig 2.3 The process of perception

Individuals have their own 'mental' view of reality. Despite the fact that a group of people may 'physically' see or hear the same thing, each person has his or her own version of what is seen or heard. A person's pattern of behaviour is shaped in response to how that person perceives a particular situation. The process of perception is essential, therefore, to an understanding of human behaviour. Consider, for example, the shape in Figure 2.4.[23] **Write down exactly what you see**. Do this before reading further. We shall return to this later.

Perceptual ambiguity

A well-known example of what might be termed a perceptual ambiguity is the shape in Figure 2.5.[24] What do *you* see?

Most people will probably see a younger, well-dressed woman looking sideways. But other people will see an older, poor looking woman facing more to the front. And some

Fig 2.4 An example of incomplete stimuli

Fig 2.5 An example of perceptual ambiguity

people will quickly see both. How can people who view the same thing 'see' something so different? This helps to explain the importance of perception.

Can you now see the other picture? If so this should help you to understand why other people have a different perception to your own. Also, once you have seen clearly both pictures your mental image may quickly jump from one to the other, causing some confusion as to what you really do see.

SCREENING AND SELECTION OF STIMULI

Because there is such a vast amount of stimuli, we cannot cope adequately with all of them so we focus on certain selected stimuli and screen or filter out others. This screening and selection of stimuli is based on a combination of internal and external factors, and the context in which the stimuli occur (see Figure 2.6).

Internal factors

Internal factors relate to the characteristics of the individual such as personality, attitudes, learning, motives, needs and preferences, interests, expectations and previous experiences. People usually perceive stimuli that are likely to satisfy their needs or prove pleasurable. People may also learn to ignore mildly disturbing stimuli but respond to more important ones. For example, a manager may screen out the constant movement of people, ringing telephones and other forms of activity, but respond quickly to a guest complaining to a receptionist.

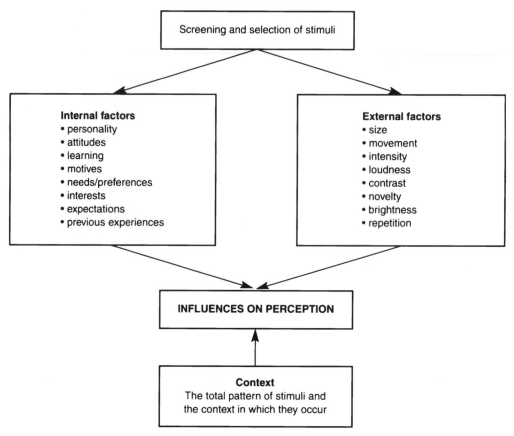

Fig 2.6 Factors influencing perception

External factors

External factors refer to the nature of the stimuli themselves. People will usually give more attention to stimuli which are, for example, large, moving, intense, loud, contrasted, bright, novel, repeated or standing out from the background. An example is the distinctive red 'pie-man' sign of Little Chef Travelodges. As another example, a fire extinguisher should be immediately visible and stand out clearly from its surroundings.

Only certain stimuli enter into an individual's perception. An intended customer entering a hotel reception area sees a member of staff having an angry exchange with a guest and walks away without booking. The customer sees only the argument and disregards the many positive features of the hotel. Another intended customer for a restaurant notices only that it is crowded and noisy and leaves without seeing the empty spaces at the back, and unaware that the food and service are excellent.

The importance of context

Any number of stimuli may be present at a given time or situation. It is, therefore, the total pattern of stimuli and the **context in which they occur** that influence perception.

The sight of a rack of muddy wellington boots is likely to be perceived quite differently in the entrance to a working farm offering bed and breakfast accommodation than in the reception area of a city-centre conference hotel.

Look now at the example in Figure 2.7.[25] Which centre black circle is the larger – A or B?

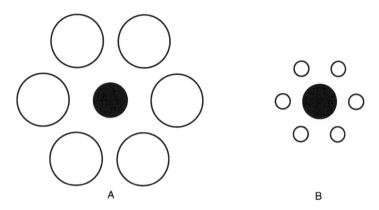

Fig 2.7 An example of context

In fact both circles are the same size and many of you might have guessed this to be the answer. However, because circle B is framed by smaller circles it certainly **appears** larger to the vast majority of people.

Organisation and arrangement of stimuli

Once incoming stimuli have been screened, they are organised and arranged in such a way that provides meaning and significance to the individual. The organisation and arrangement of stimuli can be influenced by continuity, proximity or similarity, that is **the principle of grouping**.

For example, in Figure 2.8(a) guests in a dining room are more likely to be perceived as 16 individuals, or possibly one large group. But in Figure 2.8(b) the guests are more likely to be perceived as four distinct sets or groups of people. And this perception may well influence the manner of the delivery of service.

The principle of closure

When people have incomplete or ambiguous stimuli there is a tendency to 'close' the information in order to complete the mental picture and create a meaningful image. Let us now return to Figure 2.4 (page 45).

It is probable that most people will perceive the shape either as an unconnected letter B or the unconnected number 13. However, some people may see the shape as no more than 11, or a series of, discrete blobs. For other people the shape may be perceived as some different meaningful object, for example a butterfly. Among responses from hotel and catering management degree students are a clown, a dog, a face, a series of letters of the alphabet, or a golf course (Figure 2.9, page 49). We may have difficulty in understanding

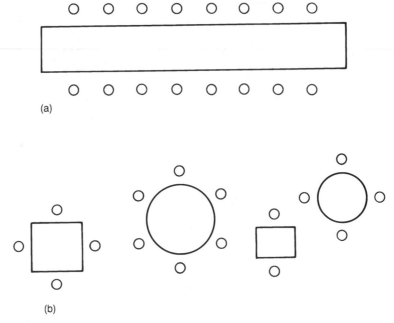

Fig 2.8 An example of the principle of grouping

how other people could possibly see such objects **but this is what they perceived the shape to be**.

The principle of closure is important as it applies not only to visual stimuli but to our other senses. We can probably all think of an example when we have 'got hold of the wrong end of the stick' as a result of our perception from overhearing only part of a conversation.

APPLICATIONS WITHIN THE HOSPITALITY INDUSTRY

As people are selective in the stimuli which determine their responses and patterns of behaviour it is important to be aware of those factors most likely to influence perception and create the desired image in the minds of customers. For example, many large hotel and catering groups adopt a standard colour scheme and layout for each of their individual establishments. This helps to influence customer perception through instant recognition and familiarity, and through helping the customer to know what to expect and to feel at home. The aim is to reinforce identification with the group and to generate repeat business.

Visual effects

Perception is influenced strongly by the appropriate use of visual effects which create a feeling of, for example, warmth or cold, intimacy or formality, large or small, cluttered or spacious. The design and layout and the lighting, patterns and colour schemes of

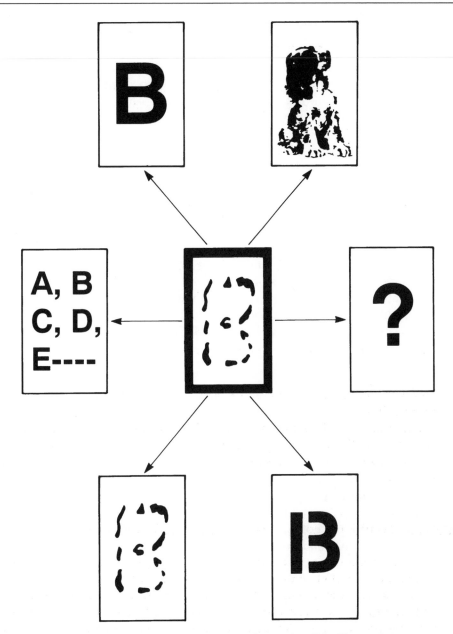

Fig 2.9 Examples of responses from the incomplete stimuli in Figure 2.4

premises, accommodation, restaurants and bars have a major impact on ambience and the atmosphere that is created.[26] Perception is also important in terms of how customers respond to the appearance and presentation of food, and to the arrangement, balance of colour and size as well as the aroma, texture and taste.

Importance of first impressions

First impressions are important. If a telephone enquiry from a potential new customer is received in a friendly, courteous and efficient manner by the receptionist the customer is likely to receive good 'vibes' and form a favourable perception of the establishment as a whole. Equally, the one curt, unhelpful receptionist can create an unfavourable perception of what is, in every other respect, a very friendly, pleasant and well-managed establishment.

A surprising number of people make a decision not to return to a hotel before they even enter the bedroom. This is linked to dissatisfaction arising from the arrival process: first impressions, the speed of check-in, the welcome, the smile, the acknowledgement, the porter service.[27]

Dress and appearance

Dress and appearance are important factors in perception, and again first impressions are important. The style of dress or uniform of the staff helps to create an image of the organisation and influences perception of the standards of service and staff–customer relationships. For example, the cleanliness of the chefs' whites influences perceptions of hygiene in the kitchen. The traditional black suits worn by the staff at Claridges convey an indication of high-class service and rather formal staff–customer relationships.

Perceiving other people

The hospitality industry is very much a people business. The way in which people perceive other people – that is the process of interpersonal perception – is clearly of particular importance. It is essential that managers and staff have a highly developed sense of people perception and understand the reasons for perceptual distortions and errors discussed below.

An understanding of perception should help us to avoid making hasty decisions about other people before thinking fully about the situation. Snap judgements can impair the 'accuracy' of perception. For example, in Figure 2.5 above it often takes time to see both the old woman and the young woman in the same picture.

Staff should be given proper guidance and training in social skills. They should be perceptually aware of customers' needs and expectations, and quick to recognise any indications that facilities or services are not up to the required standards.

Good customer care starts with good staff care.[28] It is equally important that managers also have a positive attitude towards caring for staff, and their needs and expectations at work. The manager's perception of the workforce is a major influence on the style of managerial behaviour which is adopted. (Managerial behaviour is discussed in Chapter 5.)

INTERPERSONAL PERCEPTION

The principles of perceptual differences discussed above reflect the way we perceive other people and are the source of many problems in the work situation. The process of interpersonal perception can influence both the manager-subordinate relationship and the staff-customer relationship. The perception of other people is a major determinant of behaviour and standards of service delivered.

Judgements about other people

Judgements made about other people can be influenced by perceptions of stimuli such as role or status, occupation, physical factors and appearance, and body language, for example eye contact, facial expression or tone of voice. For instance, the estimated height of a person may vary with that person's perceived status.

In a study with American college students, an unknown visitor from England was introduced briefly to five separate groups. The visitor was described with a different academic position to each group before leaving the room. Students were then asked to estimate the height of the visitor. As ascribed academic status increased, so did the group's estimate of the height of the visitor.[29]

Every person sees things in his or her own way and, as perception becomes a person's reality, this can lead to misunderstandings. There are three main factors which can create particular difficulties with interpersonal perception and cause problems in dealings with other people – selective perception, the halo effect and stereotyping.

SELECTIVE PERCEPTION

Because of their own internal characteristics, people are selective about the information to which they pay particular attention. They see and hear only what they want to see and hear. This selectivity gives rise to perceptual defence. People may tend to select information which is supportive of their point of view and choose not to acknowledge contrary information. Consider the following example.

A manager has on a number of occasions expressed dissatisfaction with the head chef, with whom there have been a number of personality clashes. On leaving the restaurant the manager enquires of a regular guest who was entertaining some business colleagues whether they enjoyed the meal. The guest replies with a smile and pointing at a colleague says: 'Peter would have preferred his steak cooked a little less, he likes it really raw so he can put a piece on his black eye.' Then with a straight face, the guest continues: 'Apart from that it was an excellent meal and we all enjoyed it, thank you.'

The manager 'hears' only the comment that the steak could have been cooked a little less and does not 'see' the accompanying smile or gesture. The manager then reports back to the chef that there has been 'another' complaint and a customer's steak was overcooked.

Another manager who has experienced no difficulties with the chef, and who gets on well with the chef, could perceive the guest's comments quite differently. The comments about the steak could be seen simply as a joke against Peter. The manager is pleased to hear that it was an excellent and enjoyable meal and reports this back to the chef.

THE HALO EFFECT

This arises when the judgements made about another person are formulated on the basis of particular characteristics or impressions that are readily available. The halo effect tends to influence perceptions of the rest of that person, either positively or negatively, and results in assumptions and generalisations from limited information.

A well-known example is with selection interviewing. A candidate arrives punctually, is smart in appearance, well-spoken and friendly. All positive characteristics – but these may well influence the perception of selectors of the candidate as a whole person. Because of the halo effect the selectors may tend to assume the candidate will perform well, and as a result place less emphasis on checking experience and technical ability.

The rusty halo effect

The process may also work in reverse (the rusty halo effect). This is where general judgements about a person are formulated from the perception of a negative characteristic. For example, a candidate is seen arriving late for an interview. There may be a very good reason for this and it may be completely out of character. But on the basis of that one particular event the person may be perceived as a poor timekeeper and unreliable.

Significance for managers

The halo effect has particular significance for managers and supervisors who may observe only a limited aspect of the behaviour or activities of staff. A single trait, such as good or bad timekeeping, may become the main, or even the sole, criterion for judging overall performance. A manager observing a member of staff performing a single task particularly well or badly may tend to see this as a judgement of that person's overall level of competence.

A danger associated with the halo effect is that the perceiver may become 'perceptually blind', and screen and shut out subsequent observations or information at variance with the original perception. For example, a manager who has recently refused to promote a member of staff despite the recommendations of the head of department may then tend to ignore favourable information about that member of staff and select only information which supports the decision not to agree to the promotion.

Another danger is that of **projection**. This is the tendency of people to project their own feelings, motives or characteristics to their perception of other people. A manager may make a more favourable judgement about members of staff who have characteristics largely in common with, and easily recognised by, the manager.

STEREOTYPING

This is the tendency to ascribe positive or negative characteristics to a person on the basis of a general categorisation and perceived similarities. Stereotyping is a form of typecasting. It is a means of simplifying the process of perception and making collective judgements of other people, rather than the recognition of each person as an individual.

Stereotyping results in the tendency to classify people according to easily recognisable characteristics and perceived common groupings according to, for example, nationality, gender, age, skin colour, speech, appearance and style of dress. For example, in some hotels male guests are required to wear jackets and ties in the restaurant. Other establishments will not admit people wearing jeans or studded jackets. In each case there is a collective stereotyping of suitable or unsuitable clientele on the basis of their dress.

Perceiving each person as an individual

We all tend to make use of stereotypes. And they *may* be helpful in enabling us to make quick predictions of likely patterns of behaviour, and reducing stress in dealing with people we do not know as individuals. However, although there is likely to be some truth in underlying stereotypes (this is why they exist) they are simplistic over-generalisations.

People of the same generalised 'grouping' do not necessarily fit into the stereotype. It is important, therefore, to be receptive to personal aspects of attitudes and behaviour. Initial perceptions based on stereotyping may need to be revised in order to perceive each person as an individual in his or her own right.

SEX STEREOTYPING AND GENDER

The (then) HCITB report on the image of hotel and catering work highlights the importance of sex stereotyping which is well established and persistent. Jobs are still perceived as being male or female and the distinction is seen as relevant in making a job choice which must be of the appropriate gender.

> The jobs which people consider suitable show substantial sex stereotyping, jobs in reception, accommodation services and the job of kitchen counter assistant being mentioned as suitable primarily by women, reception work also clearly being the most popular alternative overall. Men dominate responses concerned with management and portering. It may thus be desirable to counter established sex stereotyping and encourage women into training for management.[30]

The perception of women

Although the HCITB report demonstrated the existence of sex stereotyping, the image is grounded in reality. It is possible to predict who is most likely to be meeting customers at the reception desk, who will be cleaning their rooms and who will be cooking their meals. Typically, a woman will meet the customers, clean the rooms and serve the meals; and a man will cook the meals, repair any defects and manage the hotel.

> Statistics show that women dominate the industry, particularly at an operational level in part-time jobs. However, at a management level men outnumber women. Sex segregation can be seen in operation within some hotel departments; kitchens being almost exclusively male and housekeeping departments female.[31]

Why such distinct roles?

Why is it that men and women have such distinct roles within hotels? Is it that these roles suit their abilities or are there other explanations? Is it the women themselves who lack the ambition to become managers, or do the tradition and beliefs of the industry (the cultural milieu) exclude women? Are the ways in which management is perceived and the ways managers are developed the key to understanding the sex stereotyping of women in the industry?

In one respect it could perhaps be perceived that hotels typify the stereotype of 'women's work'. Hotels are temporary homes where staff have to anticipate and care for the physical needs of guests in terms of sleep, food and comfort. In such an environment it might be expected that women should be perceived to hold the necessary abilities, knowledge and understanding to perform well – and to attain managerial positions in large numbers.

Lack of women in management positions

For the past decade 75% of all students on higher-level hotel management courses have been female. Hence one might reasonably expect a greater proportion of women than men in management positions. However, a (then) HCITB report revealed that women are not well represented in general management positions but tend to opt for specialist career routes. Barriers exist for women, particularly with regard to differences in training opportunities.[32]

The research team also pointed out that barriers can exist 'within' women themselves and felt there was a lack of confidence shown both in their aspirations and in their career planning. However, it would seem that the study exaggerated the differences between men and women, at least in terms of their long-term ambitions, and tended to accept uncritically the 'fast' masculine route as being ideal.

Practical skills and personality

Hotel managers are expected to be multi-skilled and to be available at all times. A recurrent theme of the hotel industry is the 'traditional' style of operations characterised by a high level of activity linked to an emphasis on technical and craft skills.[33] Recent studies also confirm that hotel management is concerned primarily with the demonstration of practical skills and the personality to act as 'mine host'.[34]

If multi-skills are taken to refer to the skills of the kitchen rather than the housekeeping department, then clearly women would be disadvantaged. The food and beverage department has always held a key position in hotels, but women frequently do not receive experience or training in this section.[35] The notion of 'mine host' suggest connotations of a personality which in the past has always been associated with a male image. A number of studies have found personality to be the essential criterion in the selection and promotion of managers.[36]

The assessment of personality, however, is very subjective, it is open to interpretation and can be more concerned with whether the individual fits into the culture of the hotel. Career progression rests not only on the development of skills, or with a set of personality traits, but may be more related to whether the persona of an individual matches the culture of the hotel.

Kanter has shown that in this respect women are disadvantaged because they do not fit the conventional male profile.[37] Hicks in her research demonstrated that women were perceived in non-managerial terms, that management work was interpreted in a masculine framework and that not only was encouragement given predominantly to male trainees but females did not have an easy access to informal networks.[38]

Informal relationships and networks

Building alliances and networks are considered to be key factors in the career development and effectiveness of managers.[39] Career progression in the hotel industry is highly dependent on the managers of hotels assessing promising trainees and ensuring they receive the necessary guidance and experience. Using their own networks hotel managers ensure the progression of trainees and reinforce the significance of the maxim 'it is not what you know, but who you know'. Research has indicated that managers expect their male trainees to be committed to a career in hotel management whereas they suspect that the females are more likely to leave the industry. Thus certain trainees, typically male, are pushed towards new opportunities and advancement.[40]

Action on employment practices

According to Jagger and Maxwell, many current employment practices discriminate covertly against women. Positive action is possible, however, to prevent such discrimination. This requires attention to practices and procedures relating to job evaluation, recruitment and selection, training, management development, career planning, appraisal systems, re-entry policies, tertiary education and childcare responsibilities.[41]

Concern is becoming more widespread about the 'cloning' of organisations and that typically a board of directors consists of white, middle-class, middle-aged males. Recent attention is being given to the idea that diversity is important for the success of organisations and hence women's contributions are regarded as being paramount.[42] Positive action can therefore be seen to lie with senior managers. There is no doubt that sexism is damaging for individuals and organisations. 'Until the more powerful own the responsibility for prejudice, it will continue to cripple us all.'[43]

TRANSACTIONAL ANALYSIS

We have seen that the ability to relate effectively to other people is a particularly important feature of work in the hospitality industry. One means of helping to understand interpersonal behaviour at work is the concept of transactional analysis which has been popularised by writers such as Berne[44] and Harris.[45] Transactional analysis is a development of the ideas of Sigmund Freud and basically entails a means of applying sources of personality to provide a simplistic categorisation of social interactions.

Transactional analysis expresses an individual's personality in three patterns of feelings and behaviours, or ego states: parent, adult and child.

- **The parent state** relates to feelings about right and wrong, and how to care for and relate to other people. The parent state results from earlier conditioning and what has been learnt from external sources. It is associated with superiority and authority. For example: 'Why can't you remember to enter telephone bookings for the restaurant straight away like I've told you before. You know what happens if . . .'

- **The adult state** represents the objective, rational, thinking and reasoning aspects of personality and behaviour. Transactions are based on unemotional and calculative behaviour, and factual discussions. For example: 'We seem to have a problem with the recording equipment in the conference room. Do you think we will be able to have it repaired by this evening or should we consider alternative arrangements?'
- **The child state** is characterised by responses developed through childhood experiences. This state may be associated with wanting, having fun, playing, impulsiveness, rebelliousness, spontaneous behaviour and emotional responses. For example: 'I can't get this silly computer to work. Anyway it's not my problem, you're the one supposed to be in charge of the front office.'

An understanding of human behaviour

These states have nothing to do with chronological age but according to Berne represent aspects of psychological positions, or ego, common to everyone. All people are said to behave in each of these states at different times. The three ego states exist simultaneously within each individual although at any particular time any one state may dominate the other two. If the transactions are parallel (that is parent–parent, adult–adult or child–child) they may continue indefinitely.

However, in the adult state a person processes transactions in a reasonable and unemotional manner and responds to the other party as a responsible and sensible person. In the *majority* of work situations, therefore, the most effective form of communication is when each individual perceives the other as an adult and both adopt an adult ego state so that an adult stimulus is followed by an adult response. This form of transaction is more likely to encourage a rational, problem-solving approach and reduce the possibility of emotional conflict. There may, however, be certain situations in which different transactions may be more effective, for example a manager deliberately playing the parent state to help restore the confidence of a new member of staff who has made a mistake and is adopting a child state.

In addition to the analysis of verbal interactions, for example vocabulary and tone of voice, transactional analysis includes the perception of non-verbal communications such as posture, body language and facial expressions. Crossed transactions tend to inhibit effective communication and can lead to conflict situations. By focusing attention on the interactions occurring within a relationship, transactional analysis can aid the understanding of personality states and human behaviour. It can help to improve communication skills by assisting in interpreting a person's ego state and which form of state is likely to be the most appropriate response. This should lead to an improvement in both customer relations and management–subordinate relations.

PERCEPTION OF 'SELF'

An important factor of interpersonal behaviour and relationships with other people is perception of self, or self-image. This is how people see and think of themselves, and their evaluation of themselves. People tend to have an ideal image of themselves and how they would like to be. This is the image that is projected in dealings with other people.

The responses of other people, and their approval or disapproval, influences the development of self-image. Approval from other people will serve to reinforce that image and will contribute to an individual's self-esteem. People tend to come to see themselves how other people come to know and expect them to be. Self-esteem is the extent to which people approve of and accept themselves, and their feelings of self-respect.

Role relationships

Self-image is influenced by the different roles that people play both inside and outside the work environment. A role is an expected pattern of behaviour and forms part of the network of activities and relationships with other people. Each individual will have a number of role relationships – a 'role-set' which comprises the range of associations or contacts with whom the individual has meaningful interactions.

The expected pattern of behaviour of a hospitality manager will influence the manager's self-image. And certain characteristic features associated with this self-image will tend to persist outside the work environment, for example smart appearance and courteous behaviour in dealings with other people. (The importance of role relationships is discussed in more detail in Chapter 9.)

THE JOHARI WINDOW

In order to achieve effective interactions with other people it is necessary for individuals to be aware of their own personality characteristics and patterns of behaviour. A simple framework for looking at self-insight and the individual's own self-examination is the 'Johari window' (Figure 2.10).[46] This presents four views of personality and classifies behaviour in matrix form between:

- what is known–unknown to self; and
- what is known–unknown to others.

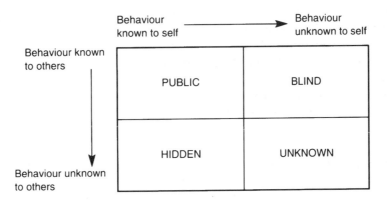

Fig 2.10 The Johari window

- **Public** is the open area containing things known both to the individual and to other people. This is the part of 'self' shared with others and where there is free disclosure of information and feelings. The larger the public area, the more effective are likely to be interactions with other people.
- **Blind** is the area containing information unknown to the individual but known to other people. This blind spot can be, for example, attitudes, mannerisms, way of speaking, body language, or the way of relating to other people. In the blind area other people may perceive readily modes of behaviour which are not obvious to the individual.
- **Hidden** is the area of behaviour which the individual wishes to conceal from, or not to communicate to, other people. An individual may try to disguise his or her real self, for example by attempting to hide shyness or nervousness behind a façade of confidence.
- **Unknown** is the area containing information unknown to both the individual and other people. Certain things may still be present but are not apparent. For example, an individual may have some 'hidden' ability, talent or past experiences.

Changes in behaviour

In order to help individuals to understand themselves better and to improve their interactions with other people it is necessary to expand the individual's public area and reduce the hidden and blind areas. To reduce hidden behaviour it is necessary to encourage greater self-disclosure in a non-threatening environment and an atmosphere of confidence and trust. To reduce blind behaviour requires feedback which the individual is prepared to accept on how other people perceive the individual's behaviour.

FRUSTRATED-INDUCED BEHAVIOUR

The behaviour and actions of people at work result from the desire to achieve some goal in order to satisfy certain needs or expectations. This is the basis of a person's motivational driving force and a major influence on the nature of interpersonal relationships. Needs and expectations at work include the satisfaction of economic rewards, for example pay and security; intrinsic satisfaction, for example variety and an interesting job; and social relationships, for example comradeship and a feeling of belonging. (Motivation, and the needs and expectations of people at work, are discussed in Chapter 8.)

When a person's motivational driving force is blocked before reaching a desired goal there are two possible sets of outcomes: constructive behaviour or frustration (Figure 2.11). Even if a person engages in constructive behaviour it could be said that the person was 'frustrated', if only mildly or in the short term. The term 'frustration', however, is usually interpreted as applying to negative behavioural responses to a barrier or blockage which prevents satisfaction of a desired goal.

Constructive behaviour

This is a positive reaction to the blockage of a desired goal and can take two main forms: problem-solving or restructuring. These are not necessarily exclusive forms of reaction,

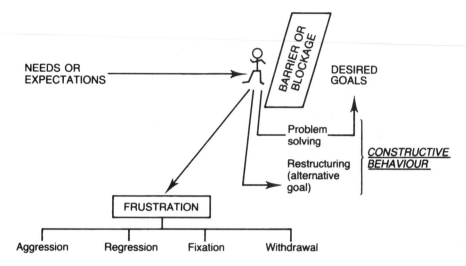

Fig 2.11 Behavioural responses to frustration
Source: Mullins L J, *Management and Organisational Behaviour*, Third edition, Pitman (1993), p. 446

and constructive behaviour may involve a combination of problem-solving and restructuring.

- **Problem solving** entails removal of the barrier, for example: by-passing an uncooperative colleague; repairing broken equipment; undertaking training or gaining a qualification, persuading the manager to grant promotion, finding an alternative method of working.
- **Restructuring** involves the substitution of an alternative goal, although such a goal may be of a lower order or priority. Restructuring may also entail compromise between the satisfaction of conflicting goals, for example: requesting a transfer to another department or to a different shift, taking an additional part-time job, accepting a less interesting job because the hours of work are more convenient.

Frustration

This is a negative response to the blockage of a desired goal and results in a defensive form of behaviour. There are many possible reactions to frustration but these can be summarised under four broad headings: aggression, regression, fixation, and withdrawal.[47] Again, these categories are not mutually exclusive and most forms of frustrated-induced behaviour at work are a combination of aggression, regression and fixation.

- **Aggression** is a physical or verbal attack on some person or object, for example: striking a supervisor, damaging equipment, destroying documents, shouting or using abusive language, spreading malicious gossip about a colleague. This form of behaviour may be directed against the person or object perceived as the actual blocking agent and the source of frustration.
- **Regression** is reverting to childish or a more primitive form of behaviour, for example: screaming, tantrums, crying, sulking, refusing to co-operate with colleagues or

listen to reasoned arguments, constantly moaning, displaying neurotic behaviour, striking or kicking broken equipment or machinery.

- **Fixation** involves persisting in a form of behaviour which has no adaptive value and continuing to repeat actions which have no positive results, for example: continually trying to operate equipment which obviously will not work, insisting on applying for promotion to a position for which clearly not suited, being excessively critical, refusing to accept change or new ideas.
- **Withdrawal** is apathy, giving up or resignation, for example: losing interest in the job, poor timekeeping, increasing sickness and absenteeism, refusing to accept responsibility, passing work over to colleagues, avoiding decision-making, failing to give support to colleagues, refusing to join in group or social activities, leaving the job altogether.

Displaced aggression

Frustrated-induced behaviour may often result in displaced aggression. This may occur when the source of the frustration is not clear or specific or where the source is feared such as a powerful superior. With displaced aggression the person may find an easier or 'safer' person or object as an outlet of frustration, for example: being short-tempered with subordinates, slamming doors, kicking the waste-paper basket, being irritable with friends.

The concept of displaced aggression has particular significance in the hospitality industry. Staff may well be expected to act in accordance with a doctrine of 'the customer is *always* right' and, however trying or demanding the circumstances, should not give vent to their frustration in public view of customers or guests. By the same token, however, managers and colleagues should be understanding when staff need to find some alternative outlet as a scapegoat for their frustration.

Factors influencing frustration

There are many factors which influence the feeling of frustration and an individual's reactions, for example the importance of the desired goal and strength of the need, cultural values, the perceived nature of the barrier or blocking agent, the pressure under which the individual is working, previous experience, the personality characteristics and social skills of the individual.

It must also be remembered that most people do not necessarily separate their working lives from their domestic or social lives. And neither is it reasonable to expect them to do so.[48] The behaviour and actions of people are influenced by problems and frustrations outside as well as inside the work organisation. Managers have a social responsibility to recognise that people cannot always leave their personal difficulties behind when they come to work.

SUMMARY

- Effective management is all about working with people and this is particularly important in the hospitality industry. People differ in their attitudes or orientations to work. The behaviour of people at work is influenced by a combination of factors and cannot be understood in terms of the study of a single discipline. It is more appropriate to adopt an applied, interdisciplinary approach including attention to the importance of cultural influences.

- A high level of interpersonal skill is important for effective work performance. Managers should focus attention on improving the people–organisation relationship and creating a climate in which staff work willingly and effectively. Two major influences on the people–organisation relationship are recognition of the psychological contract and the informal organisation.

- A major determinant of behaviour of particular importance within the hospitality industry is the process of perception. Interpersonal perception influences both the manager–subordinate relationship and the staff–customer relationship. Two main problems with interpersonal perception are the halo effect and stereotyping. Sex stereotyping is well established and persistent within the industry.

- One means of helping to understand interpersonal behaviour at work is the concept of transactional analysis. This can help to improve communication skills and reduce emotional conflict. An important factor of interpersonal behaviour and relationships with other people is the perception of 'self' or self-image.

- If a person's motivational driving force is blocked this can result in two possible sets of outcomes: constructive behaviour or negative responses (frustrated-induced behaviour). The main reactions to frustration can be summarised as aggression (including displaced aggression), regression, fixation and withdrawal.

REVIEW AND DISCUSSION QUESTIONS

1 Suggest main headings under which to view influences on behaviour in work organisations. From your own experience, give brief practical examples under each heading.

2 Comment critically on the role of social science within the hospitality industry. Explain your understanding of behavioural science as an interdisciplinary approach to the study of behaviour. Provide your *own examples* of the importance of cultural differences.

3 Explain what is meant by the psychological contract. Give practical examples of: (a) expectations that might be held by individuals; and (b) expectations that might be held by the hotel (or other hospitality organisation). Give examples of your own expectations that you would hope to see covered by the psychological contract.

4 What do you understand by the informal organisation and how does it arise? What important functions are served by the informal organisation?

5 Why is the study of perception of particular importance within the hospitality industry? Explain what is meant by perceptual illusions, and the screening and selection of perceptual stimuli.

6 Discuss the factors which influence the judgements we make of other people. Explain the main sources of distortions and errors in interpersonal perception. As a hospitality manager, how you would attempt to overcome sex stereotyping?

7 Discuss the value to the hospitality manager of an understanding of transactional analysis. Suggest how managers might become more aware of their perception of 'self' and self-image, and bring about changes in their behaviour.

8 Explain what is meant by frustrated-induced behaviour. Distinguish between constructive behaviour and frustration. From your own experience, give practical examples of both types of behaviour.

ASSIGNMENT 1

We all tend to be guilty of distortions and errors in interpersonal perception, and of making hasty decisions about the behaviour and actions of other people before thinking fully about the situation.

(i) Consider honestly the biases, prejudices and attitudes that you have about certain people. Explain how you attempt to guard against these biases, prejudices and attitudes in order to make a fair and objective assessment of others.
(ii) Relate examples of judgements you have made about other people on the basis of:
   (a) the halo effect;
   (b) the rusty halo effect; and
   (c) stereotyping.
(iii) Give a brief account of situations when you have:
   (a) made a judgement about another person on the basis of **selective perception**; and
   (b) assumed too much from **limited information** and when there was a reasonable, alternative interpretation which differed from your first reaction.

Be prepared to share and discuss your experiences in self-selecting groups of four to six. Make notes of what you feel has been learnt from undertaking this assignment.

ASSIGNMENT 2

From your own experience, provide a short account of an actual problem or difficulty you have encountered in working with other people in the hospitality industry. Explain clearly:

(i) the exact nature of the problem or difficulty;
(ii) the behaviour/actions of the person(s) involved;
(iii) the steps taken to help overcome the situation and with what results, *and/or* the actions you would now propose be taken.

CASE STUDY 1

John Adams

John Adams was on duty as a member of the night service staff with ABC Hotel. After an overseas guest clicked her fingers and whistled for service Adams lost his temper. 'You're not the only guest in this hotel.' He then warned the guest that if she did not stop her obnoxious behaviour no one would provide her or anyone else with service. Next day the guest complained to a room attendant. Adams was reprimanded by the personnel manager of the hotel and threatened with dismissal. In his defence Adams admitted that heated words were exchanged with the guest when she left the lounge late that night to go to her room. 'I did not swear at her but I did allow her to rile me. She started causing trouble as soon as she came into the lounge after the bar had closed. The day staff warned me about her when they went off duty. She was clicking her fingers and whistling for service all night. She threw the tray back at me when I took food to her room at 3 o'clock in the morning. I told her it was about time she stopped behaving like that. I just had enough of everything. I told her she would not get any more service if she treated people like that.'

(i) **Analyse the main issue(s) of management and organisational behaviour identified in this situation.**

(ii) **Suggest how the issue(s) might best be resolved. Assuming you are the general manager of ABC Hotel what action would you propose to take?**

CASE STUDY 2

What happened next?

Richard Jackson is an outgoing person with a keen sense of humour who enjoys talking with other people. He has spent the majority of his working life in the catering trade, largely in public houses. After moving from London, Jackson was pleased to accept the opportunity of a partnership in managing The River View, a public house and restaurant situated on the coast. The other partner, Tony Wheeler, was a younger man with a degree in Business Studies. It was agreed that Jackson would have particular responsibility for the kitchen and food preparation, and assisting with bar work when necessary.

At first all seemed to be going well. After meals had finished being served Jackson would often help behind the bar. He regularly joined customers drinking and laughing with them, and quickly became a very popular figure. The partnership had been in operation for about a year when, much to Jackson's surprise, Tony Wheeler announced his engagement to Belinda Daniels, a divorcee some years older than Wheeler. Jackson could not hide a certain feeling of unease at this development. As Belinda Daniels started to spend a greater amount of time at The River View, Jackson became more and more disillusioned.

Jackson felt that he was increasingly expected to undertake too much of behind-the-scenes work with little involvement in the management decision-making. When a member of the kitchen staff left, Wheeler was reluctant to appoint a replacement, claiming that Jackson could undertake more of the work. Relationships with Wheeler became very strained.

As a result, Jackson applied for, and was both delighted and surprised to obtain, a position of chef at The Hollow, a nearby golf and country club hotel. Jackson immediately informed Wheeler that he was withdrawing from the partnership and left The River View the same week.

The Hollow has 75 bedrooms in a modern building with conference facilities for 180 people. It is set in beautiful countryside and with a high-standard golf course and leisure centre. Well-known local celebrities and sportspeople are frequent customers at the hotel. The Hollow is located in a high-wage area and suffers from a constant shortage of staff, especially during the summer months.

Jackson quickly struck up a friendship with the restaurant manager and gained a reputation for being a more-than-competent chef, conscientious and uncomplaining at the long hours of work. However, two months after Jackson was appointed the restaurant manager, who started at The Hollow four months ago, left at short notice. Much to his obvious pleasure Jackson was offered the position. This did not please the assistant restaurant manager, a younger but more highly qualified person than Jackson, who had been in the post for the last 10 months.

Jackson seemed to revel in his new appointment. One of his first actions was to remove the desk from the restaurant entrance where customers would book or confirm their reservations. This was 'to create more open space as a welcome to customers'. Jackson could constantly be seen chatting and laughing with customers. He would greet them at the door of the restaurant and often take their orders personally.

One evening, after finishing the main dish, a regular and well-known customer, accompanied by a number of guests, asked to speak to Jackson. There were obvious signs of merriment from the customer's table.

'I don't like to have to say this but the meat was overcooked, the plates far too hot to touch and service was very slow. And the soup was certainly not up to standard. Last time we were here the meal was not all that great. I didn't want to complain before in case it upset you, but – sorry – this is just not good enough.'

Jackson offered reassuring words and went immediately into the kitchen. Shortly afterwards he returned with a bottle of wine. He pulled up a chair from a nearby table.

'Sorry for the hiccup. Bit of an off-night for the kitchen staff, I'm afraid. Please accept another bottle of house wine with my compliments, and there is a free choice of sweet on the house.'

'Thanks very much' responded the guest. 'We knew you would sort this out for us.'

'That's OK. Now – anything else I can do for you moaning minnies?' said Jackson in a mock-serious tone.

'No, thank you. As we said, we didn't want to upset you.'

'Good. Now you can let me have a glass of that wine I've just brought you.'

'Sure thing,' replied one of the guests, who with a smile poured a glass of wine and handed it to Jackson.

Jackson then happened to look round and to his surprise noticed the hotel manager standing quietly in a corner near the entrance to the restaurant.

The following morning in the hotel manager's office

An apprehensive Jackson is standing in front of the manager, who is sitting behind the desk.

'It seems there have been a number of complaints from the restaurant lately. Also, I am told that because of problems with delivery, on more than one occasion staff have had to go to the off-licence to buy wine for the customers. I believe yesterday was the chef's day off, and the only part of the meal he prepared was the soup of the day before. You know that, however well anyone knows their job, you can't work on your own here but as a member of a group.'

'You mean everything by rules and committee,' responded Jackson.

'No,' replied the manager. 'I mean the need for co-operation and teamwork. Anyway, we need to talk more about that later.'

The manager then left the desk, and beckoned Jackson to sit in a nearby chair. Jackson wasn't sure, but wondered if he detected a change in the expression on the face of the manager, who said, 'Now, about last night . . .'

(i) Analyse the main issues which appear to be raised in this case.

(ii) Assuming you are the manager of The Hollow, explain fully what actions you would now propose to take.

NOTES AND REFERENCES

1. See, for example, Arnold J, Robertson I T and Cooper C L, *Work Psychology*, Pitman (1991).
2. Forte, Charles (Lord), *Forte: The Autobiography of Charles Forte*, Sidgwick & Jackson (1986), p. 123.
3. For example, see Luthans F, *Organizational Behavior*, Fifth edition, McGraw-Hill (1989).
4. Goldthorpe J H *et al.*, *The Affluent Worker: Industrial Attitudes and Behaviour*, Cambridge University Press (1968).
5. Dodrill K and Riley M, 'Hotel Workers' Orientations to Work: The Question of Autonomy and Scope', *International Journal of Contemporary Hospitality Management*, vol. 4, no. 1, 1992, pp. 23–25.
6. Mullins L J, 'The Organisation and the Individual', *Administrator*, vol. 7, no. 4, April 1987, pp. 11–14.
7. Mercer K, 'Psychology at Work in the Hotel and Catering Industry', *HCIMA Review*, vol. 4, 1978, pp. 207–217.
8. Atkinson P E, 'Applications of the Behavioral Sciences Within the Hospitality Industry', *Hospitality*, September 1980, pp. 7—3.
9. For example, see Hornsey T and Dann D, *Manpower Management in the Hotel and Catering Industry*, Batsford (1984).
10. See, for example, Weaver P A and Oh H C, 'Do American Business Travellers Have Different Hotel Service Requirements?', *International Journal of Contemporary Hospitality Management*, vol. 5, no. 3, 1993, pp. 16–21.
11. Slattery P, 'Social Science Methodology and Hospitality Management', *International Journal of Hospitality Management*, vol. 2, no. 1, 1983, pp. 9–14.
12. Wood R C, 'Against Social Science?', *International Journal of Hospitality Management*, vol. 7, no. 3, 1988, pp. 239–250.
13. Lennon J J and Wood R C, 'The teaching of Industrial and Other Sociologies in Higher Education: The Case of Hotel and Catering Management Studies', *International Journal of Hospitality Management*, vol. 11, no. 3, 1992, pp. 239–253.
14. See, for example, Drake R and Smith P, *Behavioural Science in Industry*, McGraw-Hill (1973).
15. Cowling A G *et al.*, *Behavioural Sciences for Managers*, Second edition, Edward Arnold (1988,) p. 1.
16. Mintzberg H, 'The Manager's Job: Folklore and Fact', *Harvard Business Review Classic*, March–April 1990, pp. 163–176.
17. See, for example, Ferguson D H and Berger F, 'Restaurant Managers: What Do They *Really* Do?', *Cornell HRA Quarterly*, vol. 25, no. 1, May 1984, pp. 26–36.
18. Venison P, *Managing Hotels*, Heinemann (1983), p. 18.
19. See, for example, Schein E H, *Organizational Pyschology*, Third edition, Prentice-Hall (1988).
20. Robinson S, 'The Learning Curve', *Inside Hotels*, April/May 1992, pp. 40–45.
21. For a detailed account of the informal organisation, see Gray J L and Starke F A, *Organizational Behavior: Concepts and Applications*, Fourth edition, Charles E. Merrill (1988).
22. Stewart R, *The Reality of Management*, Second edition, Pan Books (1986), p. 127.
23. Morgan C T and King R A, *Introduction to Psychology*, Third edition, McGraw-Hill (1966), p. 343.
24. Hill W E, *Puck*, 6 November 1915.
25. Hellriegel D, Slocum J W and Woodman R W, *Organizational Behavior*, Fourth edition, West Publishing (1986), p. 90.
26. For example, see: Jones P, *Food Service Operations*, Holt, Rinehart & Winston (1983).

27. Hubrecht J and Teare R, 'A Strategy for Partnership in Total Quality Service', *International Journal of Contemporary Hospitality Management*, vol. 5, no. 3, 1993, p. iii.

28. Klein S, 'Customer Care Needs Staff Care', *Proceeding of The International Association of Hotel Management Schools Symposium*, Leeds Polytechnic, November 1988.

29. Wilson P R, 'Perceptual Distortion of Height as a Function of Ascribed Academic Status', *Journal of Social Psychology*, no. 74, 1968, pp. 97–102.

30. Ellis P, *The Image of Hotel and Catering Work*, HCITB (1981), p. 26.

31. *Women in the Hotel and Catering Industry*, HCITB (1987).

32. *Women's Path to Management in the Hotel and Catering Industry*, HCITB (1984).

33. Guerrier Y and Lockwood A, 'Developing Hotel Managers – A Reappraisal', *International Journal of Hospitality Management*, vol. 8, no. 2, 1989, pp. 82–89.

34. Baum T, 'Toward a New Definition of Hotel Management', *Cornell HRA. Quarterly*, Educators' Forum 1988, pp. 36–39.

35. *Women's Path to Management in the Hotel and Catering Industry*, HCITB (1984).

36. See, for example, Hicks L, 'Excluded Women: How Can This Happen in the Hotel World?', *The Services Industries Journal*, vol. 10, no. 2, April 1990, pp. 348–363.

37. Kanter R B, *Men and Women of the Corporation*, Basic Books (1977).

38. Hicks L, 'Gender and Culture: A study of the attitudes displayed by managers in the hotel industry', Unpublished Phd dissertation, University of Surrey, 1991.

39. Kotter J P, 'What Effective General Managers Really Do', *Harvard Business Review*, Vol. 60, No. 6, November–December 1982, pp. 156–167.

40. Hicks L, 'Gender and Culture: A study of the attitudes displayed by manager in the hotel industry', Unpublished PhD dissertation, University of Surrey, 1991.

41. Jagger E and Maxwell G, 'Women in Top Jobs', *Proceedings of the International Association of Hotel Management Schools Symposium*, Leeds Polytechnic, November 1988.

42. Caulkin S, 'Minorities Get The Vote', *The Observer*, Sunday 14 November, 1993.

43. Quote by Gloria Steinem in Reardon, K, 'The Memo every woman keeps in her desk', *Harvard Business Review*, March–April 1993, pp. 16–22.

44. Berne E, *Games People Play*, Penguin (1966).

45. Harris T A, *I'm OK – You're OK: A Practical Guide to Transactional Analysis*, Harper & Row (1969).

46. Luft J, *Group Processes: An Introduction to Group Dynamics*, Second edition, National Press (1970). (The term 'Johari Window' was derived from a combination of the first names of the original authors, Joseph Luft and Harry Ingham.)

47. Brown J A C, *The Social Psychology of Industry*, Penguin (1954 and 1986).

48. See, for example, Hornsey T and Dann D, *Manpower Management in the Hotel and Catering Industry*, Batsford (1984).

3

ORGANISATIONAL DESIGN AND STRUCTURE

INTRODUCTION

It is by means of structure that the work of the hospitality organisation is carried out. Structure provides the framework for the organisation's pattern of management. It affects economic performance and the behaviour of staff. The development of organisation theory has highlighted the importance of structural design and the management of human resources.

This chapter looks at:

- The importance of organisational structure
- Approaches to organisation, structure and management
- The classical approach
- Scientific management
- Bureaucracy
- Human relations approach
- The systems approach

- The contingency approach
- The shamrock organisation
- The relationship between structure and people
- Design of structure
- Span of control and scalar chain
- Line and staff structure
- The value of organisation charts

THE IMPORTANCE OF ORGANISATIONAL STRUCTURE

The application of the process of management and the execution of work take place within the structure of the hotel or other hospitality organisation. Structure is the pattern of relationships among positions in the hotel and among members of the hotel. Structure creates a framework of order and command through which the activities of the hotel are planned, organised, directed and controlled.

It is structure, therefore, that gives shape to a hotel, and provides the basis for organisational processes and the execution of work. The purpose of structure is to define:

- the division of work;
- tasks and responsibilities;
- work roles and relationships; and
- channels of communication.

In the very small hotel there are likely to be fewer problems with structure. The distribution of tasks, the definition of authority and responsibility, and relationships among members of staff can be established on a personal and informal basis. But all hotels, of whatever type or size, require some form of structure by which people's interactions and efforts are channelled and co-ordinated. With larger hotels there is a greater need for a carefully designed and purposeful form of structure.

An outline of typical key activities and division of work is given in Figure 3.1.

Structure and effective performance

In order to achieve its goals and objectives the work of the hotel has to be divided among its members. The resulting structure should be that which is most appropriate to the objectives of the hotel.[1] Structure is necessary for the effective performance of key activities and to support the efforts of staff. It provides accountability for areas of work undertaken by groups and individual members of the hotel. Structure therefore involves the organisation of human assets.[2]

The correct design of structure is a major determinant of effective organisational performance. Drucker, for example, makes the point that:

> Good organisation structure does not by itself produce good performance. But a poor organisation structure makes good performance impossible, no matter how good individual managers may be. To improve organisation structure . . . will therefore always improve performance.[3]

There is also a need for the continual review of structure to ensure that it is the most appropriate form for the particular hotel, and in keeping with its change and development. The quality of structure will affect the grouping of functions, the allocation of responsibilities, decision-making, co-ordination, control and reward. These are all fundamental requirements for the continued operation of an organisation.[4]

The structure of a hotel will affect not only its economic efficiency and performance, but also the morale and job satisfaction of the staff. Managers need to consider how structural design and methods of work organisation influence the behaviour and performance of members of the hotel. Structure is also a major component of an effective corporate strategy.[5]

APPROACHES TO ORGANISATION, STRUCTURE AND MANAGEMENT

Organisation structure, the process of management and the behaviour of people at work are inextricably linked. Underlying the development of management theory and practice are contrasting ideas on structural design and attitudes towards people. Identification of major trends in the study of organisations and management will help to provide a perspective on concepts and ideas discussed in subsequent chapters.

Much has been written about different approaches to improving the effectiveness of work organisations. It is usual, therefore, to categorise the work and ideas of writers into various 'approaches' based on their views of structure and management. This provides a framework in which to direct study and focus attention.

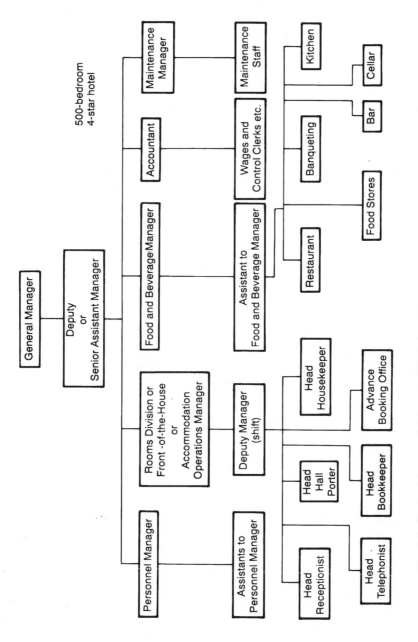

Fig 3.1 Typical key activities and division of work for a 500-bedroom four-star hotel

It is important, however, to emphasise that no single approach provides all the answers. It is the comparative study of different approaches which yields benefits for the manager. The skill of organisational design lies in taking from the different approaches those ideas which suit best the particular situation and requirements of the hotel.

Categorisation of approaches

There are many different ways of attempting to categorise these various approaches. For example, Gullen and Rhodes refer to the traditional, empirical, human relations, decision-theory and formalism approaches.[6] On the other hand, Keiser identifies the classical scientific, classical organisation, human relations, management science, contingency and Japanese approaches.[7]

Whatever the broad classification of main approaches it is possible to identify a number of possible cross-groupings and sub-groupings. Some of these sub-groupings might be seen as mutually exclusive whilst others might be viewed as sub-divisions of broader approaches.[8]

In order to provide a convenient framework as a basis for our discussion we will use a broad four-fold categorisation of:

● the classical approach – including scientific management and bureaucracy;
● the human relations approach – including the structuralists;
● the systems approach; and
● the contingency approach (Figure 3.2).

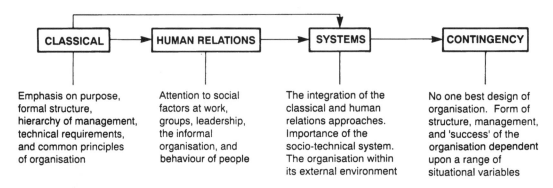

Fig 3.2 Main approaches to organisation, structure and management

THE CLASSICAL APPROACH

The classical approach is associated with work carried out initially in the early part of this century. Classical writers placed emphasis on purpose and structure, and on the technical requirements of the organisation. Identification of general objectives would lead to clarification of purposes and responsibilities at all levels of the organisation, and to the most effective structure.

Attention is focused on the division of work, reporting relationships, the clear definition of duties and responsibilities, and maintaining specialisation and co-ordination. The emphasis is on structure based upon a hierarchy of management and formal organisational relationships.

Principles of organisation

The classical writers were concerned with improving the process of management and organisation structure as a means of increasing efficiency. Emphasis was placed on the importance of a common set of principles for the design of a logical structure. Most classical writers had their own set of principles but probably the leading authority was Urwick, who specified ten principles of organisation.[9]

1. **The principle of the objective:**
   Every organisation and every part of the organisation must be an expression of the purpose of the undertaking concerned, or it is meaningless and therefore redundant.'
2. **The principle of specialisation:**
   'The activities of every member of any organised group should be confined, as far as possible, to the performance of a single function.'
3. **The principle of co-ordination:**
   'The purpose of organisating *per se*, as distinguished from the purpose of the undertaking, is to facilitate co-ordination and unity of effort.'
4. **The principle of authority:**
   'In every organised group the supreme authority must rest somewhere. There should be a clear line of authority to every individual in the group.'
5. **The principle of responsibility:**
   'The responsibility of the superior for the acts of the subordinate is absolute.'
6. **The principle of definition:**
   'The content of each position, both the duties involved, the authority and responsibility contemplated and the relationships with other persons should be clearly defined in writing and published to all concerned.'
7. **The principle of correspondence:**
   'In every position, the responsibility and the authority should correspond.'
8. **The principle of span of control:**
   'No person should supervise more than five, or at the most, six direct subordinates whose work interlocks.'
9. **The principle of balance:**
   'It is essential that the various units of an organisation should be kept in balance.'
10. **The principle of continuity:**
    'Re-organisation is a continuous process: in every undertaking specific provision should be made for it.'

The definition of responsibilities

Another major contributor of the classical approach, Brech, attempts to provide a practical approach to organisation structure based on tried general principles as opposed to concentrating on specific cases or complex generalisations.[10] Brech places emphasis on the importance of formal relationships, written definition of responsibilities and the value of job descriptions as an aid to effective structure and delegation. His work builds on the ideas of earlier writers and therefore provides a comprehensive view of the classical approach.

Relevance and applications

The classical writers have been criticised generally for not taking sufficient account of personality factors, and of creating an organisation structure in which people can exercise only limited control over their work environment. Research studies have also expressed doubts about the effectiveness of the classical approach when applied in practice.[11]

However, although the work of the classical writers is sometimes regarded as an out-of-date approach, it does focus attention on important factors in the study of organisational design. Good structure is necessary for efficiency and an essential factor in improving performance.

The idea of common sets of principles has been subject to much criticism. Simon, for example, states that:

> Organisational design is not unlike architectural design. It involves creating large, complex systems having multiple goals. It is illusory to suppose that good designs can be created by using so-called 'principles' of classical organisation theory.[12]

Many of the principles are expressed as bland statements in non-operational terms and give little basis for specific managerial action. Nevertheless, the principles are still relevant and they do provide general guidelines on the design and structuring of organisations. It is also of interest to note that, despite the criticisms, many of the more recent writings on the subject appear to be based on the original work of the classical writers.

The basic concepts can be of value to the hotel manager if modified to suit the demands of the particular situation. The application of these principles needs to take account of:

- the particular situational variables of the hotel; and
- the psychological and social factors relating to the people who work within the structure.

Two major 'sub-groupings' of the classical approach of particular importance for organisational design and structure are:

- scientific management; and
- bureaucracy.

SCIENTIFIC MANAGEMENT

Scientific management places emphasis on obtaining increased productivity from individual workers through the technical structuring of the work organisation. The major contributor to this approach was F.W. Taylor (1856–1917), who believed that in the same way that there is a best machine for each job, so there is a best working method by which people should undertake their jobs.[13]

Taylor was concerned with finding more efficient methods and procedures for the co-ordination and control of work. He also believed in the rational-economic needs concept of motivation. The provision of monetary incentives was the primary motivator for higher levels of output. Workers would be motivated by obtaining the highest possible wages through working in the most efficient and productive way.

Principles of scientific management

Scientific management was based on the principles of:

- the scientific selection, training and development of workers;
- the clear division of work and responsibilities between management and workers; and
- close management control over the actual processes of work.

Taylor considered that all work processes could be analysed into discrete tasks and that by scientific methods it was possible to find the 'one best way' to perform each task. Each job was broken down into component parts, each part timed, and the parts rearranged into the most efficient method of working.

Criticisms of scientific management

Scientific management is often referred to as a machine theory model. It adopts an instrumental view of human behaviour together with the application of specialisation and standard procedures of work. Workers were viewed less as isolated individuals and more as units of production to be handled in much the same way as machines. The scientific study of work can lead to jobs becoming repetitive, boring and requiring little skill.

The ideas behind scientific management have been largely discredited by subsequent management writers. There has been strong criticism of scientific management as representing close management control over workers. By removing decisions about how their work is carried out, by division of labour, and by dictating precise stages and methods for every aspect of work performance, management could gain control of the actual process of work. The rationalisation of production processes and division of labour tends to result in the de-skilling of work, and this may be a main strategy of management.[14]

The question of de-skilling would appear to have particular significance in hotel and catering where in recent years there have been many examples of the de-skilling of work.[15] (See also the discussion on the shamrock organisation later in this chapter.)

Relevance to the hospitality industry

Despite the criticisms, the underlying approach of scientific management still has some relevance to the hospitality industry. Taylor and his followers introduced the concept of a systematic approach to management. They have left to modern management the legacy of practices such as job analysis, systematic selection and training, work study, payment by results, production control and management by exception. The adoption of such practices has a significant effect on hospitality management.

Managers need to find the most efficient and productive methods of work. In particular, the efficiency of 'production' areas, such as food preparation and service and housekeeping is likely to benefit from a clear division of work and responsibilities, prescribed methods of working and labour-saving approaches.

Standard recipes and performance standard manuals including photographs of finished dish presentations are widely used in the industry. With chain hotels in particular it is common to have a prescribed standard layout for each room with training based on procedure manuals and the one best way. Staff are expected to clean a given number of rooms per shift with financial incentives for additional rooms. What is important, however, is the context and manner in which such practices are put into effect and whether there is any scope for personal initiative.

BUREAUCRACY

A common form of structure, especially in large-scale organisations, is bureaucracy, though today the term has common connotations of rigidity and red tape. However, in the study of organisation and management it is important that the term is seen not *necessarily* in a deprecative sense but as applying to certain structural features of formal organisation.

The German sociologist, Weber, showed particular concern for what he called 'bureaucratic structures'. He argued that the decisive reason for the growth of bureaucratic organisation was its purely technical superiority over any other form of organisation.[16] Although Weber did not actually define bureaucracy, he did attempt to identify the main characteristics of this type of organisation.

Main features of bureaucracy

Bureaucracy is characterised by:

- clear role definitions of duties and responsibilities;
- division of labour and a high level of specialisation;
- a hierarchical structure of authority;
- uniformity of decisions;
- an elaborate system of rules, procedures and regulations;
- employment based on technical qualifications and formally attested merit;
- impartiality in undertaking duties and responsibilities.

Four main features of bureaucracy are summarised by Stewart as: specialisation, hierarchy of authority, a system of rules, and impersonality.[17]

- **Specialisation** applies more to the job than to the person undertaking the job. This makes for continuity, as the job usually continues if the present job holder leaves.
- **Hierarchy of authority** makes for a sharp distinction between management and workers. Within the management ranks there are clearly defined levels of authority.
- **A system of rules** aims to provide for an efficient and impersonal operation. The system of rules is generally stable although some rules may be changed or modified over time. Knowledge of the rules is a requisite of holding a job in a bureaucracy.
- **Impersonality** means that allocation of privileges and the exercise of authority is in

accordance with the laid-down system of rules. In more highly developed bureaucracies there may be carefully defined procedures for appealing against certain types of decisions. According to Stewart, the characteristic of impersonality is the feature of bureaucracy which most distinguishes it from other types of organisation. A bureaucracy should not only be impersonal but it should be seen to be impersonal.

Criticisms of bureaucracy

These features provide an accurate account of how many organisations actually do function. However, bureaucratic structures have a number of potential disadvantages and are subject to severe criticisms, including the following.

- The over-emphasis on rules and procedures. Record-keeping and paperwork may become more important in their own right rather than as a means to an end.
- Members may develop a dependence upon bureaucratic status, symbols and rules.
- Initiative may be stifled and there is lack of flexibility or adaption to changing circumstances.
- Hierarchical position and responsibilities in the organisation can lead to officious bureaucratic behaviour.
- Impersonal relationships can lead to stereotyped behaviour and a lack of responsiveness to individual situations or problems.

Among the strongest critics of bureaucratic organisation, and the demands it makes on the worker, is Argyris. He claims that the formal, bureaucratic organisation restricts the pyschological growth of the individual. It causes feelings of failure, frustration and conflict. Argyris argues that the organisation should provide a more 'authentic' relationship with its members and provide:

- a significant degree of individual responsibility and self-control;
- commitment to the goals of the organisation;
- productiveness and work; and
- an opportunity for individuals to apply their full abilities.[18]

Hotels as bureaucracies

The growth of bureaucracy has come about through the increasing size and complexity of modern work organisations and the associated demand for effective operations. Greater emphasis has been placed on the careful design of structure, and the definition of individual duties and responsibilities. Greater specialisation and expertise, and applications of technical knowledge, have highlighted the need for laid-down procedures.

As a result, many hotels, especially large-scale ones, reflect – at least in part – similar characteristics to a bureaucratic form of organisation. This view is supported by Lockwood and Jones:

> On looking at organisation structures within hotels, we find an emphasis on a mechanistic or bureaucratic format, such as the classical kitchen brigade. This structure is based on tradition, with a breakdown of the operations into specialist occupational areas. It is also influenced by the need for a formal framework within which the uncertainty and instability of the guest input can be handled – all staff know their respective roles and positions and therefore the basis of their reactions to customers' requests.[19]

In practice, however, few organisations fit neatly into any particular model of organisational design and structure. Most are a hybrid and will lie somewhere on a continuum between bureaucracy and more organic forms of structure. The hotel organisation in particular seems unlikely to fit fully into the bureaucratic model of structure.[20]

Much of the criticism of bureaucracy is undoubtedly valid, but much also appears to be unfair comment. In any case, many staff working in the hotel industry are generally conservative by nature. They feel more comfortable working within a rigid structure and 'knowing where they stand'. The main point, however, is that whatever the validity of the criticisms it is difficult to envisage how modern large-scale hotels could function effectively without exhibiting at least some of the features of a bureaucratic structure.

THE HUMAN RELATIONS APPROACH

The main emphasis of the classical approach was on structure and the formal organisation as the basis for achieving high levels of work performance. But during the 1920s greater attention began to be given to the social factors at work and to the behaviour of people in the organisation – that is, to human relations. Whereas the classical approach adopted more of a managerial perspective, the human relations approach strove for a greater understanding of people's psychological and social needs at work as well as improving the process of management. It is usually regarded as the first major approach to organisation and management to show concern for industrial sociology. The major impetus to the human relations approach came with the famous Hawthorne studies at the Western Electric Company in America (1924–1932).

There were four main phases to the Hawthorne studies: the illumination experiment, the relay assembly test room, the interviewing programme and the bank wiring observation room.

The illumination experiment

This investigation was conducted to test the belief that improvements in physical working conditions, such as the intensity of lighting, would improve productivity. The results of the tests were inconclusive as production varied with no apparent relationship to the level of lighting, but actually increased when conditions were made worse. Production also increased in the control group although the lighting remained unchanged. Clearly other factors influenced the level of production and this prompted a series of further experiments.

The relay assembly test room

This experiment involved six women workers who assembled telephone relays by hand. The work was boring and repetitive. The researchers selected two assemblers who were friends with each other, and they chose three other assemblers and a layout operator. The six workers were moved to a room by themselves but with the same general environmental conditions as the main assembly area. The workers were subjected to a series of planned and controlled changes such as hours of work, rest pauses, and refreshment breaks. During the experiment the observer adopted a friendly manner, consulting with the workers, keeping them informed and listening to their complaints. Following all but one of the changes there was a continuous rise in the level of production. Also, sickness and absenteeism dropped, and morale appeared to improve. The researchers formed the conclusion that the main reasons were small group working, the extra attention given to workers, and the apparent interest in them shown by management.

The interviewing programme

In an attempt to find out more about the workers' feelings towards their supervisors and conditions of work, a large interviewing programme was introduced. Initially the interviewers approached their tasks using a set of prepared questions related mainly to how workers felt about their jobs. However, this method produced only limited information, so the style of interviewing was changed to be more non-directive and open-ended. Workers were free to talk about any aspect of their work. Everything was confidential, no identification was given and no personal details were revealed to management.

The interviewers set out to be friendly and sympathetic. They adopted an impartial, non-judgemental approach and did not take sides or offer opinions. If necessary they would explain company policy and details of, for example, benefit schemes but they concentrated on listening. Using this approach the interviewers found out far more about the workers' true feelings towards the company, working conditions, supervision and management, group relations and matters outside work.

Many workers appeared to welcome the opportunity to have someone who would listen to their feelings and problems, and to whom they could 'let off steam' in a friendly atmosphere. The interviewing programme was significant in giving an impetus to present-day personnel management and the use of counselling interviews. It also highlights the importance of managers actively listening to the workers. Given the nature of the hospitality industry and the importance of good employee relations, the lessons learnt from the interviewing programme have particular significance for the manager.

The bank wiring observation room

This experiment involved the observation of a group of 14 men working in the bank wiring observation room. It was noted that the men formed their own informal organisation with sub-groups and cliques, and with natural leaders emerging with the consent of members. The group developed its own pattern of informal social relations with 'norms' of what constituted 'acceptable' behaviour together with a system of sanctions against those members who did not conform with the group norms. Group pressures on individual workers restricted the level of work achieved despite financial incentive schemes offered by management. The importance of informal working practices and group 'norms' is discussed further in Chapter 9.

Evaluation of the human relations approach

The Hawthorne studies have been subject to criticism and to a number of different interpretations.[21] But, however the results are regarded, the studies have important implications for organisational structure. They generated new ideas on social interaction, output restrictions and individuals within work groups. As Nailon, for example, points out: 'Most managers have experienced antagonism when any suggestion is made for the composition of groups to be changed.'[22]

The human relations approach marked a change in emphasis away from the precision of scientific management and led to ideas on increasing productivity by humanising the work organisation. The classical approach sought to increase production through means of formal structure and rationalisation of the work organisation. With the human relations approach, recognition was given to the importance of the informal organisation which will always be present within the formal structure. Workers were seen as individuals and members of a social group, with their behaviour and attitudes as the key to effectiveness.[23]

Neo-human relations

The results of the Hawthorne studies and the subsequent attention given to the social organisation gave rise in the 1950s and 1960s to a group of writers who are usually categorised under the heading of neo-human relations. The major focus of concern was the personal adjustment of the individual within the structure of the work organisation, the effects of group relationships and leadership styles. Writers under this heading include Maslow, Argyris, Herzberg, McGregor and Likert. The works of these writers are examined in more detail in subsequent chapters.

A RADICAL PERSPECTIVE

Sometimes the work of Weber is associated with the ideas of writers such as Karl Marx under the sub-heading of the structuralist approach, which is a synthesis of the classical (or formal) school and the human relations (or informal) school.[24] A major line of thought was that the earlier approaches were incomplete. The structuralist approach provides a radical perspective of social and organisational behaviour. Greater attention should be given to the relationships between the formal and informal aspects of the organisation, and the study of conflict between the needs of the individual and the organisation, and between workers and management. (See also the discussion on conflict and the radical perspective in Chapter 12.)

THE SYSTEMS APPROACH

The classical approach emphasised the formal structure as a major mechanism in optimising organisational performance. The human relations approach emphasised the social needs of people at work and the importance of the informal organisation. The systems approach attempts to reconcile these two earlier approaches. Attention is focused on the total work organisation and the interrelationships of structure and behaviour. The systems approach views the organisation within its broader external environment and with multiple channels of interaction.

The systems approach draws attention to the importance of the socio-technical system. This directs attention to viewing the organisation as a whole and the relationships between technical and social variables. Changes in one part, technical or social, will affect other parts and thus the whole organisation as a system. An analysis of the hotel as an open system was discussed in Chapter 1.

THE CONTINGENCY APPROACH

The contingency approach, which can be viewed as an extension of the systems approach, highlights possible means of differentiating between alternative forms of organisation structure and systems of management. There is no one optimum state. The structure of the organisation and its 'success' are dependent upon a range of situational factors.

The contingency approach takes the view that there are a large number of variables or situational factors which influence organisational design and performance. There is therefore no one best, universal structure. The most appropriate structure is dependent upon the contingencies of the situation for each individual hotel. It is these situational factors which account for variations in the structure of different hotels.

Although contingency models have not involved the hospitality industry directly, their relevance and potential applications should be readily apparent. Managers can use these models to compare and contrast the structure and functioning of their own hotel, and to take from them those ideas which suit best their particular requirements.

An 'if-then' relationship

Contingency models can be seen as a form of 'if-then' matrix relationship.[25] If certain situational factors exist, then certain variables in organisational structure and systems of management are most appropriate. A simplified illustration of contingency relationships is given in Figure 3.3.

Situational variables may be identified in a number of different ways. Some obvious bases for comparison are the size and nature of the hotel, the quality of its staff, the range and standard of services and facilities offered, and the nature of the customers. Other important variables include technology and the environment.

Size of the hotel

Size has obvious implications for the design of structure. Size is not simple variable, and it can be measured in different ways. The most common indication of size is usually the number of bedrooms, perhaps associated with the number of staff employed. In other cases, however, different factors such as the range of facilities provided might be a better indicator. As an example, Foxhills Golf and Country Club has only 16 bedrooms but is set in a 400-acre estate, and offers a wide range of sports and leisure facilities.

In the very small hotel, for example with only six bedrooms and run by a husband and wife with some family help, there is little need for a formal structure. But with increasing size and complexity of operations, a hotel may be divided into distinct departments with defined tasks and responsibilities, more formalised relationships, and greater use of rules and standardised procedures.

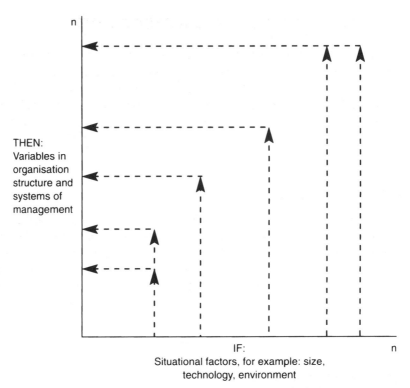

THEN:
Variables in
organisation
structure and
systems of
management

IF:
Situational factors, for example: size,
technology, environment

Fig 3.3 A simplified illustration of the 'if–then' contingency relationship
Source: Mullins L J, *Management and Organisational Behaviour*, Third edition, Pitman (1993), p. 339

Technological processes

From a major study of management organisations, Woodward draws attention to the relationships between technology, organisation structure and business success.[26] the classical approach and the idea of principles of organisation appeared to fail in providing a direct and simple basis for relating structure and success.

Patterns of organisation were found to be related more to similarity of objectives and the technology of production. Among the organisational characteristics showing a direct relationship to technology were the ratio of managers to total staff, the shape of the structure, the span of control and the number of levels of authority.

Environment influences

Two important studies have focused on the effects of uncertainty and a changing environment on the organisation and its management and structure. These are:

● Burns and Stalker – mechanistic and organic organisations; and
● Lawrence and Lorsch – differentiation and integration.

MECHANISTIC AND ORGANIC ORGANISATIONS

Burns and Stalker investigated the relationship between the pattern of structure, the nature of the external environment and economic performance.[27] They identified two ideal types of organisation at opposite extremes of a continuum – the 'mechanistic' organisation and the 'organic' organisation. These represented the polar extremes of the form which organisations could take when adapted to technical and commercial change. In practice, most organisations are likely to be a mix of both mechanistic and organic structures.

The mechanistic organisation

The mechanistic organisation resembles a bureaucracy and has a rigid, hierarchical structure. It is characterised by closely defined duties, responsibilities and technical method, the specialisation of tasks, knowledge centred at the top of the hierarchy, instructions from superiors and vertical interaction between superior and subordinates.

The mechanistic organisation is unable to deal adequately with rapid change. It is therefore more appropriate for stable environmental conditions. An example might be a traditional, high-class and expensive hotel operating along classical lines and with an established reputation and type of customer.

The organic organisation

The organic organisation is more flexible and has a fluid structure. It is characterised by a network structure of control and authority, lateral communications based on information and advice, the contribution of special knowledge and expertise throughout the organisation, the continual redefinition of tasks, and commitment to the common task of the organisation.

The organic organisation is required when new problems and unforeseen circumstances arise constantly. It is therefore more appropriate for uncertainty and changing environmental conditions. An example could be a holiday or tourist hotel with an unpredictable demand and many different types of customer. Another example could be a country club hotel specialising in a range of different functions, such as wedding receptions and corporate sports days, which require the erection of marquees and provision of other facilities according to particular requirements.

DIFFERENTIATION AND INTEGRATION

Lawrence and Lorsch analysed the internal structure of organisations in terms of 'differentiation' and 'integration'.[28]

Differentiation

Differentiation refers to differences among departments of the organisation in terms of their goals, timespans, interpersonal relations and formality of structure. it was recognised that different departments could have their own distinctive forms of structure according to the nature of their tasks, the different demands of the environment and the different levels of uncertainty.

Integration

Integration refers to the degree of co-ordinaton and co-operation between different departments and attempts to achieve unity of effort. The mechanisms to achieve integration include policies and procedures, teamwork and formal lateral relations, committees and project teams, and liaison officers.

Demands of the environment

Lawrence and Lorsch suggest that the extent of differentiation and integration in effective organisations will vary according to the demands of the environment. In an unstable and dynamic environment the more effective organisation would be highly differentiated and highly integrated. This study would seem to have particular relevance to the hotel industry because of the different orientations and demands among departments such as the kitchen, front office, security and maintenance.

THE RELEVANCE OF CONTINGENCY MODELS

Contingency models of organisation draw attention to the situation factors which account for variations in structural design. They are more concerned with differences among organisations than with similarities. The contingency approach tends to assume, however, that organisational performance is dependent upon the extent to which the structure of the organisation matches prevailing contingencies.

As with other approaches to organisation and management, contingency theory has been subject to a number of criticisms.[29] It does run the risk of concluding that 'it all depends on everything' and there is the danger of over-emphasis on differences between organisations and the exclusion of similarities. There must be a balance.[30]

Greater understanding of organisation and structure

Despite the criticisms and limitations, contingency theory has provided a further insight into our understanding of relationships among factors influencing the structure, management and operations of organisations. it can help our thinking about how hotels should be organised.

Based on the distinction between mechanistic and organic organisations, Shamir suggests that hotels tend to resolve the conflict between the demands for bureaucracy and hospitality service by the mixture of informal, organic systems of control and a lateral pattern of communication which lies behind the facade of a formal, mechanistic structure. Apart from those managers who have responsibility for co-ordinating the work of a number of different departments, most large hotels appear to lack formal integrating mechanisms at the organisational level.[31]

Contingency models draw attention to the importance of different structures for different organisations and for different activities of the organisation. Nailon, for example, feels that most theories have helped to provide a greater understanding of the catering industry and that: 'choosing the appropriate form of organisation will prevent the problems created by inappropriate structures.[32]

THE SHAMROCK ORGANISATION

One particular approach to structural design which appears to have interesting applications for the hospitality industry is Handy's concept of the 'shamrock' organisation.[33] The three leaves to each stem of the shamrock are symbolic of the organisation which is seen as made up of three distinct groups of people who are managed, organised and paid differently, and who have different expectations: the professional core, the contractual fringe and the flexible labour force (see Figure 3.4).

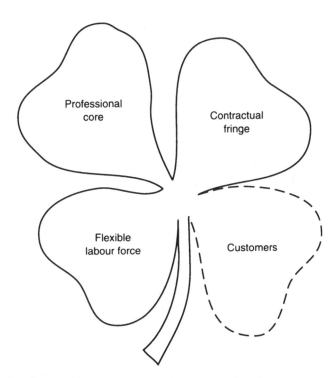

Fig 3.4 Representation of Handy's shamrock organisation

- **The professional core** comprises qualified professionals, technicians and managers essential to the existence and effective performance of the organisation. Collectively these people own the knowledge which distinguishes the organisation. The professional core are expensive and the tendency has been for organisations to restructure in order to reduce their numbers.
- **The contractual fringe** comprises those people, or other organisations, outside of the organisation who provide specialist services and undertake all non-essential work

which can be done by somebody else, and in theory are able to do it better for less. It is wise for the shamrock organisation to put boring and repetitive work out to contract, specifying the results expected and then paying the fee.

- **The flexible labour force** represents all those part-time and temporary workers which are the fastest growing group in the pattern of employment. It provides for flexibility in human resourcing. People are brought in as occasional extra part-time labour or temporary staff as changing work situations demand.

According to Handy, organisations now have three significant workforces each with a different kind of commitment to the organisation and a different set of expectations, and each workforce needs to be managed in different ways.

IMPLICATIONS FOR THE HOSPITALITY INDUSTRY

Economic pressures, rapid developments in information technology and the need for review of structural design have highlighted the significance of these different groups. Organisations have reduced the size of their workforce, especially full-time staff, and have flatter structures with fewer levels of authority. The concept of the shamrock organisation can encourage hospitality managers to question the operation of their organisations. It gives rise to important decisions concerning what activities and which people should belong to the core, to the management and control of subcontracting and to the flexible workforce.

The increasing tendency to make use of subcontracting and the buying-in of convenience or standardised food products raises important questions of management control over performance and results. Contracting out can arguably lead to a reduction in the range of customer choice and the potential de-skilling of jobs. For example, many hotels and restaurants now buy in their pastry products and as a result no longer have the need for their own specialist pastry chef as part of the core.

Customers as the fourth leaf?

Handy also refers to the growing practice of saving labour in the core by introducing another, informal and unpaid, form of subcontracting – that of getting customers to do some of the work of the organisation. In the hospitality industry there are many examples of this 'serve yourself' philosophy. Examples are the provision of shoe cleaning equipment or machines, hotel guests making their own tea and coffee in their rooms, restaurant self-service breakfast and buffet meals, standard meals and beverages in fast-food outlets with help-yourself condiments and customers expected to clear their own meal tables, the provision of vending machines for snacks and beverages.

A number of American motels also have microwaves for guests to heat popcorn or other snacks purchased from the vending machines. Other American restaurants invite customers to purchase their steak or seafood in the restaurant but then cook their meal themselves.

Managing the flexible labour force

The increase in the flexible labour force is particularly noticeable with the growth of service industries. As discussed in Chapter 1, services are created and consumed simultaneously. Unlike manufacturing, services are time-perishable and cannot be stored. The flexible labour force has increasingly been used as a cheaper and more convenient means of dealing with the peaks and troughs of demands, and as a means of adjusting the level of service to match changing customer requirements.

Although casual and part-time staff are unlikely to have the same degree of commitment or ambition as the core it is important that they are taken seriously and regarded as a valuable part of the organisation. The flexible workforce should be treated with respect, given fair and equitable treatment, adequate training and status, and decent pay and conditions. If casual and part-time staff are to respond in a positive way and provide a high standard of service then they have to be managed in a considerate and effective manner.

THE RELATIONSHIP BETWEEN STRUCTURE AND PEOPLE

Whatever the overall shape of the organisation, the effectiveness of the hotel will be affected both by sound structural design and by the individuals filling the various positions within the structure. The views of the human relations writers remind us of the importance of the human element in the design of structure. managers need to consider how structural design and methods of work organisation influence the behaviour and performance of staff.

The functions of the formal structure, and the activities and defined relationships within it, exist independently of the members of staff who carry out the work. Personalities, however, are an important aspect of the working of the hotel. The actual operation of the hotel and success in meeting its objectives will be dependent upon the behaviour of people who work within the structure, and who give shape and personality to the framework. 'Organisational structure is but a simplification of complex patterns of human behaviour.'[34]

Lord Forte has drawn attention to the importance of the human element in structure:

> . . . the human aspect in a business is vital: you can keep drawing squares and lines, but within these squares you must have people and they must be deeply involved with the business. If this does not happen, then the lines and squares and the diagrams mean nothing.[35]

Maintaining the socio-technical system

In Chapter 1 we referred to the importance of the relationships between technical efficiency and social considerations. Structure must be designed, therefore, to maintain the effectiveness of the socio-technical system and of the hotel as a whole. Attention must be given to the interactions between both the structural and technological requirements of the hotel, and human factors and the needs and demands of people.

DESIGN OF STRUCTURE

In the final analysis, however, there is an underlying need to establish a framework of order and command by which the activities of the hotel are accomplished successfully. This demands that attention be given to certain basic considerations in the design of structure (Figure 3.5).

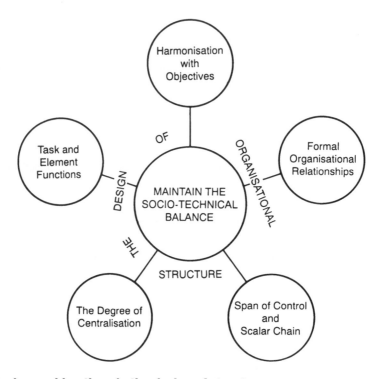

Fig 3.5 Basic considerations in the design of structure

HARMONISATION WITH OBJECTIVES

Structure must harmonise with the goals and objectives of the hotel. Only when the objectives have been clearly stated and agreed can alternative forms of structure be analysed and compared. A clear definition of goals and objectives provides a basis for the division of work and grouping of activities into sub-units. The objectives for these sub-units must be related to the overall strategy of the hotel in order that an appropriate pattern of organisation structure is established.

For example, Schaffer emphasises the importance of lodging organisations continuously engaging in the process of matching their competitive strategies and organisation structures to changes in the environment. In order to achieve effective performance, strategy must be adjusted to suit the environment. And organisation structure and processes must then be created that properly support that strategy.[36]

TASK AND ELEMENT FUNCTIONS

In her study of the management organisation of firms in the United Kingdom, Woodward distinguishes between 'task' functions and 'element' functions.[37] Task functions are those basic activities which are related to the actual completion of the 'productive' process, and directed towards specific and definable end-results. These are the essential functions that the organisation must perform and involve: developing the product/facility/service, providing the product/facility/service, marketing it, and financing the organisation.

Element functions are those activities which are not directed towards specific and definable ends but are supportive of the task functions and form an intrinsic part of the management process. These include, for example, planning, management services, administrative support, quality control and maintenance.

Structure based on task functions

Within the formal structure, duties and responsibilities have to be divided among members and different jobs related to each other. The difference between task and element functions forms the basis for the division of work and has important implications for organisation.

> Organisation is a function of purpose and the complexity of the hotel business arises because it is concerned with several distinct products, services and facilities, which are offered in various combinations.[38]

Structure should therefore be centred around the key activities which relate directly to the products, services and facilities offered by the hotel. These task functions are likely to relate to such activities as front office and reception, food and beverage, accommodation, conferences and banqueting, marketing or sales, and other direct customer facilities or services, for example leisure facilities or laundry and valeting. Support services are likely to include, for example, accounting, security, works and maintenance, and administration.

Need to distinguish task and element functions

Failure to distinguish between task and element functions can lead to confusion and difficulties in relationships among members. Woodward comments on the bad relationships between management accountants and other managers. The accountants tended to assume responsibility for end-results that were not properly theirs. They saw their role as a controlling and sanctioning one, rather than as a servicing and supportive one. Activities concerned with raising funds for the business, keeping accounts and determination of financial policy are task functions. But management accounting is an element function. Relationships seemed better when the two functions were organisationally separate.

The personnel function

The personnel function is generally identified as one of the element functions of an organisation. But in the hotel industry the importance of staff contact to customer satisfaction means that personnel can be seen as associated closely with a task function (see Chapter 6).

CENTRALISATION AND DECENTRALISATION

The division of work and grouping together of activities raises the question of the extent of centralisation or decentralisation. This arises at two levels:

- to individual hotel managers within a chain or group, for example the extent of authority for local purchasing, or to recruit or dismiss staff; and
- specific delegation to sub-units, departments or sections within the individual hotel, for example a central kitchen, or decentralisation of some of the food preparation.

The underlying issue is the measure of devolved autonomy, independence and freedom of action enjoyed by the hotel manager or by the individual sub-units.

Advantages and disadvantages

The general advantages claimed for centralisation usually include identification of a corporate image, better decision-making, easier implementation of a common policy for the chain/group or the hotel as a whole, improved co-ordination and control, economies of scale and reduction in overhead costs, and use of specialisation, including better facilities and equipment.

There are, however, a number of contrary arguments against centralisation. It creates a more bureaucratic structure and may result in a longer chain of command. The decision-making process may be cumbersome when needing to be cleared through top, and perhaps distant, management. Too much centralisation can stifle initiative and the sense of responsibility.

In addition, there are positive arguments in favour of decentralisation. It enables decisions to be made closer to the operational level of work and according to immediate needs. Support services are more likely to be effective if provided closer to the activities they serve. Decentralisation provides greater opportunities for management training and development. Also, it usually has a positive effect on the motivation and morale of staff.

The extent of centralisation or decentralisation should be considered in terms of the size and nature of the hotel, geographical location and particular circumstances, and the quality of staff. It is a question of balance and managerial choice. The growth of international hospitality organisations has drawn particular attention to the question of the extent and manner of decentralisation and empowerment related to design of structure and management control.[39]

SPAN OF CONTROL AND SCALAR CHAIN

Two of the most specific, and related, principles of good organisational design are: (a) the span of control; and (b) the scalar chain. The span of control arises in line authority and refers to the number of subordinates who report *directly* to a given manager or supervisor. It does not refer to the total number of subordinate operating staff. Hence the term 'span of responsibility' or 'span of supervision' is sometimes preferred.

Limits to span of control

The classical writers placed emphasis on the span of control but tended to suggest that this should be limited to a definite figure. Graicunas emphasised that the number of subordinates who can effectively be supervised is based on the total number of direct and cross relationships.[40] He developed a mathematical formula for the span of control:

$$R = n \left(\frac{2^n}{2} + n - 1 \right)$$

where n = number of subordinates and R = number of interrelationships.

With five subordinates the total number of interrelationships requiring the attention of the manager is 100; with six subordinates the number of interrelationships is 222.

Importance of span of control

If the span of control is too narrow it increases the number of levels of authority. A narrow span of control can result in too close a level of supervision and failure to make best use of potential managerial talent. But with too wide a span of control it becomes difficult to supervise subordinates effectively. Sub-groups or cliques and informal leaders may evolve. A wide span of control places more demands on the manager with less time to carry out all activities properly. It may also limit opportunities for promotion.

In discussing the span of control, Venison comments that:

> The hotel general manager has an impossible task to perform because it is generally beyond the behavioural range of most human beings and the sufferer has been the hotel guest – since guest contact and, to a large degree, staff contact have often been lost in the process.[41]

This observation illustrates the importance of good organisation structure including attention to span of control.

Practical considerations

In practice, however, it is not feasible to lay down a single, ideal, span of control: there are many situational variables which influence the limit of how many subordinates one person can control successfully. These include the nature of the hotel and facilities/services offered, standardisation of methods and procedures, the ability of the manager, the quality, training and motivation of subordinates, communication and control systems, geographical or physical location, and length of the scalar chain.

The scalar chain

The 'scalar chain' refers to the number of different levels in the structure of the hotel, the chain of hierarchical command. The scalar chain establishes the vertical graduation of authority and responsibility, and the framework for superior–subordinate relationships. The very act of creating structure introduces the concept of the scalar chain.

All members of staff must know their position within the organisation structure. A clear line of authority and responsibility is necessary for the effective operation of the hotel. It is generally accepted, however, that there should be as few levels as possible. Too long a scalar chain can have an adverse effect on morale, decision-making and communications.

Need for balance

There is a general movement towards flatter organisation structures. However, if efforts are made to reduce the number of levels, this may bring about an increase in the span of control. The design of structure therefore necessitates maintaining a balance between span of control and scalar chain. It is the combination of span of control and scalar chain which determines the overall pyramid shape of the hotel and whether the hierarchical structure is 'flat' or 'tall'.

ORGANISATIONAL RELATIONSHIPS

Within the structure of the hotel the defined pattern of duties and responsibilities creates certain formal organisational relationships between individual members. These *individual* relationships establish the nature of the superior–subordinate hierarchy, flows of authority and responsibility, and patterns of role relationships.

Line relationships

Managers who have responsibility for the primary objectives or essential activities of the hotel, for example front office, accommodation, food and beverage, are usually known as 'line' managers. Line managers have authority and responsibility for the activities of their own department. Line relationships are the most simple and direct form of structure. There is a direct vertical relationship between superiors and subordinates, and each subordinate reports to only one person. Authority flows down through the structure from, for example, the general manager to departmental (line) managers, section supervisors and other staff. Each level of the hierarchy has authority over the level below it.

Staff relationships

As hotels develop in size and work becomes more complex, the range of activities and functions undertaken increases. The line structure may then be supplemented by specialists who provide a common advisory function, horizontally, throughout all departments of the hotel. Such specialist advisory functions are often known as 'staff'.

They should serve to support the primary activities of the hotel and the work of the line managers. Staff functions include, for example, personnel, management accounting, marketing, maintenance and administration.

People in a 'staff' relationship have little or no direct authority over employees in other departments: this is the responsibility of the line manager. However, as the role and responsibilities of the staff positions would have been established by top management, line managers might be expected to accept the specialist advice which is given. Staff managers may also be assigned a specific responsibility which gives direct authority over other workers, for example if the personnel manager is appointed as health and safety officer for the hotel as a whole. And within their own group there is still a line relationship between functional specialists and their own subordinates and superior.

LINE AND STAFF STRUCTURE

When staff positions are created they have to be integrated into the managerial structure. A 'line and staff' structure attempts to make full use of specialists while maintaining the concept of line authority (Figure 3.6). But this form of structure can present potential

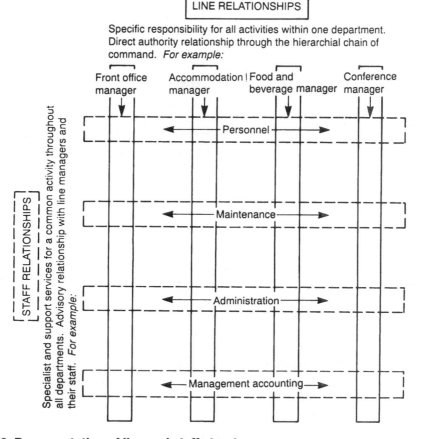

Fig 3.6 Representation of line and staff structure

difficulties, and friction often occurs between line and staff managers. A major source of difficulty is often to persuade line managers to accept, and to act upon, the advice and recommendations which are offered.

Line managers may feel that staff managers have an easier and less demanding job because they have no direct responsibility for providing facilities or services to the customer. Staff managers are often criticised for unnecessary interference in the work of the line manager, and for attempting to impose their views and advice. Line managers are often criticised for resisting the attempts of staff managers to provide assistance and co-ordination, and for making unnecessary demands for departmental independence. Staff managers may also feel that their own difficulties and work problems are not appreciated fully by the line manager.

Need for effective co-operation

It is not always easy to distinguish clearly between what is directly essential to the operation of the hotel, and what might be regarded only as a support function. The distinction between a line manager and a staff manager is not absolute. The important thing is that both line and staff recognise fully the purpose and role of the other. If the hotel is to be successful, line and staff need to work together and establish effective co-operation. The more staff managers can demonstrate the practical benefits of their specialist advice to line managers, the more such advice is likely to be heeded – and actively sought in the future.

THE VALUE OF ORGANISATION CHARTS

It is usual for the structure of the hotel to be depicted in the form of an organisation chart. This can be very useful in providing a pictorial presentation of the structural framework of the hotel and its main area of activities. It is helpful, for example, as part of a staff induction manual. The chart may also be used as a basis for the analysis and review of structure, for training and management succession, and for formulating changes. An example of an organisation chart is given in Figure 3.7.

An organisation chart may show, at a given moment in time, how work is divided, spans of control, the levels of authority, lines of communication, and formal relationships. But charts vary greatly. Some are intended to give a minimal amount of information, perhaps for example only an outline of the management structure of the hotel. Others give a range of additional detail – for example, all main positions in the structure, names of senior post holders, and a broad indication of the duties and responsibilities of the various sections.

Organisation charts are usually displayed in a traditional, vertical form such as those given in this chapter. They can, however, be displayed in other ways, for example either horizontally with the details reading from left to right,[42] or concentrically with top management at the centre. Some charts add a rider, for example: 'The chart indicates lines of communication and not necessarily lines of authority.'

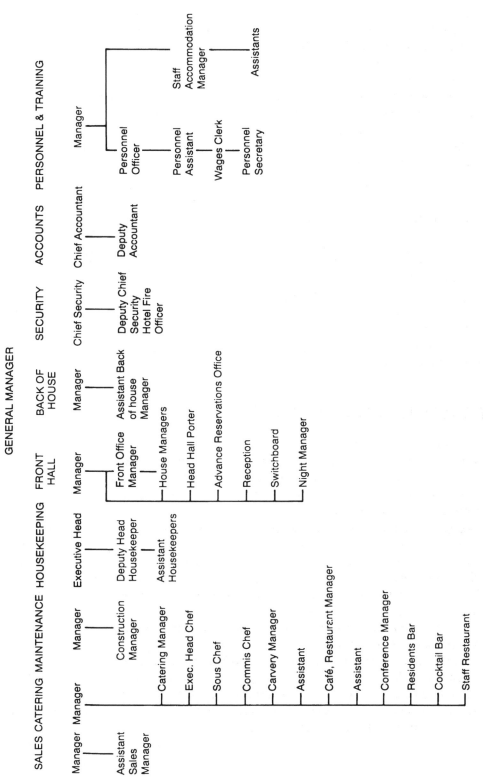

Fig 3.7 Organisation chart for a large international London hotel (882 bedrooms; 350 full-time staff)
Reproduced by permission of Trusthouse Forte Hotels

Limitations

There are a number of limitations with most organisation charts. They depict only a static view of the hotel and what the structure should be. They do not show, for example, comparative authority of positions on the same level, lateral contacts, personal delegation from superior to subordinates, or relationships between line and staff positions. A chart does not show the informal organisation, how the hotel actually works, or the behaviour of people.

The informal organisation

You will recall that in Chapter 2 we discussed the importance of the informal organisation. The underlying difference between the formal and informal organisation is the extent to which they are structured. The formal organisation is deliberately planned and created. It is hierarchically structured with the division of tasks, and defined relationships of authority and responsibilities. An organisation chart, for example, gives a representation of the formal structure of the hotel.

Within the formal structure an informal organisation will always be present. The informal organisation arises from the interactions of people and their social needs. People will modify the formal organisation, the operations of the hotel and actual working practices. What happens in practice will vary from the formal structure. The informal organisation is flexible, loosely structured and characterised by the development of groups with their own relationships and norms of behaviour. The nature of informal groups is discussed in Chapter 9.

SUMMARY

- Structure provides the basis for organisational processes and the execution of work. The structure of the hotel will affect both economic performance, and the morale and job satisfaction of staff. Underlying the development of management theory are contrasting ideas on organisation and structural design.
- The classical approach places emphasis on purpose, technical structure and hierarchy of management, and includes scientific management and bureaucracy. The human relations approach gives attention to social factors and human behaviour at work including the informal organisation. The systems approach attempts to integrate these two earlier approaches and views the organisation with multiple channels of interaction.
- The contingency approach highlights variations in the structure of different hotels and the influence of situational variables. One particular approach to structural design is the concept of the shamrock organisation. This draws attention to the constitution of the professional core, and to the management and control of subcontracting and the flexible labour force.
- It is important to remember the human element and to consider how structural design can influence the behaviour and performance of staff. Attention must be given to maintaining the socio-technical system and to the interactions between structure and technological requirements and to the needs and demands of people.

- In order to establish a system of order and command it is also important to give attention to certain basic considerations in the design of structure: harmonisation with objectives, task and element functions, centralisation and decentralisation, the span of control and scalar chain, and formal organisational relationships. The formal structure of the hotel will also be modified by the informal structure.

REVIEW AND DISCUSSION QUESTIONS

1 What is the importance of organisation structure? How does structure relate to the effective performance of hospitality operations?

2 Contrast approaches to improving organisational performance based on attention to technical and structural features, with those based on concern for psychological and social factors.

3 Explain your understanding of scientific management. Assess critically the relevance of scientific management for the hospitality industry today.

4 Despite the criticisms of bureaucracy, it is difficult to envisage how modern large-scale hotels could function effectively without exhibiting at least some of the features of a bureaucratic structure. Discuss critically the validity of this contention.

5 What are the main conclusions that can be drawn from the human relations approach to organisation, structure and management? Evaluate the practical applications of the human relations approach to the hospitality industry.

6 Explain what is meant by contingency models of organisation. Contrast mechanistic and organic systems of management practice and structure, and suggest ways in which a hotel organisation of your choice tends towards one type of system or the other.

7 Explain, with supporting practical examples, the main factors to be considered in the design of organisation structure. Assess the implications for the hospitality industry of the shamrock organisation.

8 Discuss critically the contention that a logical structure of organisation is better for efficiency and morale than a structure allowed to develop around personalities.

ASSIGNMENT

Investigate a hotel or other hospitality organisation of your choice and obtain, or prepare, a chart depicting the structural design of the hotel.

(i) Comment critically on:
- the relationships between task and element functions;
- the extent of centralisation and decentralisation;
- span of control and scalar chain; and
- formal organisational relationships.

(ii) Applying your knowledge of contingency models of organisation, comment on the apparent effectiveness of the structure of the hotel and/or particular departments of the hotel.

(iii) Identify and explain what you believe to be good and poor examples of structural design.

(iv) Explain, with supporting reasons, the changes you would recommend to the organisation structure. Where appropriate, prepare a revised organisation chart.

CASE STUDY

Hazel Wood Court

1.1 Introduction

Hazel Wood Court was built in 1958, when its owners claimed that it was one of the first motels to be opened in Britain. The motel is situated in south-east England on the outskirts of a large seaport and within easy reach of a major trunk road and the motorway system. It lies about five miles north of a busy cross-Channel ferry service terminal and is also within four miles of an expanding industrial estate. Hazel Wood Court stands on the site of a ruined sixteenth-century inn, where the original tavern known as the 'King's Retreat' still remains, and is still in everyday use as a public bar. The bar is very popular because of its authentic period character which is derived from a large open fireplace, wooden settees, and low ceilings supported by thick oak beams. Such is its attraction that the local people who use the bar still refer to it as 'The Retreat' nearly 30 years after it started trading under the name of Hazel Wood Court.

1.2 Other facilities

As well as the popular 'King's Retreat' public bar, the motel's other facilities include 51 bedrooms, a conference suite with seating for 40 delegates, a restaurant capable of serving up to 160 covers, and an attractive cocktail bar with seating for 55 persons. Hazel Wood Court is surrounded by extensive, well-kept gardens on three sides and there is a large free car park at the rear of the motel.

The motel is AA and RAC appointed with a three-star classification.

1.3 Accommodation

Only 25 bedrooms were included in the original design of the motel, but as the reputation of the Hazel Wood Court grew this total was increased to 40 rooms in 1968, and a new wing was built in 1976. The 51 bedrooms include 31 twin-bedded, 12 double, and eight rooms with three beds in each which can be converted into 'quads' if required.

All the rooms have private bathrooms, coloured television, radio and tea- and coffee-making facilities. It should be noted that despite the company's attempts to 'standardise' the accommodation units, the management has had to contend with numerous complaints, mainly from regular customers, since soon after the final extension was completed in 1976. The substance of most of these complaints is that the tariff charges do not reflect the allegedly different standards of accommodation provided by the motel.

1.4 Sources of revenue

Revenue is obtained from the following main sources:

(a) **Local business trade:** Uses the restaurant to entertain guests for luncheon and dinner, makes frequent use of the conference suite, and provides a steady flow of reservations for overnight accommodation.
(b) **Tour operators:** Accommodation is also provided for various tour operators, on a dinner, room and breakfast basis, and several groups of 30–60 people (mainly American, Dutch, Australian and German) arrive at the motel each week during the summer season.

(c) **Visiting business trade:** Close proximity to the motorway system makes the motel an ideal stopping-off point for visiting business people, and 'regulars' stay at the motel at least one night every week, booking accommodation many months in advance.

(d) **Casual trade:** Because of the easy access to a cross-Channel ferry terminal there is a regular demand during the high season for overnight visitors travelling to and from the continent. Special arrangements are made for the service of early breakfasts for these visitors if required.

(e) **Wedding receptions/functions:** A steady trade has been developed mostly at weekends.

(f) **Bar trade:** The cocktail bar provides steady revenue from resident guests and diners in the restaurant, in contrast to the 'King's Retreat' which derives most of its sales from the local inhabitants and chance trade. Snack-bar meals are a popular feature.

1.5 Fluctuations in trade

Apart from a general seasonal fall in demand for the motel's services outside the June–September period, there are also weekly fluctuations in demand which result in services being well utilised from Monday through to Friday morning throughout the rest of the year. Various attempts have been made to increase trade in the motel on Friday and Saturday nights, and on Sundays during the off-season period. Sustained local advertising has created a heavy demand for dinner on Saturday evenings and luncheon on Sundays.

Sunday nights, however, continue to be regarded as what are known in the trade as 'dead nights'. Despite these difficulties an annual guest occupancy of between 70 and 75% is generally achieved in Hazel Wood Court and none of these fluctuations affects trade in the 'King's Retreat'.

1.6 Group structure

The Hazel Wood Court is owned by a large group of companies. The group's interests are split into different divisions which are controlled by numerous subsidiary companies, most of which are also based in London. The relationship between hotels and motels like Hazel Wood Court and the parent company is shown in Figure 3.8.

The subsidiary company has its own board of directors and is run by a managing director, who is directly responsible to the board of directors of the parent company. The subsidiary company consists of hotels and motels throughout Britain which are divided into four areas. The general manager of a hotel/motel in any one of these areas is responsible to the Catering Adviser for all food and beverage operations and to a District Manager for the overall profitability of the hotel.

Communication between the hotel/motel general manager and these district executives is normally confined to one visit per month in the case of the Catering Adviser, and to one visit per week from the District Manager.

1. 7 Hazel Wood Court organisational structure

The staff at the Hazel Wood Court consists of 50 full- or part-time personnel, all of whom are ultimately responsible to the motel general manager, as shown in Figure 3.9 (page 99).

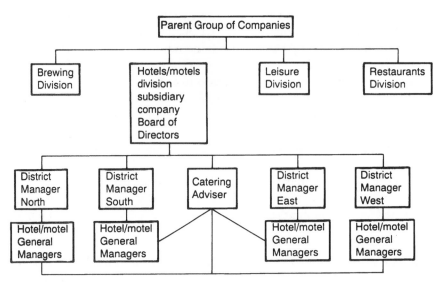

Fig 3.8 Group structure

2.1 A new general manager is appointed

Mid-way through 198– Mr Jack Cox, who had been general manager of Hazel Wood, was promoted to the position of Catering Adviser for all the hotels and motels operating under the subsidiary company's banner. Numerous applications were received when Mr Cox's position was advertised in the trade press and the board eventually decided to appoint Mr Pat Squires as the new general manager of the motel from August onwards.

Mr Squires possessed nearly 32 years' experience in the hotel and catering industry, including six years as an officer of field rank in the Army Catering Corps. He had previously been general manager of a small chain of three motels in south-west England, but had decided to accept what was on paper a less demanding position at the Hazel Wood Court, after his doctor had advised him to reduce his workload.

Mr Squires was appointed by the Managing Director of the subsidiary company who informed him that, as general manager, he would be jointly responsible to the newly appointed Catering Adviser for food and beverage operations and to the District Manager for the overall profitability of the motel.

Mr Squires' remuneration included a substantial salary, plus a 5% commission on net profitability, which would be progressively reduced to 2% as net profits increased beyond agreed targets. Accommodation for Mr Squires and his family would also be provided above the 'King's Retreat' public bar.

The Managing Director forewarned Mr Squires that the restaurant manager, Mr Ray Welsh, and head housekeeper, Mrs Brenda Cox, might find it difficult to adjust to his appointment, as both employees were inclined to be temperamental and had enjoyed considerable privileges under the previous general manager. The Managing Director added that Mrs Brenda Cox was, in fact, the wife of Mr Jack Cox, the newly appointed Catering Adviser. He urged Mr Squires to do what he could to develop a new team spirit, but stressed that if this proved to be impossible, disciplinary action was not to be taken against either employee without his prior permission.

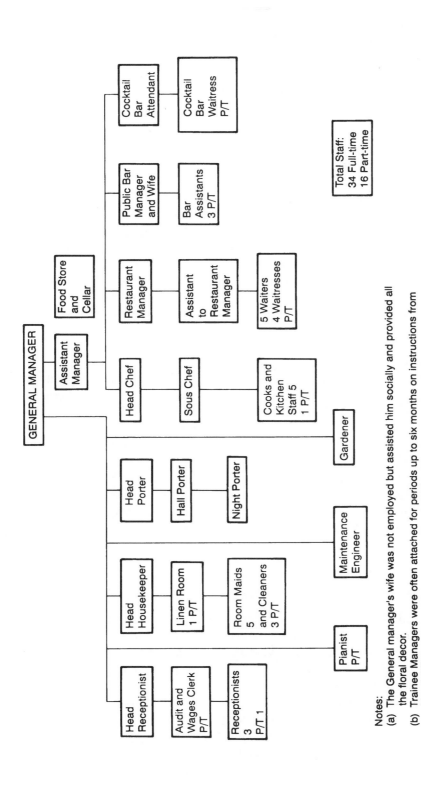

Fig 3.9 Organisation structure of Hazel Wood Court

Notes:
(a) The General manager's wife was not employed but assisted him socially and provided all the floral decor.
(b) Trainee Managers were often attached for periods up to six months on instructions from Head Office.
(c) Additional part-time waitresses were employed if required.

2.2 Other key positions at hazel wood court

When Mr Pat Squires took up his position as general manager of Hazel Wood Court the key positions were filled by the following personnel:

(a) **Assistant general manager:** Mr Ted Gascoigne, a local man in his early 20s with limited experience, whose wife, Frances, was employed as head receptionist.
(b) **Head chef:** This position was held by Mr John Drury, aged 45, who had been with the motel for six years, and was regarded as a very conscientious member of staff.
(c) **Public bar management:** This was jointly held by another husband and wife team, Lee and Beryl Marks, who had only recently taken up the appointment.

2.3 Mr Squires' first year as general manager

This was considered to be an unqualified success. Revenue was increased above the budgeted figure on both accommodation and food and beverage sales by over 15%.

Several ways of increasing revenue over weekends during the off-peak season were also introduced. Mr Squires worked particularly hard at maintaining high morale amongst the motel staff and, although he had found it necessary tactfully to censure Mrs Cox's behaviour on various occasions during the year, he was quietly optimistic about the relationships he had built up with Mr Welsh, the restaurant manager, and the rest of the staff at the motel.

2.4 An unhappy second year

Things began to go wrong for Mr Squires during his second year as general manager. At first the problems seemed to be small ones which could quickly be corrected. They began when the District Manager drew Mr Squires' attention to the fact that although revenue continued to rise, profitability could have been even higher if the labour costs at the motel were reduced to the same level as those at other hotels and motels in the District Manager's area.

Mr Squires was unsure that like was being compared with like, but he conceded that labour costs could be reduced if both Mrs Cox and Mr Welsh reduced their staff levels, especially with regard to part-time employees. Mr Squires was requested to submit a report on the situation which the District Manager promised to raise in confidence with the Managing Director.

2.5 Summary of confidential report on Mrs Cox's performance

Attention was drawn to the following problems:

(a) Mrs Cox had always taken every Saturday and Sunday off since she joined the company, and was never available to supervise her staff during weekends.
(b) Her department had always been overstaffed by at least two operatives.
(c) Overtime was offered to her staff on an indiscriminate basis and often when double-time rates had to be paid.
(d) She was inefficient in checking rooms and this had resulted in guests complaining on several occasions about the standard of cleanliness, etc.
(e) She ordered cleaning materials and other cleaning equipment without prior approval and authorisation from the manager.

In conclusion Mr Squires expressed the view that, had he not been specifically advised by the Managing Director to retain Mrs Cox's services, it would not have been necessary to write a report on her performance as she would have been replaced soon after his appointment because of her general inefficiency.

2.6 Summary of confidential report on Mr Welsh's performance
With regard to the restaurant manager, Mr Squires stated that in his opinion Mr Welsh had recently adopted an arrogant approach to the management, his own staff and visitors alike.

Other main problems were as follows:

(a) Mr Welsh, having been employed at the motel since it had opened, was apparently of the opinion that he could run his department as he wished, irrespective of demand. The restaurant was overstaffed at most times; however, when staff were needed at peak periods they were not all available.
(b) Mr Welsh's unfavourable attitude to guests, other than regular well-liked customers, was becoming more obvious and in some cases it had brought complaints from diners about some of his remarks which appeared to be bordering on the offensive.

Mr Squires was fully prepared to resolve these difficulties with Mr Welsh, but was of the opinion that he could no longer entirely count on his loyalty.

2. 7 Bar problems
Bar and stocktaking was carried out at agreed intervals of approximately six weeks by a firm from London which had been appointed by the parent company. Normally this took place on a Monday afternoon with two representatives commencing work at 2 p.m. and finishing at approximately 5 p.m. They obtained all the sales figures and 'goods inwards' information from the weekly returns sent to Head Office by the motel. Their results were received approximately two to three weeks after each stocktake. The cocktail bar and wine cellar produced excellent figures, indicating that they were being run in accordance with good commercial practice.

The public bar results caused Mr Squires considerable concern because deficiencies occurred on the cellar reconciliation figures, and the external stocktakers concluded that these shortages mainly concerned the public bar.

It was decided that all goods were delivered to the main cellar, and that each bar requisitioned from the food and beverage manager, who issued the items daily. These requisitions were then aggregated over the stocktaking period and were added to the stocks for each bar. For total cellar stocks to be reconciled, the opening cellar stock with all the purchases added, less the total of all the requisitions etc., had to equal the closing stock of each item in the cellar, and it was these discrepancies, amounting to nearly 3% of turnover, which were serious and could never be explained adequately by either the bar manager or his wife.

As the refrigerated cold room, which housed all the beers, was within the cellar compound, there had to be access for deliveries, maintenance, cleaning of the pipes and the replacement of kegs, etc.

The bar manager therefore had a set of keys for this purpose, but not to the section housing the spirits, liqueurs, aperitifs, etc., which were stored in a separate cage in the main cellar. Mr Squires and his Assistant Manager shared the view that the entrance to the main cellar was too easily accessible, being located behind the service counter of the public bar.

Between them they devised a tactful system of monitoring staff movements, and were disturbed to notice that Mr Welsh, the restaurant manager, who was on very friendly terms with Mr Marks and his wife, made regular visits to this part of the motel outside normal working hours. Mr Squires reported his concern to both the District Manager and the Catering Adviser as, even though the case against Mr Welsh was purely circumstantial and far from proven, they should be aware of the situation in case corrective action eventually had to be taken.

2.8 The response of the district manager
After discussing Mr Squires' complaints with the Managing Director, the District Manager informed him that two courses of action would be taken:

(a) Mrs Cox would be interviewed by the District Manager in the presence of Mr Squires and, unless she provided a satisfactory explanation for her behaviour, would receive a verbal disciplinary warning from the company.
(b) No action would be taken against Mr Welsh for the time being, but stocktaking in the public bar and cellar would be carried out at more regular intervals, possibly unannounced.

3.1 Disciplinary proceedings against the head housekeeper
The District Manager kept his word, and Mrs Cox was requested to attend disciplinary proceedings in the presence of Mr Squires. The meeting was well conducted by the District Manager, who kept proceedings at a low key, raised each complaint calmly, allowed Mrs Cox the opportunity to defend herself, and remained impartial throughout. Mrs Cox was denied the opportunity to turn the meeting into an angry debate and ended up by admitting responsibility for all of the criticisms raised against her by Mr Squires.

The meeting closed with the District Manager quietly insisting that a change of attitude was called for from Mrs Cox, who should communicate more frequently and in a more co-operative way with Mr Squires in the future; she should also introduce a more effective system of supervision to cover weekend work.

3.2 Additional public bar and main cellar stocktake by external auditors
Within three weeks of the previous stocktake a further audit was carried out by the same two representatives. The surprise element of the check was lost when the firm telephoned the public bar manager on the day before to enquire if an afternoon visit would be acceptable. The stocktake was completed in under two hours and the senior auditor advised Mr Squires that no significant discrepancy had been discovered. Mr Squires enquired how it was possible to carry out a detailed audit of this proportion in such a short time and draw such conclusions, but his question was received in embarrassed silence.

He later communicated his dissatisfaction to the District Manager at Head Office, but was informed that the additional audit had been accepted by the board and the complaints against Mr Welsh would be dropped and the matter closed. By persisting, Mr Squires did receive a begrudging acceptance from the outside firm of stocktakers that he or his assistant should be present at all audits in the future.

3.3 Complaints from the Catering Adviser

During the months that followed the Catering Adviser, who had previously been satisfied with the improvements that Mr Squires had introduced, began complaining about unacceptable profit margins on the food sales at the motel.

Normal procedure was for the Catering Adviser to call once a month for a meeting with Mr Squires, but he suddenly began appearing every week at unconventional hours. An unpleasant situation occurred when he arrived at the motel at 7 o'clock one Saturday evening and remonstrated with Mr Squires because he was not on duty. The explanation that Mr Squires had only shortly left the motel for a rest after officiating at a large wedding reception all the afternoon, leaving his assistant on duty, was not accepted. Mr Cox insisted that as Saturday evenings were extremely busy he should have been there personally to see that everything was progressing satisfactorily.

He also broadened his criticism of Mr Squires for complaining to Head Office about the newly introduced 'Country Style' menu, before this experiment had been given a fair chance to prove itself. Mr Squires denied this allegation by pointing out that in the past Hazel Wood Court had enjoyed a very good reputation for its a la carte menu. He had tried to enhance this reputation during his time as the manager. The 'Country Style' menu experiment, which entailed prepacked frozen foods being despatched from London for re-processing and serving to the motel's clientele, had not been successful. The meals were reasonably priced, but the choice was extremely limited and every regular customer had complained about this change in policy. All Mr Squires had done was to pass these complaints on to the District Manager in the usual way. The Catering Adviser again refused to accept this explanation and left the motel in an angry mood.

3.4 The restaurant manager's response

Relations between the restaurant manager and the general manager deteriorated thereafter and Mr Squires formed the opinion that Mr Welsh took every opportunity to 'fan the flames' of the growing conflict between the motel manager and the Catering Adviser.

Matters came to a head between Christmas and the New Year when the motel advertised a Christmas luncheon at a fixed charge, to which Mr Welsh added a 10% service charge while Mr Squires was indisposed with flu. This caused numerous complaints and Mr Squires had to rise from his sick bed to calm the situation and authorise the necessary refunds.

During the following week when Mr Squires had recovered and was entertaining some prominent members of the local business community to dinner, a *flambé* dish was ordered by several guests, but this was presented so far below the accepted standard by the restaurant manager that Mr Squires' party suffered considerable embarrassment.

3.5 Mr Squires decides to resign

Mr Squires informed his wife soon afterwards that he had decided to seek another position. His wife was relieved as she had never settled in the limited accommodation provided, and she was of the opinion that a flat above a public bar was no place to raise a teenage daughter.

Quite fortunately Mr Squires met an old army colleague at a hotel and catering exhibition in London a few weeks later, who was now employed as chief catering officer for a large county council in the Midlands. A vacancy as catering consultant had arisen at the county's largest teacher training college, and Mr Squires was urged to apply.

Mr Squires' application and interviews were successful and he was offered the appointment, subject to a satisfactory medical which took another two months to arrange.

Although Mr Squires was in sound health, he decided not to hand in his notice until after the medical. Somehow word of this intended move leaked out, and about 10 days later he was surprised by an unexpected visit from the District Manager, who mentioned that word had been received that Mr Squires wished to leave, and a decision had been taken by the Managing Director that he should depart in four weeks' time. Mr Squires responded by pointing out that he was entitled to four weeks' holiday by the company which he would take and leave at the end of that week. He left with a letter from the District Manager confirming that he had been given four weeks' notice 'because of staff re-organisation'.

The following week Mr Squires signed on as unemployed and received benefit for three weeks before this was stopped by the Department of Employment because his former employers had stated that he had resigned from his position. Mr Squires produced the letter stating that he had been asked to leave and was able to obtain unemployment benefit for a further five weeks until he could take up his new appointment.

Postscript

Mr Squires is still employed in a catering consultancy role by a Higher Education Institution in the Midlands and he has since taken on more responsibility.

He was replaced at Hazel Wood Court by a young graduate who, before taking up his appointment, telephoned Mr Squires at home to ask his advice about running the motel. As a consequence the new manager insisted that the head housekeeper should be transferred or dismissed before he would accept the appointment, and that he would also be given a free hand to make any decision he felt was necessary regarding the running of the restaurant and public bar. These requests were granted.

The Head Housekeeper decided to resign to concentrate more on her home life, during the week before the new manager arrived, and the restaurant manager took an early retirement a few months later. Shortly after these changes, the parent company were taken over by an international organisation and both the District Manager and the Catering Adviser left the company.

Source: McEwan T and Mullins L J, *Horae*, Portsmouth Business School, Hotel and Catering Research Unit Review, vol. 1, no. 1, Summer 1989, pp. 3–13.

NOTES AND REFERENCES

1. Gullen H V and Rhodes G E, *Management in the Hotel and Catering Industry,* Batsford (1983).
2. See, for example, Boella M J, Human Resource *Management in the Hotel and Catering Industry*, Fourth edition, Hutchinson (1987).
3. Drucker P F, *The Practice of Management,* Pan Books (1968), p. 273.
4. Child J, Organisation: A Guide to Problems and Practice, Second edition, Harper & Row (1984).
5. Schaffer J D, 'Structure and Strategy: Two Sides of Success', in Rutherford D G (ed), *Hotel Management and Operations*, Van Nostrand Reinhold (1990).
6. Gullen H V and Rhodes G E, *Management in the Hotel and Catering Industry,* Batsford (1983).
7. Keiser J R, *Principles and Practices of Management in the Hospitality Industry,* Second edition, Van Nostrand Reinhold (1989).
8. For a detailed account, see Mullins L J, *Management and Organisational Behaviour,* Third edition, Pitman (1993).
9. Urwick L, *The Elements of Administration,* Second edition, Pitman (1974).
10. Brech E F L, *Organisation: The Framework of Management,* Second edition, Longman (1965).
11. Woodward J, *Industrial Organization: Theory and Practice,* Second edition, Oxford University Press (1980).
12. Simon H A, *Administrative Behavior,* Third edition, Free Press (1976), p. xxii.
13. Taylor F W, *Scientific Management,* Harper & Row (1947).
14. See, for example, Gospel H F and Littler C R (eds), *Managerial Strategies and Industrial Relations,* Heinemann (1983).
15. For an interesting debate on de-skilling and work flexibility, see Wood R C, *Working in Hotels and Catering,* Routledge (1992).
16. Weber M, *The Theory of Social and Economic Organization,* Collier Macmillan (1964).
17. Stewart R, *The Reality of Management,* Second edition, Pan Books (1986).
18. Argyris C, *Integrating the Individual and the Organization,* Wiley (1964).
19. Lockwood A and Jones P, *People and the Hotel and Catering Industry,* Holt, Rhinehart & Winston (1984), p. 173.
20. Shamir B, 'Between Bureaucracy and Hospitality: Some Organisational Characteristics of Hotels', *Journal of Management Studies,* vol. 15, no. 3, October 1978, pp. 285–307.
21. See, for example, Rose M, Industrial Behaviour, Second edition, Penguin (1988).
22. Nailon P, 'A Theory of Organisation in the Catering Industry', *HCIMA Journal,* vol. 61, 1977, p. 7.
23. Torrington D, Weightman J and Johns K, *Effective Management: People and Organisation,* Prentice-Hall (1989).
24. See, for example, Etzioni A, *Modern Organizations,* Prentice-Hall (1964).
25. See, for example, Luthans F, *Organizational Behavior,* Fifth edition, McGraw-Hill (1989).
26. Woodward J, *Industrial Organization: Theory and Practice,* Second edition, Oxford University Press (1980).
27. Burns T and Stalker G M, *The Management of Innovation,* Tavistock (1966).
28. Lawrence P R and Lorsch J W, *Organization and Environment,* Irwin (1969).
29. See, for example, Child J, *Organization: A Guide to Problems and Practice,* Second edition, Harper & Row (1984).
30. Robey D, *Designing Organizations,* Third edition, Irwin (1990).
31. Shamir B, 'Between Bureaucracy and Hospitality: Some Organizational Characteristics of Hotels', *Journal of Management Studies,* vol. 15, no. 3, October 1978, pp. 285–307.
32. Nailon P, 'A Theory of Organisation in the Catering Industry', *HCIMA Journal,* vol. 61, 1977, p. 9.
33. Handy C B, *The Age of Unreason,* Business Books (1989).
34. Meyer M W, *Theory of Organizational Structure,* Bobbs–Merrill (1977), p. 44.
35. Forte, Charles (Lord), *Forte: The Autobiography of Charles Forte,* Sidgwick & Jackson (1986), p. 122.
36. Schaffer J D, 'Structure and Strategy: Two Sides of Success', in Rutherford D G (ed), *Hotel Management and Operations*, Van Nostrand Reinhold (1990).
37. Woodward J, *Industrial Organization: Theory and Practice,* Second edition, Oxford University Press (1980).
38. Medlik S, *The Business of Hotels,* Second edition, Heinemann (1989), p. 74.
39. See, for example, Goss-Turner S, 'Human Resource Management', in Jones P and Pizam A (eds), *The International Hospitality Industry: Organizational and Operational Issues,* Pitman (1993), pp. 152–164.
40. Graicunas V A, 'Relationships in Organisation', in *Papers on the Science of Administration,* University of Columbia (1937).
41. Venison P, *Managing Hotels,* Heinemann (1983), p. 33.
42. For an example, see Medlik S, *The Business of Hotels,* Second edition, Heinemann (1989), p. 83.

4

THE NATURE OF MANAGERIAL WORK

INTRODUCTION

It is through the process of management and the execution of work that the activities of the hospitality organisation are carried out. The task of management is to get work done through other people. It is the cornerstone of the people–organisation relationship. Management is essentially an integrating activity which permeates every facet of hospitality operations.

This chapter looks at:

- The nature of management
- Management as an integrating activity
- The process of management
- Essential nature of managerial work
- Principles of management
- Managerial roles
- Managerial work in the hospitality industry
- The managerial wheel

- The flexibility of managerial work
- Key result areas of hotel management
- Applications of general management theory
- Managerial job stress
- The managerial environment
- Managerial effectiveness
- Output measures of effectiveness

THE NATURE OF MANAGEMENT

Management is a generic term and subject to many possible interpretations. It is also frequently the subject of debate and discussion.[1] For our purposes, however, we are concerned with management as:

- taking place within a structured work organisation and with prescribed roles;
- directed towards the attainment of goals and objectives;
- achieved through the efforts of other people; and
- using systems and procedures.

The setting of objectives and formulation of policy take place at different levels in an organisation but as part of the same process. The board of directors, or their equivalent, establish objectives and formulate policy for the hotel as a whole. Management is responsible for the implementation of policy decisions and for the execution of work designed to meet these objectives.

The importance of management

The responsibility and importance of management are widely, and rightly, recognised. Among the leading writers emphasising this is Drucker.

> The responsibility of management in our society is decisive not only for the enterprise itself but for management's public standing, its success and status, for the very future of our economic and social system and the survival of the enterprise as an autonomous institution.[2]

The importance of management within the hospitality industry is also widely acknowledged.

> Effective management is one of the most important factors in the success or failure of any business. This applies to hotel, catering and institutional services as much as any other industry particularly as their managers need a balance of technical and management knowledge and skills acquired through a blend of education and experience.[3]

Authority over other people

Responsibility for the execution of work involves managers looking beyond their own activities, and exercising formal authority over the behaviour and performance of other people. The manager can be seen as someone who has the power and authority to make things happen and to get things done. Managers are judged not just on their own work performance but on the results achieved by subordinate staff.

The concept of a manager is usually seen therefore in terms of a person who has more work than he or she can perform personally, and who arranges for some of this work to be carried out by others through delegation to subordinate staff.[4]

One of the most popular ways of defining management is that it involves getting work done second-hand, that is *through the efforts of other people*. Stewart, for example, attempts to integrate the various definitions of management and summarises the manager's job, broadly defined as: 'deciding what should be done and then getting other people to do it.'[5]

MANAGEMENT AS AN INTEGRATING ACTIVITY

Management is not a separate, discrete function. It cannot be departmentalised or centralised. A hotel, or other hospitality organisation, cannot have a department of management in the same way as a department for other functions such as, for example, front office, food and beverage, housekeeping, personnel, marketing, reception, conferences. And management is not homogeneous. The nature of management is variable. It relates to all activities of the hotel, it takes place in different ways and is undertaken at all levels of the hotel.[6]

It is difficult to think of any aspect of the functioning of a hotel (or other hospitality organisation) or the behaviour of people which does not concern, or relate back to, management in some way or another. For example, a personality clash between two members of staff could possibly be traced back to management procedures for recruitment and selection, induction and training, delegation or the level or style of supervision.

And personality clashes are likely to have an adverse affect on the work performance of the individuals concerned, the morale of other staff and possibly the standard of customer service.

The cornerstone of organisational effectiveness

Management is concerned with arrangements for the carrying out of organisational processes and the execution of work. It is the task of management to weld a coherent pattern of activities best suited to the environment in which the hotel is operating, to harness the efforts of its members, and to ensure fair and equitable systems of motivation, job satisfaction and rewards. Management is therefore the cornerstone of organisational performance and effectiveness (Figure 4.1).

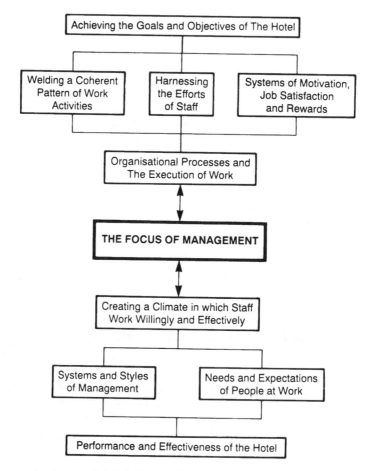

Fig 4.1 Management as an integrating activity

Attention should be focused on improving the people–organisation relationship and creating a climate in which people work willingly and effectively. Management is an integral part of this relationship. It is essentially an integrating activity which permeates every facet of the operations of the hotel. Management is seen best, therefore, as a process common to all other functions carried out within the hotel.

The importance of management to effective organisational performance has been illustrated by Lord Forte.

> Success rests first and foremost on the activities of the manager on the spot, whether of a hotel, restaurant, cafe or motorway area. It is his or her ability to run the enterprise effectively and to inspire and guide the staff that is decisive. A hotel or restaurant is only as good as its manager. If the manager is good the staff is good, if the staff is good, the hotel or restaurant is good.[7]

THE PROCESS OF MANAGEMENT

It is through the process of management that the efforts of members of the hotel are channelled, co-ordinated and guided towards the achievement of organisational goals and objectives. But what does the process of management involve and what activities does it encompass?

There are many ways of looking at management. One approach is to search for the common activities which are applicable to managers in all organisations. This approach gives rise to many different descriptions of management, although on closer study they often show a basic similarity. The inclusion or exclusion of a particular aspect of management tends to revolve round the use and interpretation of different terms, and the emphasis placed upon them.

Management as a social process

Among the best-known analysis is that given by Brech, who defines management as:

> A social process entailing responsibility for the effective and economical planning and regulation of the operation of an enterprise, in fulfilment of given purposes or tasks, such responsibility involving:
>
> (a) judgement and decision in determining plans, and in using data to control performance and progress against plans;
> (b) the guidance, integration, motivation and supervision of the personnel composing the enterprise and carrying out its operations.[8]

This is a useful definition in that it draws attention to management as a 'social process', to the responsibilities of a manager and to the importance of the people–organisation relationship

As part of a debate on the need for a framework for the study of hospitality management (discussed in Chapter 1), Wood also draws attention to the recognition of the essentially **social** nature of management. The social and therefore variable nature of management as an activity precludes the evolution of any 'systematic' theory or theories of such activities.[9]

The tasks and contribution of a manager

Another approach to describing management is provided by Drucker, who identifies three tasks, equally important but essentially different, that have to be performed:

- fulfilling the specific purpose and mission of the institution, whether business enterprise, hospital or university (and we can add 'or hospitality organisation');
- making work productive and the worker achieving; and
- managing social impacts and social responsibilities.[10]

The work of the manager requires a combination of analytical ability, synthesising ability, integrity, human perception and insight, and social skill.

Drucker also suggests that managers can be defined by their function and by the contribution they are expected to make:

> The function that distinguishes the manager above all others is the function no one but the manager can perform. The one contribution a manager is uniquely expected to make is to give others vision and ability to perform. It is vision and moral responsibility that, in the last analysis, define the manager.[11]

ESSENTIAL NATURE OF MANAGERIAL WORK

The overall responsibility of management can be seen as the attainment of the given objectives of the hotel. The essential nature of managerial work is not easy to describe, however, because aspects which may be common in many applications might escape us in others. And neither can you identify, necessarily, a manager by what people are called or by their job title. There are people whose job title may not include the term 'manager' (for example head chef or controller and, of course, maître d') but who, in terms of the activities they undertake, are very much a manager.

'Managing' distinguished from 'doing'

However, if you look at how staff actually spend their time you should be able to see a difference between those whose main occupation is the carrying out of discrete tasks and the actual doing of work themselves; and those who spend proportionally more of their time in deciding what is to be done, determining the work to be undertaken by others, planning and organising their work, issuing them with instructions and giving advice, and checking on their performance.

From a study of 65 Irish hotels, Baum found that managers were actively involved in supervision, and frequently in the operation of such areas as front office, restaurant, bar and kitchen. Time was spent on tasks that craft or semi-skilled employees could perform and this suggested little awareness or concern for cost-effective use of time. However, central to the operational focus of the managers was the 'mine host' concept. More than half the managers defined their job as being essentially concerned with satisfying the needs of guests.[12]

Main activities of management

The particular nature of the hospitality industry means that certain managers might be seen to be spending somewhat more time 'doing' than managers in other types of organisations. Nevertheless, the basis of the distinction between 'managing' and 'doing' still applies and this enables us to see the main activities of management (Figure 4.2) as:

- the clarification of objectives and policy;
- the planning of work to be carried out;
- organising the distribution of activities and tasks to other people;
- directing and guiding subordinate staff; and
- controlling the performance of other people's work.

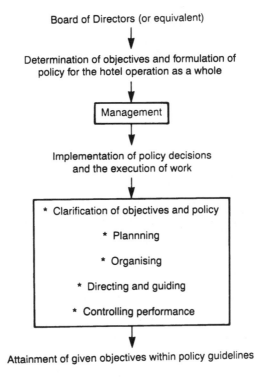

Fig 4.2 The essential nature of managerial work

Clarification of objectives and policy

Objectives are the aims to be achieved and the desired end-results. Policy provides guidelines for the operations of the hotel and determines the course of action to follow. The clarification of objectives and policy is a prerequisite if the process of management and execution of work is to be effective. If not, the manager has no secure basis for decision making and the management of subordinate staff.

Planning of work

Planning sets out the courses of action to be followed in order to meet objectives and achieve desired end-results, for example in relation to occupancy rates, financial measures or sales performance. Good forward planning is essential if staff are to know what to do and what is expected of them, for example the timing and sequencing of operations, methods by which the operations are to be carried out and standards of performance.

Organising

The work of the hotel has to be divided among its members. Organising involves the structuring of related areas of work activities such as reception, accommodation, kitchen and restaurant. Organisation provides the framework within which the process of management takes place. It makes possible the execution of work and involves the allocation of tasks and responsibilities, levels of hierarchical authority, formal relationships and co-ordination among individuals, groups and departments.

Directing subordinate staff

It is the responsibility of managers to encourage staff to work willingly and effectively. This is often referred to as motivation. It is certainly part of a manager's job to motivate staff and to provide them with job satisfaction, but it involves more than this. Subordinate staff also need development and guidance. They need to be motivated to **perform well in the right areas**. Their efforts should be directed towards the achievement of given objectives within stated policy guidelines. The manager has a responsibility to see that staff are effective as well as efficient in what they do.

Controlling performance

Control is a necessary part of the process of management. It involves gauging the measure of success in achieving objectives and planned targets. Management control involves far more than a means of restricting behaviour or the exercise of authority over others. It should not be seen therefore only in a negative sense; it can have many positive effects.

Effective control systems are a means of monitoring performance and progress, providing feedback to staff and a guide to future operations and personal development. Control completes the cycle of managerial activities and is an important part of the process of management.

The role of supervisors

Supervisors may too often be regarded primarily as 'doers' or as technicians rather than managers. But supervisors, especially in the hospitality industry, are usually very much in the front line of management and have a prime responsibility for seeing that work gets done by others. Supervisors can be seen as having a particular concern with the directing, guiding and controlling performance activities of management. They need to have the required skills to motivate staff to perform well, deal first-hand with problems of production or service, handle difficulties or complaints diplomatically, and perhaps discipline staff.

Supervisors are required to act in a fair and sensitive manner and to provide both the link and the buffer between the opposing expectations of junior staff and senior management. The general movement towards flatter organisation structures and fewer levels of management has highlighted the importance of the role of the supervisor.

PRINCIPLES OF MANAGEMENT

Despite the variable nature of management, Fayol has suggested a set of 14 well-established principles to help concentrate discussion on management theory.[13]

   (i) **Division of work** – the advantages of specialisation and the division of work. However, there are limits to division of work which experience and a sense of proportion suggest should not be exceeded.

  (ii) **Authority and responsibility** – responsibility is the corollary of authority. Wherever authority is exercised, responsibility arises. The application of sanctions is essential to good management, and is needed to encourage useful actions and to discourage their opposite. The best safeguard against abuse of authority is the personal integrity of the manager.

 (iii) **Discipline** – this is essential for the efficient operation of an organisation, and is in essence the outward mark of respect for agreements between the organisation and its members. The manager must decide on the most appropriate form of sanctions for offences against discipline.

 (iv) **Unity of command** – in any action an employee should receive orders from one superior only; if not, authority is undermined and discipline, order and stability threatened. Dual command is a perpetual source of conflicts.

  (v) **Unity of direction** – in order to provide for unity of action, co-ordination and focusing of effort, there should be one head and one plan for any group of activities with the same objective.

 (vi) **Subordination of individual interests to general interest** – the interest of the organisation should dominate individual or group interests.

 (vii) **Remuneration of personnel** – remuneration should as far as possible satisfy both employee and employer. Methods of payment can influence organisational performance and the methods should be fair and encourage keenness by rewarding well-directed effort, but not lead to over-payment.

(viii) **Centralisation** – is always present to some extent in any organisation. The degree of centralisation is a question of proportion and will vary among particular organisations.

 (ix) **Scalar chain** – the chain of superiors from the ultimate authority to the lowest ranks. Respect for line authority must be reconciled with activities which require urgent action, and with the need to provide for some measure of initiative at all levels of authority.

  (x) **Order** – this includes material order and social order. The objective of material order is avoidance of loss. There should be an appointed place for each thing, and each thing in its appointed place. Social order involves an appointed place for each employee, and each employee in his or her appointed place. Social order requires good organisation and good selection.

(xi) **Equity** – the desire for equity and for equality of treatment are aspirations to be taken into account in dealing with employees at all levels.

(xii) **Stability of tenure of personnel** – generally, prosperous organisations have a stable managerial personnel. But changes of personnel are inevitable and stability of tenure is a question of proportion.

(xiii) **Initiative** – this represents a source of strength for the organisation and should be encouraged and developed. Tact and integrity are required to promote initiative and to retain respect for authority and discipline.

(xiv) **Esprit de corps** – this should be fostered as harmony and unity among members of an organisation is a great strength. The principle of unity of command should be observed. It is necessary to avoid the dangers of 'divide and rule' of one's own team, and the abuse of formal communication. Wherever possible, verbal contacts should be used.

General guidelines for the process of management

These principles provide a helpful framework within which to view organisational processes and the execution of work. They apply as much to hospitality operations as to any other type of work organisation although their applications may vary according to particular situations. For example, the principles of discipline, the scalar chain and esprit de corps might be seen to be of particular significance for hotel management.

The principles must also be flexible and adaptable to changing circumstances, and certain principles are likely to be emphasised more in certain types of operations. For example, decisions on the division of work and the extent of centralisation are likely to be more significant in large-size establishments. However, as general guidelines for the process of management, the principles are difficult to argue against.

MANAGERIAL ROLES

The classical view of the manager as someone who organises, co-ordinates, plans and controls is not always easy to relate to what we see of the work of the manager. Mintzberg, for example, believes that the classical view tells us little about what managers actually do. It is more meaningful to describe the manager's job in terms of various 'roles' or organised sets of behaviour identified with a position[14]

Based on a study of the work of five chief executives in medium-to-large organisations, Mintzberg classifies the essential functions of a top manager's job into ten interrelated roles. These roles are divided into three main groups: (i) interpersonal roles; (ii) informational roles; and (iii) decisional roles.[15]

The manager's formal status and authority give rise to the importance of interpersonal relationships. As a result of the interpersonal roles the manager is the focus for the collection and processing of information. The informational roles provide the basis for decision making (Figure 4.3).

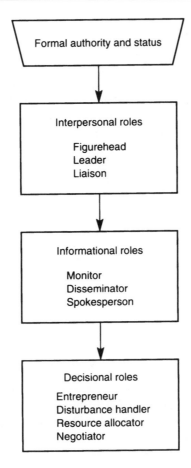

Fig 4.3 The manager's roles
Source: Mintzberg H, *The Nature of Managerial Work*, Harper & Row (1973), p. 59. Copyright © 1973 by Henry Mintzberg. Reproduced by kind permission of HarperCollins Publishers, Inc.

Interpersonal roles

Interpersonal roles are relations with other people and arise from the manager's status and authority.

(i) **The figurehead role** is the most basic and simple of managerial roles. The manager is a symbol and represents the organisation in formal matters such as signing documents or at important social occasions. The manager is also available for people who insist on access to the 'top', for example a guest with a serious complaint or a member of staff with a major grievance.

(ii) **The leader role** is among the most significant of roles and permeates all activities of a manager. This role involves a responsibility for staffing, and the motivation and guidance of subordinate staff.

(iii) **The liaison role** involves the manager in relationships with individuals and groups outside their own unit, for example other managers, or outside the organisation, for example conference organisers. This role provides a link between the organisation and its environment.

Informational roles

Informational roles relate to the sources and communication of information arising from the manager's interpersonal roles.

(iv) **The monitor role** identifies the manager in seeking and receiving information in order to develop an understanding of the working of the organisation and its environment. This could include, for example, information on occupancy rates, future bookings or levels of staff turnover.

(v) **The disseminator role** involves the manager in the transmission of external and internal information. External information, for example the results of a meeting with another manager, is passed through the liaison role. Internal information, for example a request to comply with new instructions, is passed through the leader role between subordinates.

(vi) **The spokesperson role** involves the manager as formal authority in transmitting information to people outside the unit, for example the board of directors, or to people outside the organisation such as suppliers, guests, government departments or the press.

Decisional roles

Decisional roles involve making strategic organisational decisions on the basis of the manager's status and authority, and access to information.

(vii) **The entrepreneurial role** is the manager's function to initiate and plan controlled change through exploiting opportunities or solving problems, and taking action to improve the existing situation, for example by introducing a wider range of low-season offers or improving productivity.

(viii) **The disturbance handler role** involves the manager in reacting to involuntary situations and unpredictable events. When an unexpected disturbance occurs, for example the sudden and unexplained breakdown of kitchen equipment, the manager must take action to correct the situation.

(ix) **The resource allocator role** involves the manager in using formal authority to decide where effort will be expended, and making choices on the allocation of resources such as money, time, materials and staffing; for example, a choice might be required between enlarging the leisure facilities or improving conference facilities.

(x) **The negotiator role** involves the manager in negotiation activity with other individuals or organisations, for example a new wages agreement with staff representatives or a trade union, or negotiations with a potential new supplier.

An integrated whole

Mintzberg emphasises that the set of ten roles is a somewhat arbitrary division of the manager's activities. It presents one of many possible ways for categorising the view of managerial roles. The ten roles are not easily isolated in practice but form an integrated whole. If any role is removed this affects the effectiveness of the manager's overall performance.

The ten roles suggest that the manager is in fact a specialist required to perform a particular set of specialist roles. Mintzberg argues that empirical evidence supports the contention that this set of roles is common to the work of all managers.

APPLICATIONS TO THE HOTEL MANAGER

Among the studies of the application of Mintzberg's work to the hotel manager are those by Ley, Arnaldo and Shortt.

Head office rating of managerial effectiveness

Ley undertook a detailed observation of general managers in seven medium-sized Holiday Inn hotels in America. The study was concerned with time spent on different managerial roles related to head office ratings of the managers' effectiveness.[16] After classifying the functions of the managers' jobs in terms of Mintzberg's roles, the managers were then rated by their corporate superiors. Two managers were rated highly effective, three rated effective and two rated less than effective.

Effective managers appeared to allocate their time among the roles in a manner different from less effective managers. Those managers who devoted a high proportion of their time to the **entrepreneurial** role were judged to be more effective. But managers who worked the longest hours were also rated most effective by head offices and this raises doubts about the validity of the rating system. Although all managers saw the **leadership** role as important there appeared to be no direct relationship between time spent on this role and ratings of effectiveness. The two highly effective managers actually allocated less time to the leadership role than the two less effective managers.

Time and importance assigned to roles

Arnaldo surveyed 194 American hotel general managers who were asked to classify their activities in terms of Mintzberg's ten managerial roles, and to indicate the amount of time and importance assigned to each of the roles.[17] The study asked the managers to provide a relative ranking of time and importance to the various functions within each of the three main groupings.

- Of the interpersonal roles that of **leader** clearly absorbed most time (71.7%) and was considered of most importance (86.1%).
- With the informational roles, both **monitoring** and **disseminating** were said to be relatively time-absorbing and important. The spokesperson role took up less time and was considered less important.
- Of the decisional roles, all apart from negotiating absorbed roughly equal time. The **entrepreneurial** role was clearly judged to be the most important (55.2%), although a lesser proportion of time (35.6%) was spent on this role.

From the results of this study Arnaldo suggests that the development of training programmes might emphasise the crucial activities of leader, monitor, disseminator and entrepreneur.

A similar study undertaken by Shortt concerned 62 general managers of inns in

Northern Ireland.[18] The most important roles were identified as **disturbance handler, leader** and **entrepreneur**. The least important roles were identified as **figurehead, disseminator** and **negotiator**.

MANAGERIAL WORK IN THE HOSPITALITY INDUSTRY

From a review of the literature on the nature of managerial work in the hospitality industry, which has focused primarily on hotel management, Wood summarises six principal characteristics of management work.[19]

- People enter hotel management careers via a range of routes including: formal hotel school training, training for management within the industry and late entry after an earlier career in another industry. The last appears most typical of the owner-manager but in general all three routes seem typical of career paths in the industry.
- Hotel management like other occupations and the industry itself is very insular. Students are usually separated from general business studies students and their industrial placement training serves as a means of pre-entry socialisation. There is a perceived need for an emphasis on technical skills and competence particularly in food and beverage management.
- Most senior hotel managers obtain their appointment at a relatively early age. Formal qualifications do not appear to influence either entry position, or career patterns or promotion prospects. Vocational education or time spent gaining experience of the industry are alternatives that make little difference to long-term prospects.
- Hotel management positions are gained as a result of substantial mobility. Hotel and catering managers change their jobs more frequently than managers in other industrial sectors. Experience of both front of house and food and beverage is usually essential to promotion. Experience may be gained from frequent lateral moves between hotels within the same company or from moves involving a change of company. Pay appears to be generally linked to size of hotel and this therefore provides another incentive to mobility.
- The degree of latitude given to individual managers in the running of their units is reflected in the conduct of hotel management work. Particular importance is attached to leadership and entrepreneurial roles. Hotel management is dominated by operational demands and time spent in supervision of staff and contact with customers. Managers have a preference for active management and, rather than sitting behind a desk, emphasise the 'being there' aspect of the job. The attitudes of management at unit level evidence a unitary outlook as opposed to a pluralistic perspective.
- Managers' basic remuneration, like the rest of the hotel and catering workforce, is relatively poor. Average salaries for hotel and catering managers are below those in other industrial sectors. Although hotel management careers are easier for some, the work is usually hard and the rewards are perceived, to outsiders at least, as somewhat limited.

THE MANAGERIAL WHEEL

Addressing the issue of the relationship between expected and actual behaviour, Hales and Nightingale studied managers in a wide range of organisations in the hospitality industry.[20] They identified a 'role-set' – that is, the set of people with whom the manager has contacts and the demands made upon the manager from a variety of role senders. In addition to the manager's own perception of his or her role, each member of the role-set was asked to identify the demands, requirements and expectations of the manager under study. These were recorded in a 'managerial wheel', as depicted in Figure 4.4. (The nature of role relationships and the role-set are discussed in more detail in Chapter 9.)

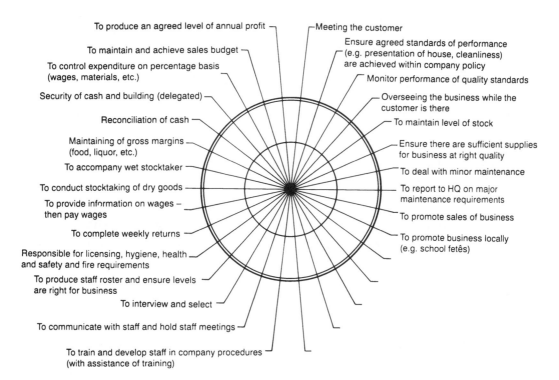

Fig 4.4 A managerial wheel: expectations of unit manager by regional general manager
Reprinted from Hales C and Nightingale M, 'What Are Unit Managers Supposed To Do? A Contingent Methodology for Investigating Managerial Role Requirements', *International Journal of Hospitality Management*, vol. 5, no. 1, 1986, p. 7 With kind permission from Pergamon Press Ltd.

As might be anticipated, the study found that the unit manager's job is subject to a range of competing and conflicting demands from a wide range of sources, both internal and external. The range of expectation of the manager varied between different sectors and different members of the role-set. A main conclusion was that the character of unit management is determined as much by the kind of unit and what is being managed as by the general characteristics of the management process.

THE FLEXIBILITY OF MANAGERIAL WORK

Based on earlier studies of managerial jobs, Stewart has developed a model for understanding managerial work and behaviour.[21] The model directs attention to the generalisations that can be made about managerial work and differences which exist among managerial jobs. It acknowledges the wide variety among different managers in similar jobs in terms of how they view their jobs and the work they do. The three main categories of the model are demands, constraints and choices. These identify the flexibility in a managerial job.

- **Demands** are what anyone in the job *has* to do. They are not what the manager ought to do, but only what must be done, for example: meeting minimum criteria of performance, work which requires personal involvement, complying with bureaucratic procedures which cannot be avoided, meetings that must be attended.
- **Constraints** are internal or external factors which limit what the manager can do, for example, resource limitations, legal or trade union constraints, the nature of technology, physical location, compliance with company philosophy, attitudes of other people.
- **Choices** are the activities that the manager is free to do, but does not have to do. They are opportunities for one job holder to undertake different work from another job holder, or to do the work in a different way, for example: what work is undertaken within a defined area, to change the area of work, the sharing of work, participation in organisational or public activities.

Stewart suggests that the model provides a framework for thinking about the nature of managerial jobs and about the manner in which managers undertake them. To understand what managerial jobs are really like it is necessary to understand the nature of their flexibility. Account should be taken of variations in behaviour and differences in jobs before attempting to generalise about managerial work.

Behaviour patterns of general managers

From a detailed study of 15 successful general managers involved in a broad range of industries, Kotter found that the managers spend most of their time interacting with other people.[22] Many of these other people were in addition to their boss or direct subordinates. Meetings provided exchanges of information over a wide range of topics in a short period of time. Many of the contacts were 'network building' and concerned more with the requirements of other managers than the manager's own needs.

How restaurant managers spend their time

Using a similar methodology to Kotter, a study of nine restaurant managers was undertaken by Ferguson and Berger. From observation and documentation of the activities of the managers, their time was categorised as being used in the following five ways:

- Desk sessions   17%
- Telephone calls   13%
- Scheduled meetings   29%

- Unscheduled meetings   35%
- Tours   6%

Ferguson and Berger see the two categories of desk sessions and scheduled meetings as suggesting a reasonable level of structure and organisation, and conducive to organising, planning and deciding. However, from their study, the activities of the restaurant managers seemed far removed from textbook descriptions of planner, organiser, co-ordinator and controller.

> Planning seems to have been eclipsed by reacting; organising might be better described as simply carrying on; co-ordination appears more like juggling; and controlling seems reduced to full time watching .[23]

KEY RESULT AREAS OF HOTEL MANAGEMENT

Jones and Lockwood suggest a model of hotel management based on key result areas, defined as 'an area of activity that must be successfully managed in order to ensure the continued existence and the ultimate success of the operation.'[24]

Three component key result areas are:

- ensuring customer satisfaction;
- maintaining employee performance; and
- protecting assets from threat.

The three components are not managed in isolation but interact and overlap with each other. This highlights other key result areas that the manager must consider, such as managing customer service, maximising productivity, maximising income and profit contribution, and managing quality (Figure 4.5).

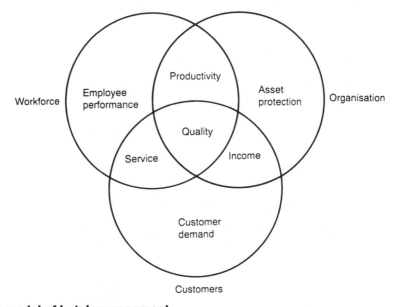

Fig 4.5 A model of hotel management
Source: Jones P and Lockwood A, *The Management of Hotel Operations*, Cassell (1989), p. 30. Reproduced by kind permission of Cassell plc.

The focus of attention or relative priority of the key result areas will vary according to particular circumstances and requirements of the hotel. The model can also be modified to suit other sectors of the hospitality industry.

APPLICATIONS OF GENERAL MANAGEMENT THEORY

You will recall from the discussion in Chapter 1 that the hospitality industry shares important common features with other business industries and faces the same general problems of management. Particular models of managerial behaviour for the hospitality industry have little relevance and, if anything, provide a constraint on an open and fluid interpretation of managerial development.[25]

In identifying major areas of activity and knowledge needed by students of the hospitality industry, *The Profile of Professional Management* has this to say about the management areas:

> Management areas cover functions common to management in any situation which have been identified as important to successful performance in hotel, catering and institutional services. Thus these areas reflect management functions which merit special emphasis in this industry and which represent the links between managements in this and other industries.[26]

Links with other industries

The common activities of management apply to a greater or lesser extent within the hotel industry. Stewart makes the point that managers' jobs vary and 'the differences are many and important' but 'we need and, with the help of research can make, useful generalisations about managerial work.'[27]

Rather than over-emphasising its uniqueness, attention should be given to ways in which ideas drawn from management theory may be applied with advantage to the industry. This point, which has been made previously by the author, is reinforced by Baum:

> While the business environment in hotels does have very distinct features, there is a danger that the emphasis which the industry places on uniqueness should not be at the cost of the application of the more general principles of good management.[28]

From a review of what hospitality managers do and how they do it, Guerrier and Lockwood conclude that:

> It is encouraging that researchers into hospitality management are increasingly drawing on the general management literature at the same time that researchers in general management are showing more interest in hospitality – clearly a consequence of the greater interest in service industries in general. Perhaps undue attention has been paid to certain theories and theorists. With the richness of management research available to draw upon, it is hoped that hospitality researchers will continue to broaden the scope of their studies.[29]

Stewart has highlighted the variations in behaviour and differences in managerial jobs. Study of managers in similar jobs indicates that their focus of attention differs.[30] And this applies as much to hotel managers as to any other group of similar managers.

Managerial work in the hospitality industry

From a review of recent studies, Dann concludes that managerial work in the hospitality industry can be seen to fit comfortably with the main body of studies in the field. The need now is to integrate the studies of managerial work connected with the hospitality industry into the general body of knowledge of managerial work.[31]

A model for future research studies

Drawing on previous studies, Dann presents a model for the better understanding of the managerial work process and a guide for the direction of further research studies. The model involves three interlinking levels: inputs and demands; conduct and choices; and ends and outputs.

- **Level 1** concerns the inputs to the position and demands that are made on the role incumbent, for example: hierarchical level, size of the role-set, demands and expectations of those in the role-set, company strategy, the inherent nature of the job environment.
- **Level 2** relates to the conduct and choices available to the individual in managing the situation, for example: development of the managerial team, patterns of contact, delegation, usage of time, choice of job functions, and effective behaviour.
- **Level 3** relates to the ends and outputs of the manager. A clear pattern of the ends managers are attempting to achieve is a factor in shaping the nature of managerial work. Managers may wish to be judged not just on quantitative factors but also, for example, on relationships with their staff, and greater account is made of external influences which affect profitability.

The three levels are not intended to be mutually exclusive or divided. They are presented as a continuum rather than as distinct and clearly defined areas, and there is an interaction between each level. According to Dann, the hospitality industry requires much more research at all three levels.

MANAGERIAL JOB STRESS

Stress appears to be generally acknowledged as an enduring feature of work in the hospitality industry. This view is supported by a study undertaken by Brymer *et al.* of over 400 middle and upper level managers in the hotel industry. The study found that managers perceived their jobs to be stressful, resulting in psychological, physiological and behavioural strains.[32] One purpose of the study was to indicate the amount of stress experienced by managers as a result of their job and their ability to manage this stress. Managers were asked to indicate the amount of stress on a 1 (very low) to 10 (very high scale). All respondents reported experiencing some level of stress and the mean response was 7.55 suggesting a high level of experienced stress.

The study examined whether managers perceived job stress as affecting attitudes or behaviours that related to bottom-line organisational costs. Results indicated that job stress has a negative effect on management and staff attitudes and behaviour. Job stress had the most significant effect on turnover, absenteeism, sickness and accidents. Job stress was also believed to decrease management and staff productivity, and job satisfaction.

Coping mechanisms

Managers were also asked to indicate on a 1 (needs improvement) to 10 (very high) scale their ability to manage stress. The mean response of 6.79 indicated that managers perceived themselves fairly well able to manage stress. However, the use of coping mechanisms did not appear to reduce the level of stress. Positive coping mechanisms (such as relaxation, hobbies, organising time, exercise) were either unrelated or positively related and did not result in alleviating stress. Negative coping mechanisms (such as avoidance, the use of alcohol, medicine, over/under eating or spending money) were, as expected, related to increased stress. Brymer *et al.* suggest the need for employee assistance and stress management programmes and increasing employee control over their work as potential ways for stress reduction and prevention.

THE MANAGERIAL ENVIRONMENT

Managers have to manage in the situation in which they find themselves. A major determinant of an individual hospitality manager's job is the environment, both internal and external, in which that manager is working.[33]

> As both an academic discipline and a set of 'real-life' practices, management is essentially a response to the demands of the wider environment and also part of it.[34]

The functioning and operation of a hospitality organisation takes place within the context of the total environmental setting. The actual process of management and execution of work is influenced by a combination of:

(i) the internal environment in which organisational processes take place, and which management is able to influence; and
(ii) the external environment of which the organisation is part, but which is outside the direct control of management.

The environment in which the manager is working will determine both the nature of the managerial roles, and the demands, constraints and choices which identify the flexibility in managerial behaviour.

The internal environment

Despite similarities in the general activities of management, the work of the manager is varied and fragmented. The jobs of individual hotel managers, for example, will differ widely and be influenced by such interrelated factors as:

- **the nature of the hotel itself** – its culture, philosophy and objectives, size, type of building, location, facilities and guests;
- **its structure** – whether mechanistic or organic, division of work, patterns of organisation and formal relationships, channels of communication;
- **the nature of the work and tasks** to be carried out;

- the 'technology' – how work is carried out, the materials, equipment and furnishings;
- its people – their knowledge, skills, and experience, attitudes and motivations, patterns of behaviour, group functioning and the informal organisation;
- the level at which the manager is working – higher-level policies or decisions, the leadership style of the manager's superior.

These differences do not just exist between different hotels but they are often more a matter of degree. Many large hotels may have more in common in their operations and management with other business organisations of the same size, than with very small hotels.

The external environment

The process of management is determined not only by internal considerations and choices, but is also influenced by a range of external factors. In Chapter 1 we saw that the hotel is an open system and in continual interaction with the external environment of which it is part (see Figure 4.6). All business organisations operate within, and are affected by, their external environment. For hotel managers the demands of the external environment, for example guests/customers, may be particularly significant.[35]

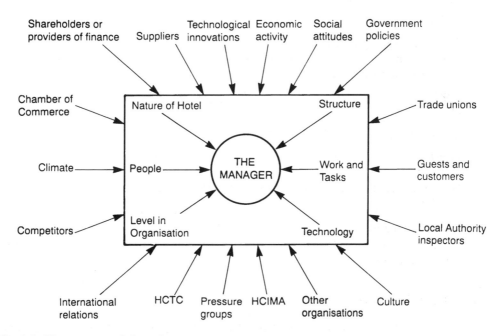

Fig 4.6 The managerial environment

Also in Chapter 1 we looked at the importance of major external factors including technological innovations, economic activity, social attitudes and government policies. There are a multiplicity of constantly changing environmental factors which are outside the control of management but which affect the operations of the hotel.

As further examples, consider how the process of management within a hotel might be affected by specific external influences such as:

- a government decision to include VAT on food;
- a total ban on all drinking and driving;
- severe restrictions on the use of water because of prolonged drought conditions;
- the building of a new hotel in close proximity by a major competitor;
- an unexpected and exceptionally high rise in the price of electricity;
- a TUC recommendation for members to boycott hotels paying below certain wage levels;
- a major advance in computer technology.

Not always easy to distinguish

It is important to note that, in practice, it is not always easy to distinguish clearly between situations that arise as a result of the internal environment or the external environment. The one tends to impinge upon the other. For example, to what extent might difficulties in recruiting high-calibre staff be due to poor selection procedures, low pay and poor working conditions (and within the control of the hotel management), or due to demographic changes in the population (and outside the control of management)?

MANAGERIAL EFFECTIVENESS

We have seen that if the hospitality organisation is to be successful there is a clear and important need for effective management. Effectiveness should be distinguished from efficiency.

- **Efficiency** is concerned with 'doing things right' and relates to inputs and what the manager does.
- **Effectiveness** is concerned with 'doing the right things' and relates to outputs of the job, and what the manager actually achieves.[36]

Effectiveness should also be distinguished from activity. Rees, for example, distinguishes between those managers who define what has to be done and get on with it, and those who seek to justify their positions by creating a flurry of activity rather than by the results they achieve.

> The great danger is that, if a manager spends too much time simply justifying himself, he may fail actually to diagnose what he should be doing and do it. Ultimately managers are much more likely to be judged by results than by anything else. Activity-centred behaviour is in any case much more likely to spring from incompetence and/or insecurity rather than adroit political behaviour.[37]

Measurements of effectiveness

Managerial effectiveness should be related to the performance of the process of management and the execution of work, and measured in terms of the results that the manager is expected to achieve. But managerial effectiveness is not easy to measure objectively. Managers are judged not just on their own performance but also on results achieved by subordinate staff. The manager's effectiveness may be assessed in part, therefore, by such factors as the strength of motivation and morale of staff, the success of their training and development, and the quality of their work performance.

However, the difficulty in applying such measurements is that they are also likely to be influenced by many important factors outside the direct control of the individual manager, for example the type, size and location of the establishment, the competitive level of the market, the general economic climate, company philosophy or general policy directives.

OUTPUT MEASURES OF EFFECTIVENESS

To be effective the manager must give attention to the outputs of the job – to performance – in terms of factors such as obtaining the best possible results in the key areas of operations, optimal use of resources, increasing profitability, and attainment of the aims and objectives of the hotel.

Criteria which *may* give some indication of managerial effectiveness include the efficiency of systems and procedures, the standard of service afforded to other departments, meeting important deadlines, adherence to quality standards, the number of recorded errors or complaints, keeping within agreed budget limits and productivity.

Again, however, there is the question of how to determine objective measurement of such criteria and to what extent they are under the control of the manager.

Outcome measures of performance

As part of a study of 63 managers from three different American hotel firms, Umbreit and Eder asked participants to record important outcome measures that a typical hotel manager should have control over, and against which their performance should be evaluated.[38] After discussion among the group, a list of 14 outcome measures was identified.

- **Guest comments** – to staff or on cards.
- **Market share** – percentage of room nights occupied in comparison to the total in the market.
- **Room nights sold** – total of rooms sold in a given period.
- **Reduction of employee turnover** – compared with a previous period.
- **Budget controlled** – sales generated and expenses controlled against budget figures.
- **Food and beverage department profit** – profit figure after deduction of expenses from departmental sales.
- **Rooms department profit** – profit figure after expenses are deducted from departmental sales.
- **Employee complaints** – about job conditions or treatment compared with a previous period.
- **Employee training course completions** – numbers formally completing a training programme during a certain time.
- **Collection of receivables** – outstanding number and amount of receivables during a given period of time.

- **Number of leadership positions held** – by a manager in the community.
- **Hotel rating** – the rating of the hotel by an outside agency.
- **Frequency of employee accidents** – reported to management compared with a previous period.
- **Adherence to productivity standards** – such as number of rooms cleaned per shift.

Behavioural dimensions of evaluation

Umbreit and Eder also suggest seven 'behavioural dimensions' for the evaluation of a hotel manager:

- handling guest complaints and promoting guest relations;
- developing market strategy and monitoring sales programmes;
- communicating with employees;
- Motivating and modifying behaviour;
- implementing policy, making decisions and delegating responsibility;
- monitoring operations and maintaining product quality;
- handling personnel responsibilities.

These seven dimensions can be applied as a basis for the performance review of a hotel manager and can provide important feedback on what behaviour is desirable to improve future performance [39]

The management of people

Criteria for assessing managerial effectiveness should be considered in terms of measuring the results that the manager is intended to achieve and over which the manager has control. But what is also important is the manner in which the manager achieves results and the effects on other people. This may well influence effectiveness in the longer term.

We have seen that there are many aspects to management in hospitality operations, but the one essential ingredient of any successful manager is the ability to handle people effectively. The manager needs to be conversant with social and human skills, and to have the ability to work with and through people. Without people there can be no organisation and no meaningful activity.[40]

Behind every action or document in a hotel there are people. The importance of the manager–subordinate relationship and the effective management of people are considered in the following chapter.

A FRAMEWORK OF MANAGEMENT

We have seen that there are many ways of looking at the nature of management and the work of a hospitality manager. A summary of the main aspects considered in this chapter is given in Figure 4.7. This provides a convenient framework in which to direct study of the subject area.

Fig 4.7 A framework for the study of management

SUMMARY

- The importance of management, including within the hospitality industry, is widely recognised. Management is responsible for the implementation of policy and the execution of work. This involves the exercise of authority over other people. Management is essentially an integrating activity – it is the cornerstone of organisational effectiveness and also a social process.
- By distinguishing 'managing' from 'doing' the essential nature of managerial work can be summarised as clarifying objectives and policy, planning, organising, directing and controlling. General principles of management provide helpful guidelines for the process of management.
- The job of a manager can be viewed in a number of ways including: as a set of inter-related roles, in terms of a role-set and the managerial wheel demands, constraints and choices and the flexibility in a managerial job and key result areas. Stress is an enduring feature of work in the hospitality industry. Attention needs to be given to potential ways for stress reduction and prevention.
- The hospitality industry has its own characteristics and features but also faces the same general problems of management. Rather than over-emphasising its uniqueness,

attention should be given to applications of general management theory and to integrating studies of hospitality management with ideas drawn from other industries.

- A major determinant of an individual manager's job is the internal and external environment in which the manager is working. Managerial effectiveness should be distinguished from efficiency and activity. Criteria for assessing the effectiveness of a hotel manager should be related to the output measures of the job and to results the manager is expected to achieve, and to the successful management of people.

REVIEW AND DISCUSSION QUESTIONS

1 Why do organisations need managers? Give your own views on the importance of management within the hospitality industry.

2 Discuss what is meant by: (i) management as an integrating activity; and (ii) the process of management.

3 Suggest how you would attempt to analyse the essential nature of managerial work. How would you distinguish the job of a hospitality manager from other jobs in the establishment?

4 Assess critically the practical relevance and applications of common principles of management within a large hospitality organisation.

5 How might the manager's job be described in terms of a set of interrelated roles? Give an example of each of these roles from the job of a senior hotel manager. What is meant by the flexibility of managerial work?

6 Discuss critically the extent to which general management theory can be applied successfully within the hospitality industry. Justify your answer with practical examples.

7 What is meant by the managerial environment? From your own experience, give *specific* examples of both internal *and* external environmental influences within hotel organisations.

8 How would you attempt to distinguish between an effective and an ineffective manager? Suggest what specific criteria you would use to assess the effectiveness of a particular hospitality manager.

ASSIGNMENT

Select a particular hospitality managerial job and observe the manager in action, preferably over an extended period of time.

(i) Make notes of how much of the manager's work and time is spent on:
  (a) the carrying out of discrete tasks and the actual 'doing' of work personally; and
  (b) deciding what work is to be done and planning, organising, directing or controlling the work of other people.
(ii) Identify clearly those factors which determine the demands, constraints and choices of the job. Comment critically on how these factors determine the flexibility in the manager's job.
(iii) Analyse particular ways in which features of the internal and external environment influence the job of the manager.
(iv) State clearly what conclusions you draw from your observations.

CASE STUDY

What *is* management?

> A thin may look specious in theory, and yet be ruinous in practice; a thin may look evil in theory, and yet be in practice excellent.   EDMUND BURKE

Adam Smith sat at his desk and reflected that it was now exactly twelve months since he had been appointed general assistant to Charles Gaynor, Managing Director of Gaynor Hotels. During this time he had been used as adviser, counsellor, internal consultant and therapist. He had investigated problems, developed concepts, established principles and generally contributed to the decision-taking process which took place in the mind of his employer, Gaynor. His attention had been attracted by an article he had been reading, which said:

> In order to maintain its internal dynamic which is essential to progress, a company needs the existence of a rebel group which is primarily concerned with challenging company policy, a group which regards as its main function the generation of sceptical attitudes towards the company's methods of operation, organisation and policies. Such a group should adopt as a working principle the slogan 'if it works it s obsolescent'. In other words the mere fact that a system is working satisfactorily should in itself be sufficient reason for its re-examination.*

Adam ruminated on this and considered that with Carson, his assistant, they really had created a two-man management services activity since they had concentrated on looking at, and solving, old problems in new ways. A pocket of rational thought in a wilderness of emotionalism – if only that were really true, thought Adam!

He felt depressed. Although he realised that some progress had been made, it seemed infinitesimal when one looked at the company as a whole. Where is the real answer to the achievement of progress, thought Adam. If only one could put one's finger on it. Particular aspects, methods, solutions and so on were looked at which all seemed part of the answer, but where was the whole answer? Charles Gaynor, although a man inculcated at an early age with the attitudes and ways of traditional hotelkeeping, was most receptive to new ideas; indeed, he could generate them himself and boasted of his preparedness to accept necessary change. But nothing much seemed to have changed in these twelve months; Gaynor Hotels was still making a profit, its managers were still 'managing' but problems continued to abound and there seemed just as many unanswered questions.

Adam leaned forward on his desk with his head in his hands. He wondered if the company was really progressing, if things were any better, and whether he was just deceiving himself. Perhaps the problem was that the company was just 'managing', that it was just getting by, just keeping its head above water. Is it really geared to grow and develop and prosper? Is it really looking ahead and ready to exploit the changing circumstances of a changing world? That's the central question, thought Adam, and I wish I could answer it confidently.

Management! It is all in the management, a handful of men cannot carry a company – it is in the strength and depth of *all* the people who form the firm. His thoughts were

*Ward, T. R., Management Services – The Way ahead, *National O & M Conference*, 1964; published as an Anbar Monograph, Anbar Publications, 1965.

interrupted by the door opening and Gaynor appearing with a benevolent smile, and a friendly 'Good afternoon, Adam.'

Gaynor: I thought I would let you know it looks as though I will have to fire a manager, or to put it euphemistically, to ask him to resign.

Adam: Who is it, sir?

Gaynor: Hedges, at the Zephyr. Nasty business and the sort of scandal I deplore. I had a letter from a Mr Coloniki; his wife is secretary to Hedges who, he asserted, has been sleeping with her. I thought there couldn't be anything in it and I referred it to our Mr Hedges never expecting anything other than a denial. Well the damn fool confirmed it as being true, he *has* been sleeping with his secretary. Doesn't leave me much alternative, does it? I can't compromise my principles and I will not have my hotel executives entering into this sort of relationship with their staff. My goodness! What sort of an example is it? Oh, the stupid man, and he was doing quite a good job for us.

Adam: Well, sir, there's an old Hungarian proverb which says that when a man's fancy is titillated his brain goes to water.

Gaynor: How very true! But a little control, a little sense of responsibility, a little maturity, that's all I ask. It isn't even as if he was serious about her; as he told me, it was just his 'little indiscretion' and he hoped that I wouldn't find out. By the way, you didn't already know about it, did you?

Adam: No, certainly not, sir. I haven't heard the slightest suggestion.

Gaynor: Well, back to the old problem of finding a new manager, as if good managers grew on trees! They are such rare animals – they take such a great deal of finding, such a great deal of raising.

Adam: How about his assistant, Gripple, do you think that he might be ready to take over?

Gaynor: He might . . . I don't know, even if we knew what job we were really picking him for; I mean, what *is* management, what is it *really*? What are we looking for?

Adam: Well, quite honestly, sir, I do not think that he's ready. I think he could develop into a manager, but he needs more time.

Gaynor: All right, we will have to find somebody. I'll tell you what we can do: you take over as manager of the Zephyr for the next month or so. During that time I will find a new manager. This *has* caught us unawares, I can't think of anybody suitable in the company at present.

Adam: But I've never actually managed a hotel!

Gaynor: Well, it will be an excellent experience for you. Anyway, I have no doubt about *your* management abilities. But you still didn't answer my question just now. What actually *is* management – do you know what it is?

Adam: Strange you should ask me that this afternoon, I think that I was going to ask myself the same question just as you walked in.

Gaynor: Fine, but can you answer it?

Adam: Well, it's obviously to do with concern for profits and its equally to do with concern for people and creating a climate where they can grow and develop.

Gaynor: That's rather vague.

Adam: Well, let me go on, sir. If it's to do with concern for profits then it is also to do with knowledge of modern management methods and techniques and how to use them. If it's to do with concern for people, then it's also to do with knowledge of human behaviour and its application.

Gaynor: You're struggling, Adam. I remember we talked about the purpose of business and it must lead on from there. We agreed that this was the satisfaction of the needs, wants and desires of those who control the business and generally, but not always, this involved a certain level of profitability. Now purpose must define or set the aims and objectives. Subsequently the policy indicates the means as to how to accomplish these. Policy acts then as the firm guide in all decision-making at an operational level. Management, therefore, is the implementation of policy to achieve company aims and objectives. Yes, I rather like that – I must remember to use it again.

Adam: I know you won't mind Mr Gaynor, but I can't agree with you.

Gaynor: Go on then, I am not very busy at the moment.

Adam: I don't disagree with what you say, but really I am concerned with the assumptions which are being made. Indeed, the business purpose sets aims or objectives but this implies that the business purpose has been established, is commonly perceived and is accepted. You next assume that policy is rationally formulated and promulgated, that managers are aware of it, and take their decisions within its limitations.

Gaynor: Perhaps that describes the ideal situation, but I would still maintain that what I said – what was it – management is the implementation of policy to achieve company aims and objectives, is a good description.

Adam: May I ask what policy Mr Hedges offended?

Gaynor: Ah, well, now, there are several. First it is unethical; second, if it became known it would damage our image and create havoc in staff relationships, and there are more besides.

Adam: But Mr Hedges took a decision, presumably with a knowledge of the policies you mention, whose effects could militate against our aims and objectives as well as damage his career.

Gaynor: And a damn fool he was, too!

Adam: Were it a less serious affair, and something which was only a minor departure from Company policy, I can't help wondering how he or we would know that a departure had occurred. For example, if a manager gave 11% commission to travel agents during the winter to obtain some preference from them, would this be stopped if you became aware of it?

Gaynor: I hope that he would have discussed this with me first, but I can appreciate the point. After all we must be flexible enough to deal with special situations.

Adam: Doesn't this, then, highlight the problem of what we mean by policy? Earlier you said that policy acts as a firm guide, but payment of commission is pretty well fixed at 10% although you would be prepared to consider exceptions. I hope I am not splitting hairs if I suggest that our policy is to pay commissions, and a procedure has been established which fixes this at 10%.

Gaynor: I think, in this case, you are tending to split hairs but I see what you are getting at; a confusion exists between policy and procedures. I must admit that I have confused these at times, yes I see the point – policy should act as a guide. But formulating policy in this way must make it so general that it cannot provide much of a guide, a paradox in fact. Another thought that occurs to me is that if the policy is to be an effective guide it should be written out and available for the manager to consult. I must say that this would be an unenviable task!

Adam: Reading textbooks about management I have found the exhortation to have a written policy a common theme. I have never actually seen one so far for a hotel and one can appreciate why this is so. At the same time I would think it comparatively easy to spell out some policies; in the financial areas, for example, this would seem a fairly straightforward exercise.

Gaynor: Yes, and I think it could be done in the operating area too. I must admit, though, that I am not sure that I would like to have an exhaustive written policy document. I feel it would be a restriction on me.

Adam: I believe this is a fairly common feeling among senior executives. Glacier Metal Company introduced a written policy and their experience was that flexibility *increased* since, when a change had to be made, everybody could be informed and a written amendment incorporated. This makes sense to me, but I have always had a sneaking feeling that they wrote a procedure manual rather than a policy handbook.

Gaynor: So you are back to your distinction between policy and procedures! Am I to take it, then, that you are advocating that we should try to produce a policy document for the Company?

Adam: No, sir, I may tend to overstate the case, but I would think that the existence of such a document represents a failure of management. At a unit level, and indeed at company level, it is essential to have *procedure* manuals since these provide a means of establishing and maintaining standards as well as a basis for training. I would also say that it is essential for a company to spend a lot of time clarifying its objectives and aims at the top level. The real problem is that many so-called policy documents are little more than a public relations handout. If a company is clear about what it wants to be, surely it should make every effort for everybody to understand and accept these aims and behave in a supportive way towards them.

Gaynor: I would have thought that having a written policy would help to do this, since people could see just what the aims are and act accordingly.

Adam: I am sure that this is partly true, but what I am trying to say is that if, starting at the top, members of an organisation demonstrate by their behaviour what the policy is, this will be reflected downwards. If the senior executives behave as though they believed the customer was important, then other employees will adopt similar behaviour.

Gaynor: In other words, people will learn by example. I am rather intrigued that you should have such a charming old-fashioned idea!

Adam: By example, yes. But it is a little more than this. Put into jargon, I would say that it is minimising corporate discrepancy. That is, reducing the difference between what a company as a collection of people say, and what in fact they do.

Gaynor: Very well, I agree with what you say but I must say there are some grave dangers of misinterpretation. If the conclusion without the supporting argument is adopted it can become an excuse for avoiding the necessary analytical thinking at the top level. We seem to have strayed a long way from my attempt to define management; taking into account all you have said we still have a good description.

Adam: I agree, but the whole problem of vocabulary in management continues to be a stumbling-block. I always remember a lecturer at college who said at his lecture to us that he had to devise a vocabulary to talk to us which we would automatically adopt, but never to attempt to use it outside. Since there is no generally accepted or defined vocabulary he had to fashion his own to communicate to us. We all forgot, of course, and it took some time to stop using our private language when we went into industry.

Gaynor: You still forget sometimes!

Adam: Sorry! If we do understand that policy and company aims and objectives are in some way related to individual interpretation, depending on the perceptions of the people involved, then I think it is a good *description*. But shouldn't a definition of this sort be a *prescription*? By saying what it is, it gives some indication of how to do it?

Gaynor: Description, prescription, you're chopping words again. I will accept, although I think you are trying to find a philosopher's stone if a definition can tell a manager how to do his job!

Adam: To come back to the definition, sir, suppose the policy is wrong or the aims and objectives are wrong. Is it true to say that an individual is managing if he keeps things going to achieve these and doesn't have the wit or the insight to besiege his superiors for a change of direction?

Gaynor: Ah! Now you are introducing value judgements about 'good' management and 'bad' management!

Adam: No, Mr Gaynor. You will accuse me of sophistry again, but I would say that a person who is a manager is managing effectively. If he is ineffective, then he is not a manager.

Gaynor: Save me from quibblers! But do go on.

Adam: When I was in America I was given an assignment to collect together as many definitions of management as I could find. It really was a fascinating exercise but eventually I found myself in a such a muddle that I could hardly think straight. The things that people have to say about this process, which hundreds of thousands of people go about for five days a week, year in and year out is amazing. The one that I remember, and considered the most banal of a very sad bunch, was 'Management is getting things done through people.'

Gaynor: Oh! I always considered that a truism.

Adam: Well, yes. But it doesn't advance our understanding. Bus conductors, waitresses and supervisors get things done through people – but they are not managers.

Gaynor: Very interesting; so you don't think supervisors are managers?

Adam: No. Managers are tacticians; that is they are people who are once-removed from the actual operators who serve the food or make the beds. Managers are concerned with the deployment of resources. A manager *says* what has to be done, a supervisor frequently *shows* people what has to be done. The supervisor is a technician, the manager is a tactician. In this sense he is *always* 'getting things done through other people' and the other people are his supervisors.

Gaynor: Well, then, why does this 'getting things done through other people' grate on you so much?

Adam: Chiefly because of its lack of prescription. Would you say that a person is an effective manager who spends all his time with his supervisors, guiding, instructing, directing and giving decisions?

Gaynor: No, certainly not. I would expect him to set the guidelines – policy, if you like – and by his selection and development of the supervisors, reach a stage where they got on with the work and left him time to think.

Adam: Exactly. I think it has been sufficiently demonstrated from studies of managers' and supervisors' behaviour that these are very different roles. We must be careful, however, about actual titles that go with a job.

Gaynor: Yes indeed. It was always a source of amusement to me, when I had the title of General Manager, to sit next to people, with the same designation, at conferences who ran a hotel with twenty bedrooms. I would be the first to insist that we belonged to the same industry, but our needs and problems were vastly different! Do we have any common ground, I wonder? The other thing that concerns me is an entrepreneurial aspect. The owner of a twenty-bedroom hotel is an entrepreneur, whereas Kimble at the Diana is a manager employed by the Company. Yet he is responsible for about twenty times the turnover of this entrepreneur!

Adam: I have often pondered about this. In many ways it is a very personal thing. Occasionally I meet people who ask me why I work for Gaynor Hotels when I could be my own boss running a small hotel in the Cotswolds and probably able to take each afternoon off for golf. But it really depends on what you mean by being one's own boss. I am sure there is great satisfaction in being personally involved with the customers in the small business, but the real boss is then the bank manager and there is a very real dependence on suppliers. I think that one can over-emphasise the differences between the entrepreneur and the manager. Probably the owner of a small hotel spends about five per cent of his time on entrepreneurial decisions and the rest of the time he is a manager. So Kimble and the proprietor have 95% of common activity if they are running similar establishments.

Gaynor: I suppose I am the professional entrepreneur of this Company, but I have never been able to find any courses which deal with this topic! But we are still groping about. You have the advantage of your research on definitions of management, what are your conclusions? After all, people like me that just manage, what time do we have for all this introspection?

Adam: Now I am in difficulties! On the one hand I am asked to offer my conclusions against your experience, and on the other hand I am asked to sit in judgement on the multitude of writers on management!

Gaynor: I thought this is what you did anyway, but please! You know that I want to know about your ideas and that I shall use my experience to challenge you where I think you are wrong. I know that you will produce research findings that I have never heard of, like rabbits from a hat. But I am still interested in your ideas.

Adam: Sorry, Mr Gaynor, but I just realised the enormity of what you asked me to do. It is one thing to make comments about a definition that somebody proposes; it is quite another thing to be asked, from limited experience, to fly in the face of the savants!

Gaynor: I quite understand, but go ahead.

Adam: Well, the early writers about management became heavily involved in trying to define management but I think because they were engineers or technologists, they wanted it cut and dried. They saw the world in mechanical terms and placed all the emphasis on what should be done to create orderliness and an organisation which works like a smoothly oiled machine.

Gaynor: Then the social scientists came along and started to demonstrate that most of the problems were centred round people who did not behave like machines. In fact they were unpredictable.

Adam: Yes, but I think that the success of techniques in advertising show that there are quite a lot of predictable elements in people's behaviour. But the effect of the behavioural scientists' findings tended to tip the balance with a lot of managers from concern for production to concern for people. In fact I sometimes think this still persists today to a large extent; from the way some people talk, one would think that the Hawthorne experiments were the only studies which have been conducted in this field.

Gaynor: You mean that a manager should be involved in maintaining a balance between his concern for people and for production?

Adam: Yes. This means that management is a process which involves achieving business goals while at the same time providing a means of satisfaction for the individual needs or goals of employees. Now I think that the real danger to maintaining this balance might be described as the return on invested time. A comparatively short time spent in replanning a layout of a kitchen, or the desirability of installing a room state indicator, can quickly produce economies. We can see that more meals can be produced or customers allocated rooms speedily. But to increase people's effectiveness requires a much greater investment in time to establish what goals they are seeking to achieve.

Gaynor: I think most managers would agree with you and that they appreciate the need for developing people, but there is always the pressure of other things to be done and the consequent shortage of time. And what about decision-taking. I would think that this is a basic and fundamental part of managing?

Adam: The problem of time is something I would like to come back to. I must admit that I feel slightly nervous when decision-taking is regarded as some prerogative of managers. After all, everybody is involved in taking decisions every day. A housewife faces a major problem in a supermarket when she has to decide between paying 28p for a family-sized pack of detergent or 32p for a special large size accompanied by a free plastic flower!

Gaynor: I see what you mean, but surely we cannot divorce this business of making decisions from a process of management? I keep reading that use of computers is likely to remove a lot of decision-taking from middle management in the future. But I don't think this will come for a long time and I certainly think that in running hotels there will continue to be a lot of decisions which would defy any computer. We will still need the reception manager who can fit an unexpected regular customer into the hotel which the computer says is full.

Adam: Yes indeed, we cannot ignore that decisions have to be taken in business organisations and it needs some careful thinking to distinguish between normal human decision taking and the special characteristics of those in business.

Gaynor: That should not be too difficult. I am sometimes very conscious of spending time collecting information in order to make a decision. In a similar way, you or the chief accountant sometimes spend time preparing briefs about the possible alternatives available and the likely results. A lot of this involves figures and projections and so on. With no disrespect to you, most of this could be done better on a computer, but I will still have to make the decision about which line to follow. I would also think that the unit managers will have to continue making similar decisions; perhaps these are less important in that a wrong one will be unlikely to damage the company, whereas mine might! In these decisions, at both levels, we have to use experience and our personal judgement.

Adam: If most of the operating decisions at unit level are to be made by computers in the future, the manager's role becomes one of a human relations mechanic.

Gaynor: I don't see it that way. I hope that they will use information from the computer in reaching operating decisions; I suppose I am agreeing with your balance between people and production. My concern, however, is that this is the only method I can see for developing executives. As you know, we are a fairly decentralised company and I want my managers to feel that they are more than what you call 'human relations mechanics'. This really goes back to what I was thinking earlier when I used the word 'policy'. One would like to feel, as a company, that decisions are made in accordance with the policy and this is the paradox you saw. I am reluctant to start writing everything down, but I do want decisions made which support what we are trying to be as a company. Perhaps it would be a better way of describing this to say that I would like to create an ethos or spirit that ensures this.

Adam: I would say that creating this environment or ethos is a very important part of the management process. It can probably be compared to the training we have as children, having confidence in social situations because we have a good idea of what is the 'right thing to do' like not putting our elbows on the table.

Gaynor: I thought only great-aunts worried about that nowadays! But I think you have something. Tell me, where does problem-solving come into all this? I certainly seem to spend a significant part of my time dealing with problems and I am sure it is the same with all managers.

Adam: Just before you came in I was thinking about this; after a year I am still involved in solving problems and I find this rather disappointing.

Gaynor: This is what I mean. Surely you can't expect problems to stop requiring solving. I would think that this is almost the core of what management is about.

Adam: This makes me feel uncomfortable. Identifying problems and solving them certainly is a significant part of managing. But I can't help feeling that this is catching hold of the wrong end of the stick. Surely if we concentrated on identifying the causes of problems and removing those we could be much more effective?

Gaynor: I am not sure I understand you.

Adam: Perhaps I can illustrate it with the problem we had at the Apollo. Rather, I should say, problems; no potential managers were being produced, there was a high labour turnover and so on. We could have attempted to solve these by introducing different methods of selection, higher pay and various other means. These might have had some effect but in the long run we hadn't identified and remedied the cause. That was Whitstone, whose autocratic behaviour as a manager was the cause of the problems.

Gaynor: Yes, I see what you mean. It is like worrying about the problem of high labour costs at Head Office when the cause is people wanting to have things in writing as a protection.

Adam: Exactly. But having said that, I am not sure just how this fits in with the management process. Undoubtedly managers are involved in solving problems and now it sounds as though I am saying they shouldn't be.

Gaynor: From what you say, and it is certainly a new slant for me, I would see this as part of the ethos. It involves analysing the cause of problems rather than saying 'we have a problem'. This reminds me of one of the British Institute of Management's luncheons when Peter Drucker spoke. It was very impressive to me when he said something like 'We are concerned with effective management rather than efficient management, because a manager can be very efficient at doing something that does not need to be done.' I remember that I was disturbed for several days afterwards!

Adam: This really typifies how one can see a whole new dimension to the task of managing by taking a step sideways and looking at the words we use. I sometimes think that words and clichés are like old slippers, they are comfortable until you notice the holes in them.

Gaynor: Comfortable, but not presentable! What about communication? I recall that we have said something about this before. It must come in somewhere.

Adam: I think on that occasion you quoted Thoreau and said, 'How can I hear what you say, when what you are keeps drumming in my ears.'

Gaynor: Ah yes! A favourite quote of mine.

Adam: Well, the way I see it is that if your ethos exists, then communication will occur. Most people in talking about communication generally emphasise the skills of writing, speaking and reading. Sometimes they also include the skill of listening. These are, of course, important, but I would think that the emotional and social context are important. Which is just what Thoreau was saying.

Gaynor: So you don't consider communication is a part of managing.

Adam: Oh, I think it is, but if we mix Drucker with Thoreau and add a dash of your observation on the ethos of the enterprise, we can see that communication is a function of the internal environment. If trust exists and people appreciate the objectives, then communication will occur. If not, then no communication.

Gaynor: In some ways I would describe it as 'good' and 'poor' communication, but I am a little worried that you might take me to task on these words! Look, I have a lunch appointment and must go in a few minutes. This has been a very interesting discussion. What shall I do, sum up what we have been saying or leave it to you to prepare a memo?

Adam: I would rather you summarised, Mr Gaynor. After all, I don't want to land myself with solving a problem of overloaded Head Office typists!

Gaynor: Your motives are suspect, but let me see. The Management Process seems to be concerned with creating an environment in which a balance between concern for production and concern for people is maintained as well as providing a guide to decision-taking. It is directed towards an analysis of the causes from which problems arise and seeks to provide for achievement of organisational objectives whilst satisfying individual needs. Is that adequate?

Adam: It really is a concise statement of what we have been talking about.

Gaynor: Does it satisfy your demands for prescription?

Adam: I think it does because it stresses the things that a manager must do. Creating the environment, for example. But I wonder how long this takes to achieve.

Gaynor: You have a chance to find out, Adam. Tell me about it when you come back from the Zephyr! Goodbye for now, and enjoy yourself.

Reprinted with permission of Professor P W Nailon and R Doswell from their book, *Further Case Studies in Hotel Management*, Century Hutchinson (1977).

NOTES AND REFERENCES

1. See, for example, Doswell R and Nailon P, 'What is Management?', in *Further Case Studies in Hotel Management*, Century Hutchinson (1977), pp. 15–26.
2. Drucker P F, *The Practice of Management*, Pan Books (1968), p. 455.
3. *The Profile of Professional Management*, Results from Research into the Corpus of Knowledge, HCIMA (1977), p. 20.
4. See, for example, Brown W, *Organization*, Penguin (1974) and Gullen H V and Rhodes G E, *Management in the Hotel and Catering Industry*, Batsford (1983).
5. Stewart R, *The Reality of Management*, Second edition, Pan Books (1986), p. 12.
6. Mullins L J, 'Management and Managerial Behaviour', *International Journal of Hospitality Management*, vol. 4, no. 1, 1985, pp. 39–41.
7. Forte, Charles (Lord), *Forte: The Autobiography of Charles Forte*, Sidgwick & Jackson (1986), p. 119.
8. Brech E F L (ed), *Principles and Practice of Management*, Third edition, Longman (1975), p. 19.
9. Wood R C, 'Theory, Management and Hospitality: A Response to Philip Nailon', *International Journal of Hospitality Management*, vol. 2, no. 2, 1983, pp. 103–104.
10. Drucker P F, People and Performance, Heinemann (1977), p. 28.
11. *Ibid.*, p. 59 28. 29.
12. Baum T, 'Toward a New Definition of Hotel Management', *Cornell HRA Quarterly*, Educators' Forum August 1988, pp. 36–39
13. Fayol H, *General and Industrial Management*, Revised edition by Gray I, Pitman (1988).
14. Mintzberg H, 'The Manager's Job: Folklore and Fact', *Harvard Business Review Classic*, March–April 1990, pp. 163–175.
15. Mintzberg H, *The Nature of Managerial Work*, Harper & Row (1973).
16. Ley D A, 'The Effective GM: Leader or Entrepreneur?', *Cornell HRA Quarterly*, November 1980, pp. 66–67.
17. Arnaldo M J, 'Hotel General Managers: A Profile', *Cornell HRA Quarterly*, November 1981, pp. 53–56.
18. Shortt G, 'Work Activities of Hotel Managers in Northern Ireland: A Mintzbergian Analysis', *International Journal of Hospitality Management*, vol. 8, no. 2, 1989, pp. 121–130.
19. Wood R C, *Working in Hotels and Catering*, Routledge (1992).
20. Hales C and Nightingale M, 'What Are Unit Managers Supposed to do? A Contingent Methodology for Investigating Managerial Role Requirements', *International Journal of Hospitality Management*, vol. 5, no. 1, 1986, pp. 3–11.
21. Stewart R, *Choices for the Manager*, McGraw-Hill (1982).
22. Kotter J P, 'What Effective General Managers Really Do', *Harvard Business Review*, vol. 60, no. 6, November-December 1982, pp. 156–167.
23. Ferguson D H and Berger F, 'Restaurant Managers: What Do They *Really* Do?', *Cornell HRA Quarterly*, May 1984, p. 30.
24. Jones P and Lockwood A, *The Management of Hotel Operations*, Cassell (1989), p. 30.
25. Mullins L J, 'Managerial Behaviour and Development in the Hospitality Industry', *Proceedings of The International Association of Hotel Management Schools Symposium*, Leeds Polytechnic, November 1988.
26. *The Profile of Professional Knowledge*, Results from Research into the Corpus of Knowledge, HCIMA (1977) pp. 16–17.
27. Stewart R, *The Reality of Management*, Second edition, Pan Books (1986), p. 20.

28. Baum T, 'Managing Hotels in Ireland: Research and Development for Change', *International Journal of Hospitality Management*, vol. 8, no. 2, 1989, p. 139.

29. Guerrier Y and Lockwood A, 'Managers in Hospitality: A Review of Current Research', in Cooper C (ed), *Progress in Tourism, Recreation and Hospitality Management*, vol. 2, Bellhaven Press, May 1990, p. 164.

30. Stewart R, *Choices for the Manager*, McGraw-Hill (1982).

31. Dann D, 'The Nature of Managerial Work in the Hospitality Industry', *International Journal of Hospitality Management*, vol. 9, no. 4, 1990, pp. 319–334.

32. Brymer R A, Perrewe P L and Johns T R, 'Managerial Job Stress in the Hotel Industry,' *International Journal of Hospitality Management*, vol. 10, no. 1, 1991, pp. 47–58.

33. See, for example, Gullen H V and Rhodes G E, *Management in the Hotel and Catering Industry*, Batsford (1983).

34. Wood R C, 'Theory, Management and Hospitality: A Response to Philip Nailon', *International Journal of Hospitality Management*, vol. 2, no. 2, 1983, p. 104.

35. For example, see Nailon P, 'Theory in Hospitality Management', *International Journal of Hospitality Management*, vol. 1, no. 3, 1982, pp. 135–143.

36. See, for example: Drucker P F, *People and Performance*, Heinemann (1977).

37. Rees W D, *The Skills of Management*, Second edition, Routledge (1988), p. 15.

38. Umbreit W T and Eder R W, 'Linking Hotel Manager Behavior with Outcome Measures of Effectiveness', *International Journal of Hospitality Management*, vol. 6, no. 3, 1987, pp. 139–147.

39. Umbreit W T, 'Developing Behaviorally-Anchored Scales for Evaluating Job Performance of Hotel Managers', *International Journal of Hospitality Management*, vol. 5, no. 2, 1986, pp. 55–61.

40. See, for example, Maher A, 'Accounting for Human Resources in UK Hotels', *Proceedings of CHME Research Conference*, Manchester Metropolitan University, April 1993.

5

THE MANAGER–SUBORDINATE RELATIONSHIP

INTRODUCTION

Managers achieve results through the efforts of other people and this involves the effective management of human resources. The behaviour of managers and their style of management will influence the effort expended and level of performance of subordinate staff. The manager-subordinate relationship is the central component of successful hospitality operations.

This chapter looks at:
- Managerial behaviour
- Managers' attitudes towards people
- The Managerial/Leadership Grid®
- Administrative or mobile type of manager
- The influence of management style
- Systems of management
- Profile of organisational characteristics
- Management by objectives
- Personality profile of hospitality managers
- The attributes of a hospitality manager
- Social and human skills
- The management of people
- Basic managerial philosophies
- The manager's use of authority
- The human cost of poor management

MANAGERIAL BEHAVIOUR

The task of management is to make the best use of staff and to ensure that they satisfactorily meet the standards required of them. It is the responsibility of management to manage. But it is people who are being managed and people should be considered in human terms. The efficiency of staff and their commitment to the aims and philosophy of the hotel are fostered by good human relationships and by the nature of managerial behaviour.

> The majority of staff come to work eager to do a good job and with the desire to perform to the best of their abilities. Where actual behaviour fails to match the ideal this is largely the result of the manner in which staff are treated by management and the perception they have of the managerial function. This places a heavy responsibility on managers.[1]

Understanding the feelings of staff, and their needs and expectations, together with a genuine concern for their welfare, go a long way in encouraging them to perform well. How managers exercise the responsibility for, and duties of, management is important. Many problems at work arise not so much from *what* management does as *the way in which it is done.*

It is not necessarily the intent of management but the manner of implementation that is often the root cause of staff unrest and dissatisfaction. For example, staff may accept, although perhaps reluctantly, that unexpected staff sickness necessitates management introducing a revised duty rota timetable. However, staff may feel resentful about the lack of consultation, failure to consider the personal needs of individual members of staff and the manner in which they were told about the new rotas. And staff may feel that management are using 'unexpected contingency' as an easy excuse for lack of adequate planning and consultation.

MANAGERS' ATTITUDES TOWARDS PEOPLE

The way in which managers approach their jobs and the behaviour they display towards subordinate staff is likely to be conditioned by predispositions about people,. human nature and work. The style of management adopted is a function of the manager's attitude towards people.

Drawing on Maslow's hierarchy of needs model, McGregor put forward two sets of suppositions based on polar assumptions about the attitudes of managers towards people at work – Theory X and Theory y.[2]

The Theory X assumptions

Theory X represents the assumptions on which traditional organisations are based and was widely accepted and practised before the development of the human relations approach. The assumptions are that:

- the average person is lazy and has an inherent dislike of work;
- most people must be coerced, controlled, directed and threatened with punishment if the organisation is to achieve its objectives;
- the average person avoids responsibility, prefers to be directed, lacks ambition and values security most of all;
- motivation occurs only at the physiological and security levels.

The central principle of Theory X is direction and control through a centralised system of organisation and the exercise of authority.

The Theory Y assumptions

At the other extreme to Theory X is Theory Y, which represents assumptions consistent with more recent approaches to human nature and behaviour. The assumptions are that:

- for most people work is as natural as play or rest;

- people will exercise self-direction and self-control in the service of objectives to which they are committed;
- commitment to objectives is a function of rewards associated with their achievement;
- if given the right conditions, the average worker can learn to accept and to seek responsibility;
- the capacity for creativity in solving organisational problems is distributed widely;
- the intellectual potential of the average person is only partially utilised;
- motivation occurs at the affiliation, esteem and self-actualisation levels as well as the physiological and security levels.

The central principle of Theory Y is the integration of individual and organisational goals. McGregor develops an analysis of the implications of accepting Theory Y in regard to performance appraisal, administration of salaries and promotions, participation, staff–line relationships, leadership, management development and the managerial team.

The manager–subordinate relationship

Although based on polar extremes and an over-simplification, Theory X and Theory Y do represent identifiable philosophies which influence the nature of the manager–subordinate relationship. The two views tend to represent extremes of the natural inclination of managers towards a particular style of behaviour.

Assumptions based on the traditional use of rewards and sanctions, close supervision and control, and the nature of the manager's power are likely to result in an exploitative or authoritarian style of management.

Most people, however, have the potential to be self-motivating. They can best achieve their personal goals through self-direction of their efforts towards meeting the goals of the organisation. Broadening educational standards and changing social values mean that people today have wider expectations of the quality of working life, including opportunities for consultation and participation in decisions which affect them.

McGregor implies that a Theory Y approach is the best way to elicit co-operation from members of an organisation. Based on practical experience of hotel management this view is supported by Venison.

> I have personally always tried to manage more in accordance with the assumptions of Theory Y than those of Theory X and my experience seems to concur with much research which indicates that Theory Y assumptions about people's attitudes are closer to the truth. Theory Y, however, does not involve abdication of management, absence of leadership or the lowering of standards. It is not a 'soft' approach to management. It is, in fact, more difficult to achieve but potentially more successful.[3]

Demands of the situation

Theory X and Theory Y tend to represent extremes of the natural inclination of managers towards a particular style of behaviour. In practice, however, the actual style of management adopted will be influenced by the demands of the situation. Even when a manager has a basic belief in Theory Y assumptions, and in the self-motivation and self-direction of subordinate staff, there may be occasions when it is necessary or more appropriate to adopt a modified approach.

When the nature of the job itself offers little intrinsic satisfaction or limited opportunities to satisfy higher-level needs, a more authoritative and controlling style of management might work best. Emergency situations, or where there is a shortage of time or other overriding factors, may demand a greater use of management authority and control in directing the tasks in hand.

Consider, for example, the hustle, heat and noise of a busy hotel kitchen where a range of fresh meals needs to be prepared for a large banquet. Many tasks must be coordinated over very short timescales and a more forceful and directed style of management may therefore be appropriate. And while such conditions persist, this form of managerial behaviour appears also to be understood by the kitchen staff.

THE MANAGERIAL/LEADERSHIP GRID®

One means of identifying and evaluating different styles of management is the Blake and Mouton Grid®, first published as the Managerial Grid®, in 1964, restated in 1978 and 1985, and republished as the Leadership Grid® in 1991.[4] The Grid provides a basis for comparison of managerial styles in terms of two principal dimensions:

(i) concern for production; and
(ii) concern for people.

Concern for production is the amount of emphasis which the manager places on accomplishing the tasks in hand, achieving a high level of production, and getting results or profits. This is represented along the horizontal axis of the Grid. **Concern for people** is the amount of emphasis which the manager gives to colleagues and subordinates as individuals, and to their needs and expectations. This is represented along the vertical axis of the Grid.

Each axis is on a scale of 1–9 indicating varying degrees of concern that the manager has for either production or for people. The manner in which these two concerns are linked together depends upon the use of the hierarchy, the 'boss' aspect, and assumptions that the manager makes about the use of power and how to achieve production.

Five basic combinations

With a nine-point scale on each axis there is a total of 81 different combinations (see Figure 5.1). The four quadrants of the Grid provide five basic combinations of concern for production coupled with concern for people. These five combinations represent the extremes of managerial behaviour.

- **Impoverished managers** (1,1 rating) tend to be remote from their subordinates and believe in the minimum movement from their present position. They do as little as they can with production or with people. Too much attention to one will cause difficulties with the other.
- **Authority-compliance managers** (9,1 rating) are autocratic and tend to rely on a centralised system and the use of authority. Staff are regarded as a means of production. If staff challenge an instruction or standard procedure they are likely to be viewed as uncooperative.

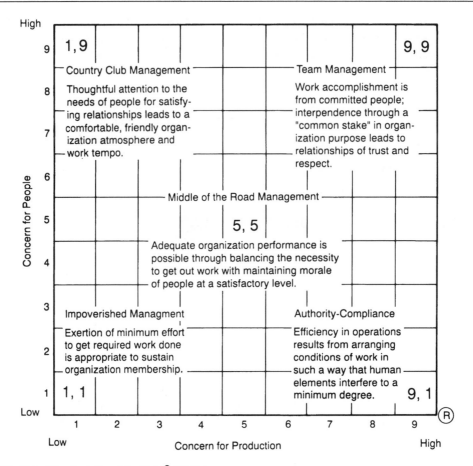

Fig 5.1 The Leadership Grid® figure.
Source: Figure from *Leadership Dilemmas – Grid Solutions*, by Robert R Blake and Anne Adams McCanse (formerly the Managerial Grid Figure by Robert R Blake and Jane S Mouton), Houston: Gulf Publishing Company, p. 29. Copyright © 1991, by Scientific Methods, Inc. Reproduced by permission of owners.

- **Country club managers** (1,9 rating) believe that a contented staff will undertake what is required of them and achieve a reasonable level of output. Production is secondary to the avoidance of conflict and maintaining harmony among the staff. Managers will seek to find compromise solutions acceptable to everyone. Innovation may be encouraged but good ideas tend to be rejected if likely to cause difficulties among the staff.

- **Middle of the road managers** (5,5 rating) adopt an approach of 'live and let live' and tend to avoid the real issues. This style of management is the 'dampened pendulum', with managers swinging between concern for production and concern for people. Under pressure this style of management tends to become task management (9,1) but, if this causes resentment from staff, pressure is eased and managers adopt a compromise approach.

- **Team managers** (9,9 rating) believe in the integration of task needs and concern for people. They believe in creating a situation whereby people can satisfy their own needs by commitment to the objectives of the organisation. Managers will discuss problems with staff, seek their ideas and give them freedom of action. Difficulties in working relationships will be handled by confronting staff directly and attempting to work out solutions with them.

Two additional Grid styles

The 1991 edition of the Grid also refers to two additional styles.

- **9+9 paternalistic 'father knows best' management** where reward and approval are granted to people in return for loyalty and obedience, and punishment is threatened for failure to comply.
- **Opportunistic 'what's in it for me' management** in which the style utilised depends on which style the manager feels will return him or her the greatest self-benefit.

The importance of team management

The Managerial Grid provides a framework in which managers can identify and review their patterns of behaviour. Blake and Mouton claim the Managerial Grid illustrates that the manager can gain the benefits of maximising, simultaneously, methods which are both production-oriented and people-oriented. The 9,9 combination of team management, although an ideal, is worth working for.

Effective team management is clearly important in any work organisation, but especially so in the hospitality industry. In hotel operations, for example, it is necessary to combine the 'production' element of speedy and efficient provision of accommodation and food and beverage, with the 'people' element of a high standard of service, and an appropriate attitude and behaviour from staff. This emphasises the need for consultation and teamwork, and for a style of managerial behaviour based on the effective integration of a high concern for production balanced with a high concern for people.

Employee performance is a key result area of management. Poor team management will have serious consequences for the morale of staff, it can prove costly and time-consuming for the manager, and it can have serious consequences for the effective operations of the hotel.[5] It is part of the manager's responsibility to develop and maintain a high level of performance from subordinate staff as members of an effective work team.

ADMINISTRATIVE OR MOBILE TYPE OF MANAGER

Venison refers to the use of a simple ten-point scale which distinguishes between an excessively administrative type of manager, and an excessively mobile and promotions-oriented manager (Figure 5.2).[6]

Applicants for hotel management positions are asked to indicate their own management style. The majority place themselves between points 3 and 4 or between points 6 and 7. This suggests that the two distinct ends of the scale are recognised clearly and that most potential hotel managers have a natural leaning towards one direction or the other.

Venison draws attention to the importance of the manager being at the 'front' of the hotel and of **'being there'**. The manager is then in a position to see employees at work

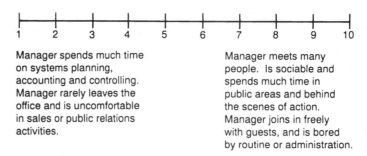

Fig 5.2 A ten-point scale for managers

and to get to know them, to check standards of service, and quickly to see trouble spots and to take corrective action.

The ideal hotel manager, however, does not sit permanently at any one point of the scale but is able to move freely from one end to the other as particular situations demand. The 'perfect' hotel manager needs to be comfortable at all positions on the scale. Success in extending the range of comfortable behaviour is an important aspect of the manager's personal development.

THE INFLUENCE OF MANAGEMENT STYLE

In the previous chapter we saw that the 'being there' style of management and a directive approach to staff is one of the principal characteristic features of hospitality management.[7] In a study of five seasonal seaside hotels, all privately owned and operated and with between 30 and 65 bedrooms, Lee-Ross investigated the influence of management style on employee job perceptions and job satisfaction.

The investigation contrasted a 'hands-on' style of management (whereby managers worked for most of the time alongside operatives and undertook similar tasks), with a 'co-ordinative' style of management (where for most of the time managers delegated tasks to operatives). It was suggested that, given the nature of hotel jobs, the hands-on managers who work alongside their staff may be expected to have similar job perceptions, be more aware of operational problems and therefore be more effective in engendering job satisfaction than co-ordinative managers.

Little effect on employee job perception

In practice, however, the concepts of hands-on and co-ordinative styles of management were often not clearly definable. Management style appeared to result from the demands of the customers, the employment policy of the hotel and the manager's departmental expertise. Managers occupied both roles and were involved at the operative level in certain departments while leaving other departments unsupervised. The study also indicated that although employees who experience a hands-on management approach are more likely to share the managers' perception of their jobs, management style has little significant effect on the way employees perceive their jobs.

SYSTEMS OF MANAGEMENT

On the basis of extensive research into a wide range of organisations, Likert views the nature of the manager–subordinate relationship in terms of a four-fold model of management systems.[9] The systems are identified by number:

- System 1 – Exploitative authoritative;
- System 2 – Benevolent authoritative;
- System 3 – Consultative; and
- System 4 – Participative group.

System 1 – Exploitative authoritative

Decisions are imposed on subordinates; motivation is based on threats; there is very little teamwork or communications; responsibility is centred at the top of the organisational hierarchy.

System 2 – Benevolent authoritative

There is a condescending form of leadership; motivation is based on a system of rewards; there is only limited teamwork or communications; there is responsibility at managerial levels but not at lower levels of the organisational hierarchy.

System 3 – Consultative

Leadership involves some trust in subordinates; motivation is based on rewards but also some involvement; there is a fair degree of teamwork and communications take place vertically and horizontally; responsibility for achieving the goals of the organisation is spread more widely throughout the hierarchy.

System 4 – Participative group

Leadership involves trust and confidence in subordinates; motivation is based on rewards for achievement of agreed goals; there is participation and a high degree of teamwork and communication; responsibility for achieving the goals of the organisation is widespread throughout all levels of the hierarchy.

PROFILE OF ORGANISATIONAL CHARACTERISTICS

Likert has also established a profile of organisational characteristics describing the nature of the four different systems of management. The profile compares the four systems in terms of a table of organisational variables under the headings of:

- (i) leadership processes;
- (ii) motivational forces;
- (iii) communication processes;
- (iv) interaction-influence processes;
- (v) decision-making processes;
- (vi) goal setting or ordering; and
- (vii) control processes.

A shorter and simpler form of the profile of organisational characteristics is provided by Likert and Likert[10] (see Figure 5.3).

Organisational variables	System 1 Exploitive Authoritative	System 2 Benevolent Authoritative	System 3 Consultative	System 4 Participative Group	Item no.
Leadership					
How much confidence and trust is shown in subordinates?	Virtually none	Some	Substantial amount	A great deal	1
How free do they feel to talk to superiors about job?	Not very free	Somewhat free	Quite free	Very free	2
How often are subordinates' ideas sought and used constructively?	Seldom	Sometimes	Often	Very frequently	3
Motivation					
Is predominant use made of 1 fear, 2 threats, 3 punishment, 4 rewards, 5 involvement?	1, 2, 3 occasionally 4	4, some 3	4, some 3 and 5	5, 4 based on group set goals	4
Where is responsibility felt for achieving organisation's goals?	Mostly at top	Top and middle	Fairly general	At all levels	5
How much co-operative teamwork exists?	Very little	Relatively little	Moderate amount	Great deal	6
Communication					
What is the usual direction of information flow?	Downward	Mostly downward	Down and up	Down, up and sideways	7
How is downward communication accepted?	With suspicion	Possibly with suspicion	With caution	With a receptive mind	8
How accurate is upward communication?	Usually inaccurate	Often inaccurate	Often accurate	Almost always accurate	9
How well do superiors know problems faced by subordinates?	Not very well	Rather well	Quite well	Very well	10
Decisions					
At what level are decisions made?	Mostly at top	Policy at top, some delegation	Broad policy at top, more delegation	Throughout but well integrated	11
Are subordinates involved in decisions related to their work?	Almost never	Occasionally consulted	Generally consulted	Fully involved	12
What does decision-making process contribute to motivation?	Not very much	Relatively little	Some contribution	Substantial contribution	13
Goals					
How are organisational goals established?	Orders issued	Orders, some comments invited	After discussion by orders	By group action (except in crisis)	14
How much covert resistance to goals is present?	Strong resistance	Moderate resistance	Some resistance at times	Little or none	15
Control					
How concentrated are review and control functions?	Very highly at top	Quite highly at top	Moderate delegation to lower levels	Widely shared	16
Is there an informal organisation resisting the formal one?	Yes	Usually	Sometimes	No ... same goals as formal	17
What are cost, productivity and other control data used for?	Policing, punishment	Reward, punishment	Reward, some self-guidance	Self-guidance, problem solving	18

Fig 5.3 Short-form profile of organisational characteristics
Adapted and reproduced from Likert R and Likert J G, *New Ways of Managing Conflict*, McGraw-Hill (1976), p. 75. With the kind permission of McGraw-Hill, Inc.

The Benefits of System 4 management

On the basis of extensive research in many organisations, Likert confirmed that the most productive departments employed management practices within Systems 3 and 4. System 4 management is based on involvement, supportive relationships and participation. Organisational decisions are improved as they are based on more accurate information and there is greater motivation to implement the decisions.

In Systems 1 and 2 organisations . . . high performance goals by superiors, coupled with high-pressure supervision using tight budgets and controls, yield high productivity initially because of compliance based on fear.[11]

However, because of unfavourable attitudes, poor communications, lack of co-operative motivation and restriction of output, the long-term result is high absence and labour turnover, and low productivity and earnings. Likert indicates strongly that the nearer the behavioural characteristics of an organisation approach System 4 the more probably this will lead to long-term improvement in labour turnover and high productivity, low scrap, low costs and high earnings.

Given the typical organisational and staffing characteristics of many hospitality operations, it would seem that managers would have much to gain from adopting a System 4 style of management. But what does System 4 management actually involve?

Likert sets out three fundamental concepts of System 4 management. These are the use of:

- the principle of supportive relationships among members of the organisation, and in particular between superior and subordinate;
- group decision-making and group methods of organisation and supervision; and
- high performance aspirations for all members of the organisation.

The principle of supportive relationships

Supportive relationships are intended to enhance self-esteem and ego building, contribute to subordinates' sense of personal worth and importance, and maintain their sense of significance and dignity. The manager's behaviour towards subordinates is regarded as supportive when this entails:

- mutual confidence and trust;
- helping to maintain a good income;
- understanding of work problems and help in doing the job;
- genuine interest in personal problems;
- helping with training to assist promotion;
- sharing of information;
- seeking opinions about work problems;
- being friendly and approachable; and
- giving recognition and credit when due.

In System 4 management interaction and decision-making rely heavily on group processes, and discussions focus on the decisions to be made. Managers should have high performance aspirations for themselves and for every member of staff. However, to be effective, high performance goals should not be imposed but they should be set by participation and involve group decision-making.

MANAGEMENT BY OBJECTIVES

One major, participative approach to management, which directly concerns the involvement and motivation of staff, is Management by Objectives (MBO). MBO attempts to relate the achievement of organisational goals to individual performance and development. The basis of MBO is the *involvement and participation* of subordinates through:

- the setting of objectives and targets;
- agreeing results to be achieved and criteria of performance; and
- the regular review and appraisal of performance.

MBO is viewed best as a continuous cycle of activities (Figure 5.4).

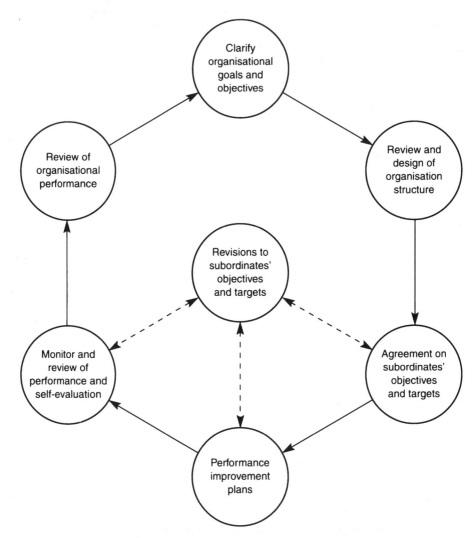

Fig 5.4 The cycle of MBO activities

Agreement on objectives and targets

The central feature of MBO is that objectives and targets should not be imposed but established and agreed between superior and subordinates. Rather than being told exactly what to do and when to do it, subordinates accept responsibility for definite targets and results to be achieved.

For each job there should be a key result analysis to identify clearly the critical areas of work activities and standards of performance which indicate satisfactory achievement of results. In support of performance improvement plans there should be an effective process of guidance, training and development for the subordinate together with a related system of rewards.[12]

Measurement of performance is in terms of the subordinates' accomplishment of results rather than the ability to follow detailed instructions on how to undertake their work. Within agreed limits and policies, subordinates are given freedom of action to decide how best to achieve these results. A system of management by objectives can be contrasted, therefore, with a style of management based on authority and control, and the adherence to rules.

MBO is sometimes likened to a system of budgetary control.[13] Although there are some broad similarities, the two systems are distinct. MBO involves agreed objectives and targets for individual members of staff as positive indicators of achievement, and not just a series of financial spending limits. Budgeting may form part of the agreed MBO targets but it is likely to be only one of the main aspects involved.

Applications to service operations

Some writers also refer to MBO as a technique[14] but it is much broader than this. MBO is more correctly described as a style or system of management. It can take a number of different forms and can be adapted to the demands of different organisations, including smaller hotel organisations.

MBO is particularly suited to service activities when it is not always easy to discern clear-cut quantified standards. In hotel operations objectives and targets could, for example, be related to the key result areas identified by Jones and Lockwood: (i) ensuring customer satisfaction; (ii) maintaining employee performance; and (iii) protection of assets.[15]

Some obvious areas in which specific MBO targets could be agreed for a stated time period could include:

- an increase in general occupancy rates or in a specific area such as return guests, conference business, restaurant trade;
- reduction in staff turnover or incidence of bad debts;
- control of costs, stock levels, breakages, wastage;
- increase in sales or spend per head in the bars or on other customer services;
- reduction in staff absence, accidents or injuries;
- increase in favourable guest comments/reduction in number of complaints;
- improved profit related to turnover or costs of purchases.

Potential benefits of MBO

MBO is therefore potentially an attractive system. It provides an opportunity for staff to accept greater responsibility and to make a higher level of personal contribution. Properly installed, and as part of a general participative style of management, there is much to recommend it to both the hospitality organisation and individual members of staff. Potential benefits of MBO include the following:

- it concentrates attention on critical areas of activity;
- subordinates know exactly what is expected of them;
- it identifies problem areas in achievement of targets;
- it improves management control information;
- it encourages review of organisation structure and aids the process of delegation;
- it aids management succession planning;
- it identifies training needs and encourages personal growth and development;
- it provides a sound basis for appraisal systems and an equitable procedure for determining rewards and promotion;
- it encourages motivation to improve individual performance.

An effective system of MBO can enhance the feeling of empowerment and encourage the exercise of greater initiative. For example, in order to increase room revenue one front office manager may prefer to follow a policy of concentrating on high tariff business with a lower occupancy rate, while another manager may opt for lower tariffs but obtain a consistently high occupancy rate. Depending on the particular environmental situation both methods could ultimately lead to the same result of achieving a specified total room revenue, which might not have been the case if the managers had been told the way in which they had to go about it.

However, despite the many potential benefits of MBO and a study commissioned by the then Hotel and Catering Training Board,[16] the introduction of MBO into hotel operations appears to be making only slow progress.[17]

Potential criticisms and limitations of MBO

- An effective system of MBO requires the full commitment and active support of top management, good superior–subordinate relationships and genuine participation by staff. It is also important to maintain the impetus of the system but without generating an excessive amount of paperwork or forms which lead to a bureaucratic approach.
- Objectives which are more difficult to specify and measure in precise terms may be neglected at the expense of an emphasis on objectives which are more easily set and monitored. A system of MBO may also be more difficult to apply where objectives are subject to continual and rapid change.
- MBO should not be applied simply as a pressure device by which superiors apply increasingly demanding targets which subordinates are expected to achieve. Placing too much emphasis on results can have an adverse affect on behaviour and performance. For example, a waiter striving to meet the objective of increased wine sales may feel obliged to use high-pressure sales techniques, even though this leads to loss of job satisfaction and may also offend some customers.[18]
- The system of MBO is usually associated with a sophisticated performance appraisal scheme and rating scales. This can give rise to a number of common problems, for example lack of comparability in performance standards or excessive emphasis on short-term achievements.[19] MBO-based appraisal schemes should not be regarded as a substitute for the successful management of people.

- Under-achievement might be the result of external environmental factors outside the control of the subordinate or the superior. It is important therefore to distinguish clearly between mere excuses and genuine reasons for the failure to obtain a satisfactory level of performance. It is also necessary to have a quick and effective procedure for the review and any necessary restatement of objectives and targets.

Attention to performance of the work group

MBO normally focuses attention on the performance of individual members of staff. In many situations, however, it is team effort and effective group working, rather than individual performance, which are important. This is especially so in many hospitality operations which tend to divide naturally into group-based work activities. Greater attention could be given therefore to agreement on objectives and targets for the members of a work group. This will help foster unity of effort and supportive relationships among group members.

PERSONALITY PROFILE OF HOSPITALITY MANAGERS

As we discussed in Chapter 1, many comments are made about the particular features of the hospitality industry and it is often assumed that because of its 'unique' nature the requirements of its managers are somehow different from those of other managers. As an example of the continual debate on the special nature of the industry, a number of studies have focused attention on the personality characteristics of hospitality managers. But to what extent are these studies likely to help in their education and development?

Shaner suggests that because of the unique demands of the hospitality industry the personal values and behaviour of its managers differ from those of managers in other industries. The most important values perceived by hospitality managers are honesty, responsibility and capability.[20] However, whilst it is difficult to argue against such values, they are of a very general nature and tell us little about the attributes required of a successful manager. Shaner also suggests that obedience and cheerfulness were considered to be of least importance compared with other values possessed by non-hospitality managers.

Based on a sample of 28 hotel general managers of the same UK hotel chain, Worsfold found that compared with general management norms, hotel managers were more assertive, venturesome and imaginative. They also placed more emphasis on people skills and group working.[21]

Particular form of behaviour

Another survey, by Stone, involved 140 UK general managers, 71 employed by hotel groups and 69 independent owner/managers.[22] From the survey Stone suggests that hotel managers display a particular form of behaviour and identifies a number of factors which distinguish them from non-hotel managers. Compared with other managers, hotel managers are:

- more calm, realistic and stable;

- more assertive, competitive and stubborn;
- more cheerful, active and enthusiastic;
- socially bolder and more spontaneous;
- more realistic, independent and cynical;
- harder to fool, more deliberate and concerned with self;
- more concerned with practical matters and detail.

It should not be assumed, however, that such personality characteristics are necessarily the most appropriate or will result in improved organisational performance. The existing managerial style may have consequences in terms of staff morale, development and retention.[23]

Stone also found that hotel managers have a lower scholastic and mental capacity. This dimension, however, is one of the most problematic. And while the finding *may* be representative of present managers, it does not necessarily apply to hotel managers of the future.

Not a new idea

The idea of looking at personality characteristics as an indicator of effective performance is not new. For example, an early approach to the study of leadership was an attempt by a number of writers to identify the common personality characteristics of 'good' or 'successful' leaders.[24]

However, extensive research into this area has revealed little to explain the nature of leadership or to help in the training of future leaders. Investigations have identified lists of traits which tend to be overlapping or contradictory and with little significant correlation (this approach is discussed more fully in Chapter 11).

A profile of 'The Perfect Hotelier'

An interesting and humorous description of the perfect hotelier, which nevertheless might appear to some people to make a serious point about the nature of the job, is given in Figure 5.5.

THE ATTRIBUTES OF A HOSPITALITY MANAGER

Rather than attempting to identify any particular, or unique, set of personality characteristics of the hospitality manager, a more constructive approach is to concentrate attention on the general attributes required of the successful manager.[25]

In order to carry out the process of management and execution of work the manager requires a combination of technical competence, social and human skills, and conceptual ability (Figure 5.6). Although a simplistic approach it does provide a useful and pragmatic framework within which to examine the attributes of the successful hospitality manager.

- **Technical competence** relates to the application of specific knowledge, methods and skills to discrete tasks, the actual 'doing' of work and day-to-day operations concerned with the actual provision of services.

The 'Perfect' Hotelier

A hotelier must be a democrat, an autocrat, an acrobat and a doormat. He must be able to entertain pickpockets, Prime Ministers, pirates, philanthropists, the police, and be on both sides of the political fence.

A footballer, tennis player, darts player, bowler and pigeon fancier. He must pick locks, take knocks but avoid the pox. And he must settle arguments and fights. He MUST be a qualified wrestler, boxer and weight lifter, sprinter and peace maker.

He must also look immaculate when drinking with bankers, swankers, commercial travellers, company reps, travel agents and wholesalers.

To be successful he must keep the bars full, house full and tanks full, the store full, the customers full, and not get himself full.

He must have hotel staff who are clean, lean, honest, quick workers and thinkers; and at all times be on the bosses' side, the customers' side and stay on the inside of the bar.

It is said that he homewrecks, signs weekly wage cheques, in other words saturates, confiscates, deteriorates and propagates.

To sum up he must be outside, inside, offside, crosseyed, glorified, sanctified, crucified and if he is not the strong type there is suicide.

The End.

Fig 5.5 A profile of 'The Perfect Hotelier'
Reproduced with permission of Mr R J Cannon, Proprietor, The Royal Hotel at Tring

- **Social and human skills** refer to interpersonal relationships in working with other people, team-work, and direction and leadership of staff to achieve co-ordinated effort and high levels of performance.
- **Conceptual ability** is required in order to view the complexities of the operations of the organisation as a whole, including external environmental influences. It also involves strategic planning and decision-making skills.

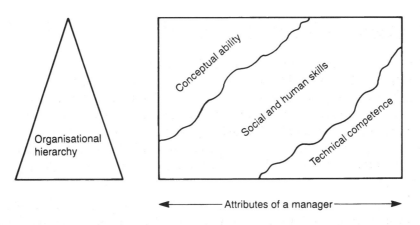

Fig 5.6 The combination of the attributes of a manager

Appropriate balance

Attempting to secure the most appropriate balance among these desirable attributes presents a constant discussion on the design and content of educational and training programmes for managers in the hospitality industry.

As the manager advances up the organisational hierarchy we would usually expect greater emphasis to be placed on conceptual ability and proportionally less on technical ability. Accordingly, the balance between technical competence and conceptual ability should be determined by the potential managers' expected level of entry into the industry and the likely pattern of their future career progression.

The nature of the industry does make particular demands upon its managers. In hotel operations, for example, managers are still often expected to have training and proficiency in craft skills and to display a high level of technical expertise as well as more general managerial ability.[26] It might be, therefore, that the requirement of perceived technical competence is greater than in other industries. This demand for technical expertise is understandable and may be in keeping with the present nature of the industry. But it must not be at the expense of general management education and development.

According to a recent HCTC report 30% of managers still have no formal qualifications.[27] In the particular areas of human resource/personnel management an investigation by Maher found that only a minority of head office staff held a professional personnel qualification. The investigation did, however, indicate an apparent increasing awareness of the importance of recruiting quality staff and a growing demand for high educational qualifications for managerial positions.[28] Technical expertise alone is not enough; it must be more than balanced by managerial competence. No amount of practical training or experience will, by itself, however, produce good managers if they do not possess the required social and human skills.

SOCIAL AND HUMAN SKILLS

Social and human skills reflect the ability to get along with other people and are, therefore, important attributes at all stages and levels of management, and in the development of staff. The ability to make the best use of people is a distinctive feature of management.

Drucker, for example, makes the point that:

> The function that distinguishes the manager above all others is the function no one but the manager can perform. The one contribution a manager is uniquely expected to make is to give others vision and ability to perform.[29]

The importance of people as a major resource of the hospitality industry is also well recognised.

> The only resources within an organisation capable of transformation are human resources. Money and materials are depleted. Meals are consumed, beds are slept in. Equipment is subject to wear and tear; it can be used well or badly, but can never perform more efficiently than it was originally designed to do. Humans only can grow and develop. Therefore, it is this resource in industry which is both the most complex to deal with and the most rewarding.[30]

The hospitality industry is very much a 'people-industry'. Many members of the workforce have direct contact with the customer and people are an essential ingredient of effective operations: they are part of the finished product that the customer is paying for. Customer satisfaction is likely to be affected as much by the attitudes and behaviour of staff as by the standard of accommodation, food and beverages, and other services provided. This emphasises the importance of the effective management of human resources.

People a common factor

Jones makes the point that the principal factor that underpins his assertion that services and managing services are different is the role of people.[31] This may be true, but at the same time it also illustrates that people are a common factor in any form of work organisation. The perceived role of people within the hospitality industry serves to emphasise the importance of the social and human skills of its managers.

Managers achieve results through the efforts of other people. An understanding of the pervasive influences which determine the behaviour of people within the work organisation should therefore form a central focus of the education and development of managers.

Theory and practice are not inseparable. For example, using accumulated knowledge of management theory, Mullins and Aldrich have constructed an integrated model of managerial behaviour and development which applies as much to the hospitality industry as to any other business organisation.[32]

THE MANAGEMENT OF PEOPLE

Whatever the debate on the personality characteristics or attributes of an effective hospitality manager, one central requirement is abundantly clear – competence in dealing with people. The one essential ingredient of any successful manager is the ability to manage people effectively. Popular books on managerial behaviour appear to take a positive view of human nature, and support an approach which gives encouragement for people to work willingly and to perform to the best of their ability.[33]

However, as many of us will have witnessed for ourselves, an understanding, people-centred approach to management seems often to be lacking in practice. It is surprising that despite the particular importance of people within the hotel industry it does not have a good reputation for adopting a caring and positive approach to the management of people.

> As an industry looking after people, we seem to make an absolute dog's breakfast of caring for employees.[34]

> Management in the hospitality industry pays considerable lip service to the notion that human resources constitute a major organisational asset . . . Although the contribution and importance of human resource decisions are often acknowledged abstractedly (i.e. 'our people are our most important asset'), the day-to-day decisions of line and top management often belie this sentiment.[35]

Autocratic style of hotel managers

Despite the lessons to be learnt from studies such as those by McGregor, Blake and Mouton, and Likert, many hotel managers still appear to adopt a more autocratic, task-oriented approach.

Using a similar set to Likert's four systems of management, White asked staff to identify the preferred style they would most like to work for – from the autocratic manager, the persuasive manager, the consultative manager or the participative manager.[36]

In manufacturing industries the most preferred style of management was consultative. However, in the hotel study the majority of responses were split between those preferring either the autocratic style or the consultative style of management.

White also asked the respondents to indicate the perceived style of their own manager. In manufacturing industries respondents identified their managers as having a variety of styles. In the hotel study, however, the majority of respondents perceived their manager as adopting an autocratic style. This can influence staff retention. White suggests that although older, long-standing staff may be happy with an autocratic style, this may lead to high levels of turnover among younger staff. He advocates a change from the prevailing autocratic style to a more consultative style.

But why do many hotel managers adopt a task-oriented, autocratic style of management? We can consider five main possible reasons.

An overriding concern for short-term results

There is a widely held view in the industry that every activity should be related directly to profitability. For example, Umbreit makes the point that:

> Traditionally, the hotel industry has had a strong operational orientation with concern primarily focussed on short-term results. Hotel managers have been evaluated on profitability measures and control of expenses.[37]

Profitability and control of expenses are clearly important aspects of effective management. But attention to results in these areas should be matched with an equal concern for the proper treatment and well-being of staff.

A high concern for front-line operations

Hotel operations combine a wide range of activities, many of which are provided simultaneously. Services are provided direct to the guests who are on the premises. A high degree of co-ordination is required, often measured over very short timescales. Managers have a high concern, therefore, with defining and organising group interactions towards the achievement of goals and objectives.

The need to maintain high standards could also, in part, explain why hotel managers often display high levels of task-oriented behaviour. For example, Worsfold points out that in the hospitality industry it is necessary:

> ... to maintain high standards (some of which are legally enforceable) in a highly variable environment with a transient product. In order to maintain these standards, it is necessary to establish rules and procedures to which staff adhere.[38]

Traditional management practices

Managers tend to rely on traditional and outdated practices, and show too much concern with perceived differences between the hospitality and other industries. This results in a blinkered approach, isolating managers from the applications of more general management theories and practices. Examples are the only comparatively recent development in the use of computers,[39] and the slow progress in recognition of the potential contribution of the concepts of management by objectives referred to above.

This might also, perhaps, be one reason why there is still some apparent reluctance from certain (but not all) hotel managers to welcome management degree course students, regarding them as too 'academic', and possibly also as a threat to their own positions. By contrast there is often less apparent resistance to the employment of diploma course students who are seen as more 'practically' oriented.[40, 41]

Failure to manage through people

A task-oriented approach may be seen as easier. People are not by nature passive, they have minds of their own and all differ as individuals. Human behaviour is capricious and scientific methods cannot be applied with reliability. People bring their own feelings and attitudes towards their duties and responsibilities. You will recall that Venison makes the point that a Theory Y style of management is not a 'soft' approach but is in fact more difficult to achieve, although potentially more successful.[42]

Too many managers appear to opt for the 'easy' approach and attempt to manage through achievement of the task, the organisational hierarchy, and systems and procedures, rather than to manage **with and through people**. Managers need to broaden their sense of people-perception and to understand the feelings of staff, and their needs and expectations as human beings. The development of human and social skills is a priority.

A vicious circle

Many hotel managers will claim that shortages of suitable staff, the nature of the working conditions, and high staff turnover demand a task-oriented approach to management. But, because management adopt such an approach this may well be, at least in part, the **underlying cause** of the staffing problems to which they claim they are reacting.

For example, we can recall that Likert found an authoritarian system of management may yield high productivity in the **short term**, but it is a participative-group system that will lead to long-term improvement in staff turnover, high productivity and improved organisational performance. We can also recall that White suggests that an autocratic style of management may lead to high levels of turnover among younger staff. We can conclude that a high level of turnover, especially among younger staff, may well be the **result** of an autocratic style of management.

High staff turnover should not, therefore, be excused as an inherent, characteristic feature of the industry. The attitude of management should be to see this as a problem area – a problem in terms of cost, time, staff morale and possible effects on the standard of service provided. Managers should be prepared to adopt a more participative style of management and to develop supportive relationships with subordinates. Managers should also be ready to learn from experiences in other industries, to review their procedures and practices, and, for example, to give greater attention to manpower planning, recruitment and selection, and induction and training.

BASIC MANAGERIAL PHILOSOPHIES

A positive policy of investment in people and an interpersonal relationship approach to management is, in the longer term, worth the effort. In the belief of the author there are a number of basic, underlying philosophies which are likely to make for the successful management of people *and* lead to improved work performance.

Consideration, respect and trust

People generally respond according to the way they are treated.[43] If you give a little you will invariably get a lot back. Make people feel important and give them a sense of personal worth. The majority of staff will respond constructively if treated with consideration and respect, and as responsible individuals who wish to serve the organisation well. 'If people feel trusted they will make extraordinary efforts to show the trust to be warranted.'[44]

From their research of outstandingly successful companies, Peters and Waterman make the following comment on the fundamental lesson of achieving productivity through people.

> Treat people as adults. Treat them as partners; treat them with dignity; treat them with respect. Treat *them* – not capital spending and automation – as the primary source of productivity gains.[45]

Recognition and credit

People can be praised to success. Give full recognition and credit when it is due and let people know you appreciate them. Too often managers are unresponsive to good performance, which may happen the vast majority of the time, and appear to take this for granted; but they are quick to criticise the few occasions when performance falls below expectations. Positive feedback on good performance is a strong motivator, *and* staff are then more likely to accept and respond to constructive criticism.

Experience from visits to hotel and catering management degree students during their training placement year has emphasised the importance of feedback on their performance. One of the most common enquiries is the desire for more information on how well they are doing. If staff are to take a pride in their work they need to know when they are performing well and to receive appropriate recognition for their efforts.

Involvement and availability

Involve yourself with the work of the staff, and make sure you fully understand the difficulties and distastes of their duties and responsibilities. Ensure an open flow of communications, and encourage participation and feedback. Take an active interest in the work of staff but without excessive supervision or inhibiting their freedom of action. Wherever possible be available to staff as a priority, rather than to administration, and remember the importance of giving time to listen to the feelings and problems of staff.

Fair and equitable treatment

Treat people fairly but according to merit. Ensure justice in treatment, equitable systems of motivation and rewards, clear personnel policies and procedures, and full observance of all laws or codes of conduct relating to employment. People expect certain outcomes in exchange for certain contributions or inputs. A feeling of inequality causes tension and motivates the person to indulge in certain forms of behaviour in order to remove or to reduce the perceived inequity.[46] Equity theory of motivation is discussed in Chapter 8.

Positive action on an individual basis

Treat members of staff as individuals. Deal with individual situations on an individual basis and avoid the 'blanket' approach. For example, it has come to the manager's attention that a couple of members of staff on the same shift have been late in arriving for work. The manager's reaction is to send a circular to *all* members of the department reminding them of the need for, and importance of, good timekeeping. This may appear to be an easy way out to the manager. But what is likely to be the reaction of staff in the department?

The two members of staff concerned might shield behind the generality of the circular and even persuade themselves that it doesn't apply particularly to them. They might even choose to believe that the manager must be referring to staff on a different shift, and take little notice of the circular. In contrast, the majority of staff in the department who do have a good record of timekeeping might well be annoyed or upset by the circular.

There could, for example, be some staff who, despite pressing personal difficulties, have taken great pride in their work and made special efforts to maintain an excellent record of timekeeping – quite possibly without any previous positive recognition from management. Again, it would be understandable if the reaction of these staff was one of resentment and disillusionment, with a possible adverse effect on their future attitude to work. The manager has more to lose than to gain from adopting a 'blanket' approach to a particular problem and from failing to take selective, positive action on an individual basis.

THE MANAGER'S USE OF AUTHORITY

Some might argue that these philosophies are too idealistic and that, given the harsh realities of the hospitality industry, managers need to adopt a more dominant stance. But it is not suggested that managers should in any way give up the right to manage: it is a question of *how* they manage and how they use their authority.

An interesting example is provided by the West German hotelier, Klaus Kobjoll, whose hotel has a 92% occupancy and a long waiting list of applicants to join an already highly motivated workforce.

. . . modern times require a basic shift in the management/employee relationship. There are three types of authority: the God-given sort of Louis XIV which many company presidents assume – but it means nothing to the guy on the shopfloor: authority gained through the exercise of professional skills: and finally authority by 'human sympathy' where you show that you care as much for employees privately as you do professionally. That's the best and highest form of authority . . . If a hotel owner says his staff are working poorly, it's him that needs to change his style.[47]

A caring attitude towards staff

The starting point for customer satisfaction is good manager–subordinate relationships. Supportive and harmonious working relationships are more likely to create a working environment which results in high levels of both staff *and* customer satisfaction.

Emphasis on the role of interpersonal skills in customer satisfaction is of great relevance to the hotel and catering industry . . . CUSTOMER CARE REALLY DOES DEPEND ON STAFF CARE BEING ATTAINED FIRST.[48]

Managers need to adopt a positive attitude towards staff and to develop a spirit of mutual co-operation. Staff should feel that they are working with the manager rather than for the manager.

As an overriding principle on which to guide managerial behaviour, it is difficult to argue against putting people first and a philosophy based on the Golden Rule of life – manage others as you would like to be managed yourself. Venison draws a striking comparison between the hotel industry and the retail industry,[49] and an interesting and enlightened example of a people approach to management based on the Golden Rule is that of Mary Kay Cosmetics in America.[50] Other enlightened examples of a caring attitude towards staff are provided by Marks & Spencer[51] and the Body Shop.[52]

Good management is not easy

No one should pretend that good management is easy. But is it really asking too much for managers to treat members of staff with courtesy and consideration? And why should this in any way detract from the managers' ability to fulfil their duties and responsibilities effectively? Provided managers are prepared to make the effort, and **have full confidence in their own abilities**, they are likely to gain much from adopting a caring approach to their staff and treating them with dignity.

Such an approach requires positive and co-operative action from both hospitality managers and staff. But it is up to management to take the initiative. If certain members of staff do not co-operate or fail to respond in a constructive way, then management should take appropriate action. Managers must be flexible and prepared, if necessary, to use their judgement in adopting different styles of behaviour in particular situations or towards particular individuals or groups.

THE HUMAN COST OF POOR MANAGEMENT

The style of managerial behaviour has an obvious and direct effect on the well-being of staff, and on their levels of work performance. Managers decide the manner in which work duties and responsibilities are to be carried out. Different styles of management may be appropriate to managing different people in different circumstances. A more autocratic style of management may not *necessarily* be a bad thing in particular individual situations.

However, an unpleasant working environment and poor manager–subordinate relationships can cause tension and stress. Increasing attention is being given to the number of health problems that are classified as stress-related and affected by working conditions. It is important to remember both the effects on organisational performance and the potentially high human cost of inappropriate managerial behaviour.[53]

SUMMARY

- People are the central focus of management. The nature of the manager–subordinate relationship is crucial to effective hospitality operations. The behaviour that managers display towards subordinate staff is conditioned by predispositions about human nature and work. One means of evaluating different styles of management is in terms of concern for production and concern for people.

- The nature of the manager–subordinate relationship can be viewed in terms of a four-fold model of management systems and a profile of organisational characteristics. A participative-group system of management practices based on involvement and supportive relationships is more likely to lead to long-term improvements in performance and organisational decisions.

- Effective team management is especially important within the hospitality industry. One major participative approach is management by objectives (MBO). MBO is particularly suited to service operations and properly installed offers a number of potential benefits. There are, however, potential criticisms and limitations of MBO and attention should be given to work groups.

- A number of studies have focused on the personality characteristics of hospitality managers. However, a more constructive approach is to concentrate on the general attributes required of the successful manager. Technical expertise must be balanced with managerial education and competence. A priority is the development of human and social skills.

- The one essential ingredient of any successful manager is the ability to manage people effectively. However, an understanding people-centred approach seems often to be lacking in the hospitality industry. Attention should be given to basic managerial philosophies and to a positive policy of investing in people. In the longer term an interpersonal-relationship approach to management is worth the effort.

REVIEW AND DISCUSSION QUESTIONS

1 Discuss how the manager–subordinate relationship can be influenced by the manager's assumptions about human nature and the behaviour of people at work.

2 Explain the Blake and Mouton Grid as a means of comparing managerial styles. What is the importance of team management in the hospitality industry?

3 How might the nature of the manager-subordinate relationship be explained in terms of a four-fold model of management systems? Explain what you understand by the principle of supportive relationships.

4 What are the potential benefits and criticisms/limitations of Management by Objectives (MBO)? Assess critically the applications of MBO to service operations.

5 It is often claimed that, because of the nature of the hospitality industry, the requirements of its managers are somehow different from those of other managers. Discuss critically the validity of this claim and suggest how you would analyse the qualities of a successful manager.

6 Suggest why it is that many hotel managers appear to adopt a task-oriented, autocratic style of management.

7 Debate critically the suggestion that there are a number of basic, underlying philosophies which are likely to make for the successful management of people and lead to improved organisational performance.

8 Give your views on the manager's right to manage and the use of authority. Why is it important to distinguish between the 'intent' and the 'implementation' of management decisions and actions?

ASSIGNMENT 1

(i) From your own experience, explain fully a situation which you believe demonstrates an effective and/or an ineffective way of dealing with subordinate staff. Comment critically on the behaviour, actions and decisions of the manager or supervisor concerned.

(ii) Explain to what extent you can relate this situation to the application of theories and/or principles of managerial behaviour.

(iii) Meet in groups of four to six to share and discuss your observations. Make notes of your colleagues' perceptions of the situation and ways in which they support, or differ from, your own observations.

(iv) Prepare a summary of your discussions to share with other groups in the class.

ASSIGNMENT 2

Using Likert's **short form profile of organisational characteristics** (see Figure 5.3), investigate a hospitality organisation of your choice.

(i) Circle what you believe to be the most accurate answer for each of the 18 questions. Where possible, give brief supporting reasons for your answers and make clear any necessary assumptions.

(ii) Summarise the pattern of your answers and the extent to which this suggests a clear indication towards one particular model of management system.

(iii) If possible, try to repeat this investigation for a different hospitality organisation.

(iv) Explain the conclusions you draw from your investigation(s).

(v) Compare your results with those of your colleagues. To what extent do you feel the investigations support the view that the most efficient organisations adopt Systems 3 or 4 management?

ASSIGNMENT 3

The following commentary represents the personal views of the former General Manager of a Golf and Country House Hotel.

Attributes of the hotel manager

I will endeavour to list a few points on what in my opinion are the attributes of being a hotel manager and where we go wrong.

Firstly, degree students expect status but there is not any. Like a war, the best generals lead from the front, not the back. So you always put yourself in the firing line. Customers like to see the manager – not deputy manager, bar manager or restaurant manager. It might be a nod, shake of the hand or a wave, but they want recognition from the top. You should lead by example. Too many managers think that they have done all the hard work getting there, and then stop.

The hotel and leisure industry is too large to bracket. You cannot classify the Savoy or Hilton with a Golf and Country-House Hotel or night-club. So therefore a manager needs different attributes. You need to have the ability to socialise with your customers. It may be a granny, newly-weds, couple on their first date, football supporter on a night out – the list is endless. You need to be able to converse with them in their language and put them at ease. So you need an ability to judge people very quickly.

Are we attracting people to the industry and giving them a false impression? It is not an easy way of earning a living. It is very hard work and stressful. You have to work split shifts, be up early, maybe in the middle of the night, and you work late at night. It is not a glamorous career where you just stand around in a dinner suit looking pretty.

It is a people industry, full stop. You have to get on well with staff and customers and put on a smile even if your mother has died. Customers are not interested, in fact they could not give a damn, but the other way round is a totally different ball game.

As a manager you are there for when problems arise. If there are no problems you would not need a manager, so hence you are busy when there are difficulties. You need an ability to make quick decisions and you may not have the time to correct them so they must be right first time. You will have no social life because of the commitment needed for the job. You have to live, eat and breathe the establishment to be successful.

The hotel industry is unique. It should not be, but it is, in various ways – but then so are most industries. A good hotel manager may not be able to manage a circus or a coal pit. If hotel workers spoke or ignored customers, like some shops, I would be out of a job within a week. Very few people would complain when out shopping – but put them in a hotel, and they change their character. So you have to have a thick skin and a long fuse. You must therefore have the ability to stay calm and composed when everything around you is burning to the ground.

I think it would be impossible to improve the standard of management without first tackling many major problems. In this country, hotel workers are always looked down upon. In France and Germany, for example, a restaurant waiter is a class job and held in high esteem. In this country if you cannot get a job you can always work in the hotel and catering industry as a last choice.

It is necessary for more of a breakdown of what makes a successful manager. In what contexts, for example making money, not receiving complaints, keeping staff, improving turnover, etc. ? The job varies if it is company or privately owned. If you manage for a company you need no vision whatsoever as you get sent memos on everything from how to answer the telephone, the correct way of opening a can of beans, positioning the vegetables on a plate, to serving a 2 oz portion of carrots. There is a standard for everything which cannot, and will not, be deviated from in any form.

So the only way to improve turnover is people-orientated again. You have to be nice to people. Large companies do not want managers but clones – they tell you how to do everything, full stop. And when you will not do it their way, you are replaced.

Large companies in their head offices have budget forecasters, company trainers, area managers, sales and marketing departments, planners, design consultants, auditors, stockbrokers, wage departments. In fact they have the lot. They tell you how to run a successful hotel, but they miss out the most important factor – life. When do you stop serving Mr Smith who is about to knife me? Or how to deal with Mrs Jones who has just collapsed?

In the end it goes back to people. They can manage the whole show from 200 miles away, but they cannot control my tone of voice. You can say the word 'Hallo' in so many different ways – gruff, abrupt, sexy, quiet, pleasant, relaxing – the list is endless.

So you possibly need to define the word 'manager'. A manager of a cafe whose bosses are living in Spain probably has to be more of a 'manager' in some contexts than someone managing a 500-room THF hotel.

Do students who go into the trade know what they want from it? If you want to make decisions, then do not work for a company.

So far I have reached the conclusion that the most important attribute of a manager is the ability to carry out what you are told to do and not question people in authority. Maybe good hotel managers should either be trained in the police or the services because the only times you make decisions, or should make them, concern people again.

We are always given the guidelines or standards. We just have to adhere to them and this is probably the case for 95% of managers. Perhaps you could analyse good managers as all yes-men?

So therefore you need a totally new approach to the whole issue. Technical ability would become extremely high on the agenda whilst strategic-planning and decision-making skills become low down on the agenda. If you do not know the technical side very well, you would not know if things were going amiss.

Now if we carry on this train of thought we come across a very big problem. Working for companies the amount of paperwork in triplicate is very high; therefore you have to spend a lot of time in the office. You have to rely on a second person or a third person, so good managers are only as good as the people around them. They therefore have to have the ability to choose a good team correctly. And we are again back to people.

So when it comes down to the nitty gritty I do not think that you can generalise. Every case is individual. Yes, you have to mix with people. You have to give orders and clear instructions, have no social life, have an eye for detail. You take flak from all directions: from guests, staff, owners or directors. It can be a very lonely life because you are always on your own. You cannot get too close to people. You must never have a relationship with anyone you work with as this will cause you problems. You must try and stay aloof.

You must be cheerful, happy, honest, and above all fair. You must always be seen to look at both points of view and never go into conversation wearing blinkers. If you are a good listener it helps, as the hotel life varies so much. For many live-in workers, it is not a job – it is their life. Everything rolled into one. It is not a job where you clock off and go home on Friday forgetting everything until Monday morning.

At the end of the day you have to **LOVE** the work and you are only as good as the weakest link in the chain. If you cannot stand the heat, get out of the kitchen, hotel, and grounds – because you will never make a successful manager.

TASKS

Meet in self-selecting groups of four to six.

(i)   Discuss critically what you see as the main points and issues which are raised in this commentary.

(ii) To what extent do you agree or disagree with the comments? Explain how these are borne out by your own experiences. How much agreement is there among members of your group?

(iii) Working as a group, suggest what actions you would propose in order to help overcome problem areas in the hotel industry identified from the commentary.

NOTES AND REFERENCES

1. Mullins L J, 'Management and Managerial Behaviour', *International Journal of Hospitality Management*, vol. 4, no. 1, 1985, p. 39.
2. McGregor D, *The Human Side of Enterprise*, Penguin (1987).
3. Venison P, *Managing Hotels*, Heinemann (1983), p. 56.
4. Blake R R and McCanse A A, *Leadership Dilemmas – Grid Solutions*, Gulf Publishing Company (1991).
5. Jones P J and Lockwood A, *The Management of Hotel Operations*, Cassell (1989).
6. Venison P, *Managing Hotels*, Heinemann (1983), p. 32.
7. Wood R C, *Working in Hotels and Catering*, Routledge (1992).
8. Lee-Ross D, 'Two Styles of Hotel Manager, Two Styles of Worker', *International Journal of Contemporary Hospitality Management*, vol. 5, no. 4, 1993, pp. 20–24.
9. Likert R, *New Patterns of Management*, McGraw-Hill (1961).
10. Likert R and Likert J G, *New Ways of Managing Conflict*, McGraw-Hill (1976).
11. Likert R, *The Human Organisation*, McGraw-Hill (1967), p. 138.
12. See, for example, Humble J W, *Management By Objectives*, Management Publications Ltd for The British Institute of Management (1972).
13. For example, see Medlik S, *The Business of Hotels*, Second edition, Heinemann (1989).
14. See, for example, Argenti J, *Management Techniques*, Allen & Unwin (1969).
15. Jones P J and Lockwood A, *The Management of Hotel Operations*, Cassell (1989).
16. Nightingale M A, *A Quest for Quality and Profitability*, HCITB (1978).
17. Boella M J, *Human Resource Management in the Hotel and Catering Industry*, Fourth edition, Hutchinson (1987).
18. Mill R C, *Managing for Productivity in the Hospitality Industry*, Van Nostrand Reinhold (1989).
19. Kane J S and Freeman K A, 'MBO and Performance Appraisal', *Personnel*, vol. 63, no. 12, December 1986, pp. 26–36.
20. Shaner M C, 'The Nature of Hospitality Managers', *Cornell HRA Quarterly*, November 1978, pp. 65–70.
21. Worsfold P, 'A Personality Profile of the Hotel Manager', *International Journal of Hospitality Management*, vol. 8, no. 1, 1989, pp. 51–62.
22. Stone G, 'Personality and Effective Hospitality Management', *Proceedings of The International Association of Hotel Management Schools Symposium*, Leeds Polytechnic, November 1988.
23. Guerrier Y and Lockwood A, 'Developing Hotel Managers – A Reappraisal', *International Journal of Hospitality Management*, vol. 8, no. 2, 1989, pp. 82–89.
24. See, for example, Mullins L J, *Management and Organisational Behaviour*, Third edition, Pitman (1993).
25. Mullins L J and Davies 1, 'What Makes for an Effective Hotel Manager?', *International Journal of Contemporary Hospitality Management*, vol. 3, no. 1, 1991, pp. 22–25.
26. Johnson P, *The Corpus of Professional Knowledge in Hotel, Catering and Institutional Services*, HCIMA (1977).
27. *Meeting Competence needs in the Hotel and Catering Industry Now and in the Future*, HCTC Research Report, September 1992.
28. Maher A, 'Accounting for Human Resources in UK Hotels', *Proceedings of CHME Research Conference*, Manchester Metropolitan University, April 1993.
29. Drucker P F, *People and Performance*, Heinemann (1977), p. 59.
30. Mercer K, 'Psychology at Work in the Hotel and Catering Industry', *HCIMA Review*, 4, 1978, p. 212.

31. Jones P (ed), *Management in Service Industries*, Pitman (1989).
32. Mullins L J and Aldrich P, 'An Integrated Model of Management and Managerial Development', *Journal of Management Development*, vol. 7, no. 3, 1988, pp. 29–39.
33. See, for example, Blanchard K and Johnson S, *The One Minute Manager*, Willow Books (1983).
34. Gunn B, 'Are Educationalists and Employers in Harmony on Hotel Management Training?', *Master Innholders' Forum*, London, June 1990. Reported in *Caterer & Hotelkeeper*, 14 June 1990, p. 14.
35. Maher A, 'Accounting for Human Resources in UK Hotels', *Proceedings of CHME Research Conference*, Manchester Metropolitan University, April 1993.
36. White M, 'Management Styles in Hotels', *HCIMA Journal*, October 1973, pp. 9–11.
37. Umbreit W T, 'Developing Behaviorally-Anchored Scales for Evaluating Job Performance of Hotel Managers', *International Journal of Hospitality Management*, vol. 5, no. 2, 1986, p. 56.
38. Worsfold P, 'Leadership and Managerial Effectiveness in the Hospitality Industry', *International Journal of Hospitality Management*, vol. 8, no. 2, 1989, p. 152.
39. For example, see Jones F, 'Computers in The Hotel', *Administrative Management*, vol. 29, no. 12, August 1980, pp. 4–6.
40. A view supported by the industrial placement officers for Hotel and Catering Management degree students at Portsmouth Business School.
41. See also Robinson S, 'The Learning Curve', *Inside Hotels*, April/May 1992, pp. 40–45.
42. Venison P, *Managing Hotels*, Heinemann (1983).
43. See, for example, Freemantle D, 'The People Factor', *Management Today*, December 1985, pp. 68–71.
44. Martin P and Nicholls J, *Creating a Committed Workforce*, Institute of Personnel Management (1987), p. 97.
45. Peters T J and Waterman R H, *In Search of Excellence*, Harper & Row (1982), p. 238.
46. See, for example, Adams J S, 'Injustice in Social Exchange', abridged in Steers R M and Porter L W, *Motivation and Work Behavior*, Second edition, McGraw-Hill (1979).
47. Tarpey D, 'Handling With Care', *Caterer & Hotelkeeper*, 12 July 1990, p. 52.
48. Klein S, 'Customer Care Needs Staff Care', *Proceedings of The International Association of Hotel Management Schools Symposium*, Leeds Polytechnic, November 1988.
49. Venison P, *Managing Hotels*, Heinemann (1983).
50. Ash M K, *On People Management*, Macdonald and Co. (1985).
51. Sieff M, (Lord Sieff of Brimpton), *Management The Marks & Spencer Way*, Fontana Collins (1991).
52. Roddick A, *Body and Soul*, Ebury Press (1991).
53. See, for example, Rockledge S, 'The Human Cost of Bad Management', *Administrator*, vol. 7, no. 1, January 1987, pp. 13–15.

6
THE PERSONNEL FUNCTION

INTRODUCTION

Whatever the structure of a hospitality organisation or the nature of its activities, an essential part of the process of management is the effective use of human resources. Proper attention to the personnel function will help to improve the efficiency of the workforce and the level of organisational performance.

This chapter looks at:
- The importance of human resources
- Human resource management
- The personnel department and the personnel function
- Personnel policies and organisation
- Teamwork and co-operation
- Employee relations
- Staffing the organisation
- Staff turnover
- Manpower planning
- Staff recruitment and selection
- Job analysis
- The selection process
- Induction and follow-up
- Education, training and development
- Effectiveness of the personnel function

THE IMPORTANCE OF HUMAN RESOURCES

Hospitality is a major industry in this country. A recent report of the HCTC indicates that in 1990 the hotel and catering industry employed 9% (2.4 million) of the total UK workforce. As the industry comes out of recession it is expected to expand rapidly and provide 72,000 new jobs by 1995 and a further 92,000 jobs by 1999.[1]

The industry is labour-intensive and its pattern of staffing is characterised by such features as mobility, seasonal and part-time work, a high proportion of unskilled, part-time and casual staff, a high labour turnover, and many trade unions but low trade union membership.

It is therefore particularly important that the industry attracts and retains staff with the right skills and attitudes to meet satisfactorily the demands of the customer. There must be effective management of human resources – there must be an effective personnel function.

The human element

The human element plays a major part in the overall success of any organisation, but especially so in a service industry such as hospitality. Many members of the workforce are in direct contact with the customer and are seen as being involved in achieving the objectives of the organisation. The quality of service offered is dependent not only upon the skills but also upon the attitudes of the staff. Both are essential if the demands of the customer are to be met satisfactorily. This places particular importance on the personnel function. This may appear to be an obvious statement. But it is worth emphasising that it is debatable how much time, care and attention is actually given to the personnel function and to the effective management of people within the hospitality industry.[2]

Personnel as a task function?

You will recall that in Chapter 3 we made the distinction between task functions – those basic activities directed towards specific and definable end results – and element functions – those activities that are supportive of the task functions. In the majority of organisations the personnel function does not normally have any direct accountability for the performance of a specific end-task. Personnel is generally identified therefore as an element or support function.

However, it is arguable to what extent this applies strictly in the hospitality industry. The people employed are more than just a means to an end, more than just inputs to a finished product. People are, at least in part, an end in themselves. They are part of the finished product for which the customer is paying. For example, the customer in the restaurant is buying not only food and beverage and the skills of the chef, but also the attention of the waiter. Should either of these give a service less than is required of them, then this will lead to customer dissatisfaction.[3]

The importance of staff contact to customer satisfaction means that personnel can be seen as closely associated with a task function. Customer satisfaction is likely to be affected as much by the courtesy, helpfulness and personal qualities of the staff as by the standard of food and beverage, accommodation or other facilities of the organisation.

HUMAN RESOURCE MANAGEMENT

The increasing emphasis on effective employee relations, and the importance of securing the involvement of staff and their commitment to the aims of the organisation, has led to the increasing use of the term 'human resources' to replace 'personnel'.

According to Willman, human resource management is concerned with:

> . . . mechanisms through which the organisation attracts candidates for employment, selects them, introduces them to the organisation's structure and culture, motivates them to perform a given set of tasks, pays them for this and seeks to identify their potential for future development. It is then concerned with systems of promotion, manpower planning, succession planning, and coping with labour turnover of one form or another.[4]

No clear distinction

There is, however, no clear distinction between personnel management and human resource management. For example, Guest suggests three ways in which human resource management has been used to distinguish it from traditional personnel management:

(i) simply to re-title personnel management to capture the new fashion;
(ii) to re-conceptualise and re-organise personnel roles, and the work of personnel departments; and
(iii) as distinctively different and offering a new approach for management.[5]

Guest goes on to describe some broad stereotypes which could be used to highlight the differences. Compared with personnel management, human resource management is concerned more with a long-term rather than a short-term perspective, with the psychological contract based on commitment rather than compliance, with self-control rather than external controls, with a unitarist rather than a pluralist perspective, with an organic rather than a bureaucratic structure, with integration with line management rather than specialist or professional roles, and with maximum utilisation rather than cost-minimisation.

According to Cuming, however, some argue that human resource management is just a new term for what most good personnel managers have already been practising. The extent to which personnel management has moved into another historical phase of human resource management is debatable.[6]

Human resource management (HRM) in the hotel industry

As part of research on the extent to which hotel companies account for human resource management, Maher questioned senior human resource managers on the perceived difference between the HR specialist and the personnel specialist. Reactions to the question were mixed and ranged from antagonism to enthusiasm for the ideas embodied in HRM.[7] Maher also found that although the HRM function had become more important in the past few years, this was seen to be because of the need to reduce costs in that area rather than as increasing recognition of the importance of the HRM function or its significance within the overall business strategy of the organisation.

It is not easy, therefore, to distinguish human resource management from personnel management. And neither does it follow that human resource management, however it is described, will necessarily lead to a higher level of organisational performance than would be achieved with a traditional personnel management approach.

For ease of reference, therefore, we shall refer to personnel management and the personnel function.

THE PERSONNEL DEPARTMENT AND THE PERSONNEL FUNCTION

The hospitality industry is made up of units which vary greatly in size and type. Smaller establishments may not justify a specialist personnel manager or a separate personnel department. **But it is still necessary to have an effective personnel *function*,** whether it be the responsibility of, for example, the owner or the general manager or shared among heads of departments.

Even the smallest establishments will have the need to recruit and train staff, to motivate and reward them, and to comply with the law relating to employment. The personnel function must still be carried out even if a unit is too small to justify, or chooses not to establish, a separate personnel department.

The importance of the personnel function has been emphasised by, among others, Venison.

> A personnel function in an hotel is required beyond any doubt. Whether that function takes up the full-time employment of one or more people, thus rendering it a service department, or whether it is the part-time responsibility of a particular member of management depends upon the size of the hotel. Irrespective of hotel size, however, and notwithstanding the style of the hotel manager, the need for the function always exists.[8]

Personnel management specialist

In the larger establishments where more time is taken up with problems of organisation and personnel, there is greater need for a specialist to whom is delegated specific responsibilities for personnel matters. A specialised personnel manager would be expected to advise top management on the implementation of clearly defined policies which permit consistent personnel practices.

There are no hard and fast rules on what size of establishment justifies a separate personnel department. One suggestion is that: 'Every good hotel with more than 300 staff deserves a personnel manager who has qualifications and/or experience both in personnel management and in hotel and catering.'[9] And in Trusthouse Forte it is usual in all units of more than 50 staff for a member of the management team to specialise in the personnel function.[10]

Other important factors

The number of staff, however, is not the only consideration. In addition to the type and nature of the organisation, there are a number of other important factors which emphasise the importance of the personnel function. These include, for example,

- the increasing level of government involvement in employment legislation;
- pressures for a greater social responsibility towards employees through schemes of worker participation, including European Commission proposals on employee involvement;
- high staffing costs;
- developments in the applications of behavioural science;
- the role of industrial tribunals and ACAS; and
- the possible growth of trade unions in the industry.

These factors all combine to suggest the increasing need for a personnel management specialist.

PERSONNEL POLICIES AND ORGANISATION

A manager achieves results through the performance of other people. Recognition of the needs and wants of staff and the nature of their grievances is a positive step in motivating them to perform well. The efficiency of staff, their commitment to the aims of the organisation, and the skills and attitudes they bring to bear on the quality of service offered are fostered by good human relationships. And success in the field of human relationships stems from good personnel policies and practices.

Although there is general agreement that 'there is a lack of established personnel practices and norms within the industry at management level',[11] it does appear that greater attention is now being given to the importance of the personnel function. Many larger hotels, in particular, have recognised the demands for personnel management as a specialist activity.

The role of top management

The overall objective of the personnel function is to create an environment in which staff work willingly and effectively. Management should attempt to maintain a level of morale and commitment of all members of staff in order to secure the optimum operational performance.

The effective management of people is influenced by the part played by top management and the attitudes which they bring to bear on relationships with staff. Personnel policies are a reflection on the overall style of management.[12] Policies should emanate from the top of the hospitality organisation. They should be defined clearly and communicated through managers and supervisors to staff at all levels.

Underlying philosophies

The formulation of personnel policies, and the implementation of personnel practices and procedures, should be based on underlying philosophies of managerial behaviour and employee relationships.

Such philosophies should embrace:

- respect for the individual;
- the recognition of people's needs and expectations at work;
- justice in treatment and equitable reward systems;
- stability of employment;
- good working environment and conditions of service;
- opportunities for personal development and career progression;
- democratic functioning of the organisation;
- full observance of all laws and codes of conduct relating to employment.

The range of the personnel function

The range and scope of the personnel function are wide. This is illustrated by the definition of personnel management given by the Institute of Personnel Management.

Personnel management is that part of management concerned with people at work and with their relationships within an enterprise. Its aim is to bring together and develop into an active organisation the men and women who make up an enterprise and, having regard for the well-being of the individual and of working groups, to enable them to make their best contribution to its success. Personnel management is also concerned with the human and social implications of change in internal organisation and methods of working, and of economic and social changes in the community.[13]

Personnel activities may be considered within the framework of the following broad headings:

- recruitment and selection;
- training and development;
- employee relations;
- organisation and manpower planning;
- pay and employment conditions.

Organisation of the personnel function

It is not easy to define closely the activities of the personnel function or of a personnel department. In a hotel group, or the larger individual establishments, these activities might be divided between two or more specialists. For example, there might be a personnel officer, a training officer, and possibly a recruitment officer, a welfare officer and an industrial relations officer.

The actual organisation and range of responsibilities will vary from one group or hotel to another, as also will the status and title of the personnel specialists, and their position in the management structure. For ease of reference we shall use the term personnel manager to refer to the person(s) with specific responsibility for personnel management activities within the hotel.

Whatever the organisation of the personnel function, a personnel manager operates through a form of delegated authority. The degree of authority given to the personnel manager is dependent upon the philosophy and attitudes of top management, the role the position is intended to perform, and the formal relationships with other managers.

The personnel and training function in Forte Hotels

Forte Hotels have recently undertaken major changes in the organisation of the personnel and training function within the company. Each Brand or Collection has District Personnel Managers and District Training Managers who look after between four and eleven units dependent on the size of the operation. These district managers report to Regional Managers who cover approximately 30 units each. (Details of the strategy for the restructuring and revised organisation of the personnel and training function in Forte Hotels are given in Appendix 1 to this chapter.)

THE PERSONNEL FUNCTION AS A SHARED RESPONSIBILITY

The Institute of Personnel Management's definition draws attention to personnel management as part of the responsibility of all managers and supervisors. Getting work done through the efforts of other people is an integral part of any managerial activity. The personnel function is part of the generality of management.[14]

For example, when the head chef ensures that the kitchen brigade are clean and that standards of hygiene are observed, this is carrying out a personnel function. If the accommodation manager reprimands a chambermaid for lateness, this is carrying out a personnel function. And if the front of house manager trains a receptionist in receiving advance reservations, this is carrying out a personnel function.

Every manager a personnel manager

It is the line managers who have the technical expertise, together with a detailed knowledge of the activities of their department and the working conditions of staff. They have the responsibility for the management of their own staff.

Line managers have both the right and the duty to be concerned with the efficiency of their own department and the well-being of their staff. Line managers are on hand to observe directly the behaviour and performance of staff. For example, the restaurant manager (or the head waiter) is in the restaurant; the chef is in the kitchen. They will actually see, and be directly affected by, the lateness of staff, unsatisfactory work, insufficient training, staff unrest or poor planning of work duties and responsibilities. It is therefore the line managers who have the immediate responsibility for personnel management. In this respect it could be said that **every manager is a personnel manager**.

The responsibility of line management

Rocco Forte has emphasised the importance of a caring and efficient personnel function to assist line managers in what is one of their primary responsibilities. The nature of Trusthouse Forte's business with many separate units of differing size, location and mix of skills means of necessity the personnel function is decentralised and prime responsibility has to be with line management.

> However, even if we had a choice, I believe we would elect to put the prime responsibility for personnel on line management rather than on specialists. The nature of our work calls for active participation by management in day to day operations and they need to have a very close relationship and understanding with their staff. Equally, staff need to know that line management has the authority and responsibility for taking actions which vitally affect them in their work and in their working environment. The link therefore must be a direct one.[15]

Functional relationship

The role of the personnel manager is to implement personnel policies throughout all departments of the organisation, to provide specialist knowledge and services for the line managers, and to support them in the performance of their work. The personnel manager should operate in terms of a 'functional' relationship with the line managers. It should not be the job of the personnel manager to manage other staff, other than any direct subordinates.

The personnel manager has no direct control over staff in other departments except where a specific responsibility is delegated directly by top management, for example for health and safety matters. In all other respects the personnel manager's responsibility with other managers and their staff should be indirect – that is, as a specialist adviser.

Specialist expertise and advice

However, although the line managers are specialists in their own areas of work, they are not necessarily specialists in personnel management. In the same way that line managers may need help and guidance on legal and accounting matters, so they may need help and specialist advice on personnel matters. Thomason suggests that the personnel manager is probably the only specialist whose role can be distinguished by the virtually exclusive concern with the management of human resources. All other managers will also have some direct concern for the management of physical assets.[16]

It is the personnel manager who has the professional expertise and specialist knowledge of personnel work. Line managers might be expected, therefore, to heed and to act upon the advice which is given. The personnel manager is responsible for the interpretation and implementation of personnel policies and procedures, and sees the overall effect throughout the hotel, for example, as a whole. It is important to keep a balance between departments, and to maintain equitable treatment for all staff and a sense of fair play.

TEAMWORK AND CO-OPERATION

If the personnel function is to be effective, there has to be good teamwork and co-operation and consultation between line managers and the personnel manager. This is made easier when top management, who retain ultimate responsibility for the personnel function, take an active part in fostering goodwill and co-operation between departments.

Top management should agree clear terms of reference for the personnel manager within a framework of sound and clear personnel policies. Within this framework the personnel function can be seen as operating at two levels: the organisational level and the departmental level (Figure 6.1).

The organisational level

At the organisational level the detailed involvement of the work activities of several departments, available time and the need for specialisation suggest that the personnel manager has a prominent role to play. The personnel manager is the main executor of personnel policies and is concerned mainly with broader aspects which affect all members of staff and the organisation as a whole.

This could include such activities as manpower planning, procedures for recruitment and selection, induction and training, health and safety, welfare, employee relations, compliance with employment legislation, dealings with trade unions or staff representatives, maintaining statistics and records, and liaison with outside bodies such as

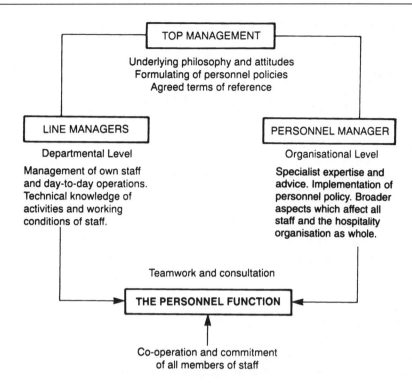

Fig 6.1 The personnel function – a shared responsibility

HCTC, HCIMA, employers' associations or ACAS. The personnel manager should act in consultation with, and taking advice from, line managers.

The departmental level

At the departmental level the line managers might assume a prominent role for day-to-day personnel matters. They would be concerned, at least in the first instance, with the operational aspects of personnel activities within their own department, for example minor disciplinary matters, poor timekeeping, unsatisfactory work performance, calling in stand-by staff, safety, on-the-job training, allocation of duties and rota schedules, communication of information, and the welfare of, and grievances from, staff. The personnel manager would be expected to act as adviser, and if necessary as arbitrator.

Commitment of all members of staff

It is clear then that the personnel function is a shared responsibility among top management, line managers and supervisors, and the personnel manager. But if the personnel function is to be implemented successfully it also requires the co-operation and commitment of all members of staff, whatever their duties or positions within the hospitality organisation. The personnel function cannot be housed within one discrete department or be the sole responsibility of selected members of staff. It permeates all levels of the organisation and all phases of its operations.

International human resource management

Goss-Turner comments on the questions facing the organisation and management of major hospitality organisations as they become increasingly global in their representation. HRM is a powerful strategic force in ensuring developments in decentralisation and empowerment for the management of business in different cultures. Key issues in attempting to develop an international HRM function include:

- a customer-oriented rather than a bureaucratic-utility approach which invades the HR philosophy;
- the development of additional skills including the area of information technology, achieved partly through training and partly through recruitment;
- strengthening team development and supportive relationships including the multi-cultural, interpersonal skills of the team;
- development of cultural awareness for HR specialists, senior line managers and management trainees, and information and briefing within the international transfer arena.[17]

EMPLOYEE RELATIONS

However the responsibilities for the personnel function are shared and whatever the respective roles of the personnel manager and line managers, the personnel function can be effective only if it is based on sound personnel policies. Good employee relations are fostered by good personnel policies.

The traditional view of industrial relations has often been associated in particular with the activities of trade unions and their officials. Trade unions may be seen as existing primarily to promote the best interests of their members and to improve the quality of working life and the general standard of living.

Good management–staff relationships are not limited, however, to trade unions and employment legislation. For this reason the broader term of 'employee relations' is now more favoured. According to an HCTC booklet, employee relations embraces:

> . . . all the factors in the relationships between employers, staff and other individuals and institutions involved in the employment process.[18]

To understand any employee relations situation it is necessary to take account of the institutions and parties involved, and their ideologies and motives.

Employee relations policy

Having well-defined and agreed policies is increasingly seen as important in establishing effective employee relations. Cuming, for example, makes the following point.

> Accepting that human resources are the most important that an organisation has, and that their effective management is essential, the principle underlying human resource management is that success is most likely to be achieved if personnel policies and practices clearly and positively contribute to the achievement of corporate objectives and strategic plans.[19]

The HCTC booklet provides a 25-point checklist which covers many of those matters about which it is useful for an employer to have a considered policy (Figure 6.2). It is important that the employer's policies and procedures are kept up to date, successfully communicated, and understood properly by all staff.[20]

DEVELOPING AN EMPLOYEE RELATIONS POLICY

Recruitment

1 What steps have you taken to produce an 'Equal Opportunity' employment policy statement?

2 Do you select on merit – regardless of sex or race?

3 Do you know that the Commission for Racial Equality and the Equal Opportunities Commission can help by giving examples of equal opportunity policies and advice on how to monitor their use?

Pay and other benefits

4 Do you plan your pay policy?

5 Do you *plan* to be a 'low' or a 'high' payer?

6 Do you know what benefits your competitors offer?

7 Is your pay structure planned and understood, or based on 'grace and favour'?

8 Do you understand and comply with current wages council orders and with the provisions of the Equal Pay Act?

Staff representation

9 What is your declared approach to staff representation?

10 Do you, where appropriate, recognise and negotiate with a trade union?

11 Do you make adequate facilities available for the representatives of your staff?

12 If you do not recognise a trade union, do your staff have adequate opportunities to represent their views?

Communication and consultation

People are often so busy that they can easily be unaware of what other working groups are doing or what problems there may be

13 What do you do to find out about these problems and to help resolve them?

14 How do you consult staff on changes that will affect them and how do you gain commitment to new policies?

Staff development and training

15 What initiatives have you taken to develop and train your staff, especially young people?

16 Do you have a policy about promotion from within the organisation and do you seek to develop staff by an effective appraisal scheme?

17 Do you select staff for training and development on the basis of merit and their needs – regardless of sex or race?

Disciplinary matters and grievances

18 Do you have adequate, readily understood procedures that are available for all to see?

19 How are these communicated?

Retirement

20 At what age do you normally retire staff?

21 How do you decide who is to retire and who can stay?

22 Are your staff aware of the policy and are they clear on whether you have a defined age of retirement?

Redundancy or lay off

23 In what circumstances will staff be made redundant or laid off?

24 What system of notification, consultation and selection will be used? (Remember that you are obliged to consult the relevant recognised trade union if one exists, and that race and sex discrimination legislation also applies to decisions about redundancy selection)

25 Are alternatives, such as work sharing or short time, built into your procedures?

Finally

Considering your employment policies in general – have they been discussed with your staff?

Even if they do not belong to a trade union, it is preferable to discuss and agree on such matters with staff or their representatives, before making rules

---

Fig 6.2 Checklist for an employee relationship policy
Reprinted, with permission, from *Employee Relations for the Hotel and Catering Industry*, Seventh edition, Hotel and Catering Training Company (1990), pp. 24–6

The value of procedures

Magurn draws attention to the value of both formal and informal procedures for regulating the working relations of people and the interests of staff in the hospitality industry. A procedure, however, is not a substitute for a policy and it is important first to have worthwhile employment policies. Procedural arrangements must be seen in perspective and managers should be aware of their limitations.

> Good procedures cannot ensure that all disputed issues will be settled peacefully. Human behaviour cannot be made to conform to prescribed rules just because they are prescribed rules. Your procedures can only be effective if they reflect a generally good relation between management and staff and a determination by both sides to use them.[21]

The importance of listening

Whatever the procedures that are used, an important part of good employee relations is managers listening to the feelings and problems of the staff. You may recall that in Chapter 3 we discussed the contribution of the interviewing programme of the Hawthorne studies to the development of a human relations approach to organisation and management. Many workers appeared to welcome the opportunity to have someone who would listen to their feelings and problems, and to whom they could 'let off steam' in a friendly atmosphere.

The interviewing programme highlighted the importance of counselling interviews and of managers actively listening to the staff. Given the nature of the hospitality industry and the importance of good employee relations, the lessons learnt from the interviewing programme have particular significance for the manager.

STAFFING THE ORGANISATION

Whatever the type, size or structure of the unit it has to be staffed with people of the right quality. The effectiveness of any hospitality organisation will inevitably depend very largely upon the staff it employs and on good management–staff relationships. Larger units may perhaps have a designated personnel manager, but this does not detract from the concern of every manager for the maintenance of good staff relations and the management of their own staff. It is only right and sensible, therefore, that managers and supervisors have at least some say in the appointment of their own staff or those staff whose work they have to supervise.

Organisational context

Within an organisational context, the prerequisites of an effective system for staffing include:

- the clarification of aims and objectives;
- the design of an effective organisation structure through which work is carried out, and to support the efforts of staff; and
- a system of manpower planning as the framework within which personnel policies and a systematic approach to recruitment and selection are planned and implemented.

The overall aim must be to select the best available staff in the first place, to train and develop them, and to retain them for a reasonable period of time.

Core and peripheral staff

Staffing of an organisation can be viewed in terms of 'core' and 'peripheral' employees, and the nature of flexible working.[22] **Core** denotes permanent, full-time employees. They undertake key activities of the organisation and are expected to be functionally flexible. Career prospects and job security are high. Peripheral denotes numerically flexible employees with fairly easy jobs, limited career opportunities and less job security. The peripheral groups surround the core employees and insulate them from the effects of changes in demand.

From a study of ten major hotel groups in the UK, Guerrier and Lockwood identify three categories of core employees and two categories of peripheral employees.[23]

- **Company core staff** have potential access to career prospects throughout the range of units within the company and consist largely of management or trainee management staff, but not usually departmental heads.
- **Unit core staff** have access to career opportunities within a single hotel, but not within the wider company, and consist of departmental heads, supervisors, certain skilled operatives and some hotel trainees.
- **Operative core** consist of staff such as receptionists, skilled kitchen staff, waiting staff and chambermaids.
- **Peripheral group 1**, by whom numerical flexibility is achieved through high turnover rate, includes highly mobile skilled kitchen and waiting staff, and students or foreign workers in the UK for a limited period.
- **Peripheral group 2** consists of part-time and casual staff, and staff who are on call, for example chambermaids.

STAFF TURNOVER

In the hospitality industry staff turnover is generally acknowledged to be high, especially in comparison with other industries. Staff turnover in the hotel and catering industry is possibly higher than in any other industry.[24] Much of the turnover is movement within the industry. Although hotels and guesthouses had the highest total turnover rate, less than half went outside the industry. But this does not alter the frequency with which staff have to be replaced or the need for retraining in particular working methods and practices. Staff turnover is highest in the first few months of employment. In the hotels and guesthouses sector almost 45% of all new workers left their employer within the first three months and 15% left within the first month.[25] Such turnover – the 'induction crisis' – is particularly disruptive and costly.

The costs of high staff turnover

A high level of staff turnover is likely to have an adverse effect on the morale, motivation and job satisfaction of staff, and on the level of organisational performance and customer satisfaction. It also has a disruptive effect on the use of managerial time. The costs of high staff turnover are emphasised by the HCTC.

> The costs of recruiting and engaging a new member of staff are considerable – not only the direct costs like advertising, agency fees, paper-work, interview time, but the many hidden or indirect costs. For example the expenses incurred in training and supervising new entrants, as well as those they are replacing, overtime that may have been paid during staff shortages, an increase in wastage and losses while new staff settle in, customer irritation and low staff morale if staff turnover is high.[26]

Reducing staff turnover

So what can be done to help overcome a high level of staff turnover, reduce costs and make more effective use of managerial time? You may recall the discussion in Chapter 5 when it was argued that high staff turnover should not be excused as an inherent, characteristic feature of the industry. The starting point, therefore, is recognition of high staff turnover as a problem area that demands management action.[27]

There is a continuing debate on the causes, true costs and other effects of high staff turnover within the hospitality industry and how best to overcome the problem. Riley, for example, suggests that it would be particularly helpful for research to focus on the relationship between organisational commitment and job satisfaction. and the intention to leave.[28]

On the basis of interviews with managers and employees in six restaurant companies and six hotel companies in America, Woods and Macaulay offer a number of remedies for staff turnover. Some are 'short-term prescriptions' which can be soon implemented and help reduce turnover fairly quickly. Others are 'long-term prescriptions' which should eventually make low turnover part of the organisation's structure.[29]

The short-term prescriptions are based on the principle that maintaining the flow of communications throughout the organisation will help the retention of staff. They involve:

- identifying the nature and character of the organisation;
- finding out why staff leave or stay;
- asking staff what they want from their jobs and providing formal opportunities for staff to voice opinions about their work; and
- developing effective recruitment, employment interviewing and orientation procedures.

The long-term prescriptions are based on organisational change and creating the type of organisation that staff want to work for. They involve:

- establishing effective socialisation, training and career-path development programmes;
- the adoption of quality circles (which are discussed in Chapter 8);
- developing profit sharing and incentive schemes;
- establishing child-care facilities and support services to attract older workers; and
- maintaining competitive pay scales.

Attention to recruitment and selection practice

Bonn and Forbringer refer to the challenge of a major personnel shortage facing the American hospitality industry and the need to give attention to methods of attracting and retaining staff. There are no easy solutions and the complexity of staff turnover demands a systemic approach for the assessment and diagnosis of the nature of the problem, and the causes and consequences for each organisation.

A strategic orientation will assist organisations in determining what solutions may be appropriate in a particular situation. The organisation can theoretically influence turnover by various intervention processes including placement and orientation, job design, leadership and supervision, job performance, and training and development. Central to all these processes is the critical activity of recruitment and selection practices.[30] (Staff recruitment and selection is discussed below.)

MANPOWER PLANNING

Human resources are the main asset of the work organisation, especially in the hospitality industry. The high level of staff turnover, the need for trained and experienced staff, and the need for management development draw attention to the importance of effective manpower planning. It is understandable, therefore, that in recent years greater recognition has been given to the importance of planning manpower resources as well as other economic resources.

A recent survey of steps taken to overcome manpower problems in 92 organisations concludes that greater priority will need to be given to manpower planning and human resource management as the availability of people and skills becomes more critical. Employers will have to continue to identify the skills needed to achieve business objectives and to restructure to make best use of the skills available. In addition they will need to devise human resource policies aimed at maintaining competitiveness in the labour market and to meeting employees' aspirations.[31]

The importance of manpower planning has been emphasised by the Hotels and Catering EDC. The industry 'produces' a service provided by people in face-to-face relationships with the customer. Manpower planning should be adopted to ensure that employment policies form an integral part of general company policy. The type of manpower planning advocated is one which stresses the way in which action and policy should be brought together.[32]

A broad approach to manpower planning

Manpower planning should not be viewed in isolation but as an integral part of the broader process of strategic planning, discussed in Chapter 1. Manpower planning is linked to the development of the organisation as a whole and should take account of external environmental factors, for example demographic changes, patterns of employment such as part-time, female or older workers, developments in the educational system, the level of competition, government initiatives on employment and training or employment legislation, and developments in information technology and automation.

It will be necessary to clarify the extent and scope of the manpower plan, the target date and the length of the forecast period, the departments, types of occupations and skills for which forecasts are to be made, and the amount of information and detail required. Management will need to determine the desired staffing levels for the various operational activities, in the case of a hotel for example, the number of cleaning staff to the number of rooms, or the number of waiting staff to the number of covers in the restaurant.

Main stages in manpower planning

Whatever the nature and scope of the manpower plan, it is possible to identify four main stages (Figure 6.3):

(i)   an analysis of present staffing resources;
(ii) an estimation of likely changes by the target date – this determines the manpower supply;
(iii) a forecast of staffing requirements for the target date – this determines the manpower demand;
(iv) measures to ensure the required staffing resources are available as and when required.

The reconciliation of supply and demand is the basis of the manpower plan and a personnel management action programme.

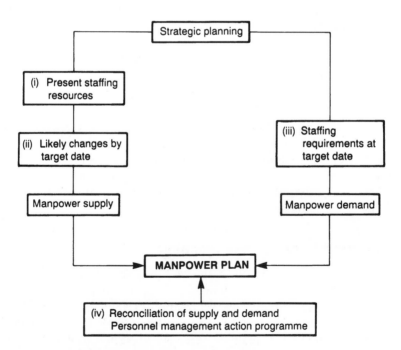

Fig 6.3 Outline of main stages in manpower planning

Manpower supply forecast

In order to determine an accurate forecast of manpower supply, it is necessary to have an effective staffing inventory and system of personnel records including details of occupational structure and staff turnover. It is important that the record system is kept up to date, including new training, experience, skills or qualifications acquired by staff. The record system should be able to indicate readily both more basic details, such as the age distribution of managerial staff, and more specific details, such as those members of staff able to converse in a foreign language.

The supply forecast must also take account of changes, additions and losses, incremental improvements in staff experience and training, and current programmes of management development.

Application of manpower planning

The underlying concepts of manpower planning are basically straightforward. Although there are a number of sophisticated quantitative techniques and computer programs available, these should be applied only when really necessary and most probably only in the larger units. Manpower planning can take a number of different forms in different organisations. In smaller hotels, for example, it can be undertaken at a more basic level. The important point is the recognition of the need for an effective system of manpower planning appropriate to the demands and requirements of the particular hospitality organisation.

Potential benefits

The use of manpower planning offers many potential benefits. An effective manpower plan will provide:

- links between objectives and organisation structure, and clarification of personnel policies;
- information on staffing requirements for forward planning at both the strategic level, for example a major extension to a hotel, and at the day-to-day operational level;
- indication of trends and likely changes in staffing resources in order to anticipate potential future difficulties while there is still a choice of action;
- a trigger for the development of effective personnel strategies and procedures, and a personnel management action programme for such activities as recruitment and selection, training and retraining, wage/salary levels, management development, transfers and redeployment, early retirements, and accommodation requirements.

Manpower planning involves considerable uncertainty and mistakes are bound to occur. Forward planning is particularly difficult in the hospitality industry, which is susceptible to changes in the external environment and consumer tastes, and seasonal patterns of demands. But manpower planning is therefore even more important. Coupled with good communications and meaningful participation, effective manpower planning will help to alleviate effects which are potentially harmful to members of staff or to organisational performance.

STAFF RECRUITMENT AND SELECTION

The nature of the hospitality industry and its pattern of staffing are such that most managers are likely to be faced frequently with the need to recruit and select staff. For example, the recent HCTC study has forecast that the hotel and catering industry will need to recruit an average of 13,000 new staff a week with 3,000 of these at skilled supervisory and management levels.[33]

The need is for effective methods and procedures of recruitment and selection.[34] It is questionable, however, to what extent performance matches the ideal. A major report by the Hotels and Catering EDC was highly critical of recruitment and selection methods. According to the report, selection methods are unsophisticated and lacking in objectivity. Managers should adopt more systematic problem-solving methods for determining their recruitment policy.[35]

Although the report was published some years ago, it appears that improvements still need to be made. From a recent study of the management of human resources in four large hotel groups, Croney found that:

> The recruitment and selection process tended to be ad hoc and informal in the majority of the groups, and even where formal procedures existed implementation at the unit level tended to be informal. Such an approach runs contrary to the 'human resource management' approach because a key feature of 'human resource management' is the importance attributed towards having sophisticated and effective recruitment and selection procedures.[36]

The important message for managers is:

- recognise the importance of a planned and systematic approach to recruitment and selection;
- assess the effectiveness of present policies and design new procedures as necessary; and
- review the methods, skills and techniques of staff selection.

A planned and systematic approach

It is possible to identify five basic stages in a planned and systematic approach to recruitment and selection.

Stage 1 – The need to know about the job to be filled

Is the job really necessary, or can it be covered adequately by reorganising or reallocating other jobs? If the job is necessary, what does it entail? What are the duties and responsibilities attached to the job?

Stage 2 – The need to know about the type of person to do the job

What qualities and attributes are required for a person to perform the job effectively?

Stage 3 – The need to know the likely means of attracting suitable applicants

Is it necessary to recruit outside? If so where are suitable applicants most likely to be found? Which are the best sources of labour and methods of recruitment?

Stage 4 – The need to know how best to assess the candidates' likely suitability for the job

How best should information be collected about the candidates? How should the selection process be planned? What are the most appropriate methods of selection?

Stage 5 – The need for induction and follow-up

How best should the socialisation process be undertaken? How should new members of staff be introduced to the policies, procedures and working practices?

Degree and application

In the smaller hospitality units an elaborate selection procedure may be neither readily practicable nor appropriate, but there is still the need for a planned and systematic approach (Figure 6.4). This provides a framework and set of principles which should underlie all recruitment and selection. Between the larger and the smaller unit there is the difference only of degree and application.

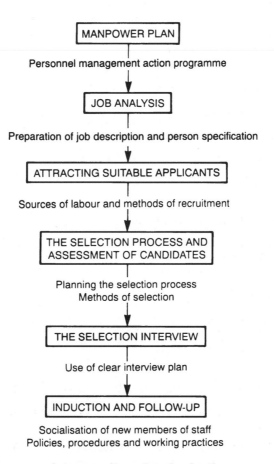

Fig 6.4 A systematic approach to recruitment and selection

Underlying considerations

Whatever the procedures for the selection of staff there are three fundamental considerations which should underlie recruitment policy.

- Recruitment and selection should not be considered in isolation, i.e. simply finding someone to do a particular job, but in the context of the overall manpower plan and personnel management action programme. It may be necessary to consider, for example, the potential for training and future promotion, and adaptability to possible future changes in working practices.
- There is a need to consider not just technical competence and the ability to perform certain tasks, but also sociability. In the hospitality industry it is especially important to consider how new members of staff are likely to fit into the social structure and membership of work groups.
- Recruitment must comply fully with all legal requirements relating to employment and follow recommended codes of practice. It is important to ensure justice and fair treatment to all applicants, and the exercise of 'social' responsibilities, for example the employment of registered disabled people and ethnic minorities.

Failure to employ ethnic minorities

The hotel industry has recently been accused by the Commission for Racial Equality (CRE) of the failure to recruit sufficient staff from ethnic minorities. From its survey of 117 hotels in England, Scotland and Wales, the CRE found that none kept records of the ethnic origins of staff or job applicants. Of those hotels who do hire from ethnic minorities, almost three out of four work as cleaners, waiters and porters.[37] Despite problems attracting and keeping suitable staff, the industry is ignoring the CRE code of practice. The industry is working against its own interests, and failing in its need to increase the number of managers and skilled workers from ethnic minorities. Note, for example, the following section.

Enhancing the recruitment and selection effort

In their discussion of interventions to manage staff turnover (discussed above) Bonn and Forbringer draw attention to the critical activity of recruitment and selection. Approaches that organisations in the American hospitality and other service industries have adopted to enhance the recruitment and selection effort include the following:

- referrals of applicants by family or friends who are given a monetary or other reward if a referred applicant is subsequently hired. An additional reward may also be given if the applicant remains with the organisation for a stated time;
- developing tactics to attract the hiring of minorities, the elderly and handicapped;
- attention to effective selection procedures including identification of the critical activities and duties of a job, and the required skills, knowledge and abilities, realistic job previews, biodata items, personality questionnaires and skills related tests;
- retention programmes such as monetary incentives including profit sharing, share ownership and suggestion schemes, educational incentives where staff can earn cash or credit for educational purposes, and parental leave and child-care programmes.[38]

JOB ANALYSIS

Before undertaking the selection process managers should ask themselves: 'If you do not know about the job to be filled or what sort of person you are looking for, how will you recognise a suitable candidate when you see one?' This underlines the importance of job analysis as central to a systematic approach to recruitment and selection.[39] The use of terms varies but it is generally agreed that 'job analysis' is the process by which you derive (i) a job description, leading to (ii) a person specification.

Job description

The job description explains **the total requirements of the job:** exactly what it is, what it entails, its purpose, duties, activities and responsibilities, and position within the formal structure. An example of a possible list of contents for a job description is given in Figure 6.5.

Job title (whether a new or replacement appointment)

Department/section and location

Wage/salary range

Duties and responsibilities – including *ad hoc* or occasional requirements.
   It may be appropriate here to give precise and detailed information or it may only be necessary to set out the general scope and level of the job. Details may be quantified wherever possible. For example, an *average* of, or perhaps a *minimum* or *maximum* of: meals produced each day, rooms to be cleaned, covers per service, bills prepared each week for departing guests.

   Duties and responsibilities can also be broken down into *approximate* percentage of time likely (or expected) to be devoted to each main activity over the *average* of, say, a week or a month, for example: % organisation of daily servicing and cleaning of guests' rooms, % training of kitchen staff, or % opening and distribution of incoming mail.

Specific limitations on authority
   For example, not to authorise cash purchases above £X per item without prior approval of General Manager; not to accept payment by cheque for bills exceeding £X without authorisation of Head Receptionist .

Responsible to – that is, the job title of immediate superior.
   (This superior would normally expect to be involved in the selection, induction and training programme for the new member of staff.)

Responsible for – that is, the number and job titles of direct subordinates.

Specific functional contacts – main lateral communications and working relationships with staff in other departments/sections.

Signature of head of department/section

Date job description prepared

Fig 6.5 Possible list of contents for a job description
Source: Mullins L J, 'Job Analysis – Know the Job and the Person to do It', *International Journal of Hospitality Management*, vol. 4, no. 4, 1985, p. 181

However, the scope of the job description and the amount of detail it provides may vary among different organisations and different types of job. (Examples of a job description for a Food and Beverage Controller and for a Senior Sous Chef are given in Appendix 2 of this chapter.)

Person specification

A person specification is an extension of the job description and provides a blueprint of **the 'ideal' person to do that job**. The person specification tells you not only about the job but also details the personal attributes and qualities associated with successful performance of the job, for example physical characteristics, experience, technical skills, formal qualifications, personality and temperament, and any special requirements such as the need for mobility. The specification could indicate those characteristics which are regarded as essential and those which are desirable. (An example of a person specification for a Meeting Point Development Manager is given in Appendix 3 of this chapter.)

Preparation of a person specification

When drawing up a person specification regard must be given to the provisions of the Sex Discrimination Act 1975 and the Race Relations Act 1976. Consideration should also be given to whether the job could be performed satisfactorily by a disabled person. From the person specification can be distilled a job advertisement and further particulars available to enquirers.

It should be remembered that you are unlikely to find the perfect or absolutely ideal candidate. The person specification should therefore be prepared in a practical manner and it should not unduly restrict the need for flexibility. 'Exit' interviews with staff can often yield useful information on the actual nature and requirements of the job, and it may be helpful to consider persons known to have performed the job successfully.

Difficulties and distastes of the job

The process of job analysis is even more meaningful if it includes considerations of the difficulties and distastes of the job. These may often go together but this is not necessarily the case.

Difficulties are those aspects of the job which are regarded as particularly demanding or hard to perform competently. Examples might be the bar manager dealing with drunken or unruly guests, waiting staff serving a large number of unexpected customers arriving together, a washer-up scrubbing heavy copper pans, a receptionist dealing with complaints or awkward guests, section heads operating within restricted budget limits.

Distastes are those aspects of the job or working conditions which are regarded as particularly tedious or unpleasant. Examples might be the waiting staff polishing silver before each service, a commis chef preparing the same vegetable day after day for a standard menu, the kitchen porter emptying swill bins, cleaning staff changing soiled bed linen, restaurant staff unblocking the toilet.

It should be recognised, however, that for some people certain perceived 'difficulties' may be an attractive feature of the job. They may enjoy what is seen as the challenge or responsibility that the difficulties of the job present. Also for some people the 'easier' aspects of the job may be disliked and seen as a distaste, for example because of the lack of variety or challenge, or because they prefer to be kept active.

Full knowledge of what the job entails

Although it may be tempting to do so, there is little to be gained from concealing the perceived difficulties or distastes of a job. This is short-sighted. If staff are appointed without full knowledge of what the job actually entails they are likely to join the numbers who leave within the first three months. This only adds to the 'induction crisis' and means starting the recruitment and selection process all over again. Even if staff do stay there is likely to be loss of goodwill, possible mistrust of management, and an adverse effect on their attitude, job satisfaction and work performance.

THE SELECTION PROCESS

The manner in which the selection process is planned and conducted is doubly important. It should of course be efficient in its own right to ensure that every effort is made to reach the 'best' decision. Equally important, however, is that for most candidates the selection process is the first point of contact with the hotel or other organisation. Candidates will tend to judge the hotel as a whole by the manner in which the selection process is conducted, looking upon this as an indication of how it manages itself and its staff. **The other side of the selection process is the candidates' acceptance of you and the hotel.**

Methods of selection

There are a variety of methods which can be used in staff selection. These include peer rating, in-tray exercises, selection tests and personality questionnaires, group exercises and individual (one-to-one), panel or board interviews.[40]

The design of the selection process is a matter of choice within each individual unit. It should be designed to meet specific requirements and matched to available facilities, both personal and physical. The choice, combination and application of methods should be appropriate to the nature and type of unit, the position, tasks and responsibilities of the vacant position and the number of candidates.

The selection interview

Although often criticised, the interview is usually the central and indispensable element of the selection process. The interview involves an interaction of personalities and perception of other people. It is important, therefore, to bear in mind the possibility of perceptual distortions and errors, such as the 'halo effect' and stereotyping, which we discussed in Chapter 2.

Candidates tend to copy the mannerisms and postures of the interviewer. A seating arrangement which is comfortable and informal helps candidates to be more at ease and reduces the element of confrontation. Candidates should be encouraged to do most of the talking and asked questions that will encourage them to describe experiences and develop ideas.

The interviewer should probe the candidates and ask meaningful, searching and practical questions. Skilled interviewers will know how to change their interview style and form of questions according to the behaviour of candidates and the extent of their social skills. Interviewers should listen carefully, observe how candidates respond to a question, and be responsive to both verbal and non-verbal cues and body language.

Interview on the move

The traditional face-to-face interview can be augmented by taking candidates round the organisation and conducting a two-way interview 'on the move'. This enables candidates to gain a fuller appreciation of the job, equipment and methods, and working conditions. It gives candidates an opportunity to meet some of the staff and to see them at work, and to ask further questions. An additional advantage of the interview on the move is that the selector is able to observe what are likely to be more natural responses of the candidates to actual situations.

The interview plan

In order to make a fair and objective assessment of candidates you must know what information is needed and how best to collect this from the interview. A clear interview plan is necessary. Two of the most popular examples of an interview plan are the Rodger Seven Point Plan[41] and the Munro Fraser Five Point Plan[42] (Figure 6.6). But whatever plan is used, by the end of the interview all points should have been covered adequately.

The important thing is that some suitable plan is used. Many organisations have their own interview plan/checklist. The plan should be appropriate to the desired characteristics of the candidates and specific interview checklists may be drawn up for particular appointments.

Each of the headings in the interview plan can be related to the requirements of the job, and to the essential and desirable characteristics looked for in candidates. It is important, however, that interviewers should avoid simply going through a list. Information should be assembled not necessarily in any set order, but under each heading as it is encountered during the interview discussion.

INDUCTION AND FOLLOW-UP

We have seen that staff turnover is particularly high during the first three months of employment – the induction crisis. We have also referred to the high costs of recruiting and engaging new members of staff. This draws attention to the importance of an effective induction programme. Induction involves the introduction and socialisation of a new member of staff to the culture of the organisation, to its policies, procedures and working practices, and to other members of staff.

The first impressions of the organisation and its managers are seldom forgotten. New members of staff face an unfamiliar working environment and have to make a number of personal adjustments. A warm welcome, initial introductions, and a properly planned and conducted induction programme will do much to reassure members, and aid their motivation and attitudes to work performance. Induction is a key factor in the longer-term retention of staff.

(a)   1   *Physical make-up*
Are there any defects of health or physique that may be of occupational importance? How agreeable are appearance, bearing and speech?

2.   *Attainments*
What type of education? How well achieved educationally? What occupational training and experience had already? How well done occupationally?

3.   *General intelligence*
How much general intelligence can be displayed? How much general intelligence ordinarily displayed?

4.   *Special aptitudes*
Any marked mechanical aptitude, manual dexterity, facility in the use of words or figures, talent for drawing or music?

5.   *Interests*
To what extent are interests intellectual, practical–constructional, physically active, social, artistic?

6.   *Disposition*
How acceptable to other people? Influence on other people? Steady and dependable? Self-reliant?

7.   *Circumstances*
What are the domestic circumstances? What do the other members of the family do for a living? Are there any special openings available?

(b)   (i)   *Impact on others* – such as an individual's appearance, speech and manner.

(ii)   *Qualifications and experience* – the knowledge and skills required by different types of work.

(iii)   *Innate abilities* – the speed and accuracy with which an individual's mind works.

(iv)   *Motivation* – the kind of work that appeals to an individual and how much effort the individual is prepared to apply to it.

(v)   *Emotional adjustment* – the amount of stress involved in living and working with other people.

Fig 6.6 Examples of selection interview plans
(a) The Seven Point Plan
Source: Adapted from Rodger A, *The Seven Point Plan*, Third edition, National Foundation for Educational Research (1970)
(b) The Five Point Plan
Source Fraser J M, *Employment Interviewing*, Fifth edition, Macdonald & Evans (1978)

The induction training programme

Induction is viewed best as a natural extension of the recruitment and selection process, starting at the interview and covering the first few months at work. The induction programme should be designed to help new members of staff to familiarise themselves with their new environment, to settle easily into their new jobs and to establish good working relationships with other members of staff.

Given the cosmopolitan nature of the hospitality industry, a particular feature of the selection process is the recognition of different cultural and ethnic values, discussed in Chapter 2. Induction training should make clear the nature of a multi-cultural working environment, and the need for integration and for people to work together harmoniously.

It is important to remember that people cannot fully absorb a large amount of information at one time, particularly in what is likely to be a strange and initially uncomfortable environment. The induction programme should therefore be planned carefully and staggered over a reasonable period of time. Video presentations can form a useful part of induction training.[43] But whatever the nature of the programme, if induction is to be effective it requires reinforcement and regular review and follow-up sessions. It will also involve the active co-operation of managers, supervisors and colleagues.

Design of the induction programme

The design and content of the induction programme is a matter of choice for each individual unit and its particular circumstances. Different members of staff will require different forms of induction depending upon, for example, their knowledge and previous experience, and the type and level of their new job. Nevertheless, it is important that some suitable form of induction is carried out for all new staff including managerial appointments.[44]

A comprehensive induction training programme could include such information as the following:

- the nature of the unit, its facilities and services, and type of guests or customers;
- requirements of the job and to whom responsible, and any subordinate staff;
- main terms and conditions of employment including circumstances which could lead to dismissal, and disciplinary and grievance procedures;
- introductions to working colleagues, and the work and functions of other relevant departments;
- the management structure including responsibilities for the personnel function;
- the physical layout of the unit and the use of equipment;
- any special policies or procedures, and any house rules such as no eating or drinking, or no-smoking areas;
- fire, health and safety regulations;
- trade union membership, staff representations, consultation and communications, suggestion schemes;
- social and welfare facilities;
- opportunities for training and personal development.

Staff induction manuals

It is helpful to provide a Staff Induction Manual or Employee's Guide which sets out and elaborates the above information. The manual could be used to incorporate checklists and a personal log book, and also to include any additional information useful to members of staff. (Details of the Employee's Guide for The Savoy are given in Appendix 4 of this chapter.)

EDUCATION, TRAINING AND DEVELOPMENT

Staff are a crucial but expensive resource and it is important to optimise their contribution to improving effective organisational performance. A significant factor in the image of the hospitality industry, in the performance and retention of employees and in levels of productivity is the extent and quality of staff education, training and development.

The ultimate purpose of training is to help the industry improve its operational effectiveness and its economic and competitive performance, including the ability to cope with future challenges. Closer links between Britain and other members of the European Union further emphasise the importance of vocational education and training. And training is clearly an important feature of international hospitality management.

Training needs within the industry

The HCTC report has drawn attention to training needs within the industry. College output from hotel and catering courses is likely to meet less than 28% of the annual replacement needs for skilled personnel in the industry and less than 70% of demand for qualified managers. Formal qualifications held by staff within the industry are generally one level lower than their equivalents in other industries. Thirty per cent of managers still have no formal qualifications compared to 12% of managers in the economy as a whole.[45]

A recent NEDC report has also indicated that productivity in British hotels is lower than that in France and Germany. In the case of Germany this is attributed largely to the attention given to vocational training and education. In order to improve productivity in Britain the industry requires an improved trained and qualified workforce.[46]

The importance of training

Training is necessary to ensure an adequate supply of staff who are technically and socially competent, and capable of career progression. The objective of training is to enhance knowledge and skills, and to develop attitudes. A central and indispensable part of the training provision is related to task and on-the-job performance and the delivery of service.

Training also forms a basis for both individual development and management succession including, for example, the acceptance and practice of delegation and empowerment, problem-solving and decision-making, teamworking and responsibility for quality standards.[47] Training for change is also vital for the long-term survival of an organisation. Increasing emphasis is being placed on both the need for continuous training to support change and on training as a vital investment for the future.[48]

It is widely accepted that training can lead to many potential benefits for both individuals and the organisation. It is a key element in the morale, job satisfaction and commitment of staff, and in improved delivery of service and customer relationships, and economic performance. However, despite an apparent recognition of the importance of training there seems doubt as to what actually happens in practice, and the extent to which the industry or employers evaluate the scope, relevance or effectiveness of its education and training programmes.[49]

An integral part of business strategy

In order to pursue a positive policy of investing in people it is necessary to demonstrate a continuous commitment to education, training and development as an integral part of business strategy.[50] There has to be active support from top management and throughout all levels of the organisation. Attention should be given to the maintenance of training standards. Training should be real, operational and rewarding.

Employees should receive positive recognition for good training achievements, for example through increased job satisfaction, higher wages or greater opportunities for career advancement. Successful training requires the co-operation of line managers, adequate finance and resources, time, skilled staff and a supporting appraisal system. In order to secure the full benefits of successful training there must therefore be a planned and systematic approach to the effective management of training.[51]

Management development

The quality of management is one of the most important factors in the effectiveness of any organisation including those in the hospitality industry. Management succession planning is necessary to ensure that a sufficient supply of appropriately qualified and capable men and women are available to meet the present and future needs of the organisation. Managers need an appropriate balance of technical, social and conceptual knowledge and skills (discussed in Chapter 5). An essential component of an effective training programme therefore is management development.

Management development is an organisational concept and should take place within the framework of a clear policy related to the nature, objectives and requirements of the organisation as a whole including the effective management of people. Managers need to be equipped to deal with the critical issues and requirements facing the particular organisation and the demands of specific managerial jobs. Linked to succession planning and management development should be a programme of planned career progression supported by a performance review system.

Mullins and Aldrich have constructed an integrated model of managerial behaviour and development[52] which applies as much to the hospitality industry as to any other business organisation.[53] However, despite the obvious importance of effective management for the hospitality industry, it is not clear how much attention is really given to management education and development. For example, Wood casts doubt about the quality and standards of hotel and catering management education, and the level of professionalisation and qualifications of its managers.[54] In order to achieve improved organisational performance the industry must ensure the development of both present and future management. There is a continual need for effective managerial development.

EFFECTIVENESS OF THE PERSONNEL FUNCTION

However the personnel function is organised, proper attention to the establishment of good personnel policies, including employee relations and training, will help to improve the efficiency of the workforce and standards of service to customers. Greater use should be made of specialist personnel managers, the involvement of line managers and modern methods of personnel management.

Attention to human resource management

Greater attention to human resource management and the personnel function will of course cost money. Unfortunately the industry has a reputation for short-term cost-consciousness and the widely held view that every activity should be seen as making a direct working contribution to profitability.

According to Umbreit, the hospitality industry traditionally has given only obligatory lip service to the concept of human resource management. Although top management express a high level of interest in human resources, the focus of the hospitality industry's efforts are on short-term profitability and market-related operational issues.[55] Hotel managers from three separate companies were asked to weight the importance of seven manager performance dimensions. Hotel managers from all three companies gave the lowest value to dimensions relating to communicating with employees and to handling personnel responsibilities.

Umbreit identifies three conditions for change: demographic shifts in the labour force, the need to be more customer-centred, and the evolving nature of hospitality education. Repeat business is crucial to the success of the hospitality operation. The quality of services to the customer provided by members of staff dictates that greater management attention be given to human resource development.

Balance between cost and long-term benefits

The ultimate measure of the effectiveness of the personnel function is the contribution it makes to the objectives of the organisation and to improved organisational performance. But achievement in the area of personnel management is difficult to measure and it is not easy to establish satisfactory methods of assessment. There is also the more general problem of assessing managerial work where the end-product results from the efforts of other people.[56]

Cost is obviously a major consideration but should not be viewed in isolation. Not every activity can be identified clearly as making a direct contribution to profitability. A balance must be kept between more easily identified financial costs of the personnel function and less readily apparent but very important long-term benefits which also make a positive contribution to the effectiveness of hospitality operations.

Contribution of the personnel function

The contributions from an effective personnel function are not always readily apparent nor are they easy to identify. Over a period of time, however, some quantified measures should provide management with an indication of its effectiveness. Possible examples include labour costs, staff turnover and stability index, complaints from customers, absenteeism/timekeeping, breakages, scrap or waste, accidents at work, promotions and staff development, discipline and grievance procedures, and dismissals.

The nature of human resource management will determine both business efficiency and the performance of individual members. Account must be taken of intangible benefits such as improved morale, job satisfaction and staff development. The attitudes, behaviour and performance of staff, and thus the performance of the hospitality organisation, will be influenced by sound personnel policies and an effective personnel function.

SUMMARY

- The human element plays a major part in customer satisfaction and in the overall success of the organisation. This places particular emphasis on human resource management. Whether or not there is a separate personnel department it is still important to give proper attention to the personnel function. Personnel policies are a reflection of the overall style of management.
- The implementation of personnel practices should be based on underlying philosophies of managerial behaviour and employee relationships. The personnel function is a shared responsibility among top management, line managers and supervisors, and the personnel manager. Sound personnel policies and practices help foster good employee relations.
- The high level of staff turnover in the industry should be recognised as a problem area which demands management attention. It is important to attract and retain staff with the right skills and abilities to satisfy the demands of the customer. An effective system of manpower planning provides the trigger for an effective management action programme.
- Most managers are likely to be faced with the frequent need to recruit and select staff. This requires a planned and systematic approach including recognition of underlying considerations. Careful attention should be given to the process of job analysis, to the planning and conduct of the selection process, and to an effective induction programme.
- A key factor in the image of the hospitality industry, staff retention and level of productivity is training including managerial development. Training should be an integral part of the business strategy of the organisation. Greater attention to the personnel function will cost money but must be balanced against the long-term benefits to improved organisational effectiveness.

APPENDIX 1: PERSONNEL AND TRAINING REORGANISATION FOR FORTE HOTELS

Introduction

Forte Hotels is an international hotel and catering company operating throughout the world with its head office in the UK.

As part of Forte PLC, the group's principal activities are the operation of an extensive network of hotels (primarily in the UK, rest of Europe and USA), a range of branded restaurants, the provision of in-flight catering services and retail services at UK airports.

Forte Hotels operates around 855 units throughout the world, ranging from Forte Travelodge to Exclusive Hotels of the World.

During 1992/93, against a background of a deepening recession in the UK which depressed domestic demand, and an uncompetitive exchange rate which deterred overseas visitors, Forte concentrated its energies on three key business objectives. They were:

- **ensuring that the products were leaders in the increasingly competitive markets** in which they operated;
- **winning market share** by enhancing sales & marketing activities; and
- **improving profit margins** by reducing costs.

As part of this strategy Forte Hotels **rebranded its hotels** to provide itself with a competitive edge. In doing this there was a clearer definition of the product which resulted from the creation of individual brands, i.e. Forte Posthouse, Forte Crest and Forte Travelodge and collections of hotels i.e. Forte Heritage, Forte Grand and Forte Exclusive.

The other main focus of activity was **cost reduction** where concentration was on **structural changes** which produced permanent cost savings, increased efficiency and in turn improvements in the standards of service offered to the customer. Examples here are the elimination of levels of management to bring decision-makers closer to the customer, more effective use of technology, and significantly the **regionalisation of support services** to decrease administration costs at individual hotels.

The personnel and training function prior to reorganisation

Up until August 1992 each brand or collection of hotels, e.g. Forte Posthouse, Forte Heritage, was co-ordinated by a personnel and training executive at head office level. Then within every hotel unit there was a personnel and training manager. The hotel personnel and training manager, although liaising with the personnel and training executives, actually reported to the hotel general manager.

This structure gave rise to a number of disadvantages and problems.

- In reality the depth of knowledge and experience of the individuals employed at the unit level varied enormously and in the majority of cases they were relatively junior individuals with limited knowledge and practical experience.
- Each unit had in the view of the hotel brand senior management team very different priorities. This meant that activities across all units were different and difficult to compare.
- Priorities identified in the local units in many cases could be out of line with company overall priorities. Each manager had their own personal agenda of what was required.
- The pressing requirement to restructure many activities across the company was considered to be prejudiced by the level of professionalism in the personnel and training 'specialists' in the hotels.
- Salary levels of personnel and training individuals varied greatly from unit to unit, and with unclear definition of how each rate was determined.
- Some of the individuals employed were at a starting point in a management career and were using the position as a stepping stone towards general management so were sometimes not committed to the specialist personnel function long term.
- To continue with the existing structure would create an ongoing programme of training junior management to become personnel and training specialists during a time when they were not sure about their future and had limited experience in management.

- This gave rise to a lack of clear direction and purpose.
- Personnel and training performance in a unit was directly linked to one individual and created a lack of consistency when people moved across units.
- Lack of local expertise created a logjam in the head office function as each head office manager looked after approximately 60 units and queries/problems came directly from the hotel general manager or the local personnel and training manager to the centre.
- There was a lack of sharing of best practices and resources as no personnel function networks had been set up to facilitate this.
- Being responsible for both personnel and training functions created a 'tug of war' effect and a very careful balancing act was needed to ensure that both of these functions were provided with due care and attention.
- The local personnel and training manager reported to the local unit general manager who may or may not have been interested in personnel and training activities. Forte is very focused on the achievement of consistent standards across all of the hotels in each brand or collection. This key senior management objective was much harder to achieve when the local manager did not dedicate much resource to the personnel and training function.
- The local personnel and training managers were sucked into the day-to-day running of the business and often ended up as duty operations managers rather than personnel and training specialists.
- There were severe cost implications with each unit having its own personnel and training manager and in larger units a team of up to seven people.
- Relatively little emphasis was placed on the growth of the specialist skills of the personnel and training manager, with any training or development given being mainly in basic skills.

All of these areas were important to consider before proposing any change but the future direction and intentions of the company were also of major significance.

Reorganisation of the personnel and training function

A project team was formed to review and discuss at length the issues and to consider ways to successfully decentralise. The brief for the group was to agree a strategy and plan its implementation and from within this group a proposal was put forward for the endorsement of the main board. On receipt of this approval the implementation of the proposal began.

The project team carefully considered the options and then put forward an initial proposal for approval from the human resources directorate. On gaining approval in principle, the agreed proposal was then worked into a detailed plan including how each part of the plan would be implemented. Again these proposals were then discussed with the human resources directorate and a project plan agreed with clear deadlines for implementation identified.

It should be noted that when first looking at this area the broader aim was to design and develop an effective organisation which would respond appropriately to change. Indeed it proved to be a launch vehicle for other significant changes within other functions of the business. By reviewing the needs of the business for the future this highlighted the growing need to have a more cost effective structure with fewer management layers and decisions being taken at a lower level to speed up responsiveness and reaction times.

It also became apparent that there had to be an effective personnel and training structure in place to facilitate future structural changes in other areas within the company, e.g. the finance function and maintenance services.

After reviewing the hotels business plan to highlight the key requirements for the personnel and training function a review was then carried out of the existing structure. As well as considering the disadvantages of the existing structure it was important to identify the positive aspects.

- Individuals were on-site at one unit and so were able to react quickly to situations arising within that unit.
- A personalised service was tailored to the needs of each individual unit.
- Staff and management had easier access to local personnel and training services.
- A personnel and training individual was able to build up close working relationships with local management and staff.
- It was easier for the personnel and training manager to get to know the local market and conditions in greater depth.
- Time was available for the personnel and training personnel to become involved in more day-to-day activities.
- The personnel and training personnel became very involved in the commercial and operational aspects of the individual unit.
- The personnel and training personnel provided hands-on assistance to the local management team.
- Personnel and training managers were directly involved in both personnel and training activities hence widening their scope of responsibility.

Objectives of personnel and training restructuring

- To put in place a structure to match the future needs of the business and to assist in major structural change and employment conditions change, i.e. the 'manpower strategy'.
- To reduce 'fixed' costs of running the business by reducing the personnel and training headcount needed to achieve these objectives.
- To enhance the professionalism of the human resources function.
- To increase the personnel and training accountability at all levels.
- To work as a team across all hotels in line with clear, agreed and consistent business objectives.
- To create consistent standards in approach and use the advantages of combined efforts.
- To provide enhanced communication channels to improve our front-line responsiveness.
- To increase specialist personnel and training networking and benefit from the sharing of best practices and experiences.

The perceived benefits of making the changes

For the company:
- higher capability of specialists available at unit level;
- more efficient and safe decision-making locally;
- greater network potential/linkage of hotels;
- part of the 'bigger team';
- reduced reliance on limited central resource;
- co-ordinated yet separate personnel and training activity;
- more planned activity/less reactivity;
- cost effective;
- integrated yet stand alone from operation;
- communication.

For the individual:
- visible and defined career path/progression;
- clear identity/job role;
- able to develop experience through qualifications;
- high level of interest/variety;
- defined level of authority/autonomy.

Reorganised structure

Building from the tasks identified the structure shown in Figure 6.7 was agreed.

In determining the number and make-up of the district teams consideration was given to the annual turnover of the properties, staff headcount and geographical locations and constraints. The final determination was that from operating about 240 hotels (UK only) they would now link into about 35 districts. These districts would be at varying levels of complexity and seniority to allow for a range of district positions to be available. In this way optimisation of current resources was possible and would also offer potential for career development and promotional prospects in the future.

From the size and complexity of the district it was also decided that in some cases a secondary role of a district personnel officer would be required and administration resources should also be considered.

Geography did play a large part in determining the new set-up as consideration had to be given to the need for district personnel managers to travel to units and long travelling distances would be expensive in both time and money.

The author is grateful to the Human Resources Department, Forte Hotels, for providing the above information.

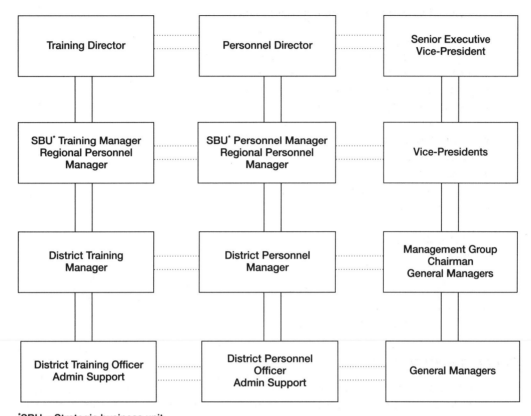

*SBU = Strategic business unit

Fig 6.7 Reorganised structure of personnel and training function at Forte Hotels

APPENDIX 2: THE COMPLEAT ANGLER HOTEL, MARLOW – JOB DESCRIPTION

(a)

Department: **Food & beverage**
Job title: **Food & Beverage Controller**
Responsible to: **Food & Beverage Manager**
Purpose of position: To provide the Food & Beverage Manager, Accountant, and Heads of Department with accurate cost of sales information. To maintain food and beverage cost control systems and procedures/to maximise profits, consistent with five star quality and service.

Overall duties:

1. *Receiving*
a) All goods must be checked in and have orders and delivery notes signed.

b) Check goods to check on any sub-standard purchase, and resolve the problem with both the deliverer and the supplier.

c) Monitor the receipt and storage of goods to respective areas, i.e. Drystores, Cellar, Glass, China, Silver and Chemicals.

2. *Storage & Issuing*

a) Ensure all goods are secured properly in locked storerooms and monitor all keys to such areas.

b) Maintain a daily, weekly and cumulative monthly account for food and beverage requisitions and of direct purchases with no requisition.

3. *Inventories of Stores*
   Take monthly inventories of china, glassware, silverware, chemicals and stationery.

4. *Ordering*
   Ordering liquor, dry stores, chemicals, stationery and tobacco.

5. *Reporting & Forecasting*

a) Cost requisitions and direct issues on a daily basis and produce daily food cost.

b) Prepare on a monthly basis food and beverage reconciliation of cost, bars and break down (long term).

c) Balance reconciliations with total purchases passed for payment.

d) Checking and verification of all food and beverage invoices and passing them for payment.

e) To submit the food invoices on relevant Food Invoice Return Sheets to the Accountant on a weekly basis.

General:
(Including scope, supervision, responsibility and authority.)

a) Must be able to deal with all levels of Management and staff.

b) Report all trends in market fluctuations to the Hotel Accountant and Food & Beverage Manager to affect purchasing.

To be fully conversant with the following:

1. The Hotel and Company Fire Procedures.

2. The Company Health and Safety policy and Hotel Health and Safety procedures.

Occasional duties:
To assist with any reasonable request that may be made by the management team regarding food and beverage.

Prepared by .... Date ....

Signature of employee ....

Date ....

(b)

Position: Senior Sous Chef
Responsible to: Executive Chef
Responsible for: Sous Chefs, Chef de Parties, Commis Chefs, Kitchen Assistants, Staff Restaurant Assistants, Storeman.
Working liaison: Restaurant and other food areas.
Scope & general purpose: To assist the Executive Chef in supervising the production and service of food to the agreed standards, ensuring complete guest satisfaction and comfort whilst ensuring maximum profitability is achieved as set out in the departmental budget.

Main duties:
1. To ensure a high standard of food presentation and service is achieved at all times in both the main kitchen and coffee shop kitchen according to the standards in the departmental S.O.P. manuals and service schedules.
2. To ensure all cleaning schedules are carried out effectively and that hygiene standards are maintained.
3. To assist the Executive Chef in weekly stocktaking.
4. To ensure that Food Hygiene Regulations are adhered to at all times, ensuring food is stored correctly, eliminating wastage and contamination.
5. To assist the Executive Chef in arranging induction and training of new staff to meet the required company standards and assisting in the maintenance of departmental training records.
6. To achieve, and maintain the agreed stock levels, by effective ordering, in line with production schedules.
7. In conjunction with the Executive Chef to be fully conversant with good gross profits, ensuring they meet the hotel's budgeted figures by careful control and monitoring of food production.
8. To ensure that a high standard of food service is maintained in the Staff Restaurant.
9. To be fully aware of all in-house food promotions.
10. To deputise for the Executive Chef, in his/her absence assuming total responsibility.
11. To ensure all cleaning materials and equipment within the department are used in accordance with the manufacturer's specifications and as laid down in the S.O.P. Manuals.
12. To aid the image of the hotel by a good personal appearance at all times, and a high standard of work presentation in the areas you are responsible for.
13. To supervise and produce varied menus for the staff restaurant ensuring a very high standard of food within the budgets.
14. To report all accidents to the Personnel Manager immediately.

Staff responsibilities:
1. To work closely with colleagues, to develop Team spirit and to achieve standards of work, as laid down in the S.O.P. Manual.
2. To put guest care as a priority, with every effort being made to meet guests' needs with all comments/complaints being actioned, following procedures laid down by Hotel Policy.
3. To aid the image of the hotel by good personal appearance, a pleasant and helpful manner and ensuring a high standard of work in the areas you are responsible for.

4. To communicate with other departments and to be aware of special promotions and facilities available in other areas, to assist the smooth running of the Operation.
5. To assist with Training of new staff within the department, as required by Company Policy.
6. To be aware of all factors relating to the care of children, as required by Company Policy.
7. To understand the procedure to follow in the event of Fire, as laid down in the Hotel Fire Plan and by the Fire Precautions Act 1971.
8. To be fully conversant with factors relating to Hygiene and Safety as outlined in the Health and Safety at Work Act 1974.
9. To work in other departments in the hotel in line with the business demand and to ensure total guest care.

Prepared by .... Date ....

Signature of employee ....

Date ....

APPENDIX 3: THE COMPLEAT ANGLER HOTEL, MARLOW – PERSON SPECIFICATION

Meeting Point Development Manager

Area of expertise	Essential	Desirable
1. Physical:	Fit, healthy	Age 25+
2. Appearance:	Smart, fresh, presentable	
3. Education/qualification:	To secondary level TS1 and TS2. Previous training experience	Previous training in hotels environment. Conference organiser
4. Intellectual ability:	Confident in product. Perceptive	Enlightened
5. Management style:	Eye for detailed accuracy. Obsessed with customer care	Empathetic
6. Technical skill:	To demonstration level with most audio-visual equipment	Carahost knowledge
7. Technical knowledge:	Full product and delivery strengths and weaknesses	Facilities of most hotels. Opportunities and threats
8. Commercial acumen:	Good risk assessor. Negotiation skills	Sales trainer
9. Skill with people (staff):	Get things done. Co-ordinated. Organised. Developer through influence	Well liked
10. Skill with people (guests):	Good listener. Fulfils promises and expectations	Well liked. Positive extrovert. Confident in a crisis
11. Communication:	Good listener. Effective in verbal and written forms. Strong presentation skills	Quick unconfused thinker
12. Motivation:	Stimulates interest in fulfilling the job	Leader
13. Circumstances:	Flexible. Clean driving licence	No regular commitments

Appendices 2 and 3 reproduced by permission of Carolyn Moth, District Personnel Manager, Forte Grand South.

APPENDIX 4: THE SAVOY HOTEL – STAFF HANDBOOK

The Staff handbook opens with the following introduction.

Director and
General Manager

> Welcome to **The Savoy.** I am delighted you have joined our team, not only as an employee but also as a custodian, to ensure preservation of the standards which make **The Savoy** the most famous hotel in the world.
>
> **The Savoy** was founded on family tradition and has always been concerned with the training and development of its staff. It is for this reason that **The Savoy** has become a cornerstone of our profession and is affectionately known at the 'University of the Industry'. Its reputation for elegance, excellence and efficient service inspires many to begin and further their careers here, and we are relying on you to continue this tradition.
>
> I trust that you will enjoy your time with us and appreciate the great social panorama of events and people you will witness. **The Savoy** has participated in history for the past one hundred years – from the first radio broadcast to the first private cable television – always aided by a staff dedicated to maintaining the tradition of the highest standards.
>
> Herbert Striessnig

This is followed by a comprehensive list of contents including information on the following:

- The Savoy – background information, and company history;
- personnel office, personal appearance, identity cards, personal property, smoking, security;
- employment – recording attendance, pay, overtime, holidays, sick pay, pension schemes, confidential information, termination of employment;
- disciplinary rules and procedures, grievance procedures;
- training and development;
- health and safety – policy and responsibilities, hygiene, first aid, reporting accidents, safety checking;
- employee of the month award, staff social activities, staff introductory bonus.

Reproduced by permission of Eric Beckley, Head of Personnel and Training, The Savoy Hotel.

REVIEW AND DISCUSSION QUESTIONS

1 Explain the importance of effective human resource management within the hospitality industry. How would you distinguish between personnel management and human resource management?

2 Discuss the nature of the personnel function as a shared responsibility. What are the justifications for personnel management specialists? To what extent do you accept the suggestion that every manager is a personnel manager?

3 Explain the importance of an effective employee relations policy. Suggest main headings for

those matters about which it is useful for an employer to have a considered policy of employee relations.

4   Give your own reasons to explain the generally high levels of staff turnover in the hospitality industry. What are the costs involved? What actions would you recommend be taken to help reduce the level of staff turnover?

5   Explain the importance and main stages of manpower planning. Discuss fully the potential benefits of manpower planning.

6   Give your views on the fundamental considerations which should underlie the recruitment and selection of staff. Outline the basic stages in a planned and systematic approach to staff recruitment and selection. In your experience, to what extent are these basic steps followed within the hospitality industry?

7   Give main headings for a possible list of contents for: (i) a job description; and (ii) a person specification. Provide your own examples of possible difficulties and distastes of hotel jobs.

8   Suggest what measures might be applied to help evaluate the effectiveness and contribution of the personnel function within the hospitality industry.

ASSIGNMENT

Assume that a vacancy has arisen for a *new* senior or supervisory position of your choice in a large hospitality organisation.

(i)   State clearly the nature of this new position and prepare a detailed job description and person specification. Include what you believe to be the likely difficulties and distastes of the job.

(ii)   Explain how you would plan and conduct the selection process, and the methods of selection that would be most appropriate for this particular appointment.

(iii) Design a suitable induction programme specifying the duration, timing and contents of the programme, including the departments and persons involved.

CASE STUDY 1

Valuation of human assets

It is easy to appreciate the financial value of professional footballers. First, note that the clubs in the football league are all limited companies with shares and shareholders, boards of directors, fixed assets, current assets and liabilities. Does it matter whether the manager and the players win or lose matches? Does it affect the number of people who pay to watch future matches? Is it only footballers we can think of as having price tags? Consider the following case.

The Regal Hotel
Two years ago Quentin bought the Regal Hotel for £600 000. He was advised that hoteliers could expect a return of 10 per cent on their capital and, as the hotel was making a profit of about £60 000 a year, the price seemed fair. He had been impressed with the high

standard of service and the excellent cuisine as well as the furniture and general appearance of the hotel.

Quentin had had no previous experience of running a hotel, nor of man management, and within a few months he started to have personality clashes with his staff. After six months he lost his highly talented chef and since then there has been a succession of mediocre chefs, none of whom has stayed more than a few months. Customers began to complain about the foods and this made it unpleasant for the waiters.

Disenchanted with the hotel business, Quentin has now gone back to the agent who sold him the business.

'I want to sell,' he says, 'I just can't get good staff. I know prices of hotels like this haven't gone up. I'll be satisfied if you sell it at the price I paid for it.'

'What profit did you make last year?' the agent asks. '£40 000,' says Quentin.

If hoteliers can expect a return of 10 per cent on their capital, how much would you pay for the Regal Hotel now?

Why do you think Quentin's profits dropped from £60 000 to £40 000?

Reprinted from Chilver J, *Finance*, Stanley Thornes Ltd (1990), p. 182. With kind permission of Stanley Thornes Ltd.

CASE STUDY 2

All change at Crown and Sceptre

Susan Kennedy has recently been appointed to head the new human resources function of the Crown and Sceptre Hotels Limited group. Until recently comprising just the one hotel, Crown and Sceptre have now added a further five properties to the company which employs a total of 650 full, part-time and casual staff. All hotels in the group are in the three-star market with between 100 and 170 bedrooms, and situated within a 30-mile radius of each other. The original Crown and Sceptre has taken over the role of head office.

Prior to the takeover, all the separate hotels had very much their own individual culture and style of operations, and there is clearly some resistance to belonging to a larger grouping. General managers appear reluctant to 'toe the corporate line', particularly if they perceive this to devalue their ability to make decisions over such matters as, for example, staffing levels and salary reviews.

The organisation of the personnel function appears to be somewhat haphazard. Kennedy herself reports to the chief accountant who, in turn, reports to the managing director. The personnel department consists of a recruitment and training officer, a personnel administration clerk and a secretary shared with the chief accountant. None of the other hotels in the group has any full-time personnel staff. Matters relating to this area are usually handled by the assistant manager and general manager's secretary, with wages being administered by each individual accounts office.

The chief accountant has, on a number of occasions, expressed concern about the organisation of the personnel function throughout the group and feels there is an urgent need for attention to such matters as standardisation, policy-making and strategic planning. The managing director, however, is wary about how the general managers will react to any suggested changes and is unsure of the scope or extent of centralisation/decentralisation which is desirable.

A main concern of the chief accountant is to determine which human resource functions should be accorded priority over the next year and during the next five years. However, the managing director seems more interested in ensuring that all staff within the enlarged group identify with corporate aims and objectives, and how they can best be inculcated into the culture of the new organisation.

Kennedy herself believes that the management of human resources is equally haphazard and considers there is a clear need for improvement, including urgent attention to modern personnel procedures and practices.

As the 'personnel specialist' Kennedy has now been asked by the managing director to put forward a detailed set of specific recommendations.

This case study has been prepared jointly with, and from original material provided by, the author's colleague Karen Meudell, University of Portsmouth.

NOTES AND REFERENCES

1. *Meeting Competence Needs in the Hotel and Catering Industry: Now and in the Future*, HCTC Research Report, September 1992.
2. See, for example, Maher A, 'Accounting for Human Resources in UK Hotels', *Proceedings of CHME Research Conference*, Manchester Metropolitan University, April 1993.
3. Mullins L J, 'The Personnel Function', *HCIMA Journal*, no. 94, October 1979, pp. 22–25.
4. Willman P, 'Human Resource Management in the Service Sector', in Jones P (ed), *Management in Service Industries*, Pitman (1989), p. 210.
5. Guest D E, 'Human Resource Management and Industrial Relations', *Journal of Management Studies*, vol. 24, no. 5, September 1987, pp. 503–521.
6. Cuming M W, *The Theory and Practice of Personnel Management*, Sixth edition, Heinemann (1989).
7. Maher A, 'Accounting for Human Resources in UK Hotels', *Proceedings of CHME Research Conference*, Manchester Metropolitan University, April 1993.
8. Venison P, *Managing Hotels*, Heinemann (1983), p. 111.
9. Agnew N, 'How to Create Management to Serve Industry's Needs', *Caterer and Hotelkeeper*, 18 January 1979, p. 55.
10. Forte R, 'How I See the Personnel Function', *Personnel Management*, August 1982, pp. 32–35.
11. Hornsey T and Dann D, *Manpower Management in the Hotel and Catering Industry*, Batsford (1984), p. 24.
12. Boella M J, *Human Resource Management in the Hotel and Catering Industry*, Fourth edition, Hutchinson (1987), p. 37.
13. Information and Advisory Services, Institute of Personnel Management.
14. Mullins L J, 'The Personnel Function – A Shared Responsibility', *Administrator*, vol. 5, no. 5, May 1985, pp. 14–16.
15. Forte R, 'How I See the Personnel Function', *Personnel Management*, August 1982, p. 32.
16. Thomason G F, *A Textbook of Personnel Management*, Fourth edition, Institute of Personnel Management (1981).
17. Goss-Turner S, 'Human Resource Management', in Jones P and Pizam A (eds), *The International Hospitality Industry: Organizational and Operational Issues*, Pitman (1993), pp. 152–164.
18. *Employee Relations for the Hotel and Catering Industry*, Seventh edition, HCTC, 1990, p. 9.
19. Cuming M W, *The Theory and Practice of Personnel Management*, Sixth edition, Heinemann (1989), p. 9.
20. *Employee Relations for the Hotel and Catering Industry*, Seventh edition, HCTC, 1990.
21. Magurn J P, *A Manual of Staff Management in the Hotel and Catering Industry*, Heinemann (1983), p. 294.
22. Atkinson J, *Flexibility, Uncertainty and Manpower Management*, Institute of Manpower Studies, 1985.
23. Guerrier Y and Lockwood A, 'Core and Peripheral Employees in Hotel Operations', *Personnel Review*, vol. 18, no. 1, 1989, pp. 9–15.

24. *Manpower Flows in the Hotel and Catering Industry*, HCITB Research Report, August 1984.
25. *Manpower Changes in the Hotel and Catering Industry*, HCITB Research Report, November 1983.
26. *Employee Relations for the Hotel and Catering Industry*, Seventh edition, HCTC, 1990, p. 43.
27. See, for example, Wasmuth W J and Davis S W, 'Managing Employee Turnover', *Cornell HRA Quarterly*, February 1983, vol. 23, no. 4, pp. 15–22, and 'Strategies for Managing Employee Turnover', *Cornell HRA Quarterly*, August 1983, vol. 24, no. 2, pp. 65–75.
28. Riley M, 'Labour Turnover: Time to Change the paradigm?' *International Journal of Contemporary Hospitality Management*, vol. 5, no. 4, 1993, pp. i–iii.
29. Woods R H and Macaulay J F, 'R for Turnover: Retention Programs that Work', *Cornell HRA Quarterly*, May 1989, pp. 79–90.
30. Bonn M A and Forbringer L R, 'Reducing Turnover in the Hospitality Industry: An Overview of Recruitment, Selection and Retention', *International Journal of Hospitality management*, vol. 11, no. 1, 1992, pp. 47–63.
31. *Manpower Planning Survey Report*, Williamm Mercer Fraser Ltd, August 1989.
32. *Employment Policy and Industrial Relations in the Hotels and Catering Industry*, Hotels and Catering EDC (1977).
33. *Meeting Competence Needs in the Hotel and Catering Industry: Now and in the Future*, HCTC Research Report, September 1992.
34. Mullins L J, 'Systematic Staff Selection', *HCIMA Journal*, May 1977, pp. 7–11.
35. *Manpower Policy in the Hotels and Restaurant Industry: Research Findings*, Hotels and Catering EDC, 1975.
36. Croney P, 'An Analysis of Human Resource Management in the UK Hotel Industry', *Proceedings of The International Association of Hotel Management Schools Symposium*, Leeds Polytechnic, November 1988.
37. *Working in Hotels: Report of a Formal Investigation into Recruitment and Selection*, Commission for Racial Equality, January 1991.
38. Bonn M A and Forbringer L R, 'Reducing Turnover in the Hospitality Industry: An Overview of Recruitment, Selection and Retention', *International Journal of Hospitality Management*, vol. 11, no. 1, 1992, pp. 47–63.
39. Mullins L J, 'Job Analysis – Know the Job and the Person to Do It', International Journal of Hospitality Management, vol. 4, no. 4, 1985, pp. 181-183.
40. For an explanation of different methods of selection, see Mullins L J, *Management and Organisational Behaviour*, Third edition, Pitman (1993).
41. Rodger A, *The Seven Point Plan*, Third edition, National Foundation for Educational Research (1970).
42. Fraser J M, *Employment Interviewing*, Fifth edition, Macdonald & Evans (1978).
43. For example, at The Waldorf two videos are shown. One introduces new employees into the company and shows information on THF outlets. Another video gives information on The Waldorf Hotel.
44. For further details on induction programmes see, for example, Hornsey T and Dann D, *Manpower Management in the Hotel and Catering Industry*, Batsford (1984,) p. 24.
45. *Meeting Competence Needs in the Hotel and Catering Industry: Now and in the Future*, HCTC Research Report, September 1992.
46. *Costs and Manpower Productivity in UK Hotels*, National Economic Development Council, 1992.
47. See, for example, Hubrecht J and Teare R, 'A Strategy for Partnership in Total Quality Service', *International Journal of Contemporary Hospitality Management*, vol. 5, no. 3, 1993, pp. i–iv.
48. *The Challenge of Change: Case Studies in the Management of Survival, Transition and Transformation*, The Training Agency and The National Economic Development Office, 1990.
49. Robinson S, 'The Learning Cuve', *Inside Hotels*, April/May 1992, pp. 40–45.
50. See, for example, Haywood K M, 'Effective Training: Toward a Strategic Approach', *Cornell HRA Quarterly*, vol. 33, no. 6, December 1992, pp. 43–52.
51. Mullins L J, 'Successful Training – A Planned and Systematic Approach', *Administrator*, July 1991, pp. 4–5.
52. Mullins L J and Aldrich P, 'An Integrated Model of Management and Managerial Development', *Journal of Management Development*, vol. 7, no. 3, 1988, pp. 29–39.
53. Mullins L J, 'Managerial Behaviour and Development in the Hospitality Industry', *Proceedings of The International Association of Hotel Management Schools Symposium*, Leeds Polytechnic, November 1988.
54. Wood R C, *Working in Hotels and Catering*, Routledge (1992).
55. Umbreit W T, 'When will the Hospitality Industry Pay Attention to Effective personnel Practices?', *Hospitality Education and Research Journal*, vol. 11, no. 2, 1987, reprinted in Rutherford D G (ed), *Hotel Management and Operations*, Van Nostrand Reinhold (1990), pp. 281–283.
56. See, for example, Tyson S and Fell A, *Evaluating the Personnel Function*, Second edition, Stanley Thornes (1992).

7
THE EXECUTION OF WORK

INTRODUCTION

In order for the hospitality organisation to function effectively the activities of members of staff need to be channelled and guided towards the achievement of corporate goals and objectives. The process of management is concerned with the utilisation of human resources, arrangements for the carrying out of organisational processes, and the execution of work.

This chapter looks at:

- The meaning of delegation
- Authority, responsibility and accountability
- The practice of delegation
- Improved use of human resources
- Difficulties and problems with delegation
- The need for management control
- Main stages in control systems

- Performance appraisal
- The regulation of behaviour
- Quality assurance
- The measurement of service quality
- Supervision and supportive relationships
- A behavioural approach to management control
- Financial and accounting controls

DELEGATION, SUPERVISION AND CONTROL

We saw in Chapter 4 that successful management involves getting work done through the efforts of other people. This entails the distribution of duties, authority and responsibilities throughout the organisation structure, and an attempt to influence the behaviour and performance of subordinate staff. It involves the processes of delegation, supervision and control .

THE MEANING OF DELEGATION

Delegation involves the passing on of authority and responsibility throughout the hierarchical structure of the hotel – or other hospitality organisation. Delegation can be seen as taking place both at the organisational or structural level, and at the individual or personal level.

The organisational level

The structure of the hotel (as depicted in an organisation chart, for example) is itself a result of delegation. As hotels grow in size the extent of delegation increases. At the organisational level delegation involves consideration of the division of work, centralisation/decentralisation and departmentalisation.

Departments or sections may be established on the basis of the task or element functions. The extent of decentralisation and divisionalisation provides the basic structural pattern of the hotel. The nature of organisation structure has already been discussed in a previous chapter. Here we are concerned with delegation at the individual or personal level.

The individual level

Within the structure of the hotel the various activities that have to be undertaken must be distributed among individual members of the workforce. At the individual level delegation is not just the issuing and following of orders or the carrying out of specified duties according to detailed instructions. It is not just the arbitrary shedding of work.

Delegation is the process of entrusting authority and responsibility to others. This involves the systematic allocation of duties and responsibilities, and undertaking activities that would otherwise be carried out by someone in a more senior position.

Delegation is necessary for organisational effectiveness. It is an essential function of management. It is possible to have delegation upwards, for example when a manager takes over from a subordinate who is experiencing difficulty in performing a particular task, or who has an exceptionally high work load, or when a manager temporarily undertakes the work of a subordinate who is absent through holiday or sickness. It is also possible to have delegation laterally to another manager on the same level. But, usually, delegation is interpreted as a movement down the organisation.

AUTHORITY, RESPONSIBILITY AND ACCOUNTABILITY

The whole basis of delegation is founded on the concepts of authority, responsibility and accountability (ultimate responsibility) (see Figure 7.1).

Authority

Authority is the right to take actions or make decisions that the manager would otherwise have taken or made. Authority legitimises the exercise of power within the structure and policies of the hotel. It enables subordinates to issue valid instructions for others to follow. Delegated duties are sometimes delegated further down the structure.

Responsibility

Responsibility involves an obligation by the subordinate to perform certain duties or make certain decisions, and having to accept possible reprimands from the manager for unsatisfactory performance.

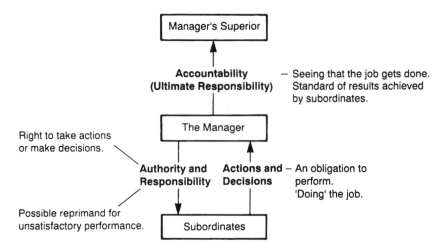

Fig 7.1　The basis of delegation

But delegation is not abdication of responsibility. The manager is still responsible for ensuring that the work gets done and is performed to a satisfactory standard. The manager is in turn accountable to a superior for the actions and decisions of subordinates.

Accountability

Accountability is interpreted as meaning ultimate responsibility. Managers have to accept ultimate responsibility for the control of their staff, for the performance of duties allocated to their department/section within the structure of the hotel, and for the standard of results achieved. **And this ultimate responsibility cannot be delegated**.

The concept of accountability means that effective delegation involves a 'dual responsibility'.

> Delegation means the conferring of a specified authority by a higher authority. In its essence it involves a dual responsibility. The one to whom authority is delegated becomes responsible to the superior for doing the job, but the superior remains responsible for getting the job done. This principle of delegation is the centre of all processes in formal organisation.[1]

Delegation of authority and responsibility

Effective delegation must embrace both authority and responsibility. It is not practical to delegate one without the other. For example, if the general manager gives the food and beverage manager authority to purchase certain items up to a given value without prior reference, then the food and beverage manager should be held responsible for the expenditure which is incurred. Responsibility is a corollary of authority. To exercise authority without accepting responsibility gives rise to the possible abuse of delegation. It can lead to complacency and a misplaced sense of security.

Equally, responsibility must be supported by the authority to take action and make decisions within the limits of that responsibility. To hold subordinates responsible for areas of performance over which they have no authority to influence is another abuse of delegation.

If people do not have sufficient power or authority to enable them to give the necessary instructions, order the required goods, or hire the necessary staff, then delegation has not been properly carried out and inefficiency will be the result.[2]

Responsibility should be sufficient to give the subordinate freedom of action within agreed terms of reference and to avoid excessive supervision. Part of the manager's job is the development of subordinates. A sense of responsibility will help in the performance of their tasks and in dealing with customers.

Parity with accountability

The delegation of authority and responsibility must, however, be kept in parity with accountability. The manager retains ultimate responsibility for the behaviour of staff and for actions taken and decisions made by subordinates. The manager remains accountable to a superior for the total operations of the department/section.

The manager must be on the lookout for subordinates who are more concerned with personal empire-building than meeting stated objectives of the hotel. The manager must prevent a strong personality exceeding the limits of formal delegation. In short, the manager must remain in control. This calls for a planned and systematic approach to the practice of delegation. But such an approach is easier said than done, and few actually achieve it.

THE PRACTICE OF DELEGATION

In order to achieve an effective system of delegation it is necessary that:

- subordinates know exactly what is expected of them, what has to be achieved, and how far they can exercise independent decision-making; and
- the manager remains accountable for the actions and decisions of subordinates.

Delegation therefore creates a special form of manager–subordinate relationship.

A planned and systematic approach

Setting up a successful system of delegation requires a planned and systematic approach involving five main stages (Figure 7.2).

- **Clarification of policies and procedures**. In order to provide a framework for the exercise of authority and acceptance of responsibility there must be clearly established policies and procedures. Managers must be clear about the opportunities and limitations of their own jobs. There should be a clear chain of command with effective communications and co-ordination between the various levels of authority within the structure of the hotel.
- **Agreement on terms of reference**. Those areas of activities which are to be delegated to subordinates should be identified clearly. Wherever possible, emphasis should be placed on the achievement of end-results rather than a set of detailed instructions. It is important to make sure that the subordinates accept both the extent of, and any restrictions on, the exercise of authority, and the responsibility delegated to them.

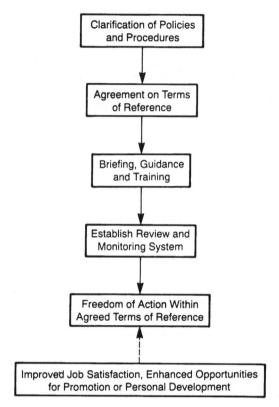

Fig 7.2 Main stages in a system of delegation

- **Briefing, guidance and training.** Once subordinates have accepted the delegation, they should be properly briefed, and given guidance and any necessary training. They should be advised where, and to whom, they can go for further advice or help. The manager should make clear to other staff the nature and extent of delegation, and obtain their co-operation. Delegation may well involve subordinates having dealings with staff in other departments or sections, in which case the manager should also communicate with the other managers.
- **An effective review and monitoring system.** The manager should make clear expected standards of achievement and how performance in each area is to be evaluated. There should be agreement on time limits for delegation (such as a target date for completion of a task, or a specified time period), and check points at which to review progress. Delegation is not an irrevocable act and can always be withdrawn.
- **Let subordinates get on with the job.** If the previous stages have been followed it should be possible, within the agreed terms of reference, to leave subordinates alone to get on with the job. This is the true nature of successful delegation.

Wherever possible, delegation should be linked to some form of 'reward' system such as improved job satisfaction, or enhanced opportunities for promotion or personal development.

Freedom of action

One of the most frustrating aspects of so-called delegation is the manager who ostensibly passes on authority but stays close behind the subordinates' shoulders, keeping a constant watch over their actions and directing their actions. This is contrary to the true nature of delegation. Managers need to be aware of the 'acceptance theory' of authority and the nature of human behaviour. It is subordinates who control the response to authority. They have the choice of undertaking a certain act or not and the manner of its performance, and of taking the consequences.[3]

If delegation is to be effective, therefore, it means that the manager must give subordinates freedom of action and must not interfere unless really necessary. Too close a level of supervision is likely to have an adverse effect on subordinates and is also failing to make the best use of the manager's time. Lord Forte, for example, makes the following point.

> I delegate wherever possible and I try to give the person to whom I delegate complete authority, with the responsibility the delegation brings. I try not to interfere. Only a very conceited man feels that he is the only one who can do a job properly. Thus the very conceited man remains very limited in his field of activity. If he is always interfering with people, he is limiting his time to do other things.[4]

IMPROVED USE OF HUMAN RESOURCES

Properly handled, delegation is a powerful and effective instrument of management. It offers many potential advantages to the hotel, to the manager and to subordinates. The main feature underlying successful delegation is that it should lead to the optimum use of human resources.

Best use of manager's time

Delegation leaves the manager free to make profitable use of time and to concentrate on the more important tasks. This should lead to a more even flow of work and a reduction in bottlenecks. It should make the manager more accessible for both customers and staff. Time is one of the most valuable but limited resources and it is important that the manager utilises time to the maximum advantage.[5]

Best use of staff

Staff are able to concentrate on those activities they perform best. Delegation encourages the development and utilisation of specialist knowledge, interests and skills.

A means of training

Delegation provides a valuable means of training and testing the subordinate's suitability for promotion. It can be used as a means of assessing the likely performance of the subordinate at a higher level in the organisation structure. Delegation thereby can help to avoid the 'Peter Principle', i.e. 'In a hierarchy employees tend to rise to their level of incompetence.'[6]

Improved strength of the workforce

Delegation can be seen as a form of participation. It gives subordinates greater scope for action, the opportunities to develop their aptitudes and abilities and increase their commitment.[7] Subordinates may develop greater confidence in themselves and experience increased motivation and job satisfaction. Delegation should lead to an improvement in the strength of the workforce.

Sound economics

Successful delegation benefits both the manager and subordinate and enables them both to play their respective roles in the effective operation of the hotel. Activities should be undertaken at the lowest level compatible with efficiency and customer satisfaction. If activities are undertaken at a higher level than necessary, they are being undertaken at greater cost than necessary. Successful delegation is therefore a matter of sound economics as well as good organisation.

DIFFICULTIES AND PROBLEMS WITH DELEGATION

Despite the many potential benefits of delegation, managers often fail to delegate successfully. There are a number of difficulties and problem areas which affect the amount of delegation and its effectiveness. Delegation is influenced by the manager's perception of subordinate staff. It is also influenced by the subordinates' perception of the manager's reasons for delegation.

Delegation: a social skill

Successful delegation is a social skill. Where managers lack this skill, two extreme forms of behaviour can result. At one extreme there is the almost total lack of *real* delegation. Subordinates are only permitted to operate within closely defined and often routine areas of activity with detailed supervision. Staff are treated as if they are incapable of thinking for themselves and given little or no opportunity to exercise initiative or responsibility, or to experience a learning situation.

At the other extreme there can be an excessive zeal for so-called 'delegation' but delegation which is often more like just 'passing the buck'. A manager may leave subordinates to their own resources, often with minimal guidance or training, and expect them to take the consequences for their own actions or decisions. And somehow, such managers seem often not to be around when difficult situations arise. The nature of the hospitality business does place particular demands upon staff who, partly through necessity, are often thrown into the deep end. But this should not be an excuse for the manager's abdication of responsibility.

Potentially stressful for subordinate staff

Poor delegation fails to take advantage of the potential benefits to both the individual and the organisation. Either of these two forms of behaviour can also be frustrating and potentially stressful for subordinate staff, and unlikely to lead to improved performance. Work stress is often caused by the failure to delegate properly and by a hierarchical structure which does not permit sufficient autonomy.[8]

Dependence upon other people

Delegation entails reliance on other people. The manager must know what to delegate, when and to whom. This involves confidence and trust – both in subordinates and in the manager's own performance and system of delegation. But learning to put trust in other people is one of the most difficult lessons for many managers, and some never learn it. Managers who claim that opportunities for delegation are limited by the nature of staffing in the hospitality industry should heed the words of Stewart.

> Managers must learn to accept their dependence upon people. A key part of being a good manager is managing that dependence. Managers who say they cannot delegate because they have poor subordinates may genuinely be unfortunate in the calibre of the subordinates that they have inherited or been given. More often this view is a criticism of themselves: a criticism either of their unwillingness to delegate when they could and should do so, or a criticism of their selection, training and development of their subordinates.[9]

In allowing freedom of action to subordinates within agreed terms of reference, managers must accept that subordinates may undertake delegated activities in a different manner from themselves. This involves the acceptance theory of authority mentioned above.

Courage – and support for subordinates

Delegation is also a matter of courage. Managers may be reluctant to delegate for fear that subordinates will not perform the job as well as they can – the 'I can do it better myself' syndrome. Mistakes will inevitably occur and the subordinate will need to be supported by the manager and protected against unwarranted criticism. Managers should protect and support subordinate staff and accept personally any reprimand for unsatisfactory performance.

The acceptance of ultimate responsibility is at the basis of the true nature of delegation. This philosophy is evidenced by the following two comments, the first from Lord Forte, the second from the West German hotelier Klaus Kobjoll.

> 'I am so sorry I have made a mistake.' 'No, you have not made a mistake,' I replied. 'We have made a mistake.'[10]

> My role is that of delegator. Each person is fully responsible for their own section and they are allowed to make mistakes and learn from them. Nobody will yell at them here.[11]

The second comment also highlights the educational aspect of the manager's job. The manager should view mistakes as part of the subordinate's training and an opportunity for further development. When mistakes do occur it is up to managers to counsel members of staff concerned and to review the effectiveness of their system of delegation.

Confidence in their own abilities

Some managers show a reluctance to delegate for fear that the subordinate will do too good a job and show the manager in a bad light. It is important that managers have full confidence in their own abilities, but they should of course remember that managing is not a solo activity. The task of management is to get work done through the efforts of other people. If a subordinate performs particularly well, this reflects favourably on the manager.

The manager needs to make full use of the technical expertise and specialist knowledge of subordinates. Failure to delegate successfully to a competent or more knowledgeable subordinate may mean that the subordinate emerges as an informal leader. This could have possible adverse consequences for the manager, and for the organisation.

THE NEED FOR MANAGEMENT CONTROL

The hotel industry is a 24-hour business. It involves a wide range of operations, many of which are provided simultaneously, and services are provided direct to the customers on the premises. Managers cannot be expected to be present at all times, or to be able to carry out all the duties which require their personal attention, as well as dealing with all the day-to-day activities.

The effective execution of work and achievement of customer satisfaction will therefore necessitate the need for delegation, for the distribution of activities and tasks to other people, and the issuing of instructions and advice. This involves the direction of staff and the checking and review of their performance.

A question of balance

The concept of ultimate responsibility gives rise to the need for effective management control. Managers must exercise control over the actions and decisions of subordinates, and be kept informed of the relevance and quality of their work. Managers need to monitor the behaviour and actions of staff in order to ensure they maintain a satisfactory standard of performance. The manager will need to keep open the lines of delegation and to have an upward flow of communication.

Control is therefore an integral part of a system of delegation. It is necessary to ensure the effective co-ordination of activities and to maintain the chain of command. But control should not be so close as to inhibit the effective operation or benefits of delegation. It is a question of securing the right balance (Figure 7.3).

The meaning and interpretation of control

The term 'control' often has an emotive connotation and is interpreted in a negative manner to suggest direction or command by the giving of orders. Staff may be suspicious of control systems and see them as emphasising punishment, an indication of authoritarian management, and a means of exerting pressure and maintaining discipline.

But this is too narrow an interpretation. There is far more to control than simply a

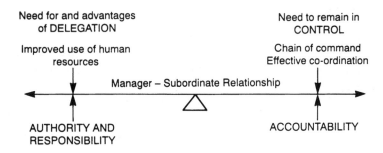

Fig 7.3 The balance between delegation and control

means of restricting behaviour or the exercise of authority over others. Control is not only a function of the formal organisation and a hierarchical structure of authority. It is also a function of interpersonal influence. Control is a general concept which is applied to both individual behaviour and effective organisational performance.

Different approaches to management control

Different approaches to organisation and management, as discussed in Chapter 3, have illustrated contrasting approaches to the nature of management control. The **classical approach** places emphasis on the technical requirements of the organisation and tends to support a high level of control as necessary for efficiency. It may be recalled, for example, that a criticism of scientific management is the high level of management control over workers and the actual process of work.

Those writers who place emphasis on a **human relations approach** and the social needs of individuals see a high level of control as self-defeating. It produces a negative response, increases internal conflict and results only in short-term improvement in performance.[12] Control should not be seen therefore only in the sense that it suggests close and constant supervision or as a constraint on freedom of action by the individual.

In terms of the **systems approach**, control relates to both the measurement of organisational effectiveness, and to the inputs and series of activities by which inputs are transformed into outputs. Control emphasises the interrelationships among the different sub-systems of the hotel. The **contingency approach** views management control as an organisational variable. The most appropriate methods of control will depend upon the contingencies of particular situations.

IMPROVEMENT IN PERFORMANCE

Control can be interpreted in different ways. It is far-reaching and can be manifested in a number of different forms. Control systems can be concerned with general results, specific actions or day-to-day operational activities, with an evaluation of overall performance of the hotel as a whole or with particular parts of it.

Whatever the different forms of management control, the underlying feature is checking and reviewing progress towards the attainment of stated objectives. The whole purpose of management control is the improvement in performance. Lord Forte, for example, makes the following point:

... we have an intensive system of controls. The word is often misinterpreted. I do not mean controls in the sense of cutting down on quality, but of setting standards and seeing that the operation conforms.[13]

Control can be seen to operate at both the individual and at the organisational level (Figure 7.4).

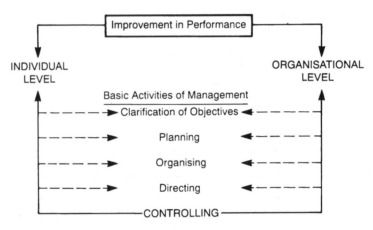

Fig 7.4 The operation of management control

The individual level

At the individual level members of staff want to know what is expected of them, and if they are performing well and in the right areas. Control is a basis for training needs, the motivation to achieve standards and for the development of individuals. Whenever a person inquires 'I would like to know how well I am doing', this can be seen in effect as asking for control. An effective control system places emphasis on the exchange of information, and feedback on actual results against planned targets.[14]

The concept of ultimate responsibility gives rise to the need for effective management control. Managers must exercise control over the actions and decisions of subordinates and be kept informed of the relevance and quality of their work. Managers need to monitor the behaviour and actions of staff in order to ensure they maintain a satisfactory standard of performance.

The organisational level

At the organisational level control completes the cycle of managerial activities. It involves reviewing the planning and organisation of the work of the hotel, and guiding and regulating the activities of staff. Management control is concerned with organisational effectiveness and determining whether the objectives of the hotel are being achieved.

The purpose of organisational control is to prevent impropriety, to monitor the use of resources, to check upon the progress of work and provide feedback on the success or failure of operations. Control is an inherent characteristic of the work situation and an important feature of the people–organisation relationship.

MAIN STAGES IN CONTROL SYSTEMS

Whatever the nature of control there are five essential stages in the design of a management control system (Figure 7.5):

1. Planning what is desired;
2. Establishing standards of performance;
3. Monitoring actual performance;
4. Comparing actual results against planned targets;
5. Rectifying and taking any corrective action.

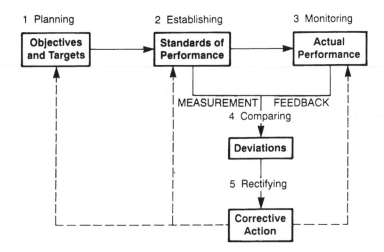

Fig 7.5 The five essential stages of management control

Clear objectives and targets

Planning provides the framework against which the process of control takes place. It is important that staff understand their duties and responsibilities, and know exactly what is required of them. Objectives and targets should be stated clearly in order to establish defined standards of performance against which the level of achievement can be determined. This requires realistic means of measurement, which wherever possible should be stated in quantitative terms.

The importance of feedback

There must be some system of feedback and reporting of information in order to monitor progress and review results. The information should be accurate, relevant, timely and easily understood by all concerned. It should be in a form which enables management to compare actual performance against planned targets, and which highlights any deviations. This information should be fed back to the staff concerned to let them know how well they are doing.

If it is to be effective, feedback should identify probable causes of any deviations and provide the basis for decisions on taking any corrective action. This might involve consideration of what can or should be done to improve the level of actual performance, revisions to the original objectives and targets, or adjustments to the standards of performance or the operation of the control system itself. Feedback and review should be a continual part of a management control system.

PERFORMANCE APPRAISAL

One method of attempting to control and improve the activities of staff and the operations of hospitality organisations is through a system of performance appraisal. For example, Boella suggests that: 'The appraisal of employees has one overriding objective and that is to improve the performance of the organisation.'[15]

An effective system of performance appraisal requires:

- careful preparation by both the appraisor and the appraisee;
- a well-planned and clearly stood procedure including design of the appraisal form;
- conducting the appraisal interview and discussion including plans for future performance;
- conclusion of the discussion and summary of key points; and
- review and follow-up.[16]

(As an example, details of the performance appraisal procedure for Swallow Hotels is given in the Appendix to this chapter.)

Uses of, and difficulties with, performance appraisal

Appraisors must make every effort to maintain objectivity. When evaluating performance it is important to avoid perceptual distortions and errors (for example the 'halo effect') discussed in Chapter 2.

Umbreit, Eder and McConnell suggest that performance appraisals have several uses, including that of a management tool, and can be used to stimulate the productivity of managers, supervisors and staff. Employees and management staff change jobs quickly and in large numbers, and hospitality operators especially need a valid method of appraising staff performance.[17]

However, Umbreit *et al.* point out that the major difficulty with most performance appraisal systems is that the judgements involved are frequently subjective, relating primarily to personality traits or to observations that cannot be verified. They suggest that any appraisal system should satisfy ten standards relating to both content requirements and to process requirements.

Content requirements

(i)   Performance standards must be based on an analysis of job requirements.
(ii) Evaluation should be based on specific dimensions of job performance, and not on single 'global measures'.
(iii) Performance standards should be objective and observable.
(iv) Ratings should be documented.
(v)   The validity of individual raters' ratings should be assessed.

Process requirements

(i)   Performance standards should be communicated to and understood by the employee.
(ii) Specific instructions for evaluators should be put in writing.
(iii) More than one evaluator should be used whenever possible.
(iv) The evaluator should review the appraisal results with the employee.
(v)   The employee should have a formal appeal procedure.

THE REGULATION OF BEHAVIOUR

By their very nature, control systems are concerned with the behaviour of people, and imply regulation and loss of individual freedom. People may be suspicious of control systems and see them as emphasising punishment and an indication of authoritarian management. Some writers support this view and even appear to suggest that organisational controls amount to exploitation of employees.[18]

Under certain conditions, however, people may actually desire control. For example, Lawler gives three reasons why employees might want to be subject to a control system:

- to give feedback on performance;
- to provide some degree of structure to tasks, and definitions of how the tasks are to be carried out, and how performance will be measured; and
- where reward systems, for example pay, are based on performance.[19]

Ambivalence towards control

Most people however, show an ambivalence towards organisational control. While they recognise the need for, and usefulness of, control systems they may not wish to have them applied to their own performance. It is important therefore not to ignore the behavioural implications. While the need for some suitable form of control is always present, the extent and manner of control is variable. Control systems can have positive as well as negative effects. They can be designed and implemented in a constructive and rewarding way.

> Although they do not readily admit it, most people probably prefer some degree of control over their lives because it gives them some stability and contributes to their general welfare and safety. Nevertheless, the negative connotation of control still exists and is amplified by the ways in which controls have been traditionally set, implemented, and used in formal organisations.[20]

QUALITY ASSURANCE

One significant aspect of management control systems of particular importance within the hospitality industry is that of quality assurance processes. In Chapter 1 we saw that profit can be seen as the incentive for the organisation to carry out its activities effectively. In order to continue in business the organisation needs to maintain growth and development, and a steady and continuous level of profitability. The successful hospitality organisation should therefore, as a matter of policy, be constantly seeking opportunities to improve the quality of its products, services and processes.

Attention to quality assurance can be seen to arise from a combination of:

- the natural outcome of good business and the need to provide high-quality goods and services in order to ensure survival, competitiveness and economic success;
- the labour-intensive nature and staffing characteristics of the industry;
- the desire to achieve and display some 'tangible' measure of quality through British Standards Institute (BSI) or International Organisations for Standardisation (ISO) certification and designation;
- the need to satisfy an absolute requirement, for example a legal liability such as that established by the Food Safety Act 1990;
- part of the exercise of the broader social responsibilities of management.

Effective systems of quality assurance

The increasing expectations of customers together with the impact of European Union directives have emphasised the importance of the hospitality industry ensuring that adequate attention is given to the planning and implementation of quality assurance systems and the review of existing practices and procedures.[21] Quality control including retrospective inspection is a necessary part of preventative systems and an important element of the quality management process.[22] However, an effective system of quality assurance involves more than just 'after the event' activities. It is concerned with demands for increased productivity, reduced costs and improved standard of the end products and services to the consumer.[23]

Quality assurance therefore relates to the entire process of management and is an integral part of the clarification of objectives and policy, planning (including design), organising, directing and guiding, and controlling performance. As an all-embracing concept quality assurance is increasingly encompassed as part of the development of a Total Quality Management (TQM) culture.[24] (TQM is discussed in Chapter 12.)

THE MEASUREMENT OF SERVICE QUALITY

Effective control systems are necessary in order to ensure that the required levels and standards of performance are maintained. In a service industry, control systems should relate to the quality of activities and processes that create customer satisfaction. One common measure is the guest questionnaire or comments card, a typical example of which is given in Figure 7.6.

However, Johnston suggests that a single measure of service quality would need to

COMMENT CARD

Dear Guest

Welcome to   Hotel. We do hope
that you will have an enjoyable stay with us,
and that means that we must ensure that every
facet of our hotel meets your expectations.
We therefore ask your assistance in completing
the *Comment Card*.

If the hotel staff are unable to rectify any problems
which you may experience, please contact the
General Manager who will be pleased to assist you.

Thank you for choosing   Hotel.

Date of arrival:
Number of nights:

	Excellent	Good	Unsatisfactory
ARRIVAL			
Reception	☐	☐	☐
Porters	☐	☐	☐
BEDROOMS			
Appearance	☐	☐	☐
Comfort	☐	☐	☐
Quality of service	☐	☐	☐
RESTAURANT			
Breakfast			
Quality of Service	☐	☐	☐
Quality of food	☐	☐	☐
Snack lunches			
Quality of Service	☐	☐	☐
Quality of Food	☐	☐	☐
Afternoon tea			
Quality of Service	☐	☐	☐
Quality of Food	☐	☐	☐
Dinner			
Quality of Service	☐	☐	☐
Quality of Food	☐	☐	☐

	Excellent	Good	Unsatisfactory
BAR			
Quality of Service	☐	☐	☐
Appearance	☐	☐	☐
LEISURE FACILITIES			
Swimming Pool	☐	☐	☐
Appearance	☐	☐	☐
Cleanliness	☐	☐	☐
Comfort	☐	☐	☐
GOLF			
Condition of Course	☐	☐	☐
GOLFSHOP			
Appearance	☐	☐	☐
Quality of Service	☐	☐	☐
GENERAL			
How did you consider the overall facilities to be?	☐	☐	☐

Have you ever stayed at before?   Yes ☐   No ☐

If not how did you select the hotel (i.e. recommended, guide book, advert etc)

Do you intend to visit us again?   Yes ☐   No ☐

YOUR COMMENTS

We would welcome any further comments or suggestions
you may wish to make regarding our facilities and overall
standards of service.

Name:
Address:

When you have completed our comment card, please seal
using the gummed edge on the right and return it to us at the
Freepost address on the reverse.

Fig 7.6 An example of a guest questionnaire

establish the degree of conformity to overall expectations and follow-up activities would need to be used to pinpoint problems and complaints. 'A single measure would ask the questions: did the service meet your expectations, or was it worse or better than expected?'[25] More comprehensive sets of measures would be based on the analysis of critical points and activities of the operations of the hotel.

Intangible nature of services

The characteristics of services mean that it is often difficult to establish specific indicators of effective performance. The intangible nature of services coupled with the individual demands of customers means that the actual delivery of services may differ widely. Benefits derived from services are associated with feelings and emotions. The quality of service in a hotel is usually identified both with its general culture and ambience, and with the disposition and attitudes of staff.

It is possible, however, to establish more specific measures of organisational effectiveness. You may recall that in Chapter 1 we considered the hotel as an open system and identified a number of possible measures of achievement. These measures could include, for example, returned customers, occupancy rates, recommendations such as 'star' ratings, cash flow and accounting ratios.

Service procedures and service conviviality

According to Martin, quality service is a complex concept and in the case of restaurants, for example, each exact definition of 'quality' service is unique as each restaurant seeks to fulfill slightly different customer needs. However, regardless of the type of service offered, service quality is always a combination of two major factors – service *procedures* and service *conviviality*.

Procedural service dimensions measure the technical systems involved in getting products and service to the customer, and comprise seven major components: flow of service, timeliness, accommodation, anticipation, communication, customer feedback and supervision. **Convivial dimensions of service** reflect the server's ability to relate to customers as people, to establish rapport and to recognise their needs as human beings. Martin suggests nine notable components of conviviality: attitude, body language, tone of voice, tact, naming names, attentiveness, guidance, suggestive selling and problem-solving.[26]

The management of total design

Drawing from the experiences of manufacturing industries, Hollins and Hollins emphasise the importance of managing the design and implementation of new service products. The concept of total design involves market research, production, accounting and selling, and also the people side, including the structure and operation of teams and their training. Specific aspects of service design include attention to queuing and the incorporation of modern technology.[27]

People part of the product

People are part of the finished product that the customer is paying for. Customer satisfaction is likely to be affected as much by the courtesy, helpfulness and efficiency of the staff as by the standard of food and beverage and accommodation.[28] As we saw in Chapter 6, the successful management of human resources is therefore an important feature of the hotel industry. The organisational and staffing characteristics of the industry might suggest the need for the exercise of a high level of management control over the behaviour and performance of staff. This, however, is not necessarily the best approach.

SUPERVISION AND SUPPORTIVE RELATIONSHIPS

Securing the right balance between delegation, individual freedom of action and control requires the correct level of supervision. A fundamental concept of participative management is the principle of supportive relationships, which we discussed in Chapter 5. Managers should have high performance aspirations for themselves and for every member of staff. A supportive relationship requires group decision-making and an employee-centred style of supervision.

In order to achieve a high level of performance it is necessary to create a manager–subordinate relationship which is supportive and intended to enhance self-esteem and ego. Subordinates should feel a sense of personal worth and importance, and maintain their sense of significance and dignity.

Employee-centred or job-centred supervision

Likert provides a contrast between employee-centred and job-centred styles of supervision and orientation towards staff. A job-centred approach to supervision is illustrated by the following point of view.

> This interest-in-people approach is all right, but it's a luxury. I've got to keep pressure on for production, and when I get production up, then I can afford to take time to show an interest in my employees and their problems.

An employee-centred approach to supervision is illustrated by this contrasting point of view.

> One way in which we accomplish a high level of production is by letting people do the job the way they want to so long as they accomplish the objectives. I believe in letting them take time out from the monotony. Make them feel that they are something special, not just the run of the mill . . . If you keep employees from feeling hounded, they are apt to pull out the necessary effort to get the work done in the required time.
>
> If people know their jobs I believe in letting them make decisions. I believe in delegating decision-making. Of course, if there's anything that affects the whole division, then the two assistant managers, the three section heads and sometimes the assistant section heads come in and we discuss it. I don't believe in saying that this is the way it's going to be. After all, once supervision and management are in agreement there won't be any trouble selling the staff the idea. My job is dealing with human beings rather than with the work . . .[29]

Likert also provides a list of 12 questions to test the extent of supportive relationships and whether a superior's behaviour is favourable (Figure 7.7).

1. How much confidence and trust do you feel your superior has in you? How much do you have in him?
2. To what extent does your boss convey to you a feeling of confidence that you can do your job successfully? Does he expect the 'impossible' and fully believe you can and will do it?
3. To what extent is he interested in helping you to achieve and maintain a good income?
4. To what extent does your superior try to understand your problems and do something about them?
5. How much is your superior really interested in helping you with your personal and family problems?
6. How much help do you get from your superior in doing your work?
   a. How much is he interested in training you and helping you learn better ways of doing your work?
   b. How much does he help you solve your problems constructively – not tell you the answer but help you think through your problems?
   c. To what extent does he see that you get the supplies, budget, equipment, etc., you need to do your job well?
7. To what extent is he interested in helping you get the training which will assist you in being promoted?
8. To what extent does your superior try to keep you informed about matters related to your job?
9. How fully does your superior try to keep you informed about matters related to your job?
10. Does your superior ask your opinion when a problem comes up which involves your work? Does he value your ideas and seek them and endeavour to use them?
11. Is he friendly and easily approached?
12. To what extent is your superior generous in the credit and recognition given to others for the accomplishments and contributions rather than seeking to claim all the credit himself?

Fig 7.7 Principle of Supportive Relationships Questionnaire
Source: Likert R, *The Human Organization: Its Management and Value*, McGraw-Hill (1967), pp. 48–9. With kind permission of McGraw-Hill, Inc.

Supportive relationships and control

The relevance of Likert's list of questions on supportive relationships, linked with the importance of maintaining control, is emphasised by Venison.

> In my experience almost every one of those questions could be asked of any hotel employee in almost any environment and at almost any level in the organisation and if the answers were negative the hotel would not be functioning as well as it could. The creation of a supportive environment should not be confused with the abdication of control or the removal of discipline. In no way is it suggested that management should absolve itself from these things. In fact

discipline is exceptionally important in achieving high standards but discipline invariably means confrontation and confrontation can be coped with within a supportive environment because people can call a spade a spade without fear of being misunderstood.[30]

THE EXERCISE OF CONTROL

The exercise of control is an expression of management systems and style. Under traditional assumptions of organisation and management, control is viewed as an essential feature of formal organisation and a hierarchical structure of authority. Controls will be based on the use of routine procedures and the exercise of rules and regulations in an attempt to create consistency and predictability in behaviour. This form of control is in keeping with a bureaucratic form of structure.

Another view of control is based on behavioural assumptions. Control is seen as a feature of interpersonal influence and takes place within a network structure of interaction and communications. Control is a function of the common commitment to the objectives of the organisation. This view of control is more in keeping with the human relations approach and the belief that the exercise of a high level of control is self-defeating.

Resentment and non-compliance

Control systems are invariably viewed with a certain amount of suspicion, and possible resentment, by members of staff. Often, control over behaviour is perceived as a threat to the need satisfaction of the individual. Even when control systems are well designed and operated there is often strong resistance and attempts at non-compliance from those members of staff affected by them. Therefore, if control systems are to be successful in leading to improved quality and performance, they require attention to the style of management and to the factors which influence human behaviour.

Assumptions about behaviour

The style of managerial leadership is a function of the manager's attitudes towards people, and assumptions about human nature and behaviour – for example McGregor's Theory X and Theory Y.[31] The central principle of Theory X is direction and control through a centralised system of organisation and the exercise of authority.

By contrast, Theory Y is based on the principle of the integration of individual and organisational goals. People can learn to accept and to seek responsibility for their own actions, and will exercise self-direction and self-control in the service of objectives to which they are committed.

A BEHAVIOURAL APPROACH TO MANAGEMENT CONTROL

If control systems are to be accepted by members of staff attention must be given to behavioural factors. The basis of a behavioural approach is founded not just on the provision of control systems but also on the meaningfulness and importance of work, and securing the motivation and commitment of staff.

People like to take pride in their work. The hospitality industry is fortunate in this respect as emphasis is usually placed on the standard of quality, rather than the quantity, of its products and services. There should be a built-in incentive for staff to produce high-quality work, for example in the preparation of food or the cleanliness of rooms. If staff derive a sense of personal satisfaction from performing a competent job there should be little need for a high level of supervision.[32]

Control systems provide an interface between human behaviour and the process of management. We have seen that underlying all control systems is the attempt to influence the behaviour of people.

> The broad objective of the control function is to effectively employ all the resources committed to an organisation's operations. However, the fact that non-human resources depend on human effort for their utilisation makes control, in the final analysis, the regulation of human performance.[33]

The control of service activities

The nature of the service industry (discussed in Chapter 1), for example the direct inter-action between employees and customers, the personal nature of activities, intangibility and the heterogeneous nature of customers, means that it is difficult to establish objective standards of effective performance. As a result managers may be tempted to revert to the exercise of control in terms of a feature of formal organisation and authority, as discussed above.

As Riley, for example, comments:

> In conditions where standards are subjective, managers always try to overcome this subjectivity by standardisation, checklists and other aids which make what is required more specific. In other words, they try to improve formal methods of control. The problem is that these can never be totally successful. What the hotel and catering manager has to realise is that the effective weapons are personal. Example and vigilance with the objective of achieving a shared value with the employees as to what constitutes 'good' in the various circumstances of the operation are effective controls. It is a trust relationship. This relationship between the nature of a job and how management can control it, leads to an important issue for the industry – control versus personal service.[34]

The effectiveness of management control systems will therefore depend upon both their design and operation, and the attitudes of staff and the way they respond to them. Control often provokes an emotional response from those affected by it. The activities of a management control system raise important considerations of the human factor and of the management of people.

IMPLEMENTATION OF A BEHAVIOURAL APPROACH

There are a number of ways in which the manager can attempt to implement a behavioural approach to control.

- **Participation**. The more that staff co-operate and participate in the setting up of control procedures, the more likely they are to accept them. If staff are involved in the decision-making process there is greater encouragement to exercise self-control over their level of performance.

- **Understanding.** Staff should understand the purpose and nature of the control systems. If staff understand and accept the reasons for control, this will help make for improved manager-subordinate relationships.

- **Motivation.** Lack of positive motivation can lead to frustrated behaviour and poor job performance, and result in a higher level of control. Recognition for a satisfactory level of attainment coupled with a suitable reward system, as integral parts of control, can do much to motivate staff and encourage good results. No amount of management control will prove effective unless employees are positively motivated to achieve a high level of performance.

- **Organisation structure.** Features of organisational design will influence the nature and operation of control systems. A 'mechanistic' structure is more likely to be characterised by directions and orders, formal rules and regulations. But with an 'organic' structure there is greater emphasis on a network system of control, communications and authority.

- **Groups and informal organisation.** The operations of groups and the informal organisation influence the functioning of control systems. Informal group 'norms' and peer pressure can be one of the most powerful forms of control. Membership of a harmonious and effective work group can lead to improved motivation and job satisfaction. Socialisation can create a feeling of commitment to the group and reduce the need for formal management control.

- **Management systems.** The character of control processes is one of the organisational variables identified in Likert's four-fold model of management systems: System 1 (benevolent authoritative), System 2 (exploitative authoritative), System 3 (consultative) and System 4 (participative group).[35] With System 1, review and control functions are concentrated with top management and exercised through the hierarchical structure. With System 4, concern for the control function is shared widely throughout the organisation, the formal and informal organisations share the same goals, and there is an emphasis on self-guidance and problem-solving.

Long-term improvement in performance

Likert's findings would appear to have particular relevance to the hotel industry. In Systems I and 2 organisations, high performance goals by superiors coupled with high-pressure supervision using tight budgets and controls yield high productivity *initially* because of compliance based on fear. However, because of unfavourable attitudes, poor communications, lack of co-operative motivation and restriction of output, **the long-term result is high absence and turnover, and low productivity and earnings**. The nearer the behavioural characteristics of an organisation approach to System 4, the more likely it is that this will lead to a long-term improvement in performance.

Maintaining freedom of action

Providing members of staff with a genuine sense of empowerment, for example through membership of autonomous project teams and quality circles and as part of a total quality management philosophy, is an important aspect of a behavioural approach to management control.[36] The more that staff feel they are sharing in a common responsibility for improving service delivery to the customers and are empowered to take corrective action when necessary, the more likely they are to develop a commitment to the quality and performance of hospitality operations.

Modern methods of management can assist the maintenance of management control without reducing the individual's freedom of action. Procedures such as management by exception, staff appraisal and management by objectives can help to maintain control without inhibiting the growth of delegation. A system of Management by Objectives (discussed in Chapter 5) may allow staff to accept greater responsibility and to make a higher level of personal contribution.

Management by Objectives as a control system

Participation is an inherent feature of an effective system of Management by Objectives (MBO). There is an assumption that most people will direct and control themselves willingly if they share in the setting of their objectives.[37] MBO can therefore be applied as a modern and effective method of control (Figure 7.8). It can be used in a positive and constructive manner to provide a control system related to performance appraisal and career progression.

Activities in Management by Objectives	Management Control System
Agree what you expect from me	Planning what is desired. Specification of objectives and targets.
Give me an opportunity to perform.	Establishing defined standards of performance.
Let me know how I'm getting on.	Monitoring and reviewing actual performance. Control information and feedback.
Give me guidance where I need it.	Comparing actual performance against planned targets. What can be done to improve performance?
Reward me according to my contribution.	Recognition of achievement. Motivation for further improvement in performance.
Control, review and adjustment.	Taking corrective action.

Fig 7.8 MBO and management control
Adapted from Humble J, *Management by Objectives*, Management Publications Ltd (1972), p. 46

FINANCIAL AND ACCOUNTING CONTROLS

Financial and accounting systems are frequently thought of as the major part of management control systems. And the reasons for this are easy to understand.

● The stewardship of financial resources and the need to demonstrate value for money is of vital concern to the organisation. Control systems are often geared to highlighting the easily identifiable performance of sales, costs and profits.

- Organisational aims, objectives and targets are often expressed in financial terms and measured in terms of profitability. Results are measured and reported in financial terms.
- Money is quantifiable and a precise unit of measurement. It is easily understood, and is often used as a common denominator and as a basis for comparison.
- Financial limits are easy to apply as a measure of control or limit to authority, and are easy to relate to. We have seen, for example, that control is a necessary part of delegation. A manager might delegate to a subordinate the authority to incur expenditure on certain items up to a given financial limit.

It is understandable, therefore, that so much attention is given to financial and accounting systems of control. Managers rely on an accurate information system as a basis for control and this information is often expressed in financial terms. Management accounting tools such as budgets, ratio analysis and standard costing provide helpful information for control of the operations of the various departments and activities of the hotel. As Venison, for example, emphasises:

> . . . the production of correct and up-to-date accounts is absolutely vital to the success of any hotel venture . . . As an hotel manager . . . you have a primary duty to ensure that somebody is effectively handling the accounts function.[38]

Attention to behavioural factors

There is of course nothing wrong with the use of financial or accounting systems of control. The important point is the manner in which such controls are applied and their effects on the behaviour of staff. Consideration must be given to the behavioural factors and the motivation for staff to improve their performance.[39]

Accounting control systems such as internal audit, management by exception and budgetary control tend to operate in a negative way and to report only on the unfavourable performance, or on variances which may have adverse consequences. As a result there is no specific recognition from management and only a limited sense of achievement for favourable performance. There is little, if any, positive motivation. Budgetary control may be perceived as a means of exerting pressure on staff and can also be seen as imposing restriction on individual freedom of action.[40]

As with other forms of control, financial and accounting systems have positive as well as negative effects. If control systems are to be successful in leading to improved performance, they should be designed and implemented in a constructive and rewarding way. To do this, they must take account of the individual, social and organisational factors which determine people's patterns of behaviour.

Concern for the whole process of management

We have commented previously that the focus of effort in the hospitality industry has traditionally been directed narrowly to profitability and short-term cost-consciousness. However, management control embraces far more than just financial or accounting considerations. It should be concerned with the whole process of management: with the extent to which the aims and objectives of the hospitality organisation are being achieved and with improvement in performance.

Control includes consideration of such factors as quality, judgement, customer satisfaction, social responsibilities, and the human factor and the effective management of people. Regrettably, however, it appears that the industry has given little attention to evaluating the contribution and worth of its human resources or to accounting for the value of its employees.[41]

SUMMARY

- For the hospitality organisation to function effectively there must be processes of delegation, supervision and control. Delegation embraces both authority and responsibility but managers retain accountability (ultimate responsibility) for the actions and decisions of subordinates. Properly handled delegation is a powerful instrument of management and should lead to improved use of human resources.
- There are, however, a number of potential difficulties and problem areas. The concept of ultimate responsibility gives rise to the need for effective systems of management control which must be kept in balance with delegation. The whole purpose of control is improvement in individual and organisational performance.
- Control is far reaching and can take a number of different forms. One method of attempting to control and improve the activities of staff is through a system of performance appraisal. A significant aspect of management control in the hospitality industry is that of quality assurance and to the products, services and processes that create customer satisfaction.
- By their very nature control systems are concerned with the behaviour of people. The exercise of control is an expression of management systems and style. Securing the right balance between delegation, freedom of action and management control requires the correct level of supervision and supportive relationships. Attention must be given to behavioural factors.
- Financial and accounting systems are an important aspect of management control but such systems need to be designed in a constructive and rewarding way. However, management control embraces far more than just financial or accounting considerations. It should be concerned with the whole process of management including accounting for the value of employees.

APPENDIX: SWALLOW HOTELS – PERFORMANCE APPRAISAL

Introduction

Swallow Hotels have reviewed their procedure for performance appraisal. The revised appraisal form (Figure 7.9) is now used for different levels of management. There are three main sections: performance review, future objectives, and training and development needs. Questions in each section are quite specific and are to be answered by both appraisor and appraisee.

- **Performance review** includes: job performance, extra achievements, objectives not achieved, changes in responsibilities, most important aspects of the job, and personal standards such as job knowledge, quality of work, communication skills, teamwork, problem-solving, decision-making, administration and planning, and social skills.
- **Future objectives** includes: utilisation of abilities, desired future achievements, and company/management support.
- **Training and development needs** includes: training and development undertaken, future areas of training and development, and long-term self-development.

SWALLOW HOTELS
PERFORMANCE APPRAISAL FORM

Name of Appraisee . . . . Place of Work . . . .

Job Title . . . . Department . . . .

Name of Appraisor/   Date of
Line Manager . . . . Appraisal Interview . . . .

Period of time this appraisal covers . . . .

NB: The appraisee is the person who is being appraised. The appraisor is the person who carries out the appraisal.

THE PURPOSE OF THE APPRAISAL

The Appraisal Interview is to enable the appraisor to have a frank and open discussion about the appraisee's job performance and his/her future. The discussion should focus on:

1 Reviewing the scope and purpose of the appraisee's job.
2 Reviewing the appraisee's job performance against the objectives set.
3 Establishing agreement on future objectives for job performance.
4 Identifying training and development needs of the appraisee.

THE PROCEDURE OF THE APPRAISAL

Before the Interview
1 The appraisee should complete the left-hand section of this form marked Appraisee Comments, at least 2–3 weeks in advance of the interview.
2 The form should then be given to the appraisor who should complete the right-hand section marked Appraisor Comments at least one week in advance of the interview.
3 The appraisee should be given an opportunity to read the appraisor's comments or be given a copy of the appraisor's remarks before the interview.
4 Both parties should be fully prepared and aware of the other person's comments on the appraisee's performance prior to the interview.

At the Interview
5 Both the appraisor and the appraisee should discuss fully the points made in each section and reach agreement/understanding on any areas of discrepancy.

Fig 7.9 Extracts from the performance appraisal form

6　At the end of the discussion the appraisor should complete the summary form indicating joint agreement on performance review, future objectives and training/development needs.

7　The appraisee should complete the general comments section and sign it.

8　The appraisor should complete the general comments section and sign it.

After the Interview

9　A copy of the appraisal form should be given to the appraisee for future reference and the original should be placed on their personal file.

10　The appraisor should monitor the progress of the appraisee to ensure follow up action is being taken on the objectives set and support required.

NB: The appraisal form consists of two types of assessment, one relating to job performance and the other relating to personal performance/development. The latter section should only be completed for Assistant Managers and Senior Employees if considered appropriate to their Appraisal.

SUMMARY

To be completed by the Appraisor at the Interview:

PERFORMANCE REVIEW (Key results and comments)

FUTURE OBJECTIVES (Key results and comments)

TRAINING AND DEVELOPMENT NEEDS (Key results and comments)

GENERAL COMMENTS BY APPRAISEE　　**GENERAL COMMENTS BY APPRAISOR**

Signed and
Agreed . . . .　　Signed and
Agreed . . . .

Date . . . .　　Date . . . .

Fig 7.9 continued

The appraisal interview

The appraisal interview focuses on each section of the form, and areas of agreement and discrepancy are discussed until an understanding is reached. At the end of the interview the summary section is completed by the appraisor and countersigned by the appraisee. This section becomes the main record of assessment and is used for future reference.

Training courses

The appraisal system is supported by two types of training courses for managers, one on appraisal interviewing and the other on effective performance appraisal.

The author is grateful to John Deighan, Personnel Director, and Fiona Hunter, Company Training Executive, Swallow Hotels, for providing this information.

REVIEW AND DISCUSSION QUESTIONS

1 Explain fully the meaning of delegation at both the organisational level and the individual level. Distinguish clearly between the concepts of authority, responsibility and account-ability. What is meant by the nature of dual responsibility in effective delegation?

2 Suggest ways in which delegation, if properly handled, should lead to the optimum use of the human resources of the hospitality organisation.

3 What is meant by the acceptance theory of authority and the nature of human behaviour? Why do you think it is that many managers often fail to delegate successfully?

4 Detail the need for management control in the hotel industry. As a departmental manager, how would you attempt to achieve the full benefits of delegation while still maintaining effective control of subordinate staff?

5 Explain the importance of quality assurance processes within the hospitality industry. Discuss the particular difficulties of the measurement of service quality.

6 Distinguish between employee-centred and job-centred styles of supervision. Discuss the importance of supportive relationships and control.

7 Control systems provide an interface between human behaviour and the process of man-agement. Explain fully how you, as a manager, would attempt to implement a behavioural approach to control.

8 Discuss critically the extent to which you believe attention should be given to financial and accounting systems of control in a hospitality organisation of your choice.

ASSIGNMENT 1

Assess critically the effectiveness of a process of delegation. Arrange to interview a manager and subordinate staff in a hospitality organisation of your choice. Give details of the nature of delegation involved and the circumstances under which it arose.

(i) Note the extent to which the five main stages in a planned and systematic approach appear to be followed.

(ii) Explain in particular: the nature of the briefing, guidance and training given, and the time limits, check points and performance standards established.

(iii) Enquire of (a) the manager and (b) the member(s) of staff concerned, the benefits each gained from the delegation, and any difficulties or problems involved.

(iv) Explain ways in which you believe the process of delegation appears to be successful or not. Where appropriate suggest ways in which the process of delegation could be made more effective.

(v) Where possible, compare and contrast your findings with your own experiences of delegation.

ASSIGNMENT 2

From your own experience of a hospitality organisation answer carefully and fully the 12 questions in Likert's Principle of Supportive Relationships Questionnaire. (Refer back to Figure 7.7 in this chapter.)

(i) Assess to what extent the principle of supportive relationships is applied well and the behaviour of the superior is favourable. Relate actual examples.

(ii) Highlight negative answers which suggest that the organisation is not functioning as well as it could. Explain fully the actual or likely consequences of these negative answers.

(iii) Summarise the results of the questionnaire, and share and discuss your answers with colleagues. What overall conclusions do you reach concerning the nature of supportive relationships in the hospitality industry?

CASE STUDY

Too hot to handle

When offered promotion to manager of the three-star Abbotts Oak hotel, Pat Morgan's reactions had been a mixture of pleasure and surprise, tempered with concern about the added responsibilities of the position. Two months after Morgan's promotion, Peter Carlton was appointed head chef at the Abbotts Oak by the joint owner, Mary Parker. Shortly after taking up his appointment Parker informed Carlton that he was expected to improve the performance of the kitchen in whatever manner he thought appropriate.

At first there were no signs of any problems and as far as Morgan was aware Carlton appeared to confirm his reputation for being very competent and hard-working. Within a matter of weeks, however, the manager started to hear rumblings of discontent among members of staff. A receptionist had mentioned to Morgan that Carlton was surly and had an offensive manner. But no one had complained formally to Morgan and customers appeared to be very pleased with the standard of the meals.

A couple of weeks passed and then the manager overheard two members of the kitchen staff talking about Carlton. They said that he worked very hard, certainly knew his job and was obviously a very good chef. But they were moaning about his disgusting behaviour, that he was swearing all the time and rude to everyone. Then, ten days later, another receptionist complained to the manager that Carlton was uncooperative, foul-mouthed and very quickly showed signs of temper.

Morgan listened carefully and then replied that trade in the restaurant was increasing and customers seemed very pleased. The manager continued: 'We are always told that good chefs tend to have a temperamental nature so I suppose we have to make some allowances. But leave it with me and I will look into things.'

Matters reached a head two weeks later, however, when Morgan felt compelled to reprimand Carlton for disparaging remarks to a waitress who had clearly been distressed. 'Now look here, we just cannot tolerate this obnoxious behaviour of yours,' said Morgan.

During the subsequent exchange Carlton became very abusive and agitated, and then threw a tin of biscuits in the direction of Morgan. Carlton refused to apologise and suggested that Morgan should pay more attention to problems nearer home. Morgan retaliated angrily: 'I won't have any of your excuses. Are you going to apologise today, or are you going to leave tomorrow?'

'If that's how you feel I'm off. You know what you can do with your job,' replied Carlton who turned sharply and hurried out of the kitchen.

After a brief pause Morgan hurried after Carlton and caught up with him walking in the direction of the car park. 'You know that if you don't work your notice you won't be entitled to any pay.' Carlton did not stop and said nothing; but grunted, and gave a wry smile.

The following day a clearly displeased Mary Parker called Morgan to her office. She reminded Morgan that Carlton had come with glowing references and that it had been necessary to offer him a high salary plus bonuses in order to secure his appointment.

Parker continued: 'You know that it is hotel policy to ask customers if they had enjoyed their meal. Since Carlton has been here there has been virtually no complaints and . . .'

'So you are saying that the ends justify the means and that customer satisfaction is more important than good staff relationships,' interrupted Morgan.

'I am saying that acceptance of responsibility involves an obligation to achieve a satisfactory level of performance,' replied Parker.

'That may be,' responded Morgan, 'but who determines the standards and the manner in which results are achieved? And what about the effects on other members of staff? Anyway, who is in charge of the kitchen, me or Carlton?'

Parker responded tersely: 'I am the one in charge here although you know that I leave the routine management and matters of staffing to you. As I hadn't heard anything to the contrary, I naturally assumed everything was running satisfactorily. But now I suppose I must intervene. And what on earth made you threaten to withold Carlton's pay?'

'It wasn't like that,' replied Morgan, 'and don't forget that the second chef is about to leave on a postponed holiday.'

'Look, until I decide what needs to be done I expect you as manager to sort out this silly personality clash and to . . .'

'So what are you telling me?' interjected Morgan.

'That I have reinstated Carton,' replied Parker.

'And what about my position? How does that make me look?' queried Morgan.

'You are still the manager here, but I have always believed that the more confident and assured a manager the easier to exercise authority and the less to fear competition from competent subordinates. The balance between successful delegation and effective control is a fine line, and . . .'

'I see,' said Morgan sharply, then left without another word while Parker was still talking.

Ten minutes later Morgan returned and without knocking entered the owner's office. The manager placed a letter of resignation on the desk in front of a disturbed-looking Mary Parker and said: 'Either he goes or I do,' and stormed out.

(i) Analyse the various issues and problems which are raised by this case.

(ii) Explain fully the actions you would recommend be taken in order to help resolve these issues and problems.

NOTES AND REFERENCES

1. Mooney J D, *The Principles of Organization*, Revised edition, Harper & Row (1947), p. 17.
2. Gullen H V and Rhodes G E, *Management in the Hotel and Catering Industry*, Batsford (1983), p. 49.
3. Newstrom J W and Davis K, *Organizational Behavior: Human Behavior at Work*, Ninth edition, McGraw-Hill (1993).
4. Forte, Charles (Lord), *Forte: The Autobiography of Charles Forte*, Sidgwick & Jackson (1986), p. 125.
5. See, for example, Drucker P F, *The Practice of Management*, Pan Books (1968),
6. Peter L J and Hull R, *The Peter Principle*, Pan Books (1970), p. 22.
7. See, for example, Vinton D, 'Delegation for Employee Development', *Training and Development Journal*, vol. 41, no. 1, January 1987, pp. 65–67.
8. Hall K and Savery L K, 'Stress Management', *Management Decision*, vol. 25, no. 6, 1987, pp. 29–35.
9. Stewart R, *The Reality of Management*, Second edition, Pan Books (1986), p. 190.
10. Forte, Charles (Lord), *Forte: The Autobiography of Charles Forte*, Sidgwick & Jackson (1986), p. 124.
11. Tarpey D, 'Handling With Care', *Caterer and Hotelkeeper*, vol. 12, July 1990, pp. 52–53.
12. See, for example, Blake R R, and Mouton J S, *The Managerial Grid III*, Gulf Publishing Company (1985).
13. Forte, Charles (Lord), *Forte: The Autobiography of Charles Forte*, Sidgwick & Jackson (1986), p. 190.
14. Mullins L and Banks G, 'How Well am I Doing?', *Euhofa Journal*, International Association of Directors of Hotel Schools, Switzerland, no. 18, June 1986.
15. Boella M J, *Human Resource Management in the Hotel and Catering Industry*, Fourth edition, Hutchinson (1987), p. 97.
16. See, for example, Mill R C, *Managing for Productivity in the Hospitality Industry*, Van Nostrand Reinhold (1989).
17. Umbreit W T, Eder R W and McConnell J P, 'Performance Appraisals: Making Them Fair and Making Them Work', in Rutherford D G (ed), *Hotel Management and Operations*, Van Nostrand Reinhold (1990), pp. 299–310.
18. See, for example, Salaman G, *Class and the Corporation*, Fontana (1981).
19. Lawler E E, 'Control Systems in Organisations', in Dunnette M D (ed), *Handbook of Industrial and Organizational Psychology*, Rand McNally (1976).
20. Luthans F, *Organizational Behavior*, Fifth edition, McGraw-Hill (1989), p 547.
21. See, for example, East J, *Managing Quality in The Catering Industry*, Croner (1993).
22. Johns N, 'Quality Management in the Hospitality Industry: Part 2. Applications, Systems and Techniques', *International Journal of Contemporary Hospitality Management*, vol. 4, no. 4, 1992, pp. 3–7.
23. Hayman K G, 'Total Quality Management and Quality Assurance within the Food and Hospitality Service Industries', *The Manager: Journal of The Institute of Commercial Management*, March 1992, pp. 10–11.
24. See, for example, Simmons P and Teare R, 'Evolving a Total Quality Culture', *International Journal of Contemporary Hospitality Management*, vol. 5, no. 3, 1993, pp. v–viii.
25. Johnston R, 'Operations Management Issues', in Jones P (ed), Management in Service Industries, Pitman (1989), p. 201.
26. Martin W B, 'Defining What Quality Service Is For You', *Cornell HRA Quarterly*, vol. 26, no. 4, February 1986, pp. 32–38.
27. Hollins G and Hollins B, *Total Design: Managing Tile Design Process in the Service Sector*, Pitman (1991).
28. Mullins L J, 'The Personnel Function', *HCIMA Journal*, vol. 94, October 1979, pp. 22–25.
29. Likert R, *New Patterns of Management*, McGraw-Hill (1961), pp. 7–8.
30. Venison P, *Managing Hotels*, Heinemann (1983), p. 64.
31. McGregor D, *The Human Side of Enterprise*, Penguin (1987).
32. See, for example, Keiser J R, *Principles and Practices of Management in the Hospitality Industry*, Second edition, Van Nostrand Reinhold (1989).
33. Reeser C and Loper M, *Management: The Key to Organizational Effectiveness*, Scott Foresman (1978), p 437.
34. Riley M, *Human Resource Management: A guide to personnel practice in the hotel and catering industry*, Butterworth-Heinemann (1991), p. 42.
35. Likert R and Likert J G, *New Ways of Managing Conflict*, McGraw-Hill (1976).
36. See, for example, Johns N, 'Quality Management in the Hospitality Industry', *International Journal of Contemporary Hospitality Management: Part 3. Recent Developments*, vol. 5, no. 1, 1993, pp. 10–15.
37. Humble J W, *Management by Objectives*, Management Publications Ltd (1972).
38. Venison P, *Managing Hotels*, Heinemann (1983), p. 107.
39. Mullins L J, 'Behavioural Implications of Management Accounting', *Management Accounting*, vol. 59, no. 1, January 1981, pp. 36–39.

40. See, for example, Prior P, 'Communicating: An Enthusiast's View', *Accountancy*, vol. 95, no. 1089, May 1984, p. 69.
41. Maher A, 'Accounting for Human Resources in UK Hotels', Proceedings of CHME Research Conference, Manchester Metropolitan University, April 1993.

8

MOTIVATING THE WORKFORCE

INTRODUCTION

The nature of the people–organisation relationship is influenced by what motivates staff to work and the satisfaction they derive from it. Managers achieve results through the efforts and performance of other people. The ability to motivate staff to work willingly and effectively is an essential ingredient of successful management.

This chapter looks at:

- The nature of motivation
- Needs and expectations at work
- Motivation and job satisfaction
- Theories of motivation
- The work of Maslow, Alderfer, Herzberg, McClelland
- Process theories of motivation

- Expectancy theories and equity theory
- Applications of motivational theories
- The nature of hospitality work
- Job design
- Restructuring of individual jobs
- Broader approaches to job design
- Quality circles

THE NATURE OF MOTIVATION

The effective management of people is influenced by the attitudes which are brought to bear on relationships with staff and to the problems which affect them. Attention should be given to the feelings of staff and to appropriate systems of motivation, job satisfaction and rewards. This is clearly important in any work organisation but especially so in labour-intensive service organisations such as those in the hospitality industry.[1]

The study of motivation is concerned with why people behave in a certain way, and with what determines the direction and persistence of their actions. Levels of work performance are determined not only by the ability of staff but also by the strength of their motivation. If staff are to perform to the best of their abilities, attention must also be given to the nature of work motivation and job satisfaction.

The opportunity to perform

Performance is a function of both ability level and the motivation to use ability.[2]

$$\textbf{Performance} = \text{function } (\textbf{ability} \times \textbf{motivation} \text{ to use ability})$$

The desire to perform well must be encouraged and supported by the **opportunity** for staff to perform and to realise their full potential. People should be able to experience a sense of achievement and personal growth in a purposeful and meaningful job. Staff are then more likely to feel motivated to perform to the best of their abilities. Motivation is derived from the fulfilment of an individual's needs and expectations.[3]

NEEDS AND EXPECTATIONS AT WORK

People's behaviour and actions are directed towards the satisfaction of certain needs and expectations which form the basis of their motivational driving force (Figure 8.1).

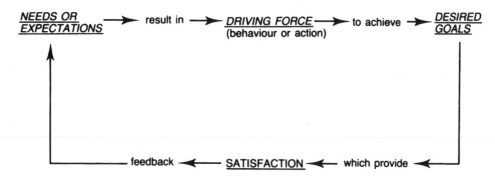

Fig 8.1 The basic motivational model

Individuals have a variety of changing, and often conflicting, needs and expectations at work which they seek to satisfy in a number of different ways. These various needs and expectations can be categorised in various ways. The following broad, three-fold framework provides a convenient starting point as a focus on work motivation and job satisfaction.

- **Economic rewards** – such as pay, perks and fringe benefits, material goods, job security and pension rights. The provision of live-in accommodation and meals at work could also be included under this heading.
- **Intrinsic satisfaction** – which is derived from the nature of the work itself and includes an interesting and challenging job, variety, a sense of involvement and achievement, and scope for personal development.
- **Social relationships** – such as the nature of the work environment, comradeship, friendship, group membership, the desire for affiliation, and a feeling of status, support or belonging.

Comparative importance

Motivation, job satisfaction and work performance will be determined by the comparative importance of these sets of needs and expectations, and the extent to which they are fulfilled (Figure 8.2).

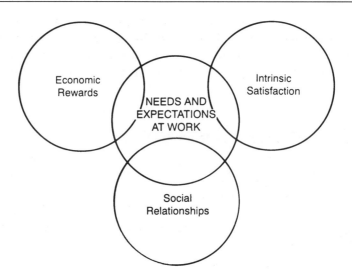

Fig 8.2 Needs and expectations of people at work

Economic rewards are clearly a motivating factor to a greater or lesser extent for all staff. But given the generally low levels of pay for the majority of staff within the hospitality industry, other motivating influences would seem to be of particular significance.

Intrinsic satisfaction will vary from job to job and often between different parts of the same job. Most of us would probably perceive a distinction between the intrinsic satisfaction of the head chef compared with a kitchen porter, or between that of serving in the bar compared with cleaning or porterage. It is difficult to generalise, however. Intrinsic satisfaction is a personal attitude which varies according to the individual and according to particular circumstances.

Social relationships would appear to be an important feature for many staff. The characteristics of the hospitality industry as a service industry, the role of people, interactions with others, and the importance of good teamwork and supportive working relationships can be strong motivators at work.

Combination and balance

Motivation at work is a very personal thing. Each individual will seek to achieve the desired combination and balance of economic rewards, intrinsic satisfaction and social relationships. For example, a low level of pay, although obviously not welcomed, may be accepted because of the strong motivating influence of an interesting job and rewarding social relationships. The comparative importance of the three sets of needs and expectations are liable to change according to the particular situation in which individuals find themselves.

Needs and motivation questionnaire

Management at The Sherlock Holmes Hotel, London, carry out an exercise with the aim of establishing exactly what motivates staff. Approximately twice a year, the personnel manager distributes a 'Needs and Motivation' form to all staff – see Assignment 1 of this chapter. The completed forms help to establish the importance of various aspects of the workplace. Attention can then be given to the most significant factors in order to help satisfy the needs of staff, and in turn to aid their retention and performance.

MOTIVATION AND JOB SATISFACTION

The motivation to work well is usually related to job satisfaction. But the nature of this relationship is not clear. Satisfaction with the job may motivate a person to achieve a high level of performance. The content theories of motivation, in particular, are related more to satisfaction. For example, Herzberg's two-factor theory (discussed below) is essentially a theory of job satisfaction. However, although the level of job satisfaction may well affect the strength of motivation, this is not always the case.

Dimensions of job satisfaction

Job satisfaction is a complex concept and not always easy to measure objectively. Satisfaction is not the same as motivation. Job satisfaction is more of an attitude, an internal state. It could, for example, be associated with a personal feeling of achievement, either quantitative or qualitative. Motivation is a process which may lead to job satisfaction.

It is not clear whether job satisfaction consists of a single dimension or a number of separate dimensions. There does appear to be a positive correlation between satisfaction and different areas of work. But some workers may be satisfied with certain aspects of their work and dissatisfied with other aspects.[4] What is clear is that the level of job satisfaction is affected by a wide range of variables related to individual, social, cultural, organisational and environmental factors. These factors all influence job satisfaction of individuals in a given set of circumstances, but not necessarily in others.

Early approaches to motivation and job satisfaction

Early approaches to motivation were based on the simple premise of the satisfaction of economic needs. You may recall that an underlying principle of scientific management (discussed in Chapter 3) was a belief in the rational-economic concept of motivation. Workers would be motivated primarily by the satisfaction of the highest possible wages. Emphasis was placed on the content of a 'fair day's work' and on optimising the level of workers' productivity. However, the definition of a fair day's work is very subjective and, if individuals work hard to increase their earnings, management might redefine the target for a fair day's work.

A range of different needs

The findings of the Hawthorne experiments and the human relations writers demonstrated that people are motivated to work in order to satisfy a range of different needs, not simply monetary reward. Emphasis was given to the importance of the satisfaction of the social needs of individuals. This in turn gave rise to the work of the neo-human relations writers and to theories of motivation based on the personal adjustment of the individual, and the content and meaning of work.

THEORIES OF MOTIVATION

Unfortunately there is no single or simple answer to the question of what motivates people to work well. Motivation is by its nature a complex subject and is influenced by a wide range of individual, social, cultural and situational variables. Motivation also varies over time and according to circumstances. It is often most acute for people at a mid-career position and especially for those who find opportunities for further advancement or promotion are limited.[5]

The complex and variable nature of work motivation has given rise to many competing ideas and theories. **But these theories are not conclusive.** They are all subject to criticism or alternative findings. It is always easy to quote an example which appears to contradict any generalised observation on what motivates people to work well.

These theories, however, help to highlight the many motives which influence people's behaviour and performance. Collectively, the different theories provide a framework within which the manager can direct attention to the problem of how best to motivate staff to work willingly and effectively. Anything which aids an understanding of how best to motivate staff must be useful.

> All managers have a duty to motivate their teams. Motivated people take more pride in their jobs and work better. But many managers don't know how to motivate their staff.[6]

Motivation in the service sector

Willman refers to the particular difficulties of motivating non-career staff in the service sector. These staff are often female, part-time non-graduates, who work in important customer-contact roles, but who infrequently move up into managerial ranks.

> Their attachment to the organisation is fleeting, their pay often low, their job content often routine. However, the problem for service businesses is that, frequently, they are all the customer sees. They define the quality of service the organisation can offer. This matters more in businesses where the service itself is the product, than where poor service may be offset by good products . . . The motivation, skills and knowledge of these staff is a key issue for the quality of service offered by an organisation.[7]

Managers can learn from the different theories and approaches to motivation. If a hospitality manager can identify different motivating factors within staff, this is likely to lead to improved attitudes to work, lower turnover and improved customer relations. The manager can judge the relevance of the different theories, how best to draw upon them and how they might successfully be applied in particular work situations. This is part of being an effective manager.

Content and process theories of motivation

Theories of motivation can be divided into two broad approaches – content theories and process theories. Content theories place emphasis on **what motivates** and attempt to explain those specific things which actually motivate the individual at work. These theories are concerned with identification of people's needs and their relative strengths, and the goals they pursue in order to satisfy these needs. Major content theories include:

- Maslow's hierarchy of needs model;
- Alderfer's continuum of needs model (ERG theory);
- Herzberg's two-factor theory; and
- McClelland's theory of achievement motivation.

Process theories place emphasis on the actual **process of motivation** and attempt to identify the relationships among the dynamic variables which make up motivation. These theories are discussed later in this chapter.

MASLOW'S HIERARCHY OF NEEDS

Maslow's theory of individual development and motivation, originally published in 1943, provides a useful starting point.[8] The basic proposition of Maslow's work is that people are wanting beings; they always desire more, and what they want depends on what they already have. He suggests that human needs are arranged in a series of levels – a hierarchy of importance. At the lowest level are physiological needs, then safety needs, love (or social) needs, esteem needs – to, at the highest level, the need for self-actualisation (Figure 8.3).

The basic premise of Maslow's theory is that once a lower-level need has been satisfied it no longer acts as a strong motivator. The needs of the next highest level in the hierarchy demand satisfaction and become the primary motivating influence. Only the unsatisfied needs motivate a person. Thus Maslow asserts that: **'a satisfied need is no longer a motivator'**.

It is important to note, however, that Maslow points out that a particular need at one level does not necessarily have to be satisfied fully before a subsequent need arises. There is a gradual emergence of a higher-level need as lower-level needs become 'largely' satisfied.

Not necessarily a fixed order

The hierarchy is not necessarily a fixed order and for some people there will be more dominant needs and a reversal of the hierarchy. To some people, for example, self-esteem may seem to be more important than love or social needs. For some innately creative people the desire to satisfy esteem needs or self-actualisation may be the prime motivating influence. This might be true for some chefs, for example.

A (then) HCITB report highlights the image of the job of the chef as very definitely seen as important, skilled and responsible. It is a challenging rather than an easy job. Although it is seen as secure, a number would prefer a more adventurous job rather than security. The most satisfying aspects of its image are that the job is seen as well respected and offering good opportunities for promotion.[9]

Fig 8.3 Maslow's hierarchy of human needs model

Relevance of Maslow's theory

Maslow's work is subject to doubts and criticisms.[10] The theory is difficult to test empirically and has been subject to various interpretations by different writers. There are also a number of problems in relating Maslow's theory to the work situation.

People do not necessarily satisfy their needs, especially higher-level needs, just through the work situation. The manager would require a complete understanding of people's private and social lives, not just their behaviour at work. Also, some rewards or outcomes at work may satisfy more than one level of need. For example, higher salary or promotion can be applied to all levels of the hierarchy.

However, despite the rather simplistic nature of the need hierarchy model, it does provide a convenient framework for viewing the different needs and expectations of people at work. The position of individual members of staff in the hierarchy will help determine the most appropriate motivators. For example, if a person's physiological and safety needs have been satisfied, giving more of the same does not provide motivation. In order to provide motivation for a change in behaviour, the manager would need to direct attention to the next highest level and the satisfaction of social needs.

It should be remembered that Maslow's theory relates to individual development and motivation in life and not just to the behaviour of people at work. The hierarchy of needs model, therefore, can also be applied to the satisfaction of the needs and expectations of hotel customers as well as to members of staff.[11]

ALDERFER'S CONTINUUM OF NEEDS MODEL

A modified need hierarchy model, applied to the organisational setting, has been presented by Alderfer. This model condenses Maslow's five levels of need into a continuum based on three core sets of needs: existence, relatedness and growth (ERG theory).[12]

- **Existence needs** are concerned with sustaining human existence and survival. They cover physiological and safety needs of a material nature.
- **Relatedness needs** are concerned with relationships to the social environment. They cover love or belonging, affiliation and meaningful interpersonal relationships of a safety or esteem nature.
- **Growth needs** are concerned with the development of potential. They cover self-esteem and self-actualisation.

A continuum of needs

Alderfer suggests that although individuals normally progress through the different levels of needs, they are more of a continuum than a hierarchy. ERG theory states that an individual may be motivated to satisfy more than one basic set of needs. Individuals may also move down to a lower level need. For example, if an individual is continually frustrated in attempting to satisfy growth needs, then relatedness needs may reassume importance as a motivating influence and become the main focus of the individual's efforts.

The results of Alderfer's work support the idea that lower-level needs decrease in strength as they become satisfied. However, lower-level needs do not have to be satisfied before a higher-level need emerges. The order of the sets of needs and their relative importance varies from individual to individual. Some people will be motivated by a strong desire to satisfy their existence needs, while others will have a high desire for satisfaction of relatedness and/or growth needs.

Flexible strategies of motivation

ERG theory appears to provide for a practical and more flexible approach to motivation. One set of needs does not operate to the exclusion of others. Therefore, if a person's needs at a particular level are blocked, then the manager should focus attention on the satisfaction of other sets of needs. Alternative strategies of motivation may be more appropriate for different departments and for different types of staff. For example, if waiters feel their growth needs are blocked through lack of opportunity for personal development, the manager should attempt to provide increased opportunities to satisfy existence and relatedness needs.

HERZBERG'S TWO-FACTOR THEORY

Herzberg's two-factor theory is essentially a theory of job satisfaction related to motivation at work.[13] The original study consisted of interviews with 203 accountants and engineers in America. They were asked to relate: (i) times when they felt exceptionally 'good' about their present job or a previous job, and (ii) times when they felt exception-ally 'bad' about their job.

From the responses to the interviews Herzberg revealed two distinct sets of factors affecting motivation and work: the two-factor theory of motivation and job satisfaction, or the motivation-hygiene theory (Figure 8.4).

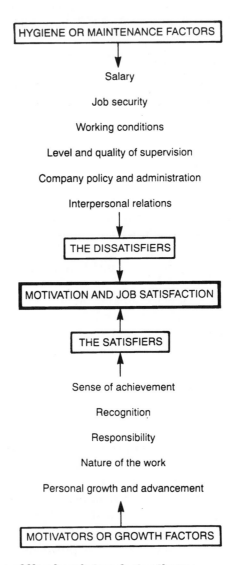

Fig 8.4 Representation of Herzberg's two-factor theory

Hygiene factors or dissatisfiers

One set of factors, known as the 'hygiene' (indicating preventative and environmental) or 'maintenance' factors, serve to prevent dissatisfaction. These factors are related to job context and include salary, job security, working conditions, level and quality of supervision, company policy and administration, and interpersonal relations.

If the hygiene factors are absent or inadequate they cause dissatisfaction. Proper attention to the hygiene factors will tend to overcome dissatisfaction and bring motivation back to normal – a zero state. But the hygiene factors do not by themselves create a positive attitude or increase the motivation to work. Accordingly, **the opposite of dissatisfaction is not satisfaction but rather no dissatisfaction**.

Motivating factors or satisfiers

To motivate workers to give of their best and to sustain higher levels of performance, the manager must give attention to a second set of factors – the 'motivators' or 'growth' factors. These factors are related to job content and include a sense of achievement, recognition, responsibility, the nature of the work itself, and personal growth and advancement. The strength of the motivators will affect feelings of satisfaction or no satisfaction, but not dissatisfaction.

Both sets of factors are important

Herzberg emphasises that both sets of factors are important, but for different reasons. Hygiene factors are not a 'second-class citizen system'. They are as important as the motivators and necessary to avoid unpleasantness at work, and to deny unfair treatment by management. The motivating factors relate to what people are allowed to do at work. They are the variables which actually motivate people.

Applications to guest satisfaction

In addition to its normal application to employee motivation, Herzberg's theory and the importance of hygiene and motivating factors can also be applied to the area of guest satisfaction.[14]

Criticisms and limitations

The two-factor theory is a source of frequent debate and controversy. It is also subject to a number of different interpretations. One general criticism relates to methodology. Describing events which gave rise to good or bad feelings is subjective and likely to influence the results. People are more inclined to attribute satisfying incidents at work, the motivators, as a favourable reflection on their own performance. The dissatisfying incidents are more likely to be attributed to external factors and to other people.

Another general, major area of criticism is the simplistic nature of the theory and the lack of allowance for individual differences. Not all workers are greatly interested in the job content of their work, or with motivators or growth factors. (See the discussion on motivating hourly workers later in this chapter.) Some staff appear content to adopt an 'instrumental' view – that is, work as a means to an end (discussed in Chapter 2). They are motivated almost solely by financial rewards and security rather than by the nature of the work or the satisfaction of social needs.[15] Other staff appear happy to work within a tightly structured framework, with closely defined work tasks and limited autonomy or responsibility.

It is often claimed that the theory has only limited application to 'manual' workers, or to people with unskilled jobs or whose work is limited in scope. Yet these are the people who often present management with the biggest problem of motivation. For example, in considering the application of Herzberg's work to hospitality staff, MacQueen comments:

> The trouble with Herzberg's motivation-hygiene theory of motivation is that it applies least to the people management most want to motivate – those with monotonous, repetitive, uninteresting jobs.[16]

Hygiene factors are more likely to be significant in the hospitality industry than in other industries. Workers who live in or take meals when on duty are more likely to be concerned with the workplace and the quality of their working conditions. It might also be that some workers have a low expectation of satisfying higher-level needs and therefore place greater emphasis on the hygiene factors.

The importance of job design

Despite doubts concerning the two-factor theory, Herzberg's work has drawn attention to wider issues which may influence motivation and job satisfaction. If managers are to provide positive motivation and improve job satisfaction, then attention must be given to both the hygiene and the motivating factors.

A particular feature of Herzberg's theory is that it drew attention to the importance of job design and the structuring of hospitality jobs. This point is acknowledged by MacQueen.

> The value of Herzberg's approach lies in its emphasis on the need for the re-design of jobs in order to bring the motivators to bear.[17]

We return to the importance of job design later in this chapter.

McCLELLAND'S ACHIEVEMENT MOTIVATION

The need for achievement underlies the higher levels of Maslow's hierarchy and is also one of Herzberg's motivating factors. The importance of achievement is emphasised by McClelland, who has developed a theory of motivation which is rooted in culture.[18] The work of McClelland is based on the concept of four main sets of needs and socially developed motives:

- the need for **affiliation**;
- the need for **power**;
- the need for **achievement**;
- the need for **avoidance**.

People possess all four needs but the relative intensity of these motives varies among individuals and different occupations. Although all four needs are important, McClelland's research had concentrated mainly on how managers can develop the need for achievement in subordinate staff.

Variations among individuals

The extent of achievement motivation varies among individuals. It is dependent upon cultural influences, occupational experiences and the type of organisation in which they work. Some people rate very highly in achievement motivation. They are challenged by opportunities and work hard to achieve a goal. Other people rate very low in achievement motivation. They do not care much and have little urge to achieve.

Characteristics of high achievers

For high achievers money may seem to be important, but it is valued more as symbolising successful goal achievement. Money may serve as a means of giving feedback on performance. People with high achievement motivation seem unlikely to remain long with an organisation that does not pay them well for good performance. For people with low achievement motivation, money may serve more as a direct financial incentive for performance.

Although it is difficult to apply objective measures, McClelland has identified four common characteristics of people with high achievement needs: the preference for personal responsibility, the setting of moderate goals, the desire for specific feedback and innovativeness.

- Personal satisfaction is derived from the accomplishment of the task itself and recognition need not come from other people. They prefer situations in which they can assume **personal responsibility** for solving problems. They like to attain success through their own efforts, rather than by teamwork or by chance factors outside their control.
- They tend to set **moderate achievement goals** with an intermediate level of difficulty, and to take calculated risks. If a task is too difficult or too risky it would reduce the chances of success and of gaining need satisfaction. If the course of action is too easy or too simple, there is little challenge in accomplishing the task and little satisfaction from successful performance.
- They want **clear and unambiguous feedback** on how well they are performing. A knowledge of results within a reasonable time is necessary for self-evaluation. Feedback enables them to determine success or failure in the accomplishment of their goals, and satisfaction from their activities.
- They are **more innovative** and tend always to be moving on to something a little more challenging. There is a constant search for variety and for information to find new ways of doing things.

Applications to the hospitality industry

There are of course potential benefits to any business organisation from the efforts and performance of high achievers. But McClelland's theory implies an individualistic approach to the motivation of staff. The hospitality industry, however, is characterised by the need for close co-operation and effective teamwork in order to provide customer satisfaction. The behaviour and performance of work groups is as important as individual motivation. Attempts to satisfy the needs of higher achievers must be matched with the requirements of the industry and this may not be an easy task.[19]

THEORY M: MOTIVATING HOURLY WORKERS

The content theories of motivation place emphasis on the importance of psychological rewards, and personal growth and achievement. According to Weaver, however, such theories have little meaning for hourly workers in the hotel and restaurant industry.[20] The work of, for example, cooks, dishwashers and waiting or housekeeping staff does not change much among different companies, so such staff feel little attachment to a particular company. Where there is little pleasure in the work itself or the job offers little opportunity for career advancement, personal challenge or growth, hourly workers are working for their pay cheque.

Motivating with money

Weaver proposes a 'Theory M' programme of motivation based on direct cash rewards for above-average productivity. A percentage base is calculated from the average performance of workers on the staff. Workers then receive a percentage of any *increase* in sales or savings to the company generated by their efforts. Although particularly suited to food and beverage operations, Weaver suggests that the programme could be extended to other hotel employees, for example a bonus payment to night-desk staff for selling as many vacant rooms as possible or a wage incentive to housekeeping staff for cleaning an above-average number of rooms in a shift.

PROCESS THEORIES OF MOTIVATION

Process theories attempt to identify relationships among the dynamic variables which make up motivation. They provide a further contribution to our understanding of behaviour and performance at work, and the complex nature of motivation. Process theories are concerned with how behaviour is initiated, directed and sustained. There are a number of different process theories but the major approach under this heading is expectancy theory.

The basis of expectancy theory

Expectancy theory provides a dominant framework in which to view motivation at work. The basis of expectancy theory is that people are influenced by the expected results of their actions. Motivation to work well is a function of the relationship between:

(i) effort expended and the perceived likely outcomes; and
(ii) the expectations that reward will be related to performance.

The level of performance depends upon the perceived expectations regarding effort expended and the desired outcome. For example, a sous chef desires higher status and seeks promotion to head chef. This desire will lead to a high level of performance only if the sous chef believes there is a strong expectation that this will lead to promotion, and that promotion will result in a satisfactory increase in status.

As another example, a personnel assistant, who is unqualified, desires a higher salary but believes this is not possible in the present job. The assistant also believes that promotion would be most unlikely without an examination qualification. In this case there is likely to be a lack of positive motivation to achieve a high level of performance.

In broader terms, however, the generally high levels of staff turnover in the industry may well mean that good performance is perceived as very likely to lead to greater opportunities for rapid promotion.

Effort, performance and rewards

The underlying premise of expectancy theory, therefore, is that motivation is determined by the perceived strength of the link between:

Effort expended – Performance achieved – Rewards obtained

A person's behaviour reflects a conscious choice between the comparative evaluation of alternative behaviour. The choice of behaviour is based on the expectancy of the most favourable consequences. And expectancy is based on the person's **perception** of the situation, irrespective of whether or not this is *de facto* the situation.

VROOM'S EXPECTANCY THEORY

Vroom's expectancy model is aimed specifically at the work situation. It is centred on three key variables: valence, instrumentality, and expectancy (VIE theory).[21] On the basis of Vroom's work it is possible to depict a general model of expectancy theory (Figure 8.5).

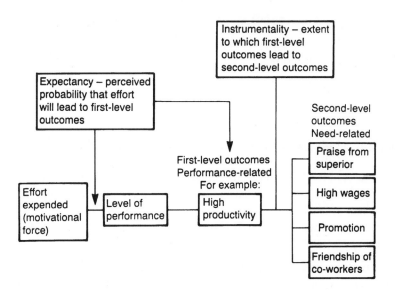

Fig 8.5 A basic model of expectancy theory

- **Valence.** This is the feelings that individuals have about specific outcomes. It is a measure of the attractiveness or preference for a particular outcome to the individual. Valence is not the same as value. Valence is **the anticipated satisfaction provided by an outcome**. This may differ from value, which is the actual satisfaction derived by an outcome.

- **Instrumentality.** This is the extent to which performance related (first-level) outcomes lead to the satisfaction of need-related (second-level) outcomes. Some people may seek to achieve a high level of performance 'for its own sake' and without thought to further expectations. Usually, however, good performance achieves valence because this will be **instrumental** in leading to the satisfaction of second-level outcomes, for example the need for higher wages, promotion or status.

- **Expectancy.** This is the perceived degree of probability that the choice of a particular action will actually lead to the desired outcome. When a person chooses between alternative forms of behaviour which have uncertain outcomes, the choice is affected not only by preference (valence) but also by the probability that such an outcome will be achieved. Expectancy is the relationship between a chosen course of action and its predicted outcome.

Motivational force

The assumption of expectancy theory is that an individual considers in a rational manner the comparative advantages of alternative choices of action and the likelihood of attaining the desired outcome from that action. It is the combination of valence and expectancy which determine a person's motivation for a given form of behaviour. This is the motivational force. Expressed as an equation, this is:

$$M \text{ (Motivation)} = V \text{ (valence)} \times E \text{ (expectancy)}$$

If either valence or expectancy is zero, then motivation is zero. There are likely to be a number of different outcomes for a given choice of action. Accordingly the measure of $V \times E$ is summed across the total number of possible outcomes to provide a single figure indicating the attractiveness for a particular choice of behaviour.

THE PORTER AND LAWLER EXPECTANCY MODEL

A development of the VIE theory has been put forward by Porter and Lawler. They present a model which extends beyond motivational force and considers performance as a whole.[22] Porter and Lawler maintain that effort expended (the motivational force) does not lead directly to performance. It is mediated by three sets of intervening variables.

- **Individual abilities and traits** – such as intelligence, skills, knowledge, training and personality. These factors affect the ability to perform a given activity.
- **The person's role perceptions** – that is, the way in which individuals view their work and the role they should adopt. This influences the type of effort expended, and the direction and level of action.
- **The nature of intrinsic and extrinsic rewards**, and perceived equitable rewards.

A representation of the Porter and Lawler model is given in Figure 8.6.

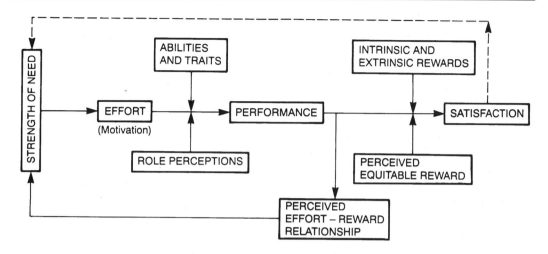

Fig 8.6 Representation of the Porter and Lawler motivation model

Intrinsic and extrinsic rewards

Rewards are desirable outcomes and both intrinsic and extrinsic rewards are important. Intrinsic rewards derive from the individuals themselves and include personal satisfaction, a sense of achievement, a feeling of responsibility and recognition. Extrinsic rewards derive from the organisation and the actions of others, and include salary, working conditions and supervision. The proportion of intrinsic and extrinsic will vary among individuals and different work situations, but there must be a minimum of both. However, Porter and Lawler suggest that intrinsic rewards are more likely to produce job satisfaction related to performance than are extrinsic rewards.

Most people have an implicit perception about the level of rewards, intrinsic and extrinsic, they should receive commensurate with the requirements and demands of the job, and the contribution expected of them. Perceived equitable reward is the level of rewards people feel they should fairly receive for a given standard of performance. The experience of satisfaction derives from actual rewards which meet or exceed the perceived equitable rewards.

Motivation, satisfaction and performance

Porter and Lawler see motivation, satisfaction and performance as separate variables, and attempt to explain the complex relationships among them. The effort, or amount of energy, a person exerts on a given activity is associated more with motivation than with performance. It does not relate to how successful a person is in carrying out an activity.

The human relations approach tended to assume that job satisfaction leads to improved performance. In contrast, Porter and Lawler suggest that job satisfaction is an effect rather than a cause of performance. Job satisfaction is more dependent upon performance, than performance is upon job satisfaction.

PRACTICAL APPLICATIONS OF EXPECTANCY THEORY

There are a number of different versions of expectancy theory and it is not always easy to understand or apply them. There are many variables which affect behaviour at work. A problem can arise in attempting to identify those variables which are most important in particular situations. Expectancy theory applies only to behaviour which is under the voluntary control of the individual. Individuals may have only limited freedom to make choices because of constraints imposed by, for example, policies and procedures, the nature of technology, the organisation structure or role prescriptions.

Complexities of work motivation

Expectancy theory does, however, draw attention to the complexities of work motivation. It provides further information in helping to explain the nature of behaviour in the work situation, and in identifying problems in motivation and performance. Research studies highlight difficulties with some of the concepts involved but do appear to provide general support for the theory.[23]

Porter and Lawler emphasise that the expectancy model is just a model. People rarely sit down and consciously list their expected outcomes, expectancies and valences. But they do consider the likely outcomes of their actions and the attractiveness of various alternatives in deciding what they will do. The expectancy model provides a means of mirroring the process and predicting its outcome.[24]

Attention by management

Expectancy theory indicates that, in order to improve the motivation and performance of staff, the manager should give attention to a number of factors including the following.

- Attempt to establish clear relationships and strong links between effort and performance, and performance and rewards.
- Review appropriateness of rewards in terms of individual performance rather than on a more general basis. Outcomes with a high valence for the individual should be used as an incentive for improved performance.
- Establish clear procedures for the monitoring and evaluation of individual levels of performance.
- Ensure subordinates have the required understanding, knowledge and skills to enable them to achieve a high level of performance.
- Give attention to intervening variables such as company policies, organisational procedures and support facilities which, although not direct motivational factors, may still affect performance.
- Minimise undesirable outcomes which may be perceived to result from a high level of performance, for example accidents, sanctions from co-workers or the imposition of increased targets. Also minimise those undesirable outcomes which result despite a high level of performance, such as a reduced level of bonus payments.

EQUITY THEORY OF MOTIVATION

One of the variables identified in the Porter and Lawler expectancy model is perceived equitable rewards. This leads to consideration of another process theory of motivation – equity theory – which adds further to our understanding of the behaviour of people at work. **Equity theory focuses on people's feelings of how fairly they have been treated in comparison with the treatment received by others**. Applied to the work situation, equity theory is usually associated with the work of Adams.[25]

People evaluate their social relationships in the same way as buying or selling an item. Social relationships involve an exchange process. People expect certain outcomes in exchange for certain contributions or inputs. Equity theory is based on this concept of exchange theory. For example, a person may expect promotion as an outcome (and in exchange for) a high level of contribution in helping to achieve an important organisational objective (input).

Comparison of outcomes and inputs

People also compare their own position with that of others. They determine the **perceived** equity of their own position. Feelings about the equity of the exchange is affected by the treatment they receive when compared with what happens to other people. Most exchanges involve a multiple of inputs and outcomes. According to equity theory, people place a weighting on these various inputs and outcomes according to how they perceive their importance.

If the ratio of a person's total outcomes to total inputs equals the perceived ratio of other people's outcomes and inputs there is equity. But when there is an unequal comparison of ratios the person experiences a sense of inequity. The feeling of inequity might arise when an individual's ratio of outcomes to inputs is either greater than or, more usually, less than that of other people.

Behavioural consequences of inequity

The feeling of inequity causes tension. This motivates the person to take action to restore equity. The magnitude of perceived inequity determines the level of tension, and the level of tension determines the strength of motivation. Adams identifies six broad types of behaviour which arise as a consequence of inequity (Figure 8.7).

- **Changes to inputs** – for example, through the amount or quality of work, timekeeping or absenteeism.
- **Changes to outputs** – for example, attempting to improve pay, working conditions, fringe benefits or perks, status and recognition, without changes to inputs.
- **Cognitive distortion of inputs or outcomes** – for example, the belief about how hard a person is really working, the value of examination qualifications, or what can be achieved with a given level of pay.
- **Leaving the field** – for example, through absenteeism, lack of interest or involvement with the work, request for transfer, or resignation from a job or the organisation.
- **Acting on others** – for example, tempting others to increase their inputs or lower their outcomes, or trying to force others to leave the field.

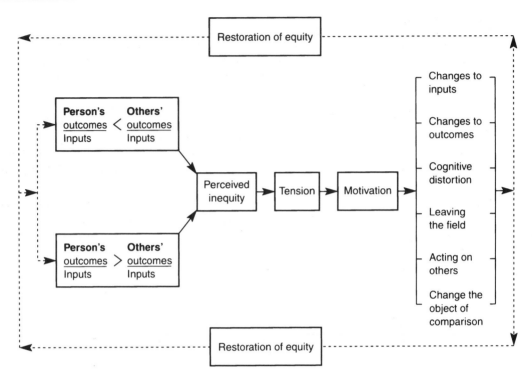

Fig 8.7 Representation of Adams's equity theory of motivation
Source: Mullins L J, *Management and Organisational Behaviour*, Third edition, Pitman (1993), p. 472

- **Changing the object of comparison** – for example, viewing people with whom comparisons have previously been made as now belonging to a different level in the organisation, and finding a new reference group with whom comparison is made.

Managers need to recognise such forms of behaviour as possible consequences of perceived inequity and to take appropriate action to reduce tension and restore a sense of equity.

APPLICATIONS OF MOTIVATIONAL THEORIES

The application of motivational theories, and a greater understanding of job satisfaction and work performance, have led to increasing interest in job design. Redesigning the nature of the work organisation and the structure of jobs can have a significant effect on the attitudes and satisfaction of staff, and their level of performance.

A major contribution of Herzberg's two-factor theory lies in the emphasis on the redesign of jobs in order to bring the motivators to bear. His belief is that people should have the opportunity to use their talents and abilities, and to exercise more self-control over the job. Inherent in the job should be a learning and growth experience.[26] Expectancy theory suggests that improving the effort–performance–reward link through job design will have a powerful motivating influence on people, especially those who place a high value on intrinsic rewards.

Alienation at work

One common approach to job satisfaction and work performance is in terms of frustration and alienation at work. Alienation refers to the feeling of detachment of individuals from their work roles. Four major dimensions of alienation are powerlessness, meaninglessness, isolation and self-estrangement.[27]

- **Powerlessness** denotes the workers' lack of control over management policy, their immediate work processes or conditions of employment.
- **Meaninglessness** stems from standardisation and the division of labour. It denotes the inability to see the purpose of work done, or to identify with the total process or completed product or service.
- **Isolation** is the feeling of not belonging to an integrated work group or to the social work organisation, or not being guided by group norms of behaviour.
- **Self-estrangement** arises from the failure to see work as an end in itself or as a central life issue. Workers experience a depersonalised detachment and work is seen solely as a means to an end.

In order to help overcome alienation, management should attempt to develop within individuals a feeling of attachment to the organisation and to the work situation. The attachment of individuals and the satisfaction derived from their jobs are influenced by the formal structure, managerial style, and the nature of technology and work organisation.

THE NATURE OF HOSPITALITY WORK

Unlike many manufacturing or administrative situations, the hospitality industry offers potentially high levels of attachment to the work.[28] As mentioned previously workers who live in or take meals on duty are especially likely to feel closely involved with their workplace. You may also recall one of the comments from a hotel manager in Assignment 3 of Chapter 5: 'For many live-in workers, it is not a job – it is their life. Everything rolled into one. It is not a job where you clock off and go home on Friday forgetting everything until Monday morning.'

Conflicting opinions

However, there appear to be conflicting opinions as to the nature of work in the hospitality industry. One view is that many jobs are monotonous, basic and routine in nature, performed under difficult working conditions and with added harassment from customers. Job enrichment may be difficult to achieve and in any case many workers do not seem greatly interested.

According to a (then) HCITB report, low status and the servile nature of jobs is a feature of work in the industry. Jobs such as those of cashier, kitchen staff and (surprisingly) receptionists lack variety and job satisfaction. The nature of the working environment deters substantial numbers of jobseekers from accepting kitchen jobs.[29]

In contrast, a later HCTC publication suggests an alternative and more positive view, that the industry offers great potential for job satisfaction. Many jobs provide satisfying contact with the customer and allow individual flair and creativity. Staff usually have close and frequent contact with their manager or supervisor, unlike the 'anonymous' nature of some factory or office situations.[30] These positive features should be built upon and developed through the restructuring of work and job design.

Likes and dislikes about working in the industry

A study of 442 recent graduates from 11 American hospitality management colleges highlighted the importance of job challenge and career advancement as a key factor of job satisfaction.[31] Responses to an open-ended question on what was liked and disliked about working in the hospitality industry were categorised into five groups of likes and six groups of dislikes (Figure 8.8).

Likes:
1. Challenge, direct involvement, autonomy, independence, rewarding work

2. People, the public, and professional contacts

3. Working environment, opportunity for growth and advancement

4. Fast pace, change

5. Benefits, travel, prestige

Dislikes:
1. Long hours, nights and weekend schedule

2. Low pay

3. Stress, demanding supervisors and duties, no personal time, quality of life

4. Routine, no advancement or growth, no import or recognition

5. Company politics, management

6. Labor shortages, poor staff, lack of employee motivation, employees' and co-workers' attitudes

Note: Each list is presented in descending order of frequency.

Fig 8.8 Hospitality jobs: likes and dislikes
Reprinted by permission of Elsevier Science Inc. from Pavesic D V and Brymer R A, 'Job Satisfaction: What's Happening to the Young Managers?, *The Cornell Hotel and Restaurant Administration Quarterly*, vol. 30, no. 4, February 1990, p. 95. Copyright 1990 by Cornell University

The most frequent response on what was liked best about the job or career referred to the challenge and direct involvement in their work. The second most frequent set of liked factors referred to interactions with others and people-related responses. Other attractions related to the nature of the work environment, including opportunities for learning and the physical surroundings, the fast pace of the industry, and for a relatively small group, benefits, travel and prestige. Women were more likely to mention likes relating to people and the public than were men, who were more likely to mention challenges and the work environment.

The most disliked factors related to the long hours involved in hotel and food-service work, particularly hours worked at evenings and weekends. Many respondents also referred to not being paid enough for working the odd hours. Other dislikes referred to the stress of the job and the demands of supervisors and their duties, the routine nature of jobs and lack of recognition, especially with lower level jobs, company politics and management, staffing shortages and the nature of the staff. Women were more likely to mention low pay and management politics than men were. But both men and women were equally likely to refer to long hours and low pay as the features most disliked about their jobs.

JOB DESIGN

Job design is concerned with the relationship between workers and the nature and content of jobs, and their task functions. It attempts to meet people's personal and social needs at work through the reorganisation or restructuring of work. There are two major, interrelated reasons for attention to job design:

- to enhance the personal satisfaction that people derive from their work; and
- to make the best use of people as a valuable resource and to help overcome obstacles to their effective performance.

There are many possible aspects of job design. We can view attention to job design in terms of two broad, related approaches (Figure 8.9):

- the restructuring of individual jobs; and
- broader approaches concerned with the wider organisational context.

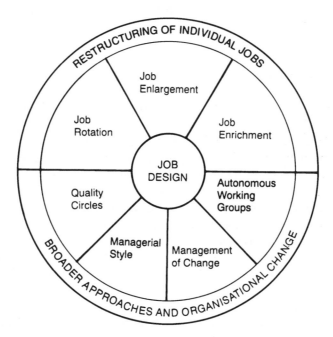

Fig 8.9 Main aspects of job design

RESTRUCTURING OF INDIVIDUAL JOBS

Earlier approaches to job design concentrated on the restructuring of individual jobs and the application of three main methods: (i) job rotation, (ii) job enlargement and (iii) job enrichment.

Job rotation

Although usually included under this heading, job rotation is not strictly job design because neither the nature of the task nor the method of working is restructured. Job rotation involves moving a person from one job or task to another, for example rotating staff from kitchen work to waiting and to reception in order to gain some understanding and experience of the work of other departments. This can benefit the hotel by increasing flexibility in staffing and reducing differences in occupational status.

Job rotation may lead to the acquisition of additional skills and can be applied as a form of training. A planned programme of job rotation is often used, for example, for hotel management students on their industrial training placements. There is also growing attention to cross-training as a means of enhancing employees' knowledge of a wider range of jobs. When business dropped dramatically during the Gulf War, staff at Portsmouth Holiday Inn accepted a four-day week and learned to undertake new jobs as an alternative to redundancies.

Job rotation should help the person to identify more with the total work of the hotel and with the completed delivery of service. It may add some variety to work and help remove monotony and boredom. Under normal circumstances, however, job rotation is often positively resisted by some staff. If the tasks involved are all very similar and routine, then once the person is familiar with new tasks the work may quickly prove boring again.

Job enlargement

This involves increasing the scope of the job and the range of tasks that the person is responsible for carrying out. It is usually achieved by combining a number of related jobs at the same level. Job enlargement is **horizontal job design**. It makes the job structurally larger. It lengthens the time-cycle of operations and may give the person greater variety – for example, allowing commis chefs to undertake a wider range of food preparation. A group of banquet waiters who each set only part of the placement for each guest could undertake the entire setting for a smaller number of guests.

Job enlargement, however, is not always very popular and may even be resisted by workers. Although it may give the person added variety and a wider range of tasks, it does little to improve intrinsic satisfaction or the development of skills. Workers may see job enlargement as simply increasing the number of routine, boring tasks they have to perform.

Job enrichment

This attempts to enrich the job by incorporating motivating or growth factors such as increased responsibility and involvement, opportunities for personal development and a sense of achievement. Job enrichment involves **vertical job enlargement**. It aims to give the person greater autonomy and authority over the planning, execution and control of their own work. Job enrichment should help provide the person with a more meaningful and challenging job, and focuses attention on intrinsic satisfaction.

Methods of achieving job enrichment can include allowing workers to undertake a full task-cycle or provide a more complete delivery of service, providing opportunities for more direct contact with the customers, giving workers greater freedom over the scheduling and pacing of their own work, reducing the level of direct supervision, and giving workers increased responsibility for the monitoring and control of their own work.[32]

For example, receptionists could be encouraged to monitor guest comment cards, and to handle complaints and develop solutions to problems rather than bringing every concern to management. Room attendants could be given greater autonomy for complying with the checklists and inspection of rooms instead of relying on a supervisor to find mistakes. Holiday Inn, for instance, have introduced a system of self-checking attendants who are responsible for supervision of their own work. Supervisors now check only a sample number of rooms to monitor the overall standard of performance. Kitchen staff could be given greater responsibility for their own budget, including ordering supplies and controlling the costs of wastage and breakages.

Stages of a job

Magurn views every job as consisting of three separate stages:

- planning and organising the job, such as use of people and equipment, standards of quality, quantities needed, and work layout;
- doing the job, such as cooking meals, waiting at tables, serving drinks and cleaning;
- control, such as evaluating what is done, inspecting, measuring and adjusting, and correcting.[33]

Most jobs in the hospitality industry are concerned only with the 'doing' stage. Attention to job design would involve exploring ways in which people could have increased autonomy and responsibility for the planning and organising, and the control stages, of their jobs.

BROADER APPROACHES TO JOB DESIGN

The restructuring of individual jobs *may* help increase motivation and job satisfaction, and lead to improved work performance. However, strategies of job rotation, job enlargement and job enrichment are only likely to be effective if they are introduced in a planned and systematic manner. Such strategies must be implemented not simply in an effort to economise on staff and increase managerial control but in the genuine believe that staff will respond in a positive manner to the acceptance of greater responsibility in their work.[34]

In the context of technological developments, attention to improved job design has spread from manipulating the tasks of individual jobs and has taken a broader perspective. Emphasis is placed on organisational change and concern for the quality of working life. The focus of attention is on the wider organisational context, the effective use of human resources and development of skills, and the way the organisation functions.

This involves the concept of a socio-technical approach (discussed in Chapter 1) and concern for people systems as well as technical systems. Broader approaches to job design include attention to autonomous work groups, the management of change, and managerial style.

Autonomous work groups

An important development in job design is a form of work organisation based on autonomous (self-regulating) work groups and teamworking. This involves a small group of workers assuming responsibility for the regulation and organisation of their jobs. Specific goals are agreed for the group, but members decide the means by which these goals are to be achieved. Group members have greater freedom and choice, and wider discretion over the planning, execution and control of their own work. The role of the supervisor is that of giving advice and support to the group as well as monitoring the standard and quality of completed work.[35]

As an example, a group of attendants may be allocated their own block of rooms for which they are collectively responsible. Group members decide on the division of work and the manner in which the various tasks are undertaken, and have discretion over when to take breaks. The group control the quality of their own work and are responsible for the standards of performance achieved.

The management of change

The increasing pace of technological and structural change has made it imperative to address the management of change in ways that would ensure the best outcomes for the organisation and its staff. It is understandable that people tend to be resistant to change. But new ideas and innovations should not be perceived as threats to members of staff. When change is being planned it is necessary to think about the work that people will do and the design of their jobs.

Improving job design needs to take account of how people perceive their present tasks, and to involve them closely in changes which affect them and their work. The way in which work is carried out and the technological processes involved should be integrated with the social needs of people at work. Management needs to adopt a clearly defined strategy for the initiation of change, and to take into account the social and human factors. The aim should be to ensure that the quality of working life is enhanced rather than undermined.

Managerial style

The potential benefits of improved job design are unlikely to be realised if attention is focused on the content of jobs alone. Equally important is the process by which re-design is carried out and the importance of managerial style. The re-design of jobs to benefit both employees and the hospitality organisation is not an easy task. It is a continuous process that requires skill, imagination and commitment. Central to improving the quality of working life is a participative, open style of management involving members of staff in decisions which affect them, their work and the nature of their jobs.

In a discussion on managerial leadership in the hospitality industry, Keegan argues that the challenge is not so much to change the job but to provide a supportive and participative relationship with employees. The manager should create an environment in which the employee's real needs are satisfied.[36] (This view is discussed in more detail in Chapter 10.)

Managers should attempt to develop an atmosphere of mutual trust with staff and encourage their active participation including involvement in problem-solving. There must be full organisational support, including the availability of information for decision-making. Personnel policies and procedures, for example those relating to pay and benefits, incentive schemes, conditions of employment and consultation, should facilitate and help new concepts of improved job design.

QUALITY CIRCLES

Although perhaps not strictly job design, a particular feature associated with part of the wider organisational context is the concept of quality circles. A quality circle is a group of people within an organisation who meet together on a regular basis to identify, analyse and solve problems relating to quality, productivity or other aspects of day-to-day working arrangements using problem-solving techniques. Quality circles are compatible, therefore, with the quality of working life and effective use of human resources in that they provide an opportunity for people at work to become more involved in matters which affect the jobs they do.

Underlying principles

The concept of quality circle groups is based on a number of underlying principles including the following.

- Membership is voluntary.
- The group usually numbers between five and ten members, normally from the same work station or concerned with similar work.
- The group selects the problems to be tackled and the methods of operation.
- The leader of the circle is usually the immediate supervisor but can be decided within the group.
- The group recommends solutions to management and where possible has authority to implement agreed solutions.
- Members receive training in the understanding of group processes, communication and problem-solving skills, and quality-control techniques.

The effective implementation of quality circles relies on the trust and goodwill of all sides. It requires full commitment and active support from top management and line managers. It also requires a participative style of managerial behaviour, full consultation with staff and the delegation of decision-making. Quality circles should not be seen as just another instrument of management. There must be a realistic time perspective for the effective operation of the group, coupled with the continuous monitoring and review of results.[37]

Potential benefits

Quality circles offer a number of potential benefits. They place emphasis on a problem-solving approach and provide for the direct participation of employees in work-related decisions which concern them. Supervisors can gain greater confidence and assume the role of communicators. Quality circles can lead to increased motivation and job satisfaction for members. They can help bring about a more positive attitude to work. In appropriate applications, quality circles can be part of a broad, long-term strategy for organisational change aimed at improving economic performance and the quality of working life. (Details of the introduction of quality circles in Scott's Hotels, as part of a total quality management programme and culture change, are given in the Appendix to this chapter.)

Quality circles do work and are used successfully by a number of British organisations. However, quality circles do not always succeed, and there may be opposition from top management, line managers or trade unions. Quality circles may also fail because of insufficient preparation or lack of positive support from management.[38]

SUMMARY

- Managers achieve results through the efforts of other people and attention must be given to systems of motivation, job satisfaction and rewards. Individuals have a variety of changing and often conflicting needs and expectations at work. These can be viewed within a broad three-fold heading of economic rewards, intrinsic satisfaction and social relationships.

- The complex and variable nature of work motivation has given rise to many competing ideas and theories. These different theories are not conclusive but help to highlight the many motives which influence people's behaviour and performance. They enable the manager to direct attention to how best to motivate staff to work willingly and effectively.

- Content theories attempt to explain those specific things which actually motivate people at work and include the work of Maslow, Alderfer, Herzberg and McClelland. Process theories attempt to identify the relationships among the dynamic variables which make up motivation and include expectancy theories and equity theory.

- The motivation to work well is usually related to job satisfaction but the nature of the relationship is not clear. There appears to be conflicting opinions about the nature of jobs and work in the hospitality industry. A key factor of job satisfaction appears to be the importance of challenges, autonomy and direct involvement in work.

- The restructuring of individual jobs and strategies of job rotation, job enlargement and job enrichment need to be planned and implemented in a positive manner. The focus of improved job design has now taken a broader organisational approach and includes attention to autonomous work groups, management of change, managerial style and quality circles.

APPENDIX: SCOTT'S HOTELS – TQM AND QUALITY CIRCLES

Background

Scott's Hotels Limited is a wholly owned subsidiary of Scott's Hospitality Incorporated, a major Canadian corporation. It is the master franchise holder for Marriott and Courtyard By Marriott hotels in the UK.

Why change?

It was identified that the burning issue for the 1990s was Total Quality Management and that the key area within TQM in our industry would be people: customers, our staff and suppliers.

We believe that the customers' needs are paramount. We can only meet their needs through clearly understanding what those requirements are and having people who work in the business who are equally committed to serving the customers' needs, and to whom we give both the skills and the authority to take whatever action is necessary to meet the customers' needs. We believe that the level of service, and the atmosphere that we can provide to our customers, through our people, will ensure that we both retain our existing customers and attract and retain new customers on a progressive basis and are able to build a reputation for ourselves that is unique within the UK hotel market.

Scott's customer care attitude has its roots firmly embedded in a Totaly Quality culture. There were three very important reasons why Scott's Hotels developed this approach. Firstly, there were new companies entering the UK market place, creating a significant shift in the competitive environment. Secondly, existing hotels were changing hands and being upgraded constantly. Thirdly, our customers were becoming increasingly demanding. They knew exactly what they wanted and how much they wanted to pay for it. We also knew that if we didn't change some of our work practices, not only would we lose our customers to the competition, but our staff as well. A quality product and service offered in a quality environment were critical to business success if we were to maintain our competitive edge, which is why we began our quest for Quality. We focused on three core elements: people involvement, customer satisfaction and changing the management style and culture of the organisation.

How?

We were committed to the belief that what we were talking about in our vision was a total change in the company's culture, a change from one of high standards achieved through a hierarchical management structure and a traditional approach to motivation and people management.

Our strategy for change had to be on an integrated basis. We could not look at one particular area of our operation in isolation. Our course of action had to have commitment throughout the organisation and include all levels.

To launch our culture change we decided to introduce Quality Circles into our hotels. We were very aware of learning from the experience of other companies in the 1980s where Quality Circles were introduced in isolation from any other quality or culture change initiatives and in many cases ultimately failed. We identified that we required external support to help with the training and implementation of Quality Circles but that this support should be in parallel with developing our own skills in this area so that we became self-supporting.

After some research we retained the National Society for Quality Circles Through Teamwork who devised a programme for each hotel that comprised preliminary meetings with general managers and their heads of departments, briefing sessions for all staff at the end of which volunteers were sought for Quality Circles and subsequently Quality Circles Leader training. A facilitator was appointed in each hotel and separate training programmes were undertaken to help them understand the requirements of their role and to acquire and develop the skills to be successful.

A Quality Circle Support Committee was established in every hotel – this ensures that middle and senior managers in each hotel are locked into the Quality Circle process in terms of help and support, and yet still have the opportunity of making decisions regarding the implementation of Quality Circle proposals.

Scott's Hotels have Circles operating in almost all their hotels throughout the UK with plans for more. The guidelines for Circles were simple – each hotel was to stick to the basic principles, i.e. process and structure. However, flexibility of approach and creativity were encouraged.

Where to now?

Despite pressures created by the Gulf War, a recession in the economy and our most significant event to date, that of rebranding, in general Circles have remained buoyant.

Circles need constant attention and it would be foolhardy to embark on this road unless management were totally committed. Motivation and enthusiasm are key factors in the success of the programme.

A Quality Support Manager was appointed from within the business to whom the facilitators within each property report on a dotted line basis. This role has given us the opportunity of having an independent view of the progress of the Quality Circle process in each hotel and support from the Human Resources Department has enabled an objective assessment of training needs to be undertaken. Facilitator meetings are held on a regular basis. These meetings, along with an objective view of training needs, have led to a training plan being produced that includes problem-solving techniques and team dynamics training for all Quality Circle participants.

The Quality Circle process, involving the handing down of responsibility, is now feeding into another key element of our TQM programme, the concept of empowerment – the handing down of responsibility to those who can make the responsibility and authority work for them. This inevitably will mean a review of management structure in the organisation. To a large extent the recommendations for these changes should come from managers themselves as part of the empowerment process. It is all too easy to be overly concerned at energising the grass roots and in the process forgetting middle line managers.

Tailor-made TQM workshops are now being run in all hotels to cover all aspects of Total Quality. They are designed to guide and motivate the team into understanding the opportunities TQM can offer them in formulating action plans in their hotels.

The author is grateful to Jan Hubrecht, Managing Director, and Paula Simmons, Quality Support Manager, Scott's Hotels, for providing the above information.

REVIEW AND DISCUSSION QUESTIONS

1 How would you attempt to explain the basic nature of work motivation? Discuss the relationship between motivation and job satisfaction.

2 Distinguish between content and process theories of motivation. Why is the study of different theories of motivation important for the hospitality manager?

3 Critically assess the practical value of Maslow's hierarchy of needs model to improving the motivation of staff in the hospitality industry.

4 Discuss critically the contention that the main factors affecting motivation and job satisfaction are high wages and good working conditions.

5 Explain your understanding of expectancy theories of motivation. What are the practical applications of expectancy theory?

6 Suggest situations when each of the following theories might have particular significance for the hospitality manager: (i) achievement motivation; (ii) equity theory.

7 What are the major reasons for increasing attention to improved job design? Given the nature of hospitality work, discuss critically the likely value of the restructuring of individual jobs.

8 Explain what is meant by broader approaches to job design. Suggest, with supporting examples, how these approaches might be applied within the hospitality industry.

ASSIGNMENT 1

Needs and motivation

Here is a list of factors that may affect your attitude to your job. Please rank them in order of their importance to you personally. There can be no ties.

In ranking these factors please put 1 against the factor that is most important to you, 2 against the next and so on to 15.

When you have rated the factors in order of importance to yourself, please consider the order in which a representative member of your work team would rate himself or herself. Complete the second column for this – Subordinate.

You		*Subordinate*
☐	Achievement	☐
☐	Advancement	☐
☐	Company policy and administration	☐
☐	Job – possibility of individual growth	☐
☐	Job interest	☐
☐	Personal relationships – with supervisors	☐
☐	Personal relationships – with colleagues	☐
☐	Personal relationships – with subordinates	☐
☐	Personal life (factors outside work)	☐

You		*Subordinate*
☐	Recognition for effective work	☐
☐	Responsibility	☐
☐	Salary	☐
☐	Security	☐
☐	Status	☐
☐	Working conditions – physical	☐

Reprinted with permission of The Sherlock Holmes Hotel, London

(i) After you have completed the form compare your responses with those of your colleagues.

(ii) Explain what conclusions you draw.

ASSIGNMENT 2

(i) Interview at least three people with different jobs in any aspect of the hospitality industry. Identify as clearly as possible, together with reasons and supporting examples:
- those aspects of the job which the person feels to be of particular importance and/or significance;
- what aspects of the job the person likes most and those aspects disliked the most; and
- what motivates each person to work well and perform to the best of his or her ability.

(ii) Select a particular department within a hospitality organisation and investigate specific causes of job dissatisfaction. Suggest how these particular problems of dissatisfaction could be tackled in a positive and practical way.

(iii) Explain what conclusions you draw from your observations and the extent to which you can relate your findings to different theories/studies of motivation and job satisfaction.

ASSIGNMENT 3

You are the newly appointed general manager of ABC Hotel. At interview you were informed that there is serious concern about the generally poor level of work performance, that morale is low and that there is a disturbingly high level of staff turnover.

(i) Explain fully the likely actions you would take to help overcome the present situation.

(ii) Indicate clearly the priorities you would have in mind.

(iii) Make clear any necessary, reasonable assumptions.

(iv) Explain how you might draw upon those theories/studies of motivation and job satisfaction you consider to be relevant.

CASE STUDY

Happy Hotels – flexible working or stretching a point?

Happy Holdings plc operate some ten four-star hotels in the UK under the trade name of Happy Hotels. Additionally within the portfolio there is also a budget chain marketed as Happy Traveller, aimed at the two- to three-star market.

Both brands operate in very different ways. Happy Hotels are traditionally managed with relatively strong demarcation lines between food and beverage, front of house and administration. Seniority is indicated by the uniform and type of name badge worn – for example, operative level staff wear a basic uniform and have a name badge engraved with their christian, or first, name; supervisory staff are given a jacket and their surname is added to their name badge. These tokens of seniority are much prized and jealously guarded, as is the perceived expertise of each job holder – gained after, in some cases, several years of specialised college and industrial training.

Conversely, Happy Traveller is managed very differently. The food and beverage operation is franchised to a national brewery chain and, to promote flexibility, the remaining staff are employed as general assistants who work as required in all other areas of the hotel.

Both operations worked effectively until Jeff Broadfield, a young and ambitious graduate, was promoted from manager of a Happy Traveller to general manager of a Happy Hotel. The hotel he left was two years old, sited on a motorway interchange and very profitable, enjoying 90 per cent occupancy rates. The hotel he inherited was ten years old, in need of a major refurbishment and suffering financially as a result of economic recession. Occupancy levels had dropped and staff were demotivated; Broadfield was under pressure both to prove himself worthy of the promotion and to restore the ailing fortunes of his new property.

His immediate action was to introduce a method of job evaluation into the hotel in an attempt to identify similar jobs in order to establish similar flexible working arrangements to those at the Happy Traveller. He felt that not only would this flexibility improve efficiency levels but that the resulting job rotation would increase job satisfaction and thus morale amongst the staff.

Constrained by finances, the job evaluation which was implemented was of a somewhat basic approach. With the aid of the personnel officer, Broadfield himself classified jobs according to skill level and the amount of training required to reach competence, the lowest level rather unfortunately being classified as 'straight off the street', implying that little or no skill was needed and training minimal to bring the job holder to full competence.

Accompanying this flexible approach was to be a change in staff uniforms; since they would be working at a variety of jobs during the working day, all staff would wear broadly the same uniform. In an attempt to promote democracy and engender feelings of equality, name badges would be changed to christian, or first, names only.

Having planned the strategy for implementing these changes, Broadfield then communicated this in a memo to head office. Unfortunately, at this stage, events overtook him: his memo was mistakenly left in the photocopier where it was discovered by a member of the maintenance team – easily the most militant and vociferous in the hotel. Events further conspired against Broadfield: the discovery of the memo coincided with his absence from the hotel on a training course. Mayhem ensued when the memo 'found' its way onto the staff canteen notice board, and irate husbands telephoning to demand why their spouses had been classified as 'straight off the street' were met with a blank wall of silence.

On his return, Broadfield was met with a deputation of staff demanding to know what was happening. He decided to call a general staff meeting to explain to the staff the reasoning behind his proposals. However, the meeting fell short of total success; his urge to communicate his ideas to staff, particularly the concept of job rotation to improve motivation, individual skills and morale, fell on stony ground.

Nevertheless, the new scheme was introduced the following week. Accounts department staff were deputed to train on bed-making, Broadfield's secretary was sent to the kitchen, the second chef was told to train as a waiter. A disgruntled maintenance engineer was heard to comment, as he cleared the potwash machine, 'So much for *my* training – I spent four years serving my apprenticeship, thirty years as a craftsman carpenter and I'm now washing pots. What can I do about it – who would want me at my age with few jobs about anyway? All this talk about job rotation, new skills and motivation is a load of rubbish – the only place he's motivated me is over a barrel and there isn't a thing that I can do about it.'

The copyright of this case study rests with the author's colleague Karen Meudell, University of Portsmouth. The case is reprinted with permission.

NOTES AND REFERENCES

1. Mullins L J, 'Management and Managerial Behaviour', *The International Journal of Hospitality Management*, vol. 4, no. 1, 1985, pp. 39–41.
2. See, for example, Vroom V H and Deci E L (eds), *Management and Motivation*, Penguin (1970).
3. See, for example, Rudolph P A and Kleiner B H, 'The Art of Motivating Employees', *Journal of Managerial Psychology*, vol. 4, no. 5, 1989, pp. i–iv.
4. Ellis P, *The Image of Hotel and Catering Work*, HCITB Research Report (1981).
5. Hunt J W, *Managing People at Work*, Second edition, McGraw-Hill (1986).
6. British Institute of Management, *Management News*, no. 64, February 1990, p. 6.
7. Willman 1', 'Human Resource Management in the Service Sector', in Jones P (ed), *Management in Service Industries*, Pitman (1989), p. 217.
8. Maslow A H, 'A Theory of Human Motivation', *Psychological Review*, vol. 50, no. 4, July 1943, pp. 370–396, and Maslow A H, *Motivation and Personality*, Third edition, Harper & Row (1987).
9, Ellis P, *The Image of Hotel and Catering Work*, HCITB Research Report (1981).
10. See, for example, Hornsey T and Dann D, *Manpower Management in the Hotel and Catering Industry*, Batsford (1984), and Mullins L J, *Management and Organisational Behaviour*, Third edition, Pitman (1993).
11. For a more detailed account of Maslow's model applied to guest behaviour, see Venison P, *Managing Hotels*, Heinemann (1983).
12. Alderfer C P, *Existence, Relatedness and Growth*, Collier Macmillan (1972).
13. Herzberg F, Mausner B and Synderman B B, *The Motivation to Work*, Second edition, Chapman & Hall (1959).
14. Balmer S and Baum T, 'Applying Herzberg's Hygiene Factors to the Changing Accommodation Environment', *International Journal of Contemporary Hospitality Management*, vol. 5, no. 2, 1993, pp. 32–35.
15. See, for example, Goldthorpe J H et al., *The Affluent Worker: Industrial Attitudes and Behaviour*, Cambridge University Press (1968).
16. MacQueen N, 'What Happened to Herzberg: Is Motivation Theory Out of Date?' *Hospitality*, no. 29, May 1982, p. 16.
17. *Idem.*

18. McClelland D C, *The Achieving Society*, Van Nostrand Reinhold (1961) (also published by Irvington, 1976), and *Human Motivation*, Cambridge University press (1988).

19. See, for example, Hornsey T and Dann D, *Manpower Management in the Hotel and Catering Industry*, Batsford (1984).

20. Weaver T, 'Theory M: Motivating with Money', *Cornell HRA Quarterly*, vol. 29, no. 3, November 1988, pp. 40–45.

21. Vroom V H, *Work and Motivation*, Wiley (1964) (also published by Krieger, 1982).

22. Porter L W and Lawler E E, *Managerial Attitudes and performance*, Irwin (1968).

23. See, for example, Graen G, 'Instrumentality Theory of Work Motivation', *Journal of Applied Psychology Monograph*, vol. 53, no. 2, 1969, part 2.

24. Porter L W, Lawler E E and Hackman J R, *Behavior in Organizations*, McGraw-Hill (1975).

25. Adams J S, 'Injustice in Social Exchange', abridged in Steers R M and Porter L W, *Motivation and Work Behaviour*, Second edition, McGrav-Hill (1979,) pp. 107–124.

26. Herzberg F, 'One More Time: How do you Motivate Employees?', *Harvard Business Review*, vol. 46, 1968, pp. 3–62.

27. Blauner R, *Alienation and Freedom*, University of Chicago Press (1964).

28. See, for example, Riley M, *Human Resource management: A guide to personnel practice in the hotel and catering industry*, Butterworth-Heinemann (1991).

29. Ellis P, *The Image of Hotel and Catering Work*, HCITB Research Report (1981).

30. *Employee Relations for the Hotel and Catering Industry*, Seventh edition, HCTC (1990).

31. Pavesic D V and Brymer R A, 'Job Satisfaction: 'What's Happening to the Young Managers?' *Cornell HRA Quarterly*, vol. 30, no. 4, February 1990, pp. 90–96.

32. See, for example, Mill R C, *Managing for productivity in the Hospitality Industry*, Van Nostrand Reinhold (1989).

33. Magurn J P, *A Manual of Staff Management in the Hotel and Catering Industry*, Heinemann (1983).

34. See, for example, Hales C, 'Quality of Working Life: job redesign and participation in a service industry: a rose by any other name?', *The Service Industries Journal*, vol. 7, no. 3, 1987, pp. 253–273.

35. See, for example, Grayson D, *Self Regulating Work Groups*, Work Research Unit, Occasional Paper no. 46, HMSO (July 1990).

36. Keegan B M, 'Leadership in the Hospitality Industry', in Cassee E and Reuland R (eds), *The Management of Hospitality*, Pergamon (1983).

37. See, for example, Simmons P and Teare R, 'Evolving a Total Quality Culture', *International Journal of Contemporary Hospitality Management*, vol. 5, no. 3, 1993, pp. v–viii.

38. For a more detailed account of quality circles, see Mullins L J, *Management and Organisational Behavior*, Third edition, Pitman (1993).

9

GROUP BEHAVIOUR AND PERFORMANCE

INTRODUCTION

Groups are an essential feature of the structure of any work organisation. Individuals seldom work in isolation from others and almost all staff in the hospitality industry will be a member of one or more groups. If performance is to be successful, the activities of staff require co-ordination through the operation of groups and effective teamwork.

This chapter looks at:
- The nature and importance of work groups
- Influences over behaviour
- Work pattern of the hospitality industry
- Formal and informal groups
- Benefits of group membership
- Developing effective groups
- Potential disadvantages of cohesive groups
- Inter-departmental conflict
- Creating team effectiveness
- The performance of groups
- Membership of successful teams
- Role relationships, role conflict and role stress
- Sociometry and interaction analysis

THE NATURE OF WORK GROUPS

The structure of the hospitality organisation is made up of groups of people. Members of a group must co-operate together in order that activities are carried out. Groups are a major influence over behaviour and the work pattern of the organisation. The manager must use groups in order to achieve a high standard of work and improve the effectiveness of hospitality operations. This requires an understanding of the functioning and processes of groups, and their influence on the behaviour and performance of people at work.

What is a group?

Most people will readily understand what constitutes a group although there appears to be no single, accepted definition. The central feature of a group is that its members regard themselves as belonging to the group. One way of defining a work group is a collection of people who share most if not all of the following characteristics:

- a definable membership;
- group consciousness;
- a sense of shared purpose;
- interdependence;
- interaction; and
- ability to act in a unitary manner.[1]

It is important to consider both the structure and processes of the group, and its effects on the behaviour of individual members. Another useful definition of the group, in psychological terms, is any number of people who:

(i)   interact with one another;
(ii) are psychologically aware of one another; and
(iii) perceive themselves to be a group.[2]

THE IMPORTANCE OF WORK GROUPS

The large majority of activities and processes in the work situation require at least some degree of group, as well as individual, effort.[3] This is an important point to emphasise. Recall that the classical approach to organisation and management tended to ignore the importance of groups and the social factors at work. Scientific management, for example, popularised the concept of the 'rabble hypothesis'. This assumed that people carried out their work, and could be motivated, as solitary individuals unaffected by others.

The human relations approach, however, drew attention to the work organisation as a social organisation. Recognition was given to the power of group membership over individual behaviour and work performance. Emphasis was placed on the importance of the informal organisation, and the influence of groups on social satisfaction and work performance.

The socio-technical approach

The systems approach also gave recognition to the importance of groups. The concept of the organisation as a socio-technical system is concerned with the interactions between psychological and social factors, as well as the structural and technical requirements of the organisation. The importance of the socio-technical system was illustrated by the introduction of technological change and new methods of working in the coal-mining industry.[4]

Small self-selecting groups of miners worked together as independent teams on one part of the coalface. The increasing use of mechanisation and the introduction of shift-working enabled coal to be extracted on a 'longwall' method. This was, technically, a more efficient and economic system. However, the new method of working disrupted the integration of the groups and brought about changes in the social relationships of the miners. As a result there was a lack of co-operation between and within shifts, an increase in absenteeism, scapegoating and signs of social stress.

The 'longwall' method was socially disruptive to the work groups and did not prove as economically efficient as it could have done with the new technology. The result was a 'composite' method of working with more responsibility taken by the team as a whole, shifts carrying out composite tasks and the reintroduction of multi-skilled roles. The composite method proved to be both more rewarding socially for the miners and also a more efficient method of working.

INFLUENCES OVER BEHAVIOUR

Groups, therefore, are a characteristic feature of all social situations. The working of groups and the influence they exert over their membership is a major feature of human behaviour and group processes. People in groups influence each other in many ways, and groups develop their own hierarchies and leaders. Group pressures to conform with 'norms' and social conventions can have a significant influence over the behaviour of individual members and their work performance.

You may recall that one experiment of the Hawthorne studies (discussed in Chapter 3) was the observation of a group of 14 men working in the bank wiring room. It was noted that the men formed their own informal organisation with sub-groups and cliques, and with natural leaders emerging with the consent of members. They would often help each other with the work and, contrary to management instructions, members would often exchange jobs.

Group values and norms of behaviour

The group developed its own pattern of informal social relations, and codes and practices ('norms') of what constituted 'proper' group behaviour:

- **not to be a 'rate buster'** – not to produce at too high a rate of output compared with other members or to exceed the production restriction of the group;

- **not to be a 'chiseller'** – not to shirk production or to produce at too low a rate of output compared with other members of the group;

- **not to be a 'squealer'** – not to say anything to the supervisor or management which might be harmful to other members of the group;

- **not to be 'officious'** – people with authority over members of the group, for example inspectors, should not take advantage of their seniority or maintain a social distance from the group.

Despite a financial incentive scheme where workers could receive more money for the more units they produced, the group decided on 6000 units a day as a fair level of output. This was well below the level they were capable of producing but group pressure was stronger than financial incentives offered by management.

It was also company policy that the supervisor should report daily on each man's output. However, the workers preferred to do their own reporting. On some days the men would actually produce more than reported in order to 'build up' extra units for days when they produced less than reported. In order to remain in favour with the group the supervisor did nothing to stop this practice.

System of sanctions

If individual members did not conform to these norms of behaviour the group had its own system of sanctions. These included ostracising members, sarcasm and verbal abuse, damaging completed work, hiding tools, and playing tricks on inspectors. Threats of physical violence were also made. The group developed a system of 'binging' which involved striking someone a fairly hard blow on the upper part of the arm. The process of binging also became a recognised method of controlling conflict within the group.

WORK PATTERN OF THE HOSPITALITY INDUSTRY

Groups are formed as a consequence of the structure of the organisation and arrangements for the division of work. They help shape the activities and work pattern of the organisation, and the attitudes of members to their jobs. The formation and operation of work groups, and the behaviour of their members, has important significance for the manager and the effective performance of activities and operations.

Likert, for example, has developed a theory of organisation based on work groups. In his discussion of group processes and organisational performance he concludes that:

> Group forces are important not only in influencing the behavior of individual work groups with regard to productivity, waste, absence and the like, they also affect the behavior of entire organisations.[5]

The need for teamwork

Work is a group-based activity and especially so in hospitality operations. How people behave and perform as a member of a group is as important as their behaviour or performance as individuals. If the hotel, for example, is to operate effectively it requires good teamwork.[6] Simmons and Teare draw attention to the emphasis on teamwork at every level of Scott's Hotels and to the importance of group working, quality improvement teams and action teams as part of a Total Quality Management approach to improved quality and performance.[7]

Not only must members of a group work well as a team but each group must also work well with other groups. It is important to reduce conflict between different groups in the hotel, and especially between front-of-house staff such as receptionists, and back-of-house staff such as housekeepers.[8]

Harmonious working relationships and good teamwork help make for a high level of both staff morale and customer satisfaction. An example of the importance placed on team-work is the extract from the introductory pages of Foxhills' staff induction manual reproduced in Figure 9.1.[9]

What is teamwork
When a group of people communicate well and clearly, work closely together and help each other with instruction and/or actual labour during work, teamwork is achieved. This means HELPING your colleagues WHENEVER and WHEREVER they need it.

Why is teamwork important
Teamwork makes everyone's job easier and makes the department a better place to work in. It also allows and promotes friendship and caring. When you help another colleague get their job done, you are helping yourself. If the customer is served by a person with a confident attitude everyone benefits. This means the co-operation of all staff is essential. It is very obvious that the waiting and barstaff are contributing to

customer service and satisfaction. There are others who will ensure a customer is comfortable and happy. The kitchen staff doing their job well is of the highest importance. There are good food waiters and waitresses but you cannot be good without a good product. Think about it!

> THE NUMBER ONE RULE IS TO COMMUNICATE CLEARLY AND EFFECTIVELY WITH YOUR COLLEAGUES

If you expect and receive instructions and help, return the favour. Before you know it everyone is not only doing their job well, but also helping others and working as part of the team.

Remember to tell people you appreciate what they are doing for you. Thank each person that helps you do your job. We all play a role in customer satisfaction.

Watch your attitude – no one wants to work with a grump or worse, if you are down you spread it around and nobody needs that.

Teamwork at Foxhills is essential to everyone's morale. Try it. Help out a fellow employee and watch it come back to you in the form of appreciation. Teamwork means helping each other and solving problems together. It is mutual respect and open communications on all levels, employee to employee, employee to manager, manager to manager.

> TEAM WORK IS WORK
> BUT IT IS WORTH IT.

Fig 9.1 The importance of teamwork
Extract from staff induction manual, Foxhills Golf and Country Club. Reproduced with permission.

Overlapping group structures

Part of the criteria for System 4 participative group management (discussed in Chapter 5) is the use of overlapping group structures. Likert suggests that the organisation functions best when members act, not as individuals, but as members of highly effective work groups. He proposes a structure based on overlapping group membership with a 'linking pin' process. The superior of one group is a subordinate member of, and the linking pin with, the next authority-level group.

A structure of vertical overlapping groups helps to develop a committed team approach and improve the flow of communications, co-ordination and decision-making. Members of one group could also serve as linking pins between different groups on the same level. This provides improved horizontal communications and co-ordination (Figure 9.2).

FORMAL AND INFORMAL GROUPS

Groups are deliberately planned and created by management as part of organisational design. An organisation chart, for example, gives a representation of the formal structure of the hotel. But groups also arise from social processes and the informal organisation, which was discussed in Chapter 2. The informal organisation arises from the interactions

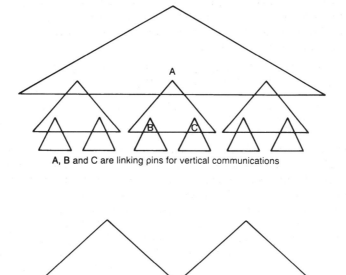

A, B and C are linking pins for vertical communications

D is a linking pin for horizontal communications

Fig 9.2 Representation of Likert's overlapping group structures

of people working within the hotel and the development of groups with their own relationships and norms of behaviour, irrespective of those defined within the formal structure. This leads to a major distinction between formal groups and informal groups.

Formal groups

Formal groups are concerned with the achievement of specific organisational objectives and with the **co-ordination of work activities** of the hotel. They are created by management with established rules, relationships and norms of behaviour. The nature of the tasks to be undertaken is a predominant feature of the formal group. People are brought together on the basis of defined roles within the structure of the hotel. Formal groups tend to be relatively permanent although there may be changes in actual membership. However, temporary formal groups may also be established by management, for example to undertake a specific task such as preparations for a special banquet.

Informal groups

Within the formal structure of the hotel there will always be an informal structure. The formal structure, and system of role relationships, rules and procedures, will be augmented by interpretation and development at the informal level. Informal groups are based more on personal relationships and agreement of group members than on defined role relationships. They serve to satisfy psychological and social needs which are not necessarily related to the tasks to be undertaken.[10]

Informal groups may arise from the same horizontal level, but they also arise vertically or diagonally. The membership of informal groups therefore cuts across the formal structure of the hotel. They may comprise individuals from different parts of the hotel and/or from different levels of the hotel. An informal group could also be the same as the formal group or it might comprise a part only of the formal group (Figure 9.3).

Characteristics of informal groups

Informal groups develop their own characteristics. They may have their own culture, status values and symbols, and their own system of communications through the 'grapevine'. Informal groups are also agents of social satisfaction and control. As a result there is often strong resistance to changes which threaten the status quo, or the environment or working practices of the group.[11]

It is possible for the leader of an informal group to be the same person as the formal leader appointed officially by management. It is more usual, however, for the group to have its own informal leader who exercises authority by the consent of the members themselves. The informal leader may be chosen as the person who reflects the attitudes and values of the members, helps to resolve conflict, leads the group in satisfying its goals, or liaises with management or other people outside the group.

You may recall the discussion on the importance of cultural influences in Chapter 2. A multi-cultural work environment may lead to the emergence of informal groups and cliques based on common nationality, religion or shared ethnic values, and with their own leaders and spokespersons. Such informal groups are not necessarily harmful to the operations of the hotel but it is important that the manager emphasises the need for effective co-operation and teamwork .

BENEFITS OF GROUP MEMBERSHIP

Individuals have varying expectations of the benefits from group membership (formal and/or informal) relating to both social processes and work performance.

- Groups provide companionship and a source of mutual understanding and support from colleagues. This can help in solving work problems or mitigating against stressful or demanding working conditions.
- Membership of the group can provide the individual with a sense of belonging. The group provides a feeling of identity, and the chance to acquire role recognition and status within the group.
- The group provides guidelines on generally acceptable behaviour. It helps to clarify ambiguous situations such as, for example, the extent to which official rules and regulations are expected to be adhered to in practice. Group allegiance can serve as a means of determining norms of behaviour, such as in the bank wiring room mentioned above.
- The combined efforts of members of a group can have a synergistic effect. The collective knowledge and expertise of members can help in problem-solving and in the performance of complex or difficult tasks.
- Groups may encourage the modification of formal working arrangements to become more to the liking of members, for example by sharing or rotating unpopular tasks. Group membership can provide opportunities for initiative and creativity.

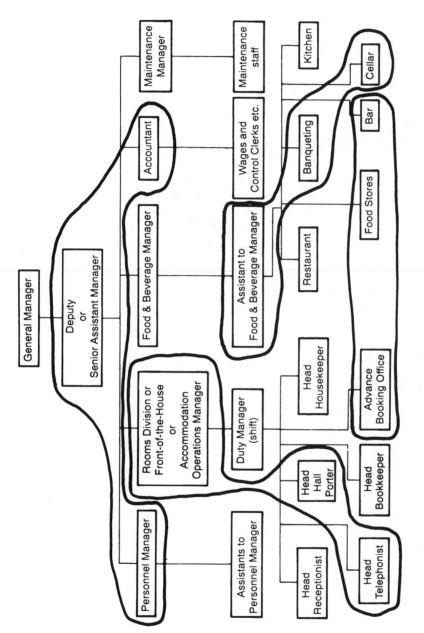

Fig 9.3 Possible examples of informal groups within the formal structure of a hotel

- The group may provide mutual support and protection for its members, for example by collaborating to safeguard their interests from outside pressures or threats.

Morale and work performance

Groups are therefore a potential source of motivation and job satisfaction, and also a major determinant of effective organisational performance. Membership of a cohesive group can be a rewarding experience for the individual and can contribute to the promotion of morale. Members of a high-morale group are more likely to think of themselves as a group and to work together effectively.

DEVELOPING EFFECTIVE GROUPS

Co-operation among members is likely to be greater in a united, cohesive group. However, cohesive groups do not necessarily produce a higher level of output. Performance varies with the extent to which the group accepts or rejects the goals of the organisation. The level of output is likely to conform to a standard acceptable as a norm by the group.[12] But cohesive groups may result in greater interaction, lower turnover and absenteeism, and often higher output.[13]

The manager's main concern is that members of a work group co-operate in order to achieve the results expected of them. The work of a hotel entails a wide range of operations, many of which are undertaken simultaneously and depend upon a high degree of co-ordination and team-work. This calls for good working relationships among staff and effective group activities.[14]

Group identity and cohesion

In order to develop the effectiveness of work groups, the manager will be concerned with those factors that contribute to group cohesiveness, or that may cause frustration or disruption to the operation and performance of the group. The manager needs to consider, therefore, both the needs of individual members of the group, and the promotion of a high level of group identity and cohesion.

Many factors contribute to group cohesiveness and performance.[15] These can be summarised under four broad headings: membership, work environment, organisational, and group development and maturity (Figure 9.4).

Membership of the group

Size of the group

It is difficult to put a figure on the ideal size of a work group and much will depend upon other variables. But it seems to be generally accepted that cohesiveness becomes more difficult to achieve when a group exceeds 10–12 members. Berger and Vanger, for example, suggest that team-building is most successful in groups of six to ten people.[16] As a group increases in size, problems arise with communications and co-ordination. Large groups are more difficult to handle and require a higher level of supervision.

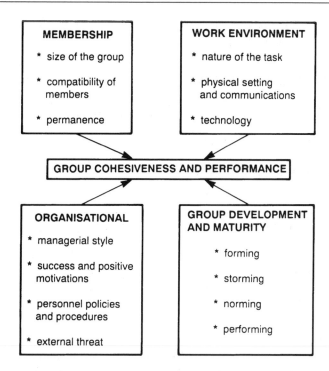

Fig 9.4 Factors contributing to group cohesiveness and performance

Absenteeism also tends to be higher in larger groups. When a group becomes too large, it may split into smaller units and friction may develop between sub-groups.

Compatibility of the members

The more homogeneous the members of a group in terms of, for example, shared backgrounds, interests, attitudes and values, the easier it is to promote cohesiveness. Differences between individual members such as personality and skills can serve to complement each other and help make for a cohesive group. However, such differences may also be the cause of disruption and conflict.

Permanence of membership

Group spirit and relationships take time to develop. Cohesiveness is more likely to be achieved when members of a group are together for a reasonable length of time and changes occur only slowly. A frequent turnover of members is likely to have an adverse effect on morale and social satisfaction, and on the cohesiveness of the group.

The work environment

The nature of the task

Where individuals are involved in similar work, share a common task or face the same problems, this may assist cohesiveness. The nature of the task may serve to bring people together. An example could be receptionists working in a large and busy international hotel.

Physical setting and communications

Where members of a group work in the same location or in close physical proximity to each other, this will often help cohesiveness. The more easily members can communicate freely with each other, the greater the likelihood of group cohesion. Members of the maintenance staff working on their own in different parts of a hotel may experience a lack of group identity. However, isolation from other workers may also tend to build cohesiveness. This may apply, for example, to a smaller number of workers on the night rota.

Technology and the manner in which work is carried out

Where the nature of the work process involves a craft- or skill-based 'technology' there is a higher likelihood of cohesiveness. For example, in a small, high-class hotel particularly noted for the standard of its cuisine, members of the kitchen brigade need to interact and work closely with each other for effective performance. (You could compare this, for instance, with the mass production technology of fast-food chain stores.)

Organisational

Managerial style

The activities of groups cannot be separated from management and the process of leadership. The style of leadership adopted will influence the relationship between the group and management, and is a major determinant of group cohesiveness. In general terms, cohesiveness will be affected by the manner in which the manager gives guidance, encouragement and support to the group, provides opportunities for participation, attempts to resolve difficulties and conflicts, and adopts a Theory Y approach.

Success and positive motivation

The more successful the group, the more cohesive it is likely to be: and cohesive groups are more likely to be successful. Success is usually a strong and positive motivational influence on the level of work performance. Success or reward as a positive motivator can be perceived by group members in a number of ways, for example, the satisfactory completion of a difficult task through co-operative action, recognition and praise from management, a feeling of high status or esteem, high wage payments from a group-based bonus scheme.

Personnel policies and procedures

Attention should be given to the effects that systems of appraisal, transfers, promotion and discipline, and opportunities for training and personal development, have on members of the group. Harmony within the group is more likely to be achieved if personnel policies and procedures are perceived to be equitable, and all members receive what they believe is fair treatment by management.

External threat

Cohesiveness may be enhanced by members co-operating with one another when faced with a common external threat, for example the introduction of new technology or changes in their method of work, or the appointment of a new supervisor. Even if the threat is subsequently removed, the group may still continue to have a greater degree of cohesion than before the threat arose. Conflict between groups will also tend to increase the cohesiveness of each group and the boundaries of the groups become drawn more closely.

Group development and maturity

Cohesiveness is also affected by the manner in which groups progress through the various stages of development and maturity. Tuckman, for example, identifies four main successive stages of group development and relationships: forming, storming, norming and performing.[17]

Stage 1: Forming

The initial formation of the group. This involves the bringing together of a number of individuals and the tentative identification of the purpose of the group, its composition and terms of reference. Consideration is given to the hierarchical structure of the group, pattern of leadership, individual roles and responsibilities, and codes of conduct. At this stage there is likely to be considerably anxiety as members attempt to create an impression, to test each other and to establish their personal identity within the group.

Stage 2: Storming

As members of the group get to know each other better they will put forward their views more openly and forcefully. Disagreements will be expressed and challenges offered on the nature of the task and the arrangements made during the forming stage. The storming stage is important because, if it is successful, there will be discussions on reforming the working and operation of the group, and agreement on more meaningful structures and procedures.

Stage 3: Norming

As conflict and hostility start to be controlled, members of the group will establish guidelines and standards, and develop their own norms of acceptable behaviour. The norming stage is important in establishing the need for members to co-operate together in order to plan, agree standards of performance and fulfil the purpose of the group.

Stage 4: Performing

When the group has progressed successfully through the earlier three stages it will have created structure and cohesiveness to work effectively as a team. At this stage the group can concentrate on the attainment of its purpose, and performance of the common task is likely to be at its most effective.

These main stages of forming, storming, norming and performing are at the basis of effective team-building.[18]

Characteristics of an effective group

The characteristics of an effective work group are not always easy to isolate clearly. The underlying feature is a spirit of co-operation in which members work well together as a united team, and with harmonious and supportive relationships. This may be evidenced when members of a group exhibit:

- a belief in shared objectives;
- a sense of commitment to the group;
- acceptance of group values and norms;
- a feeling of mutual trust and dependency;
- full participation by all members and decision-making by consensus;
- a free flow of information and communications;
- the open expression of feelings and disagreements; and
- the resolution of conflict by the members themselves.[19]

POTENTIAL DISADVANTAGES OF COHESIVE GROUPS

In order to develop effective working groups the manager should give attention to those factors which influence the creation of group identity and cohesiveness. But strong, cohesive groups also present potential disadvantages for management. The goals of the group may be at variance with the goals of the organisation. It may be remembered, for example, that in the bank wiring room experiment group norms and pressures on individual members led to unofficial working methods, and restrictions on the level of output.

It is important, therefore, that the manager attempts to influence the group during the norming stage when members are establishing guidelines and standards and their own norms of acceptable behaviour. Once a group has become fully developed, created cohesiveness and established its own culture, it is more difficult for the manager to change successfully the attitudes and behaviour of the group.[20]

Inter-group conflict

Strong, cohesive groups may develop a critical or even hostile attitude towards people outside the group or members of other groups. This can be the case, for example, when group cohesiveness is based on common status, social background, qualifications or technical expertise. Group cohesiveness may result in a lack of co-operation with other groups. Resentment and inter-group conflict may arise, to the detriment of the organisation as a whole.

A classic example is Whyte's study of the American restaurant industry and the social interactions between two groups of workers – the chefs and the waiting staff.[21] The chefs, who regarded themselves to be of high status and generally recognised as such by the staff, resented being 'told' what to do by the waitresses, who were generally regarded to be of lower status. As a result arguments resulted, disrupting performance. The conflict in status was resolved by the introduction of an ordering process by which the chefs received customers' orders without the appearance of taking instructions from the 'lower-status' waitresses.

In order to help prevent, or overcome, unconstructive inter-group conflict, the manager should attempt to stimulate a high level of communication and interaction between the groups, and to maintain harmony. Where appropriate, rotation of members among different groups should be encouraged.

However, inter-group rivalry may sometimes be encouraged as a means of helping to build stronger within-group cohesiveness.[22] The idea is that a competitive element may help to promote unity within a group. But inter-group rivalry and competition need to be carefully handled by the manager. Groups should not normally be put in a situation where they have to compete for resources, status or approval.[23] The manager should attempt to avoid the development of 'win–lose' situations. Emphasis should be placed on broader objectives of the organisation which are over and above the issues at conflict and which, if they are to be achieved, require effective co-operation of the competing groups.

INTER-DEPARTMENTAL CONFLICT

Dann and Hornsey draw attention to the prevalence of inter-departmental conflict as a distinctive feature of hotel operations. They suggest four main reasons which, either in isolation or collectively, may heighten inter-departmental conflicts:

- interdependence and the relationships between departments;
- the hotel environment and the framework within which activities occur;
- rewards and the nature of the total payment package;
- status and stigma, and the perceptions of workers within the industry.[24]

Interdependence

Interdependence arises from the nature of work flows in the industry, and the requirement for close and often immediate co-operation between two or more departments, for example the kitchen and the restaurant. A fundamental conflict may arise between the desire for autonomy and independence, and the necessity for interdependence and reliance on other people. If one department feels that the other has acted unfairly or not reciprocated a favour, there is potential for conflict. An important reason for inter-departmental conflict is goal differentiations, for example between the chef's concern for quality and that of the service staff for speed.

Social environment

The social environment of the hotel industry has a number of distinctive features which are potential sources of conflict. Departments which have direct contact with the customers adapt their attitudes and work behaviour to the situation, and this emphasises differences from other departments. The speed of operations and need for quick decisions put stress and pressure on staff. The industry is typified by authoritarian leadership styles and formal patterns of organisation. There are often strong territorial perspectives about the place of work, for example in the kitchen or the front office desk.

Reward structure

The structure of the reward system can cause perceived inequity and result in conflict between departments. The presence of tips can lead to a distorted view of differentials in earnings, and different attitudes towards the customers and management. The perceived opportunities for fiddles can also be a source of conflict between departments. Another source of conflict is perceived inequity in the allocation of scarce resources to different departments.

Perceived status or stigma

Rigid organisational hierarchies have resulted in a highly differentiated and established status system in the industry. This is based on the perception of different positions and job titles. For example, receptionists see themselves as a high-status group whilst other positions such as kitchen porters carry a distinct stigma. The status system is established by tradition and myth, and reinforced through group pressure. Perceived differences in status can also arise between different nationalities or between men and women. (You may recall the discussion on sex stereotyping and gender in Chapter 2.)

CREATING TEAM EFFECTIVENESS

The importance of people's ability to work together in the hospitality industry and the many potential benefits from successful team-building are emphasised by Berger and Vanger.

> A successful team-building effort will improve your employees' productivity. They will be better able to handle complex operations; they will respond more quickly to new situations; they will be more motivated and will make better decisions.[25]

Berger and Vanger suggest six main steps in the team-building cycle.

- **Identify the problem you wish to solve and define the objective for team-building.** An example would be to encourage a competent team to work together even more successfully or to assemble a new team for a special project. It is important to secure the willingness and commitment of staff to the team-building process.
- **Gather information about the problem.** This can be achieved through: (i) an open 'clear the air' meeting to discuss grievances; (ii) conducting a survey to establish the conflicts and difficulties the group might face; or (iii) bringing in an outside consultant.
- **Communication with group members.** Sufficient time should be allowed so that the discussion can focus on each item in turn and be free-ranging. The group leader should participate and encourage group members to join the discussion, and to elaborate their views on each topic.
- **Plan for change.** Group members should be able to work together and establish plans for eliminating blockages to the operation's effectiveness. Each member must be willing to compromise. The team should establish group objectives, the decision-making process and strategies for overcoming conflict.
- **Implement the plans.** The team should continue to function according to the guidelines it has established for itself. Other members of staff who have not been involved in the team-building sessions should be kept fully informed and involved in the plans.
- **Evaluate the group's ability as a team.** One way of measuring success is for the group to establish its own charter of procedures and to survey team members to find out how well the charter is being adhered to. Negative feedback should be addressed to the group as a whole and balanced with complimentary remarks. Reassurance and appreciation should be given when overall performance is acceptable.

Berger and Vanger claim that one of the greatest blocks to teamwork is a failure of communications. If members of staff feel isolated, they avoid talking with each other. This can result in a number of individuals, each operating according to their own concept of customer service. Such an attitude means that functioning as a team is extremely difficult and it makes for an erratic service to customers. The importance of organisational communications is discussed in Chapter 11.

THE PERFORMANCE OF GROUPS

We have seen the importance of groups to the working life of the hospitality industry, and of creating effective teamwork. But is group performance better than individual performance? It is difficult to draw any firm conclusions. An example is the process of decision-making. Certain groups may be concerned more specifically with decision-making, such as a management team, but all groups must make some decisions. Group decision making can be costly, time-consuming and possibly frustrating for members but it would appear to offer a number of advantages.

- Groups bring together a range of complementary knowledge, skills and experience.
- Interaction among members can have a 'snowball' effect, and provide an impetus for further thoughts and ideas in the minds of others.

- Group discussion leads to the evaluation and revision of possible decisions.
- Provided full participation has been facilitated, decisions will have the acceptance of all, or most, members. They are then more likely to be committed to decisions made, and to their implementation.

Given these advantages, one might expect a higher standard of decision-making to result from group discussion. However, there is the danger of compromise and decisions being made in line with the 'highest common view'. There is also the phenomenon of the so-called 'risky-shift', and the concept of 'groupthink'.

The 'risky-shift' phenomenon

This suggests that instead of the group taking fewer risks and making safer or more conservative decisions, the reverse is often the case. There is a tendency for groups to make more risky decisions than would be taken by members of the group as individuals.[26]

It is perhaps understandable that members of a group do not feel the same sense of responsibility for decisions of the group or their possible outcomes. This seems to be summed up in the belief that: 'a decision which is everyone's is the responsibility of no one'. Other possible explanations for the risk-shift phenomenon include:

- people who are inclined to be more adventurous and take more risks may be more influential m group discussions;
- the group may generate a greater range of possible solutions including those that carry greater risk; and
- risk-taking may be perceived as a desirable cultural characteristic which is more likely to be expressed in a social situation such as group discussion.

Groups do, however, appear to work well in the evaluation of ideas. They are more effective than individuals for problem-solving tasks requiring a range of knowledge and expertise. Research evidence appears to support the view that, compared with individuals, groups produce more solutions, and better solutions, to problems.[27]

Groupthink

The concept of 'groupthink' refers to in-group pressures which can result in a tendency for the group to just drift along towards decisions which may be inappropriate or not questioned fully. Janis maintains that the effectiveness of group behaviour and performance can be affected adversely by groupthink. This can result in a sense of invulnerability and an unquestioned belief in the morality of the group. The search for group consensus can lead to the suppression of minority or unpopular ideas, rationalisation and an illusion of unanimity.[28]

Brainstorming

One method of attempting to evoke full group discussion and to generate possible solutions to problems is through a 'brainstorming' approach.[29] Brainstorming is based on the assumption that creative thinking is achieved best by encouraging the natural inclinations of group members and the free association of ideas. The quantity of ideas will lead to quality of ideas. A brainstorming approach involves the group adopting a 'free-wheeling' attitude and generating as many ideas as possible. The more wild or apparently far-fetched the ideas, the better.

There are a number of basic procedures for a brainstorming approach.

- Emphasis is placed initially on the quantity of ideas generated, and not the quality of ideas.
- No matter how wild or fanciful they may appear, no individual ideas are criticised or rejected at this stage.
- Members are encouraged to elaborate or build on the ideas of others and to bounce suggestions off one another.
- There is no evaluation of any particular idea or suggestion until all possibilities have been generated.

MEMBERSHIP OF SUCCESSFUL TEAMS

What factors should be considered in deciding the membership of a management team? Based on years of research and empirical study, Belbin concludes that the most consistently successful teams comprise a range of roles undertaken by various members.[30] The constitution of the team itself is an important variable in its success. Teams composed entirely of clever people, or of people with similar personalities, display a number of negative results and lack creativity.

Key team roles

Belbin describes 'team role' as a pattern of behaviour characteristic of the way in which one team member interacts with another where performance serves to facilitate the progress of the team as a whole. There are eight useful types of contribution:

Company worker (CW)   Chairman (CH)
Shaper (SH)   Plant (PL)
Resource investigator (RI)   Monitor–evaluator (ME)
Team worker (TW)   Completer–finisher (CF)

An explanation of these team roles is given in Figure 9.5. The eight types of people identified are useful team members and form a comprehensive list. These are the key team roles and the primary characters for successful teams. Creative teams require a balance of all these roles and comprise members who have characteristics complementary to one another. Belbin claims that good examples of the eight types would prove adequate for any challenge, although not all eight types are necessarily needed. Other members may be welcome for their personal qualities, for example a sense of humour, but experience suggests there is no other team role that it would be useful to add.

Back-up team roles and functional roles

The most consistently successful teams were 'mixed' with a balance of team roles. The role that a person undertakes in a group is not fixed and may change according to

Type	Symbol	Typical features	Positive qualities	Allowable weaknesses
Company worker	CW	Conservative, dutiful, predictable	Organising ability, practical common sense, hard-working, self-discipline.	Lack of flexibility, unresponsiveness to unproven ideas.
Chairman	CH	Calm, self-confident controlled.	A capacity for treating and welcoming all potential contributors on their merits and without prejudice. A strong sense of objectives.	No more than ordinary in terms of intellect or creative ability.
Shaper	SH	Highly strung, outgoing, dynamic.	Drive and a readiness to challenge inertia, ineffectiveness, complacency or self-deception.	Proneness to provocation, irritation and impatience.
Plant	PL	Individualistic, serious-minded, unorthodox	Genius, imagination, intellect, knowledge.	Up in the clouds, inclined to disregard practical details or protocol.
Resource investigator	RI	Extroverted, enthusiastic, curious, communicative.	A capacity for contacting people and exploring anything new. An ability to respond to challenge.	Liable to lose interest once the initial fascination has passed.
Monitor – evaluator	ME	Sober, unemotional, prudent.	Judgement, discretion, hard-headedness.	Lacks inspiration or the ability to motivate others.
Team worker	TW	Socially orientated, rather mild, sensitive.	An ability to respond to people and to situations, and to promote team spirit.	Indecisiveness at moments of crisis.
Completer – finisher	CF	Painstaking, orderly, conscientious, anxious.	A capacity for follow-through. Perfectionism.	A tendency to worry about small things. A reluctance to 'let go'.

Fig 9.5 Useful people to have in a team
Reprinted, with permission, from Belbin R M, *Management Teams: Why They Succeed or Fail*, Butterworth-Heinemann (1981), p. 78

circumstances. Individuals may have a 'back-up team role' with which they have some affinity other than their primary team role. If certain roles were missing, members would call upon their back-up roles. Team roles differ from what Belbin calls 'functional roles'. These are the roles that members of a team perform in terms of the specifically technical demands placed upon them. Team members are typically chosen for functional roles on the basis of experience and not personal characteristics or aptitudes.

Revised list of nine team roles

In a follow-up publication Belbin discusses the continued evolution of team roles which now differ in a few respects from those identified in earlier research.[31] Two roles are renamed, largely for reasons of acceptability: 'co-ordinator' replaces chairman, and 'implementer' replaces company worker. The most significant change is the addition of a ninth role, that of 'specialist'. This role was added because of the significance of the importance of a given form of professional expertise in much project work and its recurring importance as an issue in career development. A description of the evolved nine team roles is given in Figure 9.6.

ROLE RELATIONSHIPS

In order that the organisation can achieve its goals and objectives, the work of individual members must be linked into coherent patterns of activities and relationships. This is achieved through the role structure. **A 'role' is the expected pattern of behaviours associated with members occupying a particular position within the organisation structure.** (The formal organisational relationships discussed in Chapter 3 can also be seen as types of role relationships.)

The concept of 'role' is important to the functioning of groups, and for an understanding of group processes and behaviour. It is through role differentiation that the structure of work groups and relationships among their members are established. The identification of distinct roles helps to clarify the structure and to define the pattern of complex relationships within the group. A suitable form of structure is necessary for teamwork and co-operation.

The role, or roles, that an individual plays within the group is influenced by a combination of:

- **situational factors**, such as the type of unit, the nature of the task, the style of leadership, other members of the group, pattern of communication network; and
- **personal factors**, such as values, beliefs, attitudes, motivation, experience, ability and personality.

A role set

In addition to the role relationships with members of their own group – superior, peers, subordinates – individuals will have a number of role-related relationships with other people. This is a person's 'role set'. A role set comprises the range of associations or contacts with whom individuals have meaningful interactions in connection with the

Roles and descriptions – team-role contribution	Allowable weaknesses
Plant: Creative, imaginative, unorthodox. Solves difficult problems.	Ignores details. Too pre-occupied to communicate effectively.
Resources investigator: Extrovert, enthusiastic, communicative. Explores opportunities. Develops contacts.	Overoptimistic.Loses interest once initial enthusiasm has passed.
Co-ordinator: Mature, confident, a good chairperson. Clarifies goals, promotes decision-making, delegates well.	Can be seen as manipulative. Delegates personal work.
Shaper: Challenging, dynamic, thrives on pressure. Has the drive and courage to overcome obstacles.	Can provoke others. Hurts people's feelings.
Monitor evaluator: Sober, strategic and discerning. Sees all options. Judges accurately.	Lacks drive and ability to inspire others. Overly critical.
Teamworker: Co-operative, mild, perceptive and diplomatic. Listens, builds, averts friction, calms the waters	Indecisive in crunch situations. Can be easily influenced.
Implementer: Disciplined, reliable, conservative and efficient. Turns ideas into practical actions.	Somewhat inflexible. Slow to respond to new possibilities.
Completer: Painstaking, conscientious, anxious. Searches out errors and omissions. Delivers on time.	Inclined to worry unduly. Reluctant to delegate. Can be a nit-picker.
Specialist: Single-minded, self-starting, dedicated. Provides knowledge and skills in rare supply.	Contributes on only a narrow front. Dwells on technicalities. Overlooks the 'big picture'.

Strength of contribution in any one of the roles is commonly associated with particular weaknesses. These are called allowable weaknesses. Executives are seldom strong in all nine team roles.

Fig 9.6 Revised list of nine team roles
Reprinted, with permission, from Belbin R M, *Team Roles at Work*, Butterworth-Heinemann (1993), p. 23

performance of their role. A role set provides a useful basis for analysing the nature of a person's job, and associated duties and responsibilities, within the structure and operation of the hotel.[32]

An example of a possible role set for a receptionist is given in Figure 9.7. The range of different expectations of these associations and contacts will have a significant influence on the behaviour and performance of the receptionist.

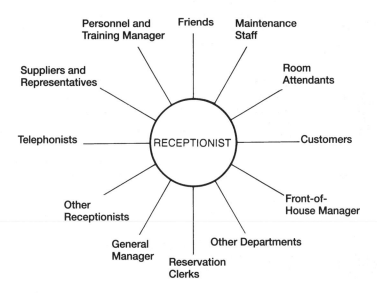

Fig 9.7 Possible role set for a receptionist

Role expectations

The role that a person plays in one work group may be quite different from the role that person plays in other work groups. However, everyone within a group is expected to behave in a particular manner and to fulfil certain role expectations. These role expectations may be established formally, or be informal, or they may be self-established.

- **Formal role expectations** indicate what the person is expected to do, and the duties and obligations. Formal role prescriptions provide guidelines for expected behaviour. Examples are a written contract of employment, rules and regulations, policy decisions or standards, compliance with legal requirements, job descriptions or directives from superiors.
- **Informal role expectations** are not prescribed formally but nonetheless are expected patterns of behaviour. These informal role expectations may be imposed by the group itself. Examples include general conduct, mutual support to co-members, attitudes towards superiors, means of communication, dress and appearance. Members may not always be consciously aware of these informal expectations, yet they still serve as important determinants of behaviour. Under this heading could be included the psychological contract, discussed in Chapter 2.

- **Self-established role expectations** arise when members have formal expectations which are specified loosely or only in very general terms. This allows members to determine their own role expectations and patterns of behaviour. Opportunities for self-established roles are more likely in senior positions, for example the general manager or senior departmental managers. They may also arise within certain professional or technical groups or where there is a demand for creativity or artistic flair, for example the head chef.

ROLE CONFLICT

Patterns of behaviour result from both the role and the personality. The concept of role focuses attention on aspects of behaviour existing independently of an individual's personality. A personality clash arises from incompatibility between two or more people as individuals, even though their roles may be defined clearly and understood fully. Role conflict, however, arises from inadequate or inappropriate role definition. A classic example is the conflict in status between chefs and waiting staff. See Whyte's study above and below.

In practice, the manner in which a person actually behaves may not be consistent with their expected pattern of behaviour. This inconsistency may be a result of role conflict. As a generic term, role conflict may include role incompatibility, role ambiguity, role overload and role underload. These are all areas associated with the creation of role expectations (Figure 9.8).

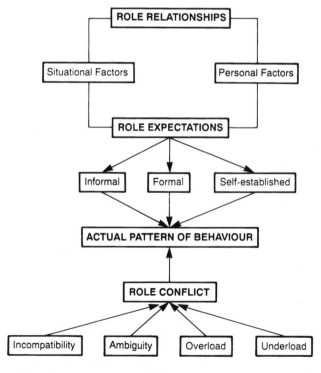

Fig 9.8 Role relationships and role conflicts

Role incompatibility

This occurs when a person faces a situation in which simultaneous different or contradictory expectations create inconsistency. Compliance with one set of expectations makes it difficult or impossible to comply with other expectations. The two incompatible sets of expectations are in conflict. A typical example concerns the person 'in the middle', such as the supervisor or section head who faces opposing expectations from subordinates and from senior management. For example, the subordinates may expect a relaxed, Theory Y approach and good working relationships, but management may expect the supervisor to adopt a more directive, Theory X approach with emphasis on achieving maximum output.

Role incompatibility may also be used to describe situations in which the person is expected to fulfil a role for which they are not suited.[33] This may arise when the values, attitudes, personality, skills or interests of the person do not equate with the demands of the role. An obvious example is a person with an introverted personality occupying a role that demands frequent dealings with people. Role incompatibility may also arise when a person accepts promotion without taking account of the different expectations of the new position. Revised working practices may result in changes to the nature and expectations of a person's role, for example from the introduction of computers into the hotel or the appointment of a new manager.

Role ambiguity

This occurs when there is lack of clarity as to the precise requirements of the role and the person is unsure what to do. The person's own perception of the role may differ from the expectations of others. The person is uncertain about the expected pattern of behaviour. This implies that insufficient information is available for adequate performance of the role. The characteristic nature of service industries, discussed in Chapter 1, gives rise to a high potential for ambiguity. Role ambiguity may result from a lack of formally prescribed expectations and often arises at times of constant change. Uncertainty may relate to such matters as the range of duties and responsibilities, the method of performing tasks, standards of work, or the evaluation and appraisal of performance.

Common examples of role ambiguity concern management trainees who may be uncertain as to how much authority they are expected to exercise over other members of staff. Management degree students on their industrial placement training may suffer from role ambiguity. It may be unclear to what extent they are expected to be involved in practical working experience at the operator level, or in gaining exposure to supervisory responsibilities. Another example could be a person appointed to a newly created position, perhaps because of the expansion or reorganisation of the hotel. The person may be uncertain about the exact nature of the new job or the authority and responsibility it involves.

Role overload

This is where a person faces too many separate roles or too great a variety of expectations. The person is unable to meet satisfactorily all expectations and some must be neglected to satisfy others. This leads to a conflict of priorities. Role overload can be distinguished from work overload. Role overload is seen in terms of the total role set and implies that the person has too many separate roles to handle at the same time. Where there are too many expectations of a single role, i.e. it is a problem of quantity rather than variety, this is work overload.[34]

An example of role overload for a hotel assistant manager is given by Lockwood and Jones. The manager is already responsible for personnel and training, but is now asked to act as duty manager, and in addition become health and safety officer, security officer and to chair the staff social committee.[35]

Role underload

This can arise when the prescribed role expectations fall short of the person's own perception of their role. The person may feel the role is not demanding enough or that it lacks variety, responsibility or challenge. It is possible, however, that the person could still suffer from work overload. Role underload may arise, for example, from the initial effects of delegation or from the appointment of an over-qualified member of staff. It may also arise from examples mentioned above such as the cases of management trainees, students on their industrial training, or members of staff appointed to a new position.

ROLE STRESS

Role conflict can result in role stress. Stress is an ever-present feature of hotel and catering work and occurs in an environment of uncertainty.[36] Although a certain amount of stress may arguably be a good thing and helps to promote a high level of performance, it is also potentially very harmful. Stress is a source of tension, frustration and dissatisfaction. It can lead to difficulties in communication and interpersonal relationships. Research evidence points to the consequences of role conflict leading to lower job satisfaction, and an adverse effect on the level of individual performance.[37]

An example of role stress is Whyte's study of chefs and waiting staff discussed above. One reason was the constant conflict between the demands of the customers to be served quickly and pressure from the chefs who were unable to produce the food in time. The waitresses were caught between two incompatible expectations and pulled both ways. As a result, a number of waitresses found the job very stressful and they often cried.

Reducing role stress

There is increasing evidence concerning stress-related illnesses and social problems, for example marriage breakdowns, which can have stress as a contributory factor. And decreasing efficiency resulting from work stress is extremely costly to organisations.[38] It is therefore important that managers make every effort to minimise the causes of stress. There are a number of ways in which management might attempt to avoid or reduce role conflict and the possibilities of role stress:

● increased clarity and specification of prescribed role expectations, for example through job descriptions;

- improved recruitment, selection and induction, the careful matching of abilities, motivations, personalities and interests to the demands of particular roles;
- a systematic approach to job training and retraining, staff development and career progression plans;
- review of organisation structure, for example the creation of new roles, assimilation of existing roles or reallocation of tasks and responsibilities;
- attention to group structures and group cohesiveness, and overcoming inter-group conflict, the possible use of autonomous working groups;
- changes in management systems and leadership style, for example a move towards System 4 management, the use of MBO, increased delegation, improved communications;
- advance notice and explanations of what is likely to happen, for example plans for a major refurbishment of the hotel, an unexpectedly large number of customers arriving together, preparations for a special banquet or conference;
- programme of medical examinations and health screening which may give early indications of potential stress-related problems.

BEHAVIOUR OF INDIVIDUALS IN GROUPS

In order to understand and to influence the functioning and operation of groups, it is necessary to study patterns of interaction, and the parts played by individual members. Two methods of analysing the behaviour of individuals in group situations are sociometry and interaction process analysis.

SOCIOMETRY

Sociometry is a method of obtaining and analysing data about social interactions and communication patterns among individuals. In the group situation, a common basis of sociometry, as proposed by Moreno, is 'buddy rating' or peer rating as a means of indicating feelings of acceptance or rejection among members.[39] Each member of the group is asked to nominate or to rate, privately, other members in terms of some given context or characteristic, for example how influential or how likeable. Questions may relate to either a work situation or a social situation. Choices may be limited to a given number and sometimes individuals may be asked to rank their choices.

Sociograms

Data derived from sociometry may be displayed by graphic means in the form of a sociogram. This is a diagrammatic representation which depicts the choices, preferences, likes or dislikes, and interactions among individual members of a group. Usually, positive choices only are recorded. The sociogram can also be used to display the structure of the group and to record the observed frequency and/or duration of contacts among members.

Figure 9.9 shows a simple illustration of a sociogram for a group of 15 members with single, positive choices only.

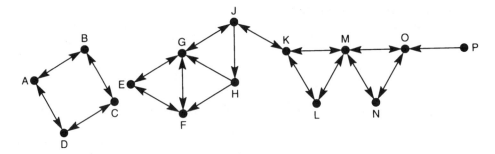

Fig 9.9 A *simple* sociogram illustrating interaction among 15 members of a group

- G and M are popular (the stars) and chosen most often.
- M is the link between two overlapping cliques, KML and MNO.
- H and P are unpopular (isolated) and chosen least.
- JKMO is a chain.
- ABCD is a sub-group and separated from the rest of the members.

It should be noted, however, that there are several methods of compiling/drawing sociograms and a number of potential criticisms and limitations with the contribution of Moreno. Problems also arise over *how* to draw the sociogram and how to interpret the roles of individual members: the drawing of a sociogram is a highly arbitrary and time-consuming task.[40] (See also the discussion on communication network analysis in Chapter 11.)

INTERACTION ANALYSIS

In addition to occupying a position within the structure of the group, each member may fulfil a distinctive role as part of the operations and processes of the group. The basic assumption behind interaction analysis is that behaviour in small groups may be analysed from the viewpoint of its function.[41] If the group is to be effective, then what-ever its structure or the pattern of interrelationships among members, there are two main sets of processes or functions that must be undertaken – task functions and main-tenance functions.

- **Task functions** are directed towards achieving the tasks and objectives of the group, and problem-solving activities. Most of the task-oriented behaviour will be concerned with 'production' activities, and the exchange and evaluation of information and ideas.
- **Maintenance functions** are directed towards maintaining the group as an effective working unit and the emotional life of the group. Most of the maintenance-oriented behaviour will be concerned with relationships among group members, giving encouragement and support, maintaining cohesiveness, and the resolution of conflict.

The appropriate combination and balance of task-oriented behaviour and maintenance-oriented behaviour is essential to the success and continuity of the group.

Classification of member roles

In addition to the fulfilment of task or maintenance functions, members of a group may say or do something to satisfy a personal need or goal. The display of behaviour in this way is termed **self-oriented (or individual) behaviour.** This gives three main types of functional behaviour which can be exhibited by members of a group: task-oriented, maintenance-oriented and self-oriented.

A popular system for the classification of member roles under these three broad headings is that devised originally by Benne and Sheats and summarised as follows.[42]

Group task roles

These assume that the task of the group is to select, define and solve common problems. Any of the roles may be performed by the various members or the group leader. Examples include initiator, information seeker, opinion giver, co-ordinator, elaborator, evaluator–critic and recorder.

Group building and maintenance roles

The analysis of member-functions is oriented towards activities which build group-centred attitudes or maintain group-centred behaviour. Contributions may involve a number of roles, and members or the leader may perform each of these roles. Examples include encourager, harmoniser, compromiser, gate-keeper, standard setter, observer and commentator.

Individual roles

These are directed towards the satisfaction of personal needs. Their purpose is not related to either group task or to the group functioning. Examples include aggressor, blocker, recognition-seeker, play actor, dominator.

Analysis of behaviour

A number of different frameworks have been designed for observers to analyse patterns of behaviour of group members. Observers chart members' behaviour on specially designed forms. These forms may be used to focus on single individuals or to record the total small-group interactions. The interaction process can become complex, especially if non-verbal behaviour is included, and headings of the observation sheet are not necessarily exclusive. It is important, therefore, to keep the framework simple, and easy to understand and to complete.[43] An example of the ten-point observation sheet used by the author is given in Figure 9.10.

The system of categorisation may distinguish between different forms of behaviour in terms of the functions they serve. Completed observation forms can be used as a basis for discussing individual contributions or the group performance related to the strength/weaknesses of different functional behaviours. Different frameworks use varying categories for studying behaviour in groups. Observation sheets can be designed to suit the particular requirements of the group situation and the nature of the activity involved.

Nature of group

Nature of activity

Date   *Name of observer(s)*

Inital arrangement of group	C D B E A F

Names of group members (or reference letters)

	A	B	C	D	E	F
Taking initiative – e.g. attempted leadership, seeking suggestions, offering directions						
Brainstorming – e.g. offering ideas or suggestions, however valid						
Offering positive ideas – e.g. making helpful suggestions, attempting to problem-solve						
Drawing in others – e.g. encouraging contributions, seeking ideas and opinions						
Being responsive to others – e.g. giving encouragement and support, building on ideas						
Harmonising – e.g. acting as peacemaker, calming things down, compromising						
Challenging – e.g. seeking justification, showing disagreement in *constructive* way						
Being obstructive – e.g. criticising, putting others down, blocking contributions						
Clarifying/summarising – e.g. linking ideas, checking progress, clarifying objectives/proposals						
Performing group roles – e.g. spokesperson, recorder, time keeper, humorist						
Other comments						

Fig 9.10 Observation sheet for behaviour in groups
Source: Mullins L J, *Management and Organisational Behaviour*, Third edition, Pitman (1993), p. 212

SUMMARY

- Groups are a characteristic feature of all work organisations and social situations. They have a major influence on individual behaviour and performance. Work is a group-based activity especially in the hospitality industry. Harmonious working relationships and good teamwork help make for a high level of staff morale and customer satisfaction.

- There are two major types of groups at work: formal, which are deliberately planned and created by management; and informal, which are based on personal relationships and serve to satisfy psychological and social needs. Individuals have varying expectations of the benefits from group membership relating to both work performance and social processes.

- Co-operation among members is likely to be greater in a strong, cohesive group. Many factors contribute to group cohesiveness and performance and can be summarised under the main headings of membership, work environment, organisational, and group development and maturity. There are, however, potential disadvantages from strong, cohesive groups.

- Group performance and the standard of decision-making can be influenced by the 'risky-shift' phenomenon and the concept of 'groupthink'. Consistently successful teams comprise a range of roles undertaken by various members. The concept of role is important to an understanding of group functioning. The manager should make every effort to minimise role conflict and role stress.

- Two methods of analysing the behaviour of individuals in group situations are sociometry and interaction analysis. The basic assumption of interaction analysis is the examination of behaviour from the viewpoint of its function. The success and continuity of a group is dependent upon the appropriate combination of task functions and maintenance functions.

REVIEW AND DISCUSSION QUESTIONS

1 Why is an understanding of the functioning and operation of work groups important for the hospitality manager?

2 Distinguish between formal and informal groups. From your own experience give practical examples of the influence of group values and norms.

3 As a manager explain what action you would take in order to develop effective group relationships and performance among members of your staff.

4 Explain why strong, cohesive groups may present potential disadvantages for management. Where possible, support your answer with practical examples.

5 What actions would you, as a hospitality manager, take in order to create successful team-building? Explain the likely characteristics of an effective work group.

6 Assess critically those factors which are likely to influence the performance of groups compared with individual performance. Give practical examples by reference to a work group to which you belong.

7   Explain fully the importance of the concept of 'role' to an understanding of group processes and behaviour. Distinguish between role conflict and a personality clash. As manager, what actions would you take to reduce the possibilities of role stress?

8   Discuss how you would attempt to analyse the parts played by, and the behaviour of, individual members in group situations.

ASSIGNMENT 1

(i)   Construct a diagram to show fully your own role-set within a work situation.

(ii)   Think of any work group(s) to which you belong, or have recently belonged. Identify clearly and give examples of your:
● formal role expectations;
● informal role expectations; and
● self-established role expectations.

(iii)   Give a detailed account of a work situation in which you have experienced role conflict. Explain what form(s) this conflict took and how you attempted to overcome or reduce the conflict.

ASSIGNMENT 2

Observe a small group at work.

(i)   Explain the extent to which the group progressed through the stages of: forming, storming, norming and performing.

(ii)   Provide examples of group values or norms which constituted 'proper' behaviour of group members.

(iii)   Attempt to construct a simple sociogram to display the structure of the group, and the frequency and duration of contacts among members.

(iv)   Summarise the extent to which the behaviour of each individual member could be classified under:
● group task roles;
● group building and maintenance roles; and
● individual roles.

(v)   Explain the conclusions you draw from your observation.

ASSIGNMENT 3

A self-perception inventory

This inventory was developed from a number of earlier versions which had been designed to give Henley members a simple means of assessing their best team-roles.

DIRECTIONS: For each section distribute a total of ten points among the sentences which you think best describe your behaviour. These points may be distributed among several sentences: in extreme cases they might be spread among all the sentences or ten points may be given to a single sentence. Enter the points in Figure 9.11.

SECTION	ITEM a	b	c	d	e	f	g	h
I								
II								
III								
IV								
V								
VI								
VII								

Fig 9.11 Points table for self-perception inventory

I. What I believe I can contribute to a team:
(a) I think I can quickly see and take advantage of new opportunities.
(b) I can work well with a very wide range of people.
(c) Producing ideas is one of my natural assets.
(d) My ability rests in being able to draw people out whenever I detect they have something of value to contribute to group objectives.
(e) My capacity to follow through has much to do with my personal effectiveness.
(f) I am ready to face temporary unpopularity if it leads to worthwhile results in the end.
(g) I can usually sense what is realistic and likely to work.
(h) I can offer a reasoned case for alternative courses of action without introducing bias or prejudice.

II. If I have a possible shortcoming in teamwork, it could be that:
(a) I am not at ease unless meetings are well structured and controlled and generally well conducted.
(b) I am inclined to be too generous towards others who have a valid viewpoint that has not been given a proper airing.
(c) I have a tendency to talk too much once the group gets on to new ideas.
(d) My objective outlook makes it difficult for me to join in readily and enthusiastically with colleagues.
(e) I am sometimes seen as forceful and authoritarian if there is a need to get something done.
(f) I find it difficult to lead from the front, perhaps because I am overresponsive to group atmosphere.
(g) I am apt to get too caught up in ideas that occur to me and so lose track of what is happening.
(h) My colleagues tend to see me as worrying unnecessarily over detail and the possibility that things may go wrong.

III. When involved in a project with other people:
(a) I have an aptitude for influencing people without pressurising them.
(b) My general vigilance prevents careless mistakes and omissions being made.
(c) I am ready to press for action to make sure that the meeting does not waste time or lose sight of the main objective.
(d) I can be counted on to contribute something original.

(e) I am always ready to back a good suggestion in the common interest.
(f) I am keen to look for the latest in new ideas and developments.
(g) I believe my capacity for judgement can help to bring about the right decisions.
(h) I can be relied upon to see that all essential work is organised.

IV. My characteristic approach to group work is that:
(a) I have a quiet interest in getting to know colleagues better.
(b) I am not reluctant to challenge the views of others or to hold a minority view myself.
(c) I can usually find a line of argument to refute unsound propositions.
(e) I have a tendency to avoid the obvious and to come out with the unexpected.
(f) I bring a touch of perfection to any job I undertake.
(g) I am ready to make use of contacts outside the group itself.
(h) While I am interested in all views I have no hesitation in making up my mind once a decision has to be made.

V. I gain satisfaction in a job because:
(a) I enjoy analysing situations and weighing up all the possible choices.
(b) I am interested in finding practical solutions to problems.
(c) I like to feel I am fostering good working relationships.
(d) I can have a strong influence on decisions.
(e) I can meet people who may have something new to offer.
(f) I can get people to agree on a necessary course of action.
(g) I feel in my element where I can give a task my full attention.
(h) I like to find a field that stretches my imagination.

VI. If I am suddenly given a difficult task with limited time and unfamiliar people:
(a) I would feel like retiring to a corner to devise a way out of the impasse before developing a line.
(b) I would be ready to work with the person who showed the most positive approach.
(c) I would find some way of reducing the size of the task by establishing what different individuals might best contribute.
(d) My natural sense of urgency would help to ensure that we did not fall behind schedule.
(e) I believe I would keep cool and maintain my capacity to think straight.
(f) I would retain a steadiness of purpose in spite of the pressures.
(g) I would be prepared to take a positive lead if I felt the group was making no progress.
(h) I would open up discussions with a view to stimulating new thoughts and getting something moving.

VII. With reference to the problems to which I am subject in working in groups:
(a) I am apt to show my impatience with those who are obstructing progress.
(b) Others may criticise me for being too analytical and insufficiently intuitive.
(c) My desire to ensure that work is properly done can hold up proceedings.
(d) I tend to get bored rather easily and rely on one or two stimulating members to spark me off.
(e) I find it difficult to get started unless the goals are clear.
(f) I am sometimes poor at explaining and clarifying complex points that occur to me.
(g) I am conscious of demanding from others the things I cannot do myself.
(h) I hesitate to get my points across when I run up against real opposition.

To interpret the self-perception inventory you should look at the Analysis sheet at the back of the book.

Reprinted with permission from Belbin R M, *Management Teams: Why They Succeed or Fail*, Butterworth-Heinemann (198l), pp. 153–156.

NOTES AND REFERENCES

1. Adair l, *Effective Teambuiding*, Gower (1986).
2. Schein E H, *Organizational Psychology*, Third edition, Prentice-Hall (1988) p. 145.
3. See, for example, Riley M, *Human Resource Management: A guide to personnel practice in the hotel and catering industry*, Butterworth-Heinemann (1991).
4. Trist E L *et al.*, *Organizational Choice*, Tavistock Publications (1963).
5. Likert R, *New Patterns of Management*, McGraw-Hill (1961), p. 38.
6. See, for example, Venison P, *Managing Hotels*, Heinemann (1983).
7. Simmons P and Teare R, 'Evolving a Total Quality Culture', *International Journal of Contemporary Hospitality Management*, vol. 5, no. 3, 1993, pp. v–viii.
8. Jones P and Lockwood A, *The Management of Hotel Operations*, Cassell (1989).
9. Reproduced by permission of Ashley Laking, Assistant General Manager, Foxhills Golf and Country Club.
10. See, for example, Gullen H V and Rhodes G E, *Management in the Hotel and Catering Industry*, Batsford (1983).
11. See, for example, Keiser J R, *Principles and Practices of Management in the Hospitality Industry*, Second edition, Van Nostrand Reinhold (1989).
12. Seashore S E, *Group Cohesiveness in the Industrial Work Group*, Institute for Social Research, University of Michigan (1954).
13. Argyle M, *The Social Psychology of Work*, Second edition, Penguin (1986).
14. Mullins L J, 'Management and Managerial Behaviour', *The International Journal of Hospitality Management*, vol. 4, no. 1, 1985, pp. 39–41.
15. See, for example, Atkinson P E, 'Developing Cohesive Working Groups', *Hospitality*, no. 29, May 1983, pp. 19–23.
16. Berger F and Vanger R, 'Building Your Hospitality Team', *Cornell HRA Quarterly*, February 1986, pp. 82–89.
17. Tuckman B W, 'Development Sequence in Small Groups', *Psychological Bulletin*, vol. 63, 1965, pp. 384–399.
18. See, for example, Adair , *Effective Teambuilding*, Gower (1986).
19. See also Jones P and Lockwood A, *The Management of Hotel Operations*, Cassell (1989).
20. See, for example, Allcorn S, 'Understanding Groups at Work', *Personnel*, vol. 66, no. 8, August 1989, pp. 28–36.
21. Whyte W F, *Human Relations in the Restaurant Industry*, McGraw-Hill (1948).
22. Staw B M, 'Organisational Psychology and the Pursuit of the Happy/Productive Worker', *California Management Review*, vol. 28, no. 4, Summer 1986, pp. 40–53.
23. Schein E H, *Organizational Psychology*, Third edition, Prentice-Hall (1988).
24. Dann D and Hornsey T, 'Towards a Theory of Interdepartmental Conflict in Hotels', *The International Journal of Hospitality Management*, vol. 5, no. 1, 1986, pp. 23–28.
25. Berger F and Vanger R, 'Building Your Hospitality Team', *Cornell HRA Quarterly*, February 1986, pp. 83–84.
26. See, for example, Kogan N and Wallach M A, 'Risk-taking as a Function of the Situation, the Person and the Group', in Newcomb T M (ed), *New Directions in Psychology III*, Holt, Rinehart and Winston (1967).
27. Shaw M E, *Group Dynamics*, McGraw-Hill (1976).
28. Janis J L, *Groupthink*, Second edition, Houghton Mifflin (1982).
29. Osborn A F, *Applied Imagination*, Revised edition, Scribner (1957).
30. Belbin R M, *Management Teams: Why They Succeed or Fail*, Heinemann (1981).
31. Belbin R M, *Team Roles at Work*, Butterworth-Heinemann (1993).
32. For an example of a role-set for a unit manager, see Hales C and Nightingale M, 'What Are Unit Managers Supposed to Do?' *The International Journal of Hospitality Management*, vol. 5, no. 1, 1986, pp. 3–11.
33. Jones P and Lockwood A, *The Management of Hotel Operations*, Cassell (1989).

34. See, for example, Handy C B, *Understanding Organizations*, Fourth edition, Penguin (1993).

35. Lockwood A and Jones P, *People and the Hotel and Catering Industry*, Holt, Rinehart and Winston (1984).

36. Wood R C, *Working in Hotels and Catering*, Routledge (1992), p. 90.

37. Filley A C and House R J, *Managerial Process and Organizational Behavior*, Scott Foresman (1969).

38. Hall K and Savery L K, 'Stress Management', *Management Decision*, vol. 25, no. 6, 1987, pp. 29–35.

39. Moreno J L, *Who Shall Survive?*, Beacon House (1953).

40. Rogers E M and Kincaid D L, *Communication networks: Towards a New Paradigm for Research*, The Free Press (1981), p. 92.

41. Bales R F, *Personality and Interpersonal Behavior*, Holt, Rinehart and Winston (1970).

42. Benne K D and Sheats P, 'Functional Roles of Group Members', *Journal of Social Issues*, vol. 4, 1948, pp. 41–49.

43. For a more detailed account of frameworks for behavioural analysis and their use, see Mullins L J, *Management and Organisational Behaviour*, Third edition, Pitman (1993).

10
MANAGERIAL LEADERSHIP

INTRODUCTION

An essential part of management is co-ordinating and directing the efforts of members of staff. A major influence on effective performance in the hospitality industry is the nature of the manager–subordinate relationship. This entails the process of leadership and the choice of an appropriate style of managerial behaviour.

This chapter looks at:

- The nature of leadership
- Management and leadership
- The leadership relationship
- The qualities or trait theories
- Are leaders born or made?
- The functional or group approach
- Needs and leadership functions
- Leadership as a behavioural category

- Managerial behaviour and leadership style
- Continuum of leadership behaviour
- The situational approach
- Contingency models of leadership
- The best style of leadership in the hospitality industry

THE NATURE OF LEADERSHIP

It is difficult to generalise about leadership. It is a complex and discursive subject area, and there are many ways of looking at leadership and the interpretations of its meaning. Essentially, however, we can see leadership as **a relationship through which one person influences the behaviour and actions of other people.** Leadership is a dynamic process and not limited to influences over people in a subordinate position. The leader–follower relationship is reciprocal, and effective leadership is a two-way process.

From a survey of managers in the hotel and restaurant industry which asked how leadership should be, it was described as: 'the ability to stimulate people to understand for themselves what they should do and be motivated to do it'.[1]

Leadership is closely associated with the activities of groups and with effective team-building. It is related to motivation, interpersonal behaviour and patterns of communications.[2] The manager's style of leadership also affects employee job satisfaction and performance.[3] However, despite the importance of leadership, the subject has received scant attention as a topic of research in the hospitality industry.[4]

MANAGEMENT AND LEADERSHIP

Sometimes management and leadership are seen as synonymous, but there is a difference. Whereas effective management involves leadership, it does not follow that every leader is necessarily a manager. The primary concern of managers is the achievement of organisational objectives through the use of systems and procedures. Management relates to people working within a hierarchy, and with prescribed positions and roles within the formal structure of the organisation.

The leadership process

The emphasis of the leadership process, however, is on interpersonal behaviour in a broader context. It is often associated with the willing and enthusiastic behaviour of followers. A leader often has sufficient influence to bring about long-term changes in people's attitudes and to make change more acceptable. Leadership therefore can be seen primarily as an inspirational process.[5] It does not necessarily take place only within the hierarchical structure. Many people operate as leaders without their role being formally established or defined.

Managers are more concerned with the 'hard' Ss of strategy, structure and systems. Leaders have an inherent inclination for utilisation of the 'soft' Ss of style, staff, skills and shared goals.[6] Managers also tend to adopt impersonal or passive attitudes towards goals. They maintain a low level of emotional involvement in their relationships with other people. Leaders adopt a more personal and active attitude towards goals. They have empathy with other people and give attention to what events and actions mean.[7]

Leadership skills and the management of people

Despite the differences, there is a close relationship between management and leadership, and it is not easy to separate them as distinct activities. For example, a Theory X or Theory Y style of managerial behaviour will have a significant influence on the nature of leadership. Many methods of management training can also be used as a means of measuring leadership style. For example, the Leadership Grid (discussed in Chapter 5) was until recently known as the Managerial Grid.

Being an effective manager involves the successful management of people. Chris Bonington, for example, suggests that the same basic skills of leadership which enabled his successful expedition to climb Everest can be learned and practised in business. There is a similarity between the leadership skills required on Everest and the same skills required by team leaders in management.[8]

To be an effective manager it is necessary to exercise the role of leadership. You may recall, for example, that one of the interpersonal roles of a manager identified by Mintzberg (discussed in Chapter 4) is that of leader. The leader role permeates all activities of a manager and includes a responsibility for the motivation and guidance of subordinate staff.[9] Leadership is therefore a part of managerial behaviour, although it is a special attribute which can be distinguished from other elements of management.

THE LEADERSHIP RELATIONSHIP

A leader may be imposed, or formally appointed or elected. The leader exercises authority as an attribute of position or because of a stated position within the hierarchical structure of the organisation. Leadership, however, is more than just adherence to a formal role prescription or a superior–subordinate relationship.

> Remember that you can be appointed a manager but you are not a leader until your appointment is ratified in the hearts and minds of those who work for you.[10]

A leader may also be chosen informally, or emerge through the wishes of the group or the demands of the situation.[11] Leadership may be exercised because of accepted knowledge or expertise, or by reputation (sapiential authority). It may also be based on the personal qualities, or charisma, of the leader and the manner in which authority is exercised.

A complex relationship among variables

Leadership is therefore a dynamic form of behaviour. McGregor, for example, suggests that leadership is not a property of the individual but a complex relationship among a number of variables. The leadership relationship is affected by:

- the characteristics of the leader;
- the attitude, needs and other personal characteristics of the followers;
- the nature of the organisation, such as its purpose, structure and tasks to be performed; and
- the social, economic and political environment.[12]

Leadership power and influence

The nature of the leadership relationship can arise in a number of different ways. Leadership influence will be dependent upon the type of 'power' that the leader can exercise over other people. The exercise of power is a social process which helps to explain how different people are able to influence the behaviour and actions of others.

French and Raven have identified five main sources of power upon which the influence of the leader is based.[13] It is important to note that these sources of power are based on the **perception** of the influence of the leader, whether it is real or not. The leader may exercise different types of power in particular circumstances and at different times. We can consider these in terms of the work situation of the hospitality organisation.

- **Reward power** is based on the perception that the leader has the ability and resources to obtain rewards for those who comply with directives, for example pay, promotion, allocation of tasks, responsibilities and hours of work, granting of privileges, praise, recognition.
- **Coercive power** is based on fear and the perception that the leader has the ability to bring about punishment or undesirable outcomes for those who do not comply with directives. This is in effect the opposite of reward power. Examples include withholding pay rises, promotion or privileges, allocating undesirable duties or

responsibilities, withdrawal of friendship or support, formal reprimands or possibly dismissal.

- **Legitimate power** is based on the perception that the leader has a right to exercise influence because of role or position. Legitimate power is based on formal authority, for example that of managers and supervisors within the hierarchical structure. The leader's influence arises from 'position' power and not from the nature of personal relationships.

- **Referent power** is based on a feeling of identification with the leader. Influence over others arises because of the perceived reputation, personal characteristics or 'charisma' of the leader. For example, a particular member of staff may not be in a position to influence rewards or punishments but may still exercise power through commanding respect or esteem.

- **Expert power** is based on the perception of the leader as someone who is competent and who has some special knowledge or expertise in a given area. Expert power is based on credibility and is usually limited to narrow, well-defined areas of activity or specialisms, for example the technical expertise of the head chef or catering manager, or the professional knowledge of the accountant or personnel manager.

The five sources of power are interrelated. The use of one type of power, for example coercive, may affect the ability to use another type, for example referent power.

THE STUDY OF LEADERSHIP

Because of its complex and variable nature there are many ways of analysing leadership. It is helpful therefore to have some framework in which to approach further study of the subject area (Figure 10.1). We can examine leadership in terms of:

- the qualities or trait theories;
- the functional or group approach;
- leadership as a behavioural category;
- styles of leadership; and
- the situational approach and contingency models.

THE QUALITIES OR TRAIT THEORIES

The qualities (or trait) approach is based on the belief that leadership consists of certain inherited characteristics, or personality traits, which distinguish leaders from their followers. This is the so called 'Great Person' theory of leadership and leads to the suggestion that leaders are born and not made. Drucker, for example (writing originally in 1955), makes the point that:

> . . . leadership is of utmost importance. Indeed there is no substitute for it. But leadership cannot be created or promoted. It cannot be taught or learned.[14]

The qualities approach focuses attention on the man or woman in the job and not on the job itself. It suggests that people with certain personality traits or characteristics would

QUALITIES OR TRAIT THEORIES

Assumes leaders are born and not made. Leadership consists of certain inherited characteristics or personality traits. Focuses attention on the person in the job and not on the job itself.

THE FUNCTIONAL OR GROUP APPROACH

Attention is focused on the functions and responsibilities of leadership, what the leader actually does and the nature of the group. Assumes leadership skills can be learned and developed.

LEADERSHIP AS A BEHAVIOURAL CATEGORY

The kinds of behaviour of people in leadership positions and the influence on group performance. Draws attention to range of possible managerial behaviour and importance of leadership style.

STYLES OF LEADERSHIP

Ways of describing behaviour adopted by managers towards subordinate staff and classifications of leadership style.

THE SITUATIONAL APPROACH

The importance of situational factors. Interactions between the variables involved in the leadership situation and patterns of behaviour. Contingency models of leadership and no single style of leadership.

Fig 10.1 A framework for the study of leadership

be successful leaders whatever the situation. Attention is given to the selection of leaders rather than to the training for leadership.

Limitations

Despite many research studies, attempts to find common personality, physical or mental characteristics of 'good' or 'successful' leaders have met with little success.[15] Investigations have identified lists of traits which tend to be overlapping, contradictory or with little correlation for most features. The lists of possible traits tend to be very long and there is not always agreement on the most important. It is noticeable, however, that such characteristics as individuality or originality usually feature in these lists of traits. This suggests that there is little in common between specific personality traits of different leaders.

There is, in any case, bound to be some subjective judgement in agreeing who is regarded as a good or successful leader. Even if it were possible to identify an agreed list of more specific qualities this would provide little explanation of the nature of leadership. It would do little to help in the training and development of future managers.

Early developments in the hospitality industry

In the early development of the hospitality industry many organisations were based upon the family unit and leadership was closely associated with ownership. Attempts to maintain the dynasty were based on the acceptance of a natural leader with the 'right' of leadership passing down to departmental levels.[16] However, as hospitality organisations have grown in size and complexity, increasing attention has been given to the need for a more broadly based approach to the appointment and development of leaders.

Leadership characteristics

Attempting to find a common list of those characteristics which make for an effective leader is likely to encounter the same limitations as the qualities approach. Walker, however, suggests that the real key to excellent leadership involves developing personality characteristics and the ability to develop the talents of other members of the organisation.[17]

Proven managers have generally developed an intuitive ability to evaluate the leadership potential of others. The objective of screening for managerial potential is to locate the individuals whose past experience and temperament show a pattern typical of successful leaders. Walker identifies the following as some of the most important indicators of the appropriate temperament for leadership.

- **Self-control** – potential leaders should be above-average in their ability to exercise self-control as this ability will be most frequently called upon.
- **Sense of values** – the greatest leaders are those who downplay materialistic values and status symbols, and instead respect the intangible, spiritual side of life.
- **Drive** – a strong drive is an advantage in any assignment and a 'doer' is preferred to the person who procrastinates.
- **Moodiness** – the manager should not be prone to inconsistency in personality but be optimistic, cheerful and generally capable of maintaining morale and team spirit.
- **Sensitivity** – people who are sensitive themselves are generally sensitive to others and have a high potential for managerial success.
- **Defence of ideas** – successful managers must be willing and able to support and defend their own ideas while remaining receptive to the ideas of others.
- **Self-awareness** – everyone needs a certain amount of appreciation from others but the person needing less recognition for *individual* contribution is generally more successful as a manager.

ARE LEADERS BORN OR MADE?

Despite the limitations of the qualities or traits approach, there is still a frequent debate about whether leaders are born or made, or whether leadership is an art or a science. The important point, however, is that these should not be viewed as mutually exclusive alternatives. Even if there are certain inborn qualities which make for a good leader, these natural talents need encouragement and further development. Even if leadership is an art, it still requires knowledge and application of special skills or techniques.

There is, then, still some interest in the qualities or trait, approach but increasing attention has been directed to other approaches to leadership. The focus now is more on what the leader does and how the functions of leadership are carried out.

The importance of the situation

A variety of people with different personalities and from varying backgrounds have emerged as effective leaders in different situations. The person who becomes the leader is regarded as most appropriately qualified, who knows best what to do and who is seen as the most suitable leader in the particular set of circumstances. This gives rise to the influence of situational factors in analysing the nature of leadership. The importance of situational factors is discussed later in this chapter.

THE FUNCTIONAL OR GROUP APPROACH

This approach is based on the process and content of leadership. Attention is focused on the functions and responsibilities of leadership, what the leader actually does and the nature of the group. Leadership is always present in any group engaged in a task. Greater attention can be given to the successful training of leaders by concentrating on those functions which lead to effective performance by the work group.

The functional approach believes that the skills of leadership can be learned, developed and perfected. In contrast to the view of Drucker (referred to above), Kotter, for example, makes the point that successful companies do not wait for leaders to come along.

> They actively seek out people with leadership potential and expose them to career experiences designed to develop that potential. Indeed, with careful selection, nurturing and encouragement, dozens of people can play important leadership roles in a business organisation.[18]

The functions and responsibilities of leadership

In order to help understand the process of leadership it is necessary to analyse the role of the leader. The functions and responsibilities of leadership require varying emphasis in different situations according to the nature of the group. It is possible, however, to identify a range of general functions which are served by the leadership position. For example, Krech provides a useful summary of 14 functions.[19]

- **The leader as executive** – co-ordinating group activities and overseeing the exection of policies.
- **The leader as planner** – deciding the ways and means by which the group achieves its objectives .
- **The leader as policy-maker** – establishing group goals, objectives and policies.
- **The leader as expert** – acting as a source of readily available information and skills, although there will be some reliance on technical expertise and advice from other members of the group.

- **The leader as external representative** – acting as official spokesperson for the group, representative of the group and the channel for communications.
- **The leader as controller of internal relations** – determining specific aspects of the group structure and functioning.
- **The leader as purveyor of rewards and punishment** – controlling group members by the use of reward power and coercive power.
- **The leader as arbitrator and mediator** – controlling interpersonal conflict among members of the group.
- **The leader as exemplar** – acting as a model of behaviour for members of the group and setting an example of what is expected.
- **The leader as symbol of the group** – enhancing the group unit by providing a cognitive focus and establishing the group as a distinct entity.
- **The leader as substitute for individual responsibility** – relieving individual members from the necessity of, and responsibility for, personal decisions.
- **The leader as ideologist** – serving as the source of beliefs, values and standards of behaviour for individual members of the group.
- **The leader as father figure** – serving as focus for the positive emotional feelings of individual members, and the object for identification and transference.
- **The leader as scapegoat** – serving as a target for aggression and hostility of the group, and accepting blame in the case of failure.

These 14 functions help illustrate the range of roles and responsibilities that the leader might be expected to fulfil. Leadership resides in the functions and not a particular person and can be shared among members of the group. When a member fulfils a particular activity which is accepted by members as relevant to the needs of the group, then this could become a leadership function.

NEEDS AND LEADERSHIP FUNCTIONS

A major contribution to the functional approach to leadership is the work of John Adair, and his ideas on action-centred leadership and the 'three circles' model.[20] The effectiveness of the leader is dependent upon meeting three key functions, or areas of need, within the work group:

- the need to **achieve the common task**;
- the need for **building and maintaining the team**; and
- the need for **developing the individual**.

These areas of need are symbolised by three overlapping circles in Figure 10.2.

Task functions involve:

- achieving the objectives of the group;
- defining group tasks and planning the work;
- allocation of resources;
- organisation of duties and responsibilities;
- controlling quality, checking performance and reviewing progress.

Fig 10.2 The core responsibility of the leader
Reprinted, with permission, from Adair J, *Effective Teambuilding*, Gower Publishing Limited, (1986), p. 121

Team functions involve:

- maintaining morale and building team spirit;
- maintaining the cohesiveness of the group as a working unit;
- setting standards and maintaining discipline;
- establishing systems of communication within the group;
- training the group and appointment of sub-leaders.

Individual functions involve:

- meeting the needs of individual members of the group;
- attending to personal problems;
- giving praise and status;
- reconciling conflicts between group needs and individual needs;
- training the individual.

The responsibilities of the leader

The elements of task, team and individual constitute the core responsibility of the leader. In order to achieve effectiveness and satisfaction, all three kinds of needs present in every group must be met to some extent. When the necessary functions are missing, group progress is slow and uneven. A function is what you do, as opposed to a quality or trait. To fulfil the three circles of responsibility certain key functions have to be performed. Although these are the responsibility of the leader, they can be shared or delegated and the leader will not undertake them all personally.

The action by the leader in any one area of need will affect one or both of the other areas of need. The ideal position is where complete integration of the three areas of need is achieved. In any work group the most effective leader is the person who sees that the task needs, the needs of the group, and those of the individual, are all adequately met. The effective leader elicits the contribution of members of the group and draws out other leadership from the group to satisfy the three interrelated areas of need.

Part of group functions and activities

The characteristics of the hospitality industry and the nature of the delivery of services place emphasis on a leadership style which should result in managers and supervisors being an integral part of the functions and activities of work groups.

Adair, however, makes the point that a leader is not there to dominate a group of people or simply to co-ordinate functions. The leader strengthens unity of a common purpose through the complementary and enhanced efforts of individuals.

> In industry, as in every other sphere where free and able people need to co-operate, effective leadership is founded upon respect and trust, not fear and submission. Respect and trust help to inspire whole-hearted commitment in a team; fear and submission merely produce compliance. Leadership involves focusing the efforts of a group towards a common goal and enabling them to work together as a team. A leader should be directive in a democratic way.[21]

Training for leadership

Although the functional approach acknowledges that there are some natural or born leaders, attention is focused on developing the skills of leadership. Training for leadership is important, whether the people trained are 'naturals' or not. Based on the idea of action-centred leadership, The Industrial Society, for example, has developed a system of training for helping managers to develop and improve their ability as leaders.[22]

The three-circle approach also serves to illustrate the close relationship between leadership and management. Building the team and satisfying individual needs would include leadership. Achieving the common task clearly involves the process of management.

LEADERSHIP AS A BEHAVIOURAL CATEGORY

This approach draws attention to the kinds of behaviour of people in leadership positions and to the influence of leadership style on group performance. There are many types of actual leadership behaviour and their effectiveness depends upon the variables in any particular situation. However, there does appear to be general agreement on two major dimensions of leadership which can also be related to studies discussed in previous chapters (Figure 10.3).

Two major research studies on behavioural categories of leadership are those relating to:

- consideration and structure; and
- employee-centred and production-centred supervision.

CONSIDERATION AND STRUCTURE

Results of a study undertaken at Ohio State University indicated two major dimensions of leadership behaviour – 'consideration' and 'initiating structure'.[23]

- **Consideration** reflects the extent to which the leader establishes trust, mutual respect and rapport with the group, and shows concern, warmth, support and consideration

McGregor, attitudes towards people	Theory X	Theory Y
Blake and McCanse, Leadership Grid	Concern for production	Concern for people
Group interaction analysis	Task functions	Maintenance functions
Ohio State leadership study	Initiating structure	Consideration
University of Michigan study	Production-centred supervision	Employee-centred supervision

Fig 10.3 Two major dimensions of leadership

for subordinates. This dimension is associated with two-way communication, participation and a human relations approach to leadership.

- **Structure** reflects the extent to which the leader defines and structures group interactions towards attainment of formal goals, and organises group activities. This dimension is associated with efforts to achieve organisational goals and objectives.

Separate behavioural categories

The two dimensions were found to be uncorrelated and separate behavioural categories. This gives rise to the development of four quadrants which illustrate the different combinations of consideration and structure (Figure 10.4). Some balance is needed between consideration and structure in order to satisfy both individual needs and formal goals. Although much depends upon situational factors, a high consideration and high structure category of behaviour appears to be generally more effective in terms of member satisfaction and group performance.

Consideration and structure can be related to the two major sets of group processes, task functions and maintenance functions, discussed in Chapter 9. Consideration can be seen to be the same as the maintenance function of building and maintaining the group as a cohesive working unit. Structure can be seen to be the same as the task function of accomplishing specific tasks of the group and achieving goals.

Leadership style of hotel general managers

Using the dimensions of consideration and initiating structure, Worsfold studied the leadership style of 31 general managers of a major UK hotel group.[24] The managers obtained a relatively high mean score for both dimensions. This indicates good interpersonal relationships with subordinates and an active role in directing group activities through planning and trying out new ideas.

Worsfold refers to the image of the hotel and catering industry as being people orientated with a need to maintain good interpersonal relations. This suggests the need for

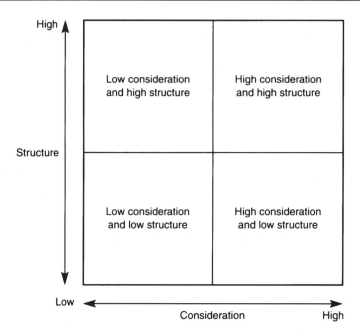

Fig 10.4 The Ohio State quadrants of leadership behaviour

high scores on consideration. But it is also necessary to maintain high standards, and to establish rules and procedures to which staff adhere. This suggests the need for effective hotel managers to demonstrate high levels of initiating structure.

EMPLOYEE-CENTRED AND PRODUCTION-CENTRED SUPERVISION

Another major research study relating to leadership behaviour was conducted at the University of Michigan. Effective supervision (measured along dimensions of group morale, productivity and cost reduction) appeared to display four common characteristics:

- delegation of authority and avoidance of close supervision;
- an interest and concern in subordinates as individuals;
- participative problem-solving; and
- high standards of performance.

The need for balance

The findings were summarised by Likert, who used the terms **employee-centred** and **production-centred supervision**.[25] (Recall the discussion on supervision and supportive relationships in Chapter 7.) These terms are similar to the dimensions of consideration and structure. The first three supervisory characteristics listed relate to consideration; the fourth characteristic exemplifies structure. And, like consideration and structure, employee-centred and production-centred supervision need to be balanced. Employee-centred supervisors who also recognise production as one of their main responsibilities tend to achieve the best results.

The importance of leadership style

Both the Ohio State University study and the University of Michigan study give support to the idea that there is no single behavioural category which is superior. These studies have drawn attention to the range of possible managerial behaviour, and the importance of leadership style. This provides another heading under which to analyse the nature of leadership.

MANAGERIAL BEHAVIOUR AND LEADERSHIP STYLE

It has become increasingly clear that managers can no longer rely solely on the use of their position in the hierarchical structure as a means of exercising the functions of leadership. In order to get the best results from subordinates, the manager must also have regard for the need to encourage high morale, a spirit of involvement and co-operation, and a willingness to work.

This gives rise to the importance of appropriate forms of managerial behaviour and leadership style for effective human resource management. Boella, for example makes the point that:

> The 'style' of leadership is therefore of vital importance in an organisation because this determines to a large extent whether employees obtain satisfaction from their jobs and whether managers will achieve their business objectives.[26]

Classifications of leadership style

Leadership style is the way in which the functions of leadership are carried out, the way in which the manager typically behaves towards subordinate staff and members of the group.

There are many possible ways of describing the behaviour adopted by managers towards subordinate staff, for example dictatorial, unitary, bureaucratic, benevolent, supportive, charismatic, consultative, participative and abdicatorial. And there are therefore a number of possible classifications of leadership styles.

The focus of power

A broad, three-fold heading, based on the focus of power, is: authoritarian (or autocratic); democratic and laissez-faire.

- **Authoritarian style** is based on the manager as the focus of power, and the issuing of orders and instructions. All interactions within the group move towards the manager. The manager alone exercises decision-making and authority for determining policy, procedures, work tasks and relationships, and control of rewards and punishments.
- **Democratic style** is based on the manager as part of a team. The focus of power is

more with the group as a whole. There is greater interaction and the leadership function is shared with members of the group. Members have a greater say in decision-making, determination of policy and the implementation of systems and procedures.

- **Laissez-faire style** is based on the focus of power being passed to the group and allowing members freedom of action. There is often confusion over the meaning of this form of behaviour. A 'genuine' laissez-faire style is where the manager observes that members of the group are working well on their own and decides not to interfere, but is readily available if help is needed and still accepts responsibility. This is to be contrasted with the manager who could not care, does not wish to get involved and leaves the group to face problems which rightly belong with the manager.

Leadership related to decision-making

An alternative classification is suggested by Magurn. He categorises the manner adopted by managers towards staff leadership in terms of four main approaches related to decision-making: autocratic, persuasive, consultative and participative.[27]

- Managers make a decision and issue instructions, and expect it to be carried out without question – an **autocratic** approach.
- Managers make a decision and expect compliance – a **persuasive** approach.
- Managers make decisions but put ideas forward for discussion and take account of staff views – a **consultative** approach.
- Managers bring staff into a problem and accept the view of the majority as the basis of the decision – a **participative** approach.

Solo leader and team leader

Belbin distinguishes between two broad contrasting or diverging styles of leadership in industry: the solo leader and the team leader.[28] The solo leader enjoys free range, and rules as if absolutely. The leader takes no risks with other people, adopts a directive approach, prefers specific tasks and goals, expects compliance and acts as a model for others to follow. In times of crisis or urgency the talented solo leaders have been effective in overcoming departmental barriers and obstacles, and implementing decisions quickly. However, when the solo leaders fail, they are discarded.

By contrast, the team leader declines to rule as if absolutely and deliberately limits his or her role. The leader creates a sense of mission, expresses greater respect for and trust in subordinates, recognises the skills and strengths of others, and is more inclined to delegate. Belbin suggests that solo leadership is familiar to most people because part of crowd psychology is to seek to be led and to have faith in the leader. However, increasing uncertainty and continuous change together with societal pressure for the sharing of power has led to increasing attention to team leadership.

Attention to styles of leadership

The development of behavioural science has drawn attention to the processes of interpersonal behaviour in the work situation and to the effects of leadership on those being led. The attention given to leadership style is based on the assumption that subordinates are more likely to work willingly and effectively for managers who adopt a certain style of leadership than for those managers who adopt alternative styles.

Attention to the manager's style of leadership has come about because of a greater understanding of individual motivation, and the needs and expectations of people at work. It has also been influenced by broader standards of education and training, changes in the value system of society, pressure for a greater social responsibility towards employees, and the concept of the quality of working life. These have all combined to create resistance against purely dictatorial styles of leadership.

CONTINUUM OF LEADERSHIP BEHAVIOUR

A popular model of leadership style is that presented by Tannenbaum and Schmidt, (Figure 10.5).[29] They suggest a continuum of possible behaviour available to the manager and along which various styles of leadership may be placed. The continuum presents a range of actions related to the degree of authority used by the manager and to the area of freedom available to subordinates. At one extreme is boss-centred (authoritarian) leadership and at the other extreme is subordinate-centred (democratic) leadership. These extreme forms of leadership behaviour can be related to McGregor's Theory X and Theory Y suppositions.

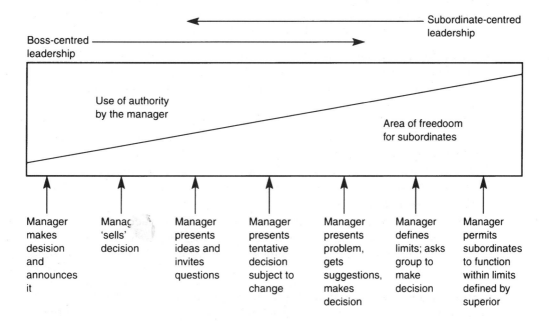

Fig 10.5 Continuum of leadership behaviour
Reprinted by permission of the *Harvard Business Review*, from 'How to Choose a Leadership Pattern' by Robert Tannenbaum and Warren H Schmidt (May/June 1973). Copyright © 1973 by the President and Fellows of Harvard College. All rights reserved.

Four main styles of leadership

Neither extreme of the continuum is absolute as there is always some limitation on the use of authority or the area of freedom. Moving along the continuum, the manager may be characterised according to the degree of control that is maintained over subordinates. This approach leads to the identification of four main styles of leadership – tells, sells, consults, joins.

- **Tells** – the manager identifies a problem, chooses a decision and announces this to subordinates, and expects them to implement it without an opportunity for participation.
- **Sells** – the manager still chooses a decision but recognises the possibility of some resistance from those faced with the decision and attempts to persuade subordinates to accept it.
- **Consults** – the manager identifies the problem but does not choose a decision until the problem is presented to the group, and the manager has listened to the advice and solutions suggested by subordinates.
- **Joins** – the manager defines the problem and the limits within which the decision must be chosen and then passes to the group, with the manager as a member, the right to make decisions.

Forces influencing the type of leadership

Tannenbaum and Schmidt suggest that there are three factors, or forces, of particular importance in deciding which types of leadership are practical and desirable. These are: forces in the manager, forces in the subordinates and forces in the situation.

- **Forces in the manager** – managers' behaviour will be influenced by their own personalities, backgrounds, knowledge and experiences. These internal forces include: value systems, confidence in subordinates, leadership inclinations, and feelings of security in uncertain situations.
- **Forces in the subordinate** – subordinates are influenced by many personality variables and individual sets of expectations about relationships with the manager. Characteristics of the subordinates include the need for independence and readiness to accept responsibility, identification with the goals of the organisation, interest in, and perceived importance of, the problem, knowledge and experience, extent of learning to share in decision-making.
- **Forces in the situation** – managers' behaviour will be influenced by the general situation and environmental pressures. Characteristics of the situation include the type and nature of organisation, group effectiveness, the nature of the problem, pressure of time.

Successful leaders are keenly aware of those forces which are most relevant to their behaviour at a particular time. They are able to behave appropriately in terms of their understanding of themselves, the individuals and the group, the organisation, and environmental influences. Successful managers are both perceptive and flexible.

THE SITUATIONAL APPROACH

The continuum of leadership behaviour draws attention to forces in the situation as one of the variables influencing the nature of managerial behaviour. The situational approach, however, concentrates on the importance of the situation as the dominant feature in considering the characteristics of leadership. Despite the more recent interest in this approach, it is interesting to note that the idea of the manager applying the law of the situation was put forward over 50 years ago.

The law of the situation

This idea was propounded by Mary Parker Follet, who considered the way orders should be given in the manager–subordinate relationship. The problem is to avoid the two extremes of (i) too great bossism in giving orders; and (ii) practically no orders given. Follett's solution was what she called the 'depersonalising of orders and obeying the law of the situation'.

> My solution is to depersonalise the giving of orders, to unite all concerned in a study of the situation, to discover the law of the situation and obey that. Until we do this I do not think we shall have the most successful business administration . . . This is, ideally what should take place between any head and subordinates. One *person* should not give orders to another *person* but both should agree to take their orders from the situation. If orders are simply part of the situation, the question of someone giving and someone receiving does not come up. Both accept the orders given by the situation.[30]

Contingency theories of leadership

More recent studies under the situational approach focus on the interactions between the variables involved in a leadership situation and patterns of leadership behaviour. This gives rise to the study of leadership-contingency theories. Contingency theories are based on the belief that there is no single style of leadership appropriate to all situations. Also, depending upon the nature of the situation, different individuals within the group may fulfil the functions of leadership.

Three major contingency models of particular relevance to the hospitality manager are those which relate to:

- the favourability of the leadership situation;
- path–goal theory; and
- the 'readiness' (or maturity) of followers.

FIEDLER'S CONTINGENCY MODEL

A major leader-situation model is that developed by Fiedler in his contingency theory of leadership effectiveness.[31] In order to measure the attitudes and effectiveness of the leader, Fiedler developed a 'least preferred co-worker' (LPC) scale. The LPC score is determined by the ratings given by leaders about the person with whom they could work least well. The questionnaire contains up to 20 bipolar items. Each item on the scale is given a single ranking of between one and eight points (Figure 10.6).

Pleasant	:_:_:_:_ 8 7 6 5	:_:_:_:_ 4 3 2 1	Unpleasant
Friendly	:_:_:_:_ 8 7 6 5	:_:_:_:_ 4 3 2 1	Unfriendly
Rejecting	:_:_:_:_ 1 2 3 4	:_:_:_:_ 5 6 7 8	Accepting
Helpful	:_:_:_:_ 8 7 6 5	:_:_:_:_ 4 3 2 1	Frustrating
Unenthusiastic	:_:_:_:_ 1 2 3 4	:_:_:_:_ 5 6 7 8	Enthusiastic
Tense	:_:_:_:_ 1 2 3 4	:_:_:_:_ 5 6 7 8	Relaxed
Distant	:_:_:_:_ 1 2 3 4	:_:_:_:_ 5 6 7 8	Close
Cold	:_:_:_:_ 1 2 3 4	:_:_:_:_ 5 6 7 8	Warm
Cooperative	:_:_:_:_ 8 7 6 5	:_:_:_:_ 4 3 2 1	Uncooperative
Supportive	:_:_:_:_ 8 7 6 5	:_:_:_:_ 4 3 2 1	Hostile
Boring	:_:_:_:_ 1 2 3 4	:_:_:_:_ 5 6 7 8	Interesting
Quarrelsome	:_:_:_:_ 1 2 3 4	:_:_:_:_ 5 6 7 8	Harmonious
Self-assured	:_:_:_:_ 8 7 6 5	:_:_:_:_ 4 3 2 1	Hesitant
Efficient	:_:_:_:_ 8 7 6 5	:_:_:_:_ 4 3 2 1	Inefficient
Gloomy	:_:_:_:_ 1 2 3 4	:_:_:_:_ 5 6 7 8	Cheerful
Open	:_:_:_:_ 8 7 6 5	:_:_:_:_ 4 3 2 1	Guarded

Fig 10.6 Least preferred co-worker (LPC) scale
Reprinted with permission of Professor F E Fiedler

Interpretation of the LPC score

The more a leader is generally 'lenient' in rating the least preferred co-worker, the higher the LPC score, and the more critical the rating, the lower the LPC score. Interpretation of the LPC score appears to be that:

- a high-rating leader derives most satisfaction from interpersonal relationships and is motivated to act in a supportive considerate manner when relationships with subordinates need to be improved;
- a leader with a low LPC score derives most satisfaction from performance of the task and achieving objectives – establishing good relationships with subordinates is a secondary motivation .

Favourability of the situation

The relationship between the LPC score and leadership behaviour is dependent upon the favourability of the situation. This is the extent to which the situation gives a leader control over subordinates. There are three major variables which determine the favourability of the situation and which affect the leader's role and influence.

- **Leader-member relations** – the degree to which the leader is trusted and liked by group members, the willingness of members to follow the leader's guidance.
- **The task structure** – the degree to which the task is clearly defined for the group, the extent to which the task can be carried out by detailed instructions or standard procedures.
- **Position power** – the power of the leader by virtue of position in the organisation, the degree to which the leader can exercise authority to influence, for example rewards and punishments, promotions and demotions.

Group–task situations and leadership style

From these three variables, Fiedler constructs eight combinations of group–task situations through which to relate favourability and leadership style. The variables are weighted and assume leader–member relations as the most important, with next task structure and then position power. As the favourability of the leadership situation varies, the leadership style varies (Figure 10.7).

When the situation is:

 (i) very favourable, with good leader–member relations, structured task and strong position power; or
(ii) very unfavourable, with poor leader–member relations, unstructured task and weak position power;

then a **task-oriented leader** (low LPC score) with a directive, controlling style will be more effective.

When the situation is:

(iii) moderately favourable and the variables are mixed;

then an **interpersonal-oriented leader** (high LPC score) with a participative approach will be more effective.

Applications to the hospitality industry

Although there appears to be some uncertainty about the interpretation of the LPC scale, and Fiedler's work may at first appear somewhat complex, it does provide a further dimension to the study of leadership. Consideration is given to the importance of organisational variables which affect leadership effectiveness.

As discussed previously, the nature of the hospitality industry does make particular demands upon its managers. The nature of managerial behaviour and style of leadership is a significant factor in both staff and customer satisfaction.

> The industry provides the manager, in most situations, with a multiplicity of tasks and very complex interrelationships between staff and customers. Together with this the nature of demand in hotels is highly fluctuating. These factors mean that the hotel manager must be highly adaptable to prevailing circumstances.[32]

Fiedler's contingency model draws attention to the importance of situational variables and leadership style, and matching changes in the leader-member relations, task structure and position power to the characteristics of the leader. The model would therefore appear to have particular significance for the hospitality manager.

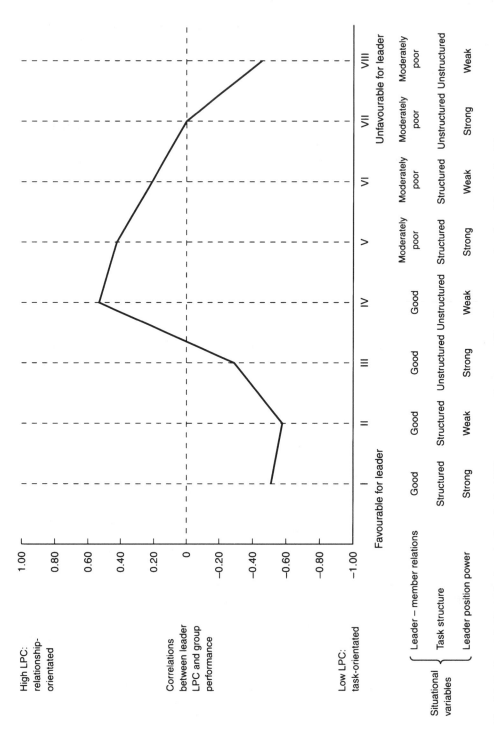

Fig 10.7 Correlations between leader's LPC scores and group effectiveness – leadership style. The appropriateness of a leadership style for maximising group performance is dependent upon the three variables in the leadership situation.
Adapted and reproduced with permission of Fiedler F E from *A Theory of Leadership Effectivenesss*, McGraw-Hill (1967), p. 146

PATH–GOAL THEORY OF LEADERSHIP

The importance of the path-goal theory for the hospitality manager is that it attempts to explain the influence of leadership behaviour on the performance and job satisfaction of subordinates. The model is based on the expectancy theory of motivation (discussed in Chapter 8). The main work in this field has been undertaken by House[33] and House and Dessler.[34]

The theory suggests that the performance of subordinates is affected by the extent to which the manager satisfies their expectations. Subordinates will see leadership behaviour as a motivating influence to the extent that it means:

(i)   satisfaction of their needs is dependent upon effective performance; and
(ii) the necessary direction, guidance, training and support, which would otherwise be lacking, is provided.

Four main styles of leadership

The path–goal approach identifies four main types of leadership behaviour.[35]

- **Directive leadership** involves letting subordinates know exactly what is expected of them and giving specific directions. Subordinates are expected to follow rules and regulations. This type of behaviour is similar to 'initiating structure'.
- **Supportive leadership** involves a friendly and approachable manner, and displaying concern for the needs and welfare of subordinates. This type of behaviour is similar to 'consideration'.
- **Participative leadership** involves consulting with subordinates, and the evaluation of their opinions and suggestions before the manager makes the decision.
- **Achievement-oriented leadership** involves setting challenging goals for subordinates, seeking improvement in their performance and showing confidence in their ability to perform well.

Situational factors

According to path-goal theory, the effect of leadership behaviour is determined by two main situational factors: the personality characteristics of subordinates; and the nature of the task (Figure 10.8).

- **The personality characteristics of subordinates** determine how they will react to the manager's behaviour and the extent to which they perceive such behaviour as an immediate or potential source of need satisfaction.
- **The nature of the task** relates to the extent that it is routine and structured, or non-routine and unstructured.

These situational factors determine the subordinates' perceptions and motivation, which in turn lead to improved goal clarity, performance and job satisfaction. The situational factors also influence the subordinates' preferences for a particular style of managerial behaviour. For example, when a task is highly structured, the goals are

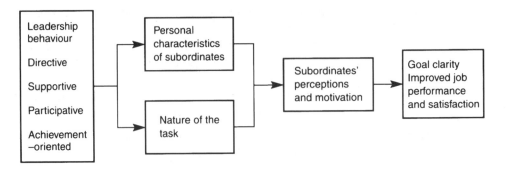

Fig 10.8 Representation of the path–goal theory of leadership

readily apparent and subordinates are confident, then a directive style of leadership may not be welcomed. However, when a task is highly unstructured, the nature of the goals is not clear and subordinates lack experience, then a more directive style of leadership may be welcomed.

Motivational leadership

Different types of behaviour can be practised by the same person at different times in varying situations. By using one of the four styles of leadership the manager attempts to influence subordinates' perceptions and motivation, and smooth the path to their goals. Effective leadership is based on both the willingness of the manager to help subordinates, and the needs of subordinates for help. Leadership behaviour will be motivational to the extent that it provides necessary direction, guidance and support, helps clarify path-goal relationships and removes any obstacles which hinder the attainment of goals.

READINESS OF THE FOLLOWERS

A major variable in the style of leadership adopted by the hospitality manager is the nature of subordinate staff. This leads to consideration of another important contingency model – the situational leadership model presented by Hersey and Blanchard.[36] The model is based on the 'readiness' level of the people the leader is attempting to influence. Readiness (formerly called 'maturity') is the extent to which followers have the ability and willingness to accomplish a specific task. It is not a characteristic of the individual, but how ready the individual is to perform a particular task.

A continuum of four levels

Readiness (R) is divided into a continuum of four levels: R1 (low), R2 and R3 (moderate), and R4 (high).

- **R1 – low follower readiness.** This refers to followers who are both unable and unwilling, and who lack commitment and motivation, or who are unable and insecure.
- **R2 – low to moderate follower readiness.** This refers to followers who are unable but

willing, and who lack ability but are motivated to make an effort, or who are unable but confident.

- **R3 – moderate to high follower readiness.** This refers to followers who are able but unwilling, and who have the ability to perform but are unwilling to apply their ability, or who are able but insecure.
- **R4 – high follower readiness.** This refers to followers who are both able and willing, and who have the ability and commitment to perform, or who are able and confident.

For each of the four levels of readiness, the appropriate style of leadership is a combination of task behaviour and relationship behaviour (Figure 10.9).

- **Task behaviour** is the extent to which the leader provides directions for the actions of followers, sets goals for them, and defines their roles and how to undertake them.

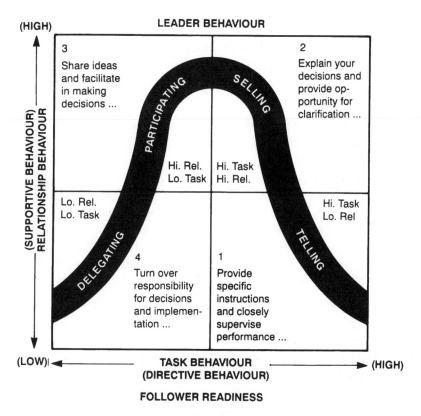

Fig 10.9 Situational leadership model
Source: Hersey P, *The Situational Leader* (1984), p. 63. Copyrighted material from Leadership Studies Inc. Used by permission. All rights reserved.

- **Relationship behaviour** is the extent to which the leader engages in two-way communications with followers, listens to them, and provides support and encouragement.

Four leadership styles

The combination of task behaviour and relationship behaviour produces four leadership styles (S): telling, selling, participating and delegating.

- **S1 – telling.** This emphasises high amounts of guidance (task behaviour) but limited supportive (relationship) behaviour. This style is most appropriate for low follower readiness (R1) .
- **S2 – selling.** This emphasises high amounts of both directive (task) and relationship behaviour. This style is most appropriate for low to moderate follower readiness (R2).
- **S3 – participating.** This emphasises a high amount of two-way communication and supportive (relationship) behaviour but low amounts of guidance (task behaviour). This style is most appropriate for moderate to high follower readiness (R3).
- **S4 – delegating.** This emphasises little direction or support with low levels of task and relationship behaviour. This style is most appropriate for high follower readiness (R4).

Flexible leadership behaviour

According to Hersey and Blanchard, the key to using situational leadership is that any leader behaviour may be more or less effective depending on the readiness of the followers whom the leader is attempting to influence. An important contribution for the hospitality manager is therefore the need for a flexible style of leadership behaviour. It is important to treat subordinates differently according to their 'readiness' (or maturity), and to treat the same subordinate differently according to changes in the situation.

The model also draws attention to the importance of developing the ability, confidence and commitment of subordinates. The manager should help subordinates to develop in readiness to the extent that they are able and willing. This development should take place by adjusting leadership behaviour through the four styles of telling, selling, participating and delegating.

THE BEST STYLE OF LEADERSHIP IN THE HOSPITALITY INDUSTRY

We have seen that different individuals may fulfil the leadership functions and that there are many alternative styles of leadership. And contingency models demonstrate the importance of situational variables. Different types of leadership may also be most appropriate at different stages in the development of a business organisation.[37] Clearly, there is no simple answer to what is the best style of leadership.

Studies on leadership in the hospitality industry appear to yield conflicting results. For example, using Fiedler's contingency model, Nebel and Stearns conducted a survey of first-line supervisors in the American hotel and restaurant industry. Their findings indicate that a task-oriented style of management leadership would be most effective.[38]

In contrast, however, is the survey by Keegan of managers in the hotel and restaurant industry. The managers identified effective leadership neither as being autocratic or dictatorial, nor as creating followers out of fear or patronising dedication. Rather, they were aware of the need for, and the trend towards, a more human relations style of leadership. Changing social values have increased the demands of employees for a 'good' job and it is the style of managerial leadership which contributes most to their satisfaction and motivation.

Keegan presents a strongly argued case for the adoption of a more supportive, behavioural approach to managerial leadership and draws the following conclusion.

> The challenge for us is not so much to change the job, but to provide the managerial leadership that would create an environment in which the employee's real needs are satisfied. Such a leadership is characterised as being personal, supportive and participative, and is firmly based on a solid relationship between the manager and employees. This managerial leadership should be an integral part of the hospitality environment, a behavioural model as it were, of how best to behave with people in general whether they be guests or employees. Such a leadership style is in many ways in direct opposition to the leadership traditionally associated with our industry. We must change and change dramatically, so let our goal be then to develop this new leadership for our industry.[39]

Variables influencing leadership effectiveness

Many research studies tend to indicate that democratic styles of leadership are more likely to produce effective performance from work groups. A human relations, people-oriented approach is more likely to lead to job satisfaction and group cohesiveness. However, it is not always the case that democratic styles of leadership are best. There are occasions when an autocratic style of leadership is more likely to be effective.

There is no one 'best' style of leadership which will result in the maintenance of morale among group members and high work performance. There are many variables which underlie the effectiveness of managerial leadership in the hospitality industry, including:

- the type and nature of the organisation, its goals and objectives, and the organisational culture and climate;
- the characteristics of the manager, personality, attitudes, abilities, value system and personal credibility;
- the characteristics of the subordinates, their needs and expectations, motivation and commitment, and their knowledge, confidence and experience;
- the basis of the leadership relation and the type of power and influence;
- the relationships between the manager and the group, and among members of the group;
- the type of problem and nature of the manager's decisions;
- the nature of the tasks to be achieved, the extent to which they are structured or routine, the technology and work organisation;
- the organisation structure and systems of management;
- the nature and influence of the external environment.

The most effective form of leadership behaviour is therefore a product of the total leadership situation. Education and training in management need to emphasise not only the interpersonal skills of leadership but also the importance of adopting a flexible and adaptable approach.

SUMMARY

- There are many ways of looking at leadership. Essentially it is a relationship through which one person influences other people, and is closely associated with the activities of groups. To be an effective manager it is necessary to exercise the role of leadership. The leadership relationship is dependent upon the perceived power which the leader can exercise over other people.

- Because of its complex and variable nature there are many ways of analysing leadership. The qualities or traits approach is based on the belief that leadership consists of certain inherited characteristics or personality traits. The functional approach focuses attention on the work group, and functions and responsibilities of leadership.

- Increasing attention has been given to leadership as a behavioural category and the importance of leadership style. Two main dimensions of leadership behaviour are consideration and structure. There are many possible classifications of styles of leadership. One approach is based on the focus of power or the degree of authority used by the manager.

- The situational approach draws attention to variables influencing the nature of managerial leadership. This gives rise to the study of leadership-contingency models. Major models of particular relevance to the hospitality manager are those which relate to the favourability of the leadership situation, path–goal theory, and the readiness of followers.

- Contingency models demonstrate the importance of situational variables and the belief that there is no, one single style of leadership appropriate to all situations. Many research studies suggest the advantages of a democratic, people-oriented approach. However, the most effective form of behaviour is a product of the total leadership situation.

REVIEW AND DISCUSSION QUESTIONS

1 Explain the meaning and nature of leadership. How would you attempt to distinguish leadership from management?

2 What is meant by the leadership relationship? Give practical examples of the different sources of leadership power and influence within the hospitality industry.

3 Critically assess the relevance of the qualities or trait theories of leadership. Suggest what you believe to be the most important characteristics of an effective leader in the work situation.

4 Explain your understanding of the functional approach to leadership. Discuss the main areas of need which constitute the core responsibility of the leader.

5 What is meant by leadership as a behavioural category? Explain how you would attempt to summarise the major dimensions of leadership behaviour.

6 Explain the meaning and importance of leadership style. Suggest ways in which leadership styles can be classified. Why do think greater attention is being given to more participative styles of managerial leadership?

7 Discuss critically the practical value of contingency models of leadership. What are the main factors which are likely to influence the most appropriate form of managerial leadership in the hospitality industry?

8 Why do you think it is that studies on leadership in the hospitality industry appear to yield conflicting results? Justify what you think is the best style of leadership.

ASSIGNMENT 1

Assume you are a departmental manager in a hospitality organisation of your choice.

(i) Using the Tannenbaum and Schmidt continuum, identify your *preferred* style of leadership. Explain fully the rationale for your preference.

(ii) Detail fully, and preferably from actual experience, an example of a particular situation when you believe a different form of managerial leadership is likely to be most effective.

ASSIGNMENT 2

Three months ago you were appointed head housekeeper at ABC Hotel. A member of your staff, several years older than yourself and with five years' service, has in recent weeks had a poor record of punctuality and sickness absence, and often a below-expected standard of work. Despite attempts to find out what might be the cause, the member of staff has been reluctant to say anything. Other members of the group have been covering for their colleague but the strain is now showing and morale is beginning to suffer. The general manager has now expressed concern at the situation. You are given clear instructions as 'leader of the group' to sort out the problem as quickly as possible. If not, action will have to be taken at a higher level.

Explain fully and with supporting reasons the actions you would propose to take.

ASSIGNMENT 3

The following items (see Figure 10.10) describe aspects of leadership behaviour. Respond to each item according to the way you would most likely act if you were the leader of a work group. Circle whether you would most likely behave in the described way:

always (A); frequently (F); occasionally (O); seldom (S); or never (N).

Scoring
1. Circle the item number for items 8, 12, 17, 18, 19, 30, 34 and 35.
2. Write the number 1 in front of a *circled item number* if you responded S (seldom) or N (never) to that item.
3. Also write a number 1 in front of *item numbers not circled* if you responded A (always) or F (frequently).
4. Circle the number 1 which you have written in front of the following items: 3, 5, 8, 10, 15, 18, 19, 22, 24, 26, 28, 30, 32, 34 and 35.

5. *Count the circled number 1s.* This is your score for concern for people. Record the score in the blank following the letter P at the end of the questionnaire.
6. *Count the uncircled number 1s.* This is your score for concern for task. Record this number in the blank following the letter T.

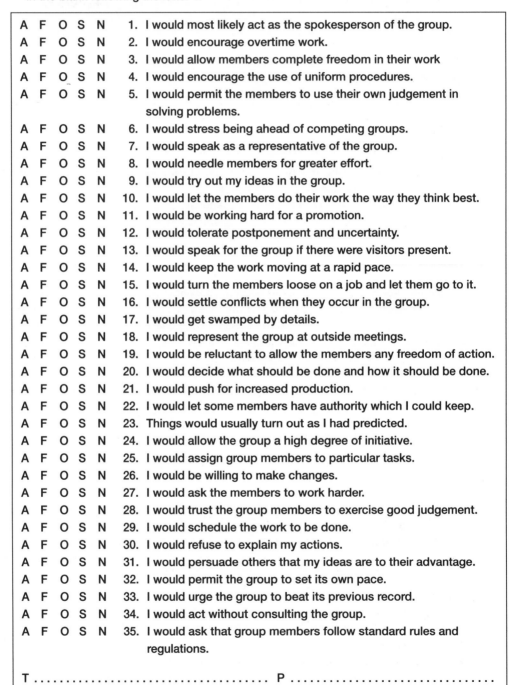

```
A  F  O  S  N     1. I would most likely act as the spokesperson of the group.
A  F  O  S  N     2. I would encourage overtime work.
A  F  O  S  N     3. I would allow members complete freedom in their work
A  F  O  S  N     4. I would encourage the use of uniform procedures.
A  F  O  S  N     5. I would permit the members to use their own judgement in
                     solving problems.
A  F  O  S  N     6. I would stress being ahead of competing groups.
A  F  O  S  N     7. I would speak as a representative of the group.
A  F  O  S  N     8. I would needle members for greater effort.
A  F  O  S  N     9. I would try out my ideas in the group.
A  F  O  S  N    10. I would let the members do their work the way they think best.
A  F  O  S  N    11. I would be working hard for a promotion.
A  F  O  S  N    12. I would tolerate postponement and uncertainty.
A  F  O  S  N    13. I would speak for the group if there were visitors present.
A  F  O  S  N    14. I would keep the work moving at a rapid pace.
A  F  O  S  N    15. I would turn the members loose on a job and let them go to it.
A  F  O  S  N    16. I would settle conflicts when they occur in the group.
A  F  O  S  N    17. I would get swamped by details.
A  F  O  S  N    18. I would represent the group at outside meetings.
A  F  O  S  N    19. I would be reluctant to allow the members any freedom of action.
A  F  O  S  N    20. I would decide what should be done and how it should be done.
A  F  O  S  N    21. I would push for increased production.
A  F  O  S  N    22. I would let some members have authority which I could keep.
A  F  O  S  N    23. Things would usually turn out as I had predicted.
A  F  O  S  N    24. I would allow the group a high degree of initiative.
A  F  O  S  N    25. I would assign group members to particular tasks.
A  F  O  S  N    26. I would be willing to make changes.
A  F  O  S  N    27. I would ask the members to work harder.
A  F  O  S  N    28. I would trust the group members to exercise good judgement.
A  F  O  S  N    29. I would schedule the work to be done.
A  F  O  S  N    30. I would refuse to explain my actions.
A  F  O  S  N    31. I would persuade others that my ideas are to their advantage.
A  F  O  S  N    32. I would permit the group to set its own pace.
A  F  O  S  N    33. I would urge the group to beat its previous record.
A  F  O  S  N    34. I would act without consulting the group.
A  F  O  S  N    35. I would ask that group members follow standard rules and
                     regulations.

T . . . . . . . . . . . . . . . . . . . . . . . . . . . . . . . . . . .    P . . . . . . . . . . . . . . . . . . . . . . . . . . . . . . . . .
```

Fig 10.10 Leadership questionnaire

To determine your style of leadership look at the Interpretation Sheet at the back of the book.

NOTES AND REFERENCES

1. Keegan B M, 'Leadership in the Hospitality Industry' in Cassee E and Reuland R (eds), *The Management of Hospitality*, Pergamon (1983), p. 78.
2. Tack A, *Motivational Leadership*, Gower (1984).
3. See, for example, Mill R C, *Managing for Productivity in the Hospitality Industry*, Van Nostrand Reinhold (1989).
4. Worsfold P, 'Leadership and Managerial Effectiveness in the Hospitality Industry', *International Journal of Hospitality Management*, vol. 8, no. 2, 1989, pp. 145–155.
5. Hunt J W, *Managing People at Work*, Second edition, McGraw-Hill (1986).
6. Watson C M, 'Leadership, Management and the Seven Keys', *Business Horizons*, March–April 1983, pp. 8–13.
7. Zaleznik A, 'Managers and Leaders: Are They Different?', *Harvard Business Review*, May–June 1977, pp. 67–78.
8. Bonington C, 'Leading to the Top: The Successful Management of People', *Office and Information Management International*, September 1988, pp. 8–9.
9. Mintzberg H, *The Nature of Managerial Work*, Harper & Row (1973).
10. Adair J, *Effective Teambuilding*, Gower (1986) p. 123.
11. For an example, see Riley M, *Human Resource Management: A guide to personnel practice in the hotel and catering industry*, Butterworth-Heinemann (1991).
12. McGregor D, *The Human Side of Enterprise*, Penguin (1987), p. 182.
13. French J R P and Raven B, 'The Basis of Social Power', in Cartwright D and Zander A F (eds), *Group Dynamics: Research and Theory*, Third edition, Harper & Row (1968).
14. Drucker P F, *The Practice of Management*, Pan Books (1968), p. 194.
15. See, for example, Jennings E E, 'The Anatomy of Leadership', *Management of Personnel Quarterly*, vol. 1, no. 1, Autumn 1961, pp. 2–9.
16. Hornsey T and Dann D, *Manpower Management in the Hotel and Catering Industry*, Batsford (1984).
17. Walker R G, 'Wellsprings of Managerial Leadership', *Cornell HRA Quarterly*, vol. 27, no. 2, August 1986, pp. 14–16.
18. Kotter J P, 'What Leaders Really Do', *Harvard Business Review*, May–June 1990, p. 103.
19. Krech D, Crutchfield R S and Ballachey E L, *Individual in Society*, McGraw-Hill (1962).
20. Adair J, *The Skills of Leadership*, Gower (1984).
21. Adair J, *Effective Teambuilding*, Gower (1986), p. 116.
22. For a summary, see Smith E P, *The Manager as a Leader* (Notes for Managers), The Industrial Society, June 1983.
23. Fleishman E A and Bass A R, *Studies in Personnel and Industrial Psychology*, Third edition, Dorsey (1974).
24. Worsfold P, 'Leadership and Managerial Effectiveness in the Hospitality Industry', *International Journal of Hospitality Management*, vol. 8, no. 2, 1989, pp. 145–155.
25. Likert R, *New Patterns of Management*, McGraw-Hill (1961).
26. Boella M J, Human Resource Management in the Hotel and Catering Industry, Fourth edition, Hutchinson (1987), p. 40.
27. Magurn J P, *A Manual of Staff Management in the Hotel and Catering Industry*, Heinemann (1983).
28. Belbin R M, *Team Roles at Work*, Butterworth-Heinemann (1993).
29. Tannenbaum R and Schmidt W H, 'How to Choose a Leadership Pattern', *Harvard Business Review*, May–June 1973, pp. 162–180.
30. Follett M P 'The Giving of Orders', in Pugh D S (ed), *Organization Theory*, Penguin (1971), pp. 154–155.
31. Fiedler F E, *A Theory of Leadership Effectiveness*, McGraw-Hill (1967).
32. Hornsey T and Dann D, *Manpower Management in the Hotel and Catering Industry*, Batsford (1984), p. 108.

33. House R J, 'A Path–Goal Theory of Leadership Effectiveness', *Administrative Science Quarterly*, vol. 16, September 1971, pp. 321–338.

34. House R 1 and Dessler G, 'The Path–Goal Theory of Leadership', in Hunt J G and Larson L L (eds), *Contingency Approaches to Leadership*, Southern Illinois University Press (1974).

35. House R 1 and Mitchell T R, 'Path–Goal Theory of Leadership', *Journal of Contemporary Business*, vol. 3, Autumn 1974, pp. 81–97.

36. Hersey P and Blanchard K, *Management of Organizational Behavior*, Fifth edition, Prentice-Hall (1988).

37. See, for example, Clarke C and Pratt S, 'Leadership's Four-Part Progress', *Management Today*, March 1985, pp. 84–86.

38. Nebel E C and Stearns K, 'Leadership in the Hospitality Industry', *Cornell HRA Quarterly*, vol. 18, no. 3, November 1977, pp. 69–76.

39. Keegan B M, 'Leadership in the Hospitality Industry', in Cassee E and Reuland R (eds), *The Management of Hospitality*, Pergamon (1983), pp. 69–93.

11
COMMUNICATION IN ORGANISATIONS

Tom McEwan

INTRODUCTION

Most people take it for granted that communication permeates every aspect of their relations with others. Effective communication is an essential requirement of the numerous formal and informal contacts that occur each day in hospitality organisations between managers and staff, or with customers, competitors or even strangers.

This chapter looks at:

- Developments in communication theory
- The everyday use of the concept of communication
- Communication and organisational behaviour theory
- Three main approaches to human communication theory
- The linear approach to human communication

- Interactional approaches to communication
- The relational and systems-interactive approaches
- Dyadic and triadic relationships
- Prescribed and emergent communication networks
- Communication network analysis
- Practical applications

DEVELOPMENTS IN COMMUNICATION THEORY

The tendency to undervalue the necessity of communication is never more apparent than in the countless face-to-face exchanges that take place with relatives, colleagues, friends and acquaintances at home, at work, or elsewhere during leisure time activities. However, communication at work is just as extensive. It involves contacts with other people who may be separated by time, distance and season, at the other end of a telephone or 'fax', as well as by language, race, religion, economic, political or other cultural differences.

Anyone familiar with developments in higher education in the UK would agree that the influential Crick formula for business education was amended in an important way in the early 1980s when the study of sociology was replaced by an array of new subjects such as behavioural studies/science, industrial psychology and organisational behaviour/analysis.[1] The preferred subject was usually organisational behaviour although, for reasons which are outside the scope of this chapter, this was also regarded as a contentious replacement for sociology.

Several factors account for the growing popularity of organisational behaviour.

- By focusing on the study of organisations, the subject has been included on vocational courses which seek to prepare students for careers in, for example, the hotel and catering industry.
- Previous textbooks on organisational behaviour have tried to simplify the study of human behaviour. However, they usually exclude a broad discussion of the different approaches to human communication, which are relevant to understanding how organisations evolve as collectivities and help to explain how their members achieve common objectives.
- The long-standing incompatibility between organisational behaviour theory and organisational communication theory was rarely discussed, and attempts have only recently been made to show that both subjects can be integrated if an open systems perspective is applied to developments in communication theory, such as communication network analysis.

THE EVERYDAY USE OF THE CONCEPT OF COMMUNICATION

Before discussing these theoretical issues, it is worth considering the different practical usages attributed to the word 'communication' in everyday life. The word 'communication' is derived from the Latin 'munio' meaning service to, or mutual help in, the community. Thus, the old who were no longer able to give service were granted 'immunity', whereas those who refused to help or participate were sometimes 'excommunicated' from society. The *Oxford English Dictionary* defines communication as 'the act of imparting, or conveying information or evoking understanding', yet the word has also been used in 12 other ways since it first entered the English language in 1392. These include 'a piece of information', 'a means of access', 'a line of connexion', 'common participation', 'personal/sexual intercourse', 'the act of recognising a quality shared in common', 'the Christian sacrament of Holy Eucharist', 'a conference of the Freemasonry fraternity', 'the discipline developed by the Ancient Greeks known as Rhetoric' and as 'a combination' term in artefacts such as 'a communication-cord' or a 'communication-valve'. Additional, more abstract meanings of the word 'communication' include the 'conversing', 'exchanging' or 'interchanging' of information between at least two people.

A pervasive characteristic

Despite this wide diversity, most people apparently spend much of their lives engaging in different forms of communication with others, without wondering too much about what goes on during these encounters. For most of us, communication is such a pervasive characteristic of the social world we inhabit that we are either hardly ever aware of it, or never need to be reminded of its crucial importance, unless perhaps we experience the painful effects of its absence as a result of prolonged isolation from other human beings.

In short, if it is not too absurd to compare communication with the air around us, or even with the water in which fish need to be immersed if they are to survive, this is because we engage in it whenever we are in the company of at least one other person, go shopping, attend meetings, join groups, teams or crowds, or merely perform our jobs in small firms, public-sector institutions or large multinational corporations. Yet if communication occurs whenever people associate in these ways, why should it be so difficult to isolate the phenomenon for the purposes of carrying out independent research? Furthermore, why should the views of those who study communication at the interpersonal level differ so strikingly from those who are more interested in explaining the behaviour of people who work in larger organisations?

COMMUNICATION AND ORGANISATIONAL BEHAVIOUR THEORY

Various reasons appear below why, until the late 1980s, the study of human communication in organisations was regarded as almost impossible to reconcile with organisational behaviour theory.

- The sheer pervasiveness of communication in every sphere of human activity means that it has always been regarded as a legitimate area of study in more than one academic discipline. Hence, communication is investigated in psychology, sociology, linguistics, media studies, and in more abstract subjects such as philosophy and mathematics. Hardly surprisingly, therefore, not everyone approaches the topic from the same starting point, and many end up with different, sometimes conflicting, conclusions.

- This widespread interest has led to so much diversity of opinion that agreement has never been reached on the best way to define human communication. Some regard any attempt to generate a comprehensive definition, aimed at gaining widespread support, as a futile activity because writers such as Dance and Larsen have identified nearly 200 different definitions of human communication and were unable to reduce these to fewer than 15 distinct themes or 'conceptual components'.[2]

- Faced with the prospect of confusion arising out of this complexity, caused by the availability of so many competing viewpoints and definitions from which to choose, American social scientists, in particular, opted for a systematic approach that divided the study of human communication into separate disciplines such as interpersonal communication, speech communication, philosophy of communication and organisational communication. In the last discipline, alone, Guetzkow,[3] Porter and Roberts[4] and Jablin et al.[5] have identified over 4000 studies of communication in organisations, most of them carried out after 1960.

- Whereas this division of communication studies into separate disciplines clarified many issues, it has also created several awkward problems. For example, researchers either omitted, or were unable, to separate communication from other variables in literally thousands of studies of motivation, leadership and group behaviour which provide the academic foundations of organisational behaviour. Rather than question these premises, this discovery led Porter and Roberts to conclude that:

Organisational Communication appears to be mired in an identity crisis. Researchers interested in organisations frequently confound communication in them with a host of other phenomena such as leadership and control.[6]

Perhaps such researchers did confound communication with other phenomena except their conclusion looks rather biased if the question is asked: How can you study authority, control, motivation, etc., in isolation – in the absence of communication – to be so sure?

What is interesting about Porter and Roberts' analysis is the discussion of the views of leading writers on organisational behaviour, under the four headings set out below, which reveal what they describe as a 'communication failure' between organisational theory and organisational communication (see also Chapter 3).

Classical structural approaches

In summarising the writings of classical theorists such as Taylor and Weber, they note that neither writer places explicit emphasis on communication in organisations, 'but their viewpoints suggest a concern for its channel and content aspects.' Other classical writers including Fayol, Gulick and Urwick, and Mooney and Reilly advocate only 'limited and specific communication channels for the purpose of coordinating specialised parts of the organisation in which there were detailed role prescriptions and authoritative leadership styles.'

These writers share a common belief, expressed or implied, in the paramount importance of formal communication channels as a means of achieving efficiency in organisations. Their views have influenced the early network studies of Bavelas,[7] Guetzkow and Simon,[8] Leavitt[9] and Shaw.[10] Of these, the research carried out by Bavelas is perhaps the best known, despite being dismissed as 'cage experiments' by Becker,[11] who criticised the studies for not reflecting the everyday activities that occur in organisations. Writing of the work of Bavelas and that of another early researcher, Rogers and Kincaid comment:

> However, neither of these research approaches appear to be very alive today, nor have they contributed a useful body of generalisations about communication.[12]

Human relations approaches

The Hawthorne studies, the research on group dynamics, and the Theory X–Theory Y approaches to management are also reviewed, and the absence of any specific discussion of communication in these writings is also noted. For example, McGregor states that communication is less open in Theory X than in Theory Y organisations,[13] which leads Roberts and O'Reilly to enquire:

> What does openness mean? Does it mean that there is more informal than formal communication? Does accuracy increase? If so, how? These are questions McGregor does not address.[14]

Similarly, the works of other leading writers are analysed, and their primary concern is found to be 'for individual motivation through which acceptance and commitment to organisational goals is ensured. The communication aspects of these themes are, however, given little attention.'

Even Likert only mentions communication vaguely in his ideal system of organisational structure, composed of interlocking functional groups, in which communication 'refers to a variety of different levels of activities. Some of these are causal and some intervening.'[15] Roberts and Reilly comment:

> Given Likert's emphasis on flat interlocked organisational systems, one might think he would emphasise horizontal communication. However, most of his discussion concerns superior–subordinate interaction.

Behavioural decision theorists

The work of Simon,[16] March and Simon,[17] Cyert and March,[18] Woodward,[19] Pugh *et al.*[20] and Perrow[21] is also summarised. In a telling comment discussed below, Porter and Roberts challenge Simon's assertion that:

> . . . organisations exist because the behaviour of people can be influenced by communication. Does this mean [*they ask*] all organisational phenomena are sub-sets of communication? Authority, control, motivation, etc., are clearly not aspects of communication but are expressed through communication.[22]

March and Simon assert that one of the results of 'uncertainty absorption is that incomplete information influences decision making', and note the need for communication systems in organisations to 'ensure coordination and minimise the effect of lost information . . . on overloaded feedback channels.' Surprisingly, the influential work of Woodward is mentioned yet not discussed; however, Pugh and co-workers' attempt to 'provide empirical observations of organisations as interlocking systems' is acknowledged, although they have 'not yet discussed at length the process of organisational communication. It is mentioned only briefly and indirectly . . .' Reference is also made to Perrow's research which 'gives little attention to differentiating various facets of communication', and the general conclusion is that all of these authors direct attention towards the formal blueprint of organisational communication, but 'some imply the necessity for investigating communication influences on decision-making'.

CASE EXAMPLE NO. 1

The impact of new technology on working practices in hotels

Porter and Roberts also comment on Perrow's conclusion that technology is the primary determinant of organisational structure because it suggests the testable hypothesis:

> Communication, whatever it is, should be the same at the interpersonal level in different organisational sub-units with similar technologies, and internal organisational communication should differ between units with different technologies.

McEwan tested this hypothesis by categorising all the jobs performed in two hotels into six classifications, according to the access employees had to formal information channels and the type of technology they used in carrying out their jobs. Strong support for the hypothesis was recorded for employees at both extremes of this job-classification typology.[23] For example, housekeeping chambermaids, cleaners and kitchen stewards, who used simple technology and were physically isolated from other employees for long periods in carrying out their jobs, were compared with managers and front-desk staff, who relied heavily on technological aids and interacted constantly with other employees.

New technology was also found to have altered the working conditions of most people employed in the food and beverage departments, particularly kitchen stewards, the modern-day 'plongeurs', whose work was memorably described by Orwell as a job 'which offers no prospects, is intensely exhausting, and at the same time has not a trace of skill or interest'.[24]

This transformation was initially due to the introduction of automatic washing equipment which required kitchen stewards to be retrained so that they could operate the controls, monitor the water level, temperature and steam pressure, and add the correct amounts of detergents at regular intervals.

Several other changes in traditional working practices including the need to sort kitchen utensils into different-coloured plastic containers were necessary so that the correct washing time could be allocated. The sorting of utensils actually reduced the efficiency of the washing machine, if left to a single kitchen steward, and this task was eventually shared by waiters and chefs, who all benefited from the rapid washing and return of equipment to their respective work stations. Kitchen stewards admitted to being more involved in the daily work and social activities in the hotel. For example, one male steward became engaged to a receptionist and another female steward and her fiancé chef were subsequently given transfers to the same company hotel in another town. One unexpected outcome involved two Portuguese stewards, who could speak no English, despite being employed in the same hotel for over five years, but who each had married English-speaking Philippino waitresses.

Finally, the need to use different concentrations of detergent in the automatic washing machine also resulted in the creation of a new role of stewards' supervisor, who was later given responsibility for ordering all detergents and cleaning materials used in the hotel, a task that was eventually allocated to new management trainees, who were required to carry out these duties for an initial six-month period on being appointed.

Further contact with other staff was maintained by giving these supervisors responsibility for issuing tokens, which permitted staff to obtain free food from the 'automat' in their canteen.

Conversely, the later introduction of microwave ovens and portion-control meals in the hotel kitchens caused resentment among chefs, particularly at one of the Scottish hotels, where changes in the preparation of meals were regarded as a de-skilling activity that lowered their status and resulted in staff dissatisfaction and labour turnover. On the other hand, room-service staff, who worked alone or in pairs in isolated areas of other company hotels, welcomed these changes because the use of this technology raised their status, widened the range of their activities, and made them less dependent on kitchen chefs, etc., who had previously been regarded as rather unhelpful.

Process and systems approaches

The contributions of Katz and Kahn, who state that information flows in 'limited communication networks' that define and link organisational subsystems,[25] and Weick, who 'views organisations as information processing organisms focusing on the "how" of information transmission',[26] are also reviewed. However, these writings are summarised without comment by Roberts.

Comment

It would be wrong to assume that Porter and Roberts see no need to justify their preference for a 'top-down' approach in analysing the lack of communication elements in their review of four main perspectives on organisation theory. Indeed, they argue that:

> . . . communication must be explicated within and across the domains of interpersonal interactions within and between organisational sub-units and across organisational–environmental interactions.

What is important, however, is the lack of any discussion of the 'bottom-up' viewpoint that no domain of interpersonal interaction, organisational sub-unit, or organisational–environmental interaction would exist unless individuals were first influenced by communication with other people. Yet to restate Herbert Simon's argument alongside Porter and Roberts' criticism means that any analysis of communication in organisations must remain incomplete unless it deals with both the formal and the informal aspects of the phenomenon.

Porter and Roberts cannot be criticised, however, for failing to discuss the full impact of open systems theory on our understanding of communication processes in organisations, since this perspective was not widely known at the time; it will be discussed later. However, their review would have benefited from the inclusion of a more comprehensive summary of the main communication theories.

THREE MAIN APPROACHES TO HUMAN COMMUNICATION THEORY

The main reason why Dance and Larsen[27] uncovered so many different theories of human communication is that researchers have been unable to agree on which of the following criteria should be regarded as most important:

- the 'message' itself and the characteristics of the individuals who transmit or receive this information;
- the interaction or exchange process when communication occurs;
- the environmental and social contexts in which communication develops as an overall system of relationships between people.

One reason for this disagreement is because researchers often failed to separate the five different **modes of communication** as set out in Figure 11.1.

Most of the early models of human communication tended to focus on the individual mode, which was then applied to dyadic, group, organisational or collective situations.

Writers like Krone *et al*. have addressed this problem by describing four different perspectives on communication (viz. mechanistic, psychological, interpretive–symbolic and systems-interaction) and relating these to seven different theories of organisational behaviour (viz. classical, human relations, behavioural decision theory, systems, resource dependency, population, ecology and institutional).[28]

Mode	Example
Individual	I 'debate' a topic with myself.
Dyadic	Two people discuss their manager's behaviour.
Group	More than two people share information about the same subject, e.g. when to take their holidays.
Organisational	Information about budgets is transmitted to various departments in a hotel by the general manager.
Ecological	Information from an external' source is relayed to all the head office staff, e.g. the need to boil water because of a temporary failure in the local Water Board's treatment plant.

Fig 11.1 Modes of communication

However, this approach is thought to be too specialised for the general reader, who should be able to gain a broad understanding of what is already a complicated subject if the three different broad approaches to human communication can be shown to be compatible with three perspectives on organisational behaviour theory, as presented in Figure 11.2.

THE LINEAR APPROACH (INCLUDING PSYCHOLOGICAL, INFORMATIONAL AND MECHANISTIC APPROACHES) TO HUMAN COMMUNICATION

What Rogers and Kincaid refer to as the linear model has also been described by Harré and Lamb as the informational approach,[29] and by Krone *et al.* as the mechanistic perspective at the organisational communication level. There are no major theoretical differences between the three approaches which, henceforth, will be grouped under the linear rubric for the sake of brevity.

Historically, the linear approach is the earliest attempt to define human communication, and was developed in Shannon and Weaver's mathematical theory of communication, represented in Figure 11.3, which was derived from electronic engineering research carried out in the United States.[30]

The transmission of information

Linear models attempt to describe the transmission of information as 'messages' between 'senders', or 'sources', and 'receivers' (which may include modes such as individuals, organisations and collectivities, as well as animals, or even inanimate objects such as telecommunication and electronic devices). These models are based on the assumption that information can be encapsulated, rather like the contents of a hypodermic syringe, and transmitted as words, gestures, symbols or objects to a passive 'receiver'. It follows that before the content of the message can be known and understood by a minimum of two participants, it must first be encoded by the 'sender/source' before being decoded by the 'receiver'.

Organisational theory	Characteristics	Communication perspective	Characteristics	Modes of communication	Aims
Classical	Hierarchical structure, consisting of specialised formal roles, rules and regulations, with emphasis on efficiency	Linear, including informational, psychological and mechanistic approaches.	Source–receiver, or 'top-down', directed individuals and messages through formal channels and prescribed networks	Focus on specific individuals and organisational goals.	The focus is on sending and receiving information accurately and little attention is paid to the receiver. Messages are often over-simplified and meaning can be lost because of belief that there is only one 'best way' to communicate.
Human relations	The focus is on small groups, and the job satisfaction and other social needs of individuals are emphasised as an alternative way of achieving efficiency	Interactional and interpretative–symbolic approaches.	Informal interaction and participative decision-making based on communication 'rules' within a specified organisational culture	Focus on individual, group and organisational modes.	Emphasises the intentions and roles of receivers of information so that superior–subordinate roles may be improved through more openness and trust.
Behavioural decision and open systems	The formal structure decision is modified to include open systems changing coalitions as the 'system' is adapted to achieve effectiveness by absorbing uncertainty from a turbulent environment.	Relational and system interactive approaches.	Interdependent sub-units in the system process incomplete information from a changing environment modes. through formal and informal networks.	Focus on individual, dyadic group, organisational and ecological modes.	Emergent communication networks process information as part of an evolving system which seeks to manage uncertainty.

Fig 11.2 Comparison of organisational and information theories

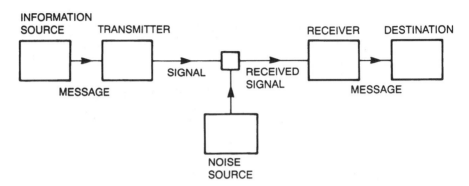

Fig 11.3 Shannon and Weaver's (1949) linear model of communication

Shannon and Weaver's theory was adopted in psychological models of communication, which became popular in the United States during the 1950s. A number of writers generally supported Newcomb's influential proposition that 'many of those phenomena of social behaviour which have been somewhat loosely assembled under the label of 'interaction' can be more adequately studied as communicative acts.'[31] Newcomb's A–B–X Communicative Act System is shown as Figure 11.4.

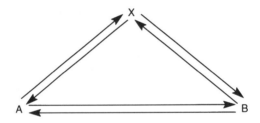

Fig 11.4 The Newcomb A–B–X Communicative Act System

According to Newcomb, in the simplest possible communicative act one person (A) transmits information to another person (B) about something (X), when such an act can then be symbolised as 'A to B re X'. The minimum components of the A–B–X system included:

(i)   A's orientation towards X, including both attitude towards X, as something to be approached or avoided, and A's cognitive attributes such as beliefs, etc.;
(ii) A's orientations towards B, in exactly the same sense as in (i) above;
(iii) B's orientations towards X; and
(iv) B's orientations towards A.

David Berlo incorporated Newcomb's Communicative Act System in his modified version of Shannon and Weaver's theory by introducing the concept of 'feedback' into his S–M–C–R model, which is shown as Figure 11.5.[32]

This was probably the most widely known linear model of communication in the United States and the UK until Berlo acknowledged criticism by Smith.[33,34] The components and general benefits of linear models of communication are considered below.

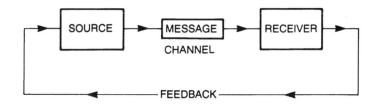

Fig 11.5 The Berlo (1960) S–M–C–R model of communication

Components of linear models of communication

The following components are included, or subsumed, in these models:

A message	Either verbal or non-verbal information.
A channel	The medium in which the message travels, e.g. radio, newsprint, television, word-of-mouth, etc.
A sender	The individual who sends the message, or the technological source of this information.
A receiver	The person who receives the message, or the technological destination of this information.
Transmission	The sending and receiving of messages through specified channels.
Encoding	The creation and transformation of any message for transmission.
Decoding	The deciphering of a message to obtain its meaning.
Feedback	The process of interpreting and, if need be, repeating and re-formulating a message until its intended meaning is understood.
Communication effects	The outcome, e.g. an observable change in behaviour, resulting from the transmission of a message.
Communication barriers	Obstacles, e.g. cultural and linguistic difficulties, that impede or slow down transmission of messages.
Communication breakdowns	Any other obstacle along the channel that brings the transmission of a message to a stop.

Advantages of the linear approach

The following general benefits are normally attributed to the linear approach to communication which, although not discussed by classical writers, is to be found in all forms of hierarchical or bureaucratic organisation structures.

- It is probably the most simple, direct, efficient and understandable method of transmitting 'formal' messages available. It allows 'concrete' information to be transmitted orally either face-to-face, at meetings, or on film/video or in writing, using memoranda, bulletins, notice boards, computerised messages, etc.

- Gatekeepers, e.g. managers, supervisors or employees, who receive information from a reliable source and relay it accurately to another receiver may also be identified.
- It permits 'message fidelity' to be maximised whenever information is transmitted accurately between a source and a receiver.
- The transmission of sensitive information can be controlled by breaking down messages into relevant elements for accurate transmission to specified receivers, employed at different levels in medium-size or large hierarchical organisations. A well-known practical application of this principle is the use of 'briefing groups', as advocated by The Industrial Society in the UK.

Criticisms of the linear approach

Despite these advantages, the linear approach is frequently criticised on logical, theoretical and even on practical grounds for misrepresenting communication. In the latter case, it is all too easy for senior managers, who may be preoccupied with strategic issues, to lose control over the day-to-day operations in any organisation. One way this can occur is for them to attach too much importance to the formal 'briefing' of selected assistants and deputies, who are then expected to relay information accurately to other employees.

For example, the use of briefing groups is advocated by The Industrial Society in the UK. Done well, day in day out, this is a highly efficient procedure; however, managers will still encounter resistance from members of powerful 'informal' networks and 'grapevines', which exist at all levels in every organisation, because people fear or believe that their views may be, or have been, misrepresented or ignored. In other words, overlap, conflict or confusions may occur between the different modes of communication which have become established in the organisation.

Procedures such as quality control circles (discussed in Chapter 8) are often used to correct these problems, and some imaginative chief executives in large companies in the UK and the United States have also made video films which are distributed to and shown simultaneously in each department or plant, so that all employees can find out what is happening in the organisation at the same time.

Cause and effect

The logical criticism of the linear approach is based on an analysis of the concepts of 'cause' and 'effect' by the Scottish philosopher, David Hume, who argued that a 'cause' can only be distinguished from an 'effect' if the mode of connection between them both is ignored, as it is not part of empirical science.[35] This creates problems, as Penman notes:

> . . . on the one hand, if we do not look at the connection between cause and effect, where is the communication process? On the other hand, if we decide we must, which connection do we look at when each person is seen as both the cause and the effect?[36]

David Berlo accepted the criticism of his S–M–C–R model, by admitting that:
> . . . our view of research and our view of communication have been contradictory . . . It could be argued that S–M–C–R was not intended as a 'model' of communication, that it met none of the tests of theoretic models, and that it was developed as an audio-visual aid to stimulate recall of the components of a communication relationship.[37]

General critique of linear models

A more general critique of linear models of communication has been developed by Kincaid[41] and by Rogers and Kincaid.[42] It is summarised thus:

- Linear models view communication as a linear one-way act (usually vertical), rather than as a cyclical two-way process over time.
- There is a source bias, which assumes dependency by the receiver, rather than focusing on the interdependency of those involved in the communication relationship.
- There is a tendency to focus on the objects as simple isolated physical objects, at the expense of the context in which they exist.
- There is a tendency to focus on messages *per se* at the expense of silence, and the punctuation and timing of messages.
- There is a tendency to view persuasion as being the primary function of communication rather than mutual understanding and consensus, etc.
- There is a tendency to focus on the psychological effects of communication on individuals and overlook the social effects and relationships among individuals in networks.
- There is a belief in one-way mechanistic causation rather than mutual causation, which recognises the fundamentally cybernetic characteristics of human information systems.

CASE EXAMPLE NO. 2

The division (and loss) of labour in hotels

McEwan notes that, since the Second World War, British hotels have usually attempted to increase efficiency and profitability through the dual policy of introducing new technology into the kitchen, reception areas, etc., and by using techniques such as Management by Objectives (MBO) to achieve the economies of scale that are associated with a division of labour.[38]

The work performed in hotels is normally divided along 'classical' lines into five functional sections. The two main 'production' activities are carried out in the food and beverage department (which includes the kitchen, bars, banquets and conferences, the restaurant and room service, etc.) and housekeeping sections (including room preparation, laundering and hotel cleaning). The three main 'servicing' departments are reception (including room sales, guests' accounts, portering, mail and telephone services, etc.), administration (including general management, marketing, accounts, personnel and security staff, etc.), and engineering (including service and maintenance of machinery, etc.).

Little imagination is required to realise that hotels should be ideal places for testing the efficiency of classical management principles by undertaking replicated empirical field studies. After all, unlike many manufacturing organisations, all activities are carried out under the same roof by small numbers of people in specified departments, who are often easily identifiable by the different clothes they wear and by the separate tasks they perform at work. Hotel labour forces are small compared with manufacturing and only 1.5 per cent of the 9740 hotels in Britain have over 200 rooms, 95.9 per cent less than

100 rooms, 84.2 per cent less than 50 rooms, and 64.6 per cent have between 11 and 25 rooms. There are also some 43 000 'small hotels' consisting of smaller guesthouses, etc. (*Financial Times UK Hotel and Catering Survey*, 18 January 1984).

Why is it, then, that the industry is so inefficient in retaining its labour force? For example, the (then) HCITB study of manpower flows shows that 78.4 per cent of the 569 000 labour force, mostly working in 'production' departments, left the industry during 1979/80[39] when the average labour wastage in manufacturing industries was 22–26 per cent per annum between 1979/80 and 1982/3 (*Employment Gazette*, 1984). There is a striking similarity between national labour turnover statistics in Britain and the United States of America during this period. Jablin, for example, reports that 'the median monthly turnover of persons employed in the United States is approximately 2% (or 24% per annum) according to the Bureau of National Affairs, 1980.[40]

An average net loss of 30 per cent of employees from the hotel and catering industry occurred each year between 1990 and 1992 (HTCTC Report, *Caterer and Hotelier*, 26 August 1993). This reduction in labour turnover was probably due to the prolonged recession, since the estimated average labour wastage in British manufacturing industries was below 10 per cent during the same period (*Employment Gazette*, 1990–1992). The working conditions of housekeeping staff, who are mostly females, offer some insights into the reasons for this anomaly, since they work alone 'upstairs' in an environment which is controlled according to MBO principles.

Each chambermaid is allocated a set number of rooms per day, which must be 'made up' by completing 40 to 45 separate bedmaking/cleaning/dusting, etc. tasks, per room. Wage rates are low but bonuses are paid when staff 'make up' additional rooms and they receive overtime if they work at weekends.

Contact with fellow employees is minimal, except at breaktimes in the canteen, and supervisors are often not seen unless they are on their 'rounds' when rooms are inspected. On her own, for the vast majority are female employees, the first thing a chambermaid usually does on entering an empty guest-room is to switch on the TV or radio 'for the company'. Most supervisors are younger, often from different ethnic backgrounds, and they usually have little direct experience of 'making up' bedrooms. Chambermaids may attend short weekly *ad hoc* meetings with the head housekeeper, but they rarely attend inter-departmental meetings. McEwan reported an annual labour turnover among chambermaids in two hotels ranging from 81 to 138 per cent and the average employment period was two months. Isolation, hard physical work, low pay and a lack of respect from staff in other departments were common reasons why these employees said they disliked or wanted to change their jobs.

INTERACTIONAL (INCLUDING INTERPRETATIVE–SYMBOLIC) APPROACHES TO COMMUNICATION

What Harré and Lamb call interactive approaches to communication rely on the same conceptual assumptions as the interpretative–symbolic perspective adopted by Krone *et al*. That is to say, the two approaches originated almost simultaneously in social psychology, on the one hand, and in symbolic interactionism in American sociology on the other. This is because both viewpoints sprang from the same intellectual roots in the

United States with the emergence of the philosophy of pragmaticism.

However, the interactive and interpretative–symbolic approaches to communication only began to emerge slowly in the 1960s and early 1970s, mainly in reaction to the psychological models discussed above. The writer who influenced the development of the interactional approach is the American social scientist, Erving Goffman, who shares in common with social psychologists a lack of interest in psychological 'universals' and an interest in gearing theories and research towards the specific settings of social behaviour.

Communication as an 'exchange'

Chiefly because interactive and interpretative–symbolic approaches cut across disciplines such as psychology, sociology and philosophy, the tendency is for various elements, or types, of communication to be discussed under separate headings, but without the use of simple models or diagrams like those developed by Newcomb or Dance. Goffman, for example, focuses on communication as an 'exchange' which he analyses under four headings:

(i)   the communicational arrangements (e.g. direct v. indirect);
(ii) the communicational conduct (e.g. the strategies that the interacting parties adopt towards each other);
(iii) the communicational constraints (e.g. the emotional, technical, intellectual and environmental factors that limit people's choice of strategy); and
(iv) the interpretational frames (e.g. the personal attributes that govern the way people perceive themselves and interpret one another's behaviour).[43]

Goffman's approach is important because it seeks to analyse various different modes of communication.

What distinguishes the interactive from the linear approach is an assumption that it is 'not so much a function of the individual's internal drives, motivations and personality as of the situation and social relationships established with others.'[44]

The interactional approach

However, the headings described by Goffman are also discussed in social psychology by Frazer under the following three types of communication:

(i)   interaction regulation;
(ii) interpersonal communication, which covers the three elements:
      (a) social and personal identities;
      (b) temporary states and current attitudes;
      (c) social relationships;
(iii) Representational communication.[45]

Similar elements appear in the interpretative–symbolic perspective in the assumptions made about the self, shared meanings and social behaviour.

Given their common antecedents and broadly similar characteristics, the three perspectives will henceforth be discussed as interactional approaches and, again with brevity in mind, the key components are summarised below.

One has to be cautious about generalising, since human relations writers provided so few references to communication, yet it is probably true that the interactional approach comes closest to representing their views on how people discuss problems and negotiate with other members of organisations.

Components of the interactional approach

- Social behaviour is emphasised rather than individual behaviour.
- Mutual understanding is assumed to occur if the participants play adaptive roles rather than act as 'senders' and 'receivers'.
- Role-taking leads to shared meaning if the goal of mutual understanding is given priority over message transmission.
- Mutual understanding involves empathetic bonding, but also an awareness by the participants of the communication constraints, **rules** or **order**, without which organised behaviour is impossible.

Interactional approaches tend to be described in words rather than in representational models, but the Kincaid convergence model of communication (Figure 11.6, probably succeeds in depicting the main components of this perspective.

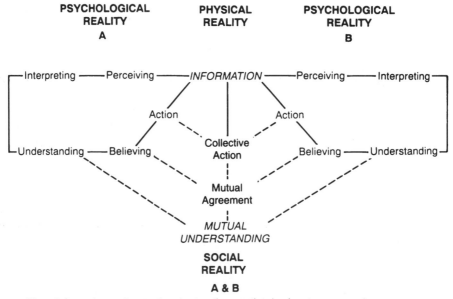

Note: Information and mutual understanding are the dominant components of the convergence model of communication. Information shared by two or more participants in the communication process may lead to collective action, mutual agreement, and mutual understanding.

Fig 11.6 Basic components of the convergence model of communication
Source: Kincaid D L, *The Convergence Model of Communication*, East-West Communication Institute, Honolulu (1979)

General benefits of using the interactional approach

- This approach allows both 'informal' and 'formal' communication procedures to be explored and re-defined to reduce 'overload'.
- If handled skilfully, it can lead to greater confidence and trust between managers, supervisors and other employees.
- It permits individual members of groups and organisations to adapt to rapid cultural and technological change.
- Information sharing can result in increased organisational knowledge, improved decision-making and more effective 'problem-solving' skills.

Criticism of the interactional approach

No detailed criticism similar to that made by Kincaid at the end of the previous section could be found in the research literature, but common sense insists that the interactional approach will inevitably be a slower, more time-consuming process than the linear approach to communication. It is also probably wiser to assume that, unlike researchers, managers will rarely be trained to think symbolically, in terms of roles, rules and shared meanings, and are therefore more likely to respond to 'concrete' issues and goals, rather than seeking spontaneously to adapt to the contrasting values and needs of those employed at different levels in an organisation.

THE RELATIONAL AND SYSTEMS-INTERACTIVE APPROACHES

The third viewpoint on communication is called the relational approach by Harré and Lamb and the systems-interactive perspective by Krone *et al*. Advocates of both approaches are critical of other theories discussed above because these are said to pay insufficient attention to the environments and social contexts in which the transfer of information, or the shared face-to-face interpretation of activities and events, takes place.

For the latter writers, communication refers to 'the overall system of relations people develop between each other and with the wider community and habitat in which they live'. These environments and social contexts are seen as constituting 'the very phenomenon of communication itself'.

Following previous practice, the heading 'relational approaches' will be used to describe both viewpoints, for the sake of brevity.

Surprisingly, although relational approaches to communication have only recently been discussed, their origins pre-date all the perspectives discussed so far, with the exception of Shannon and Weaver's linear model discussed above. It was Ruesch and Bateson who first described all behaviour as potential communication, which becomes so immediately it is perceived by others.[46]

They were supported by Birdwhistell, who asserted that:

> . . . an individual may move, make noises . . . see, smell, taste or feel, but he does not communicate . . . he engages in and becomes part of communication.[47]

For Watzlawick *et al*., not communicating in an interpersonal context is impossible since:

... all behaviour, not only the use of words, is communication, which is not the same thing as saying that behaviour is only communication, and since there is no such thing as non-behaviour, it is impossible not to communicate.[48]

Some form of meaning

It follows that any activity, or inactivity, words or silence, must convey some form of meaning when perceived by others, and this communication lasts as long as the participants remain in the same perceptual field.

Bateson extended this analysis by stating that all people, animals and other organisms form an indispensable part of communication,

> ... in the same way as they are, whether they want it or not, a part of the local or global ecosystem. They become immersed in it at the moment of their birth and do not leave it until the moment of their death.[49]

This ecological perspective may perhaps be better understood if communication is compared with the air we breathe, or the water that fish must be immersed in if they are to survive.

An all-pervasive phenomenon

There are four reasons why communication should be regarded as an all-pervasive phenomenon:

- There is an argument used in philosophy, known as Russell and Whitehead's Theory of Logical Types, which states that no class can be a member of itself (e.g. everybody agrees that the UK and Denmark are members of the United Nations, but it would not make sense to ask if the United Nations is also a member of that organisation). Distinctions must therefore be made between the different orders of reality in any relationship. With this in mind, any communication process must be regarded as of a different order of reality than the members who actually take part in this relationship.
- Open systems theory in organisational behaviour can be reconciled more easily with relational approaches than with any of the other models of communication discussed so far, because interdependency between the participants is a prerequisite of both perspectives.
- Studies carried out by Bateson, and also in the emerging field of communication network analysis, provide a growing empirical verification of relational approaches to communication.
- Bearing in mind that these views were first voiced some 40 years ago, it would appear that informed opinion has at last begun to catch up with this alternative perspective on communication, since we are now more inclined to describe the world as 'a global village', or as an 'information society', in which people are also increasingly concerned about the environment and ecology.

Relational approaches to human communication

Relational approaches to human communication have been defined by Hawes as:

> . . . a patterned, spatio-temporal circuit of concatenous events involving two or more persons who are within each other's perceptual field.[50]

Here, 'concatenous' simply means that the communication events are linked together in an organised process, or 'circuit', which is 'punctuated', with the passing of time, by interventions from one or more of the participants. Interventions occur whenever the participants try to achieve co-operation or mutual understanding, or if conflict occurs between them in, say, a dispute or an argument.

In the latter situation, Watzlawick *et al.* state that conflict would result whenever differences or disagreements affected the 'punctuation' of the communication relationship. They illustrate this in an original, yet presumably tongue-in-cheek, manner by analysing the communication episodes in a stereotyped relationship between a 'nagging' wife and her 'withdrawing' husband, which appears as Figure 11.7.

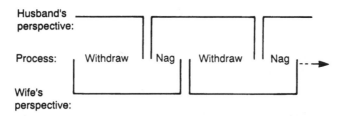

Fig 11.7 Punctuation of a communication process from the participants' perspectives

The wife might admit to 'nagging' because her husband 'withdraws' every time she wishes to discuss something with him. Conversely, the husband might admit to 'withdrawing' because his wife 'nags'. For the husband, however, 'nagging' always precedes his 'withdrawal', whereas his wife perceives her response to be a reasonable reaction to his passive behaviour.

Both participants arbitrarily 'punctuate' the communication events as self-serving episodes, which ensure that the other's behaviour is always perceived as the 'start', whereas their own marks the 'end', of each of these encounters. Neither participant is apparently able to adopt the role of impartial observer and recognise that without mutual interdependence, however hostile, the communication relationship would not be possible.

Model of relational communication

However, communication relationships are not normally dominated by conflict and disagreement and McEwan's model of relational communication, presented as Figure 11.8, also focuses on exchanges which are characterised by co-operation and mutual understanding.

Communication is depicted in the model as an irreversible, concatenous process which

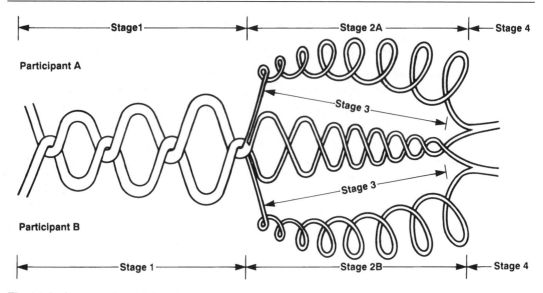

Fig 11.8 A general model of human communication
Source: McEwan T, Unpublished doctoral thesis, Cranfield Institute of Technology, UK (1988)

continues as long as the participants share the same perceptual field, and which can be analysed in four stages:

- **Stage 1** depicts the communication 'episodes' which have occurred since the Participants A and B first entered each other's perceptual field.
- **Stages 2 and 3** represent separate activities occurring simultaneously in real time.
- **Stages 2A and 2B** refer to the covert intrapersonal activities through which the communication exchange is perceived by each participant.
- **Stage 3** refers to the overt interpersonal behaviour of both participants, which could be observed by a third party.
- **Stage 4** begins all over again the convergence/divergence process depicted in Stages 2 and 3.

It follows that the more interdependence occurs through co-operation, etc., the less likely A and B would be to punctuate events, for example through conflict or withdrawal, leading to further divergence or the termination of communication. However, Stage 3 represents progressive convergence towards mutual understanding, before the next communication episode emerges in Stage 4.

DYADIC AND TRIADIC RELATIONSHIPS

Both of the above two-person, or dyadic, models can be expanded progressively to depict triadic, large group, organisation-wide or network relationships in very large collectivities. This is an important advance because it provides d sound theoretical basis for analysing all five modes of communication. However, these models usually become very complicated as they grow in size, and another technique, known as communication (or social) network analysis is used to depict these extended relationships.

Communication, or social, network analysis is related to sociometry, discussed in Chapter 9, which is credited to Moreno, although previous research was carried out by L.M. Terman in 1904, and their underlying ideas were derived from earlier writings by the German sociologist, Georg Simmel (1858–1918).

Simmel's work is generally neglected in the field of organisational behaviour, yet he was the first to show that what we understand by the term 'society' is not a corporate entity, distinct from and exerting constraints on individuals. Nor is it an aggregation of corporate entities such as organisations, elites, or classes. Rather, individuals 'form society' by entering into interaction with each other to satisfy such basic needs as companionship or the expression of aggression, and also to pursue other goals such as income, territory, salvation, education, etc. They do this through 'sociation' by forming or joining dyads, triads and progressively larger collectivities. Simmel concludes that:

> The major field of study for the student of society is therefore 'Sociation', that is the particular patterns and forms in which men associate and interact with each other.[51]

Simmel's two key concepts are the 'dyadic relationship' and the 'triadic relationship'. The dyad 'differs quantitatively from all other types of group in that each of the two participants is confronted by only one other and not by a collectivity.' Since neither of the partners can hold a group responsible for what the dyad has done or failed to do, this communication relationship can be analysed in terms of 'power dependence'.

As Rogers and Farace note, power is displayed whenever one participant tries, or fails, to maximise differences and gain control by exhibiting 'one-up' behaviour, whereas the other might be expected to yield ground and display 'one-down' behaviour.[52] Power-sharing usually occurs after both participants realise the advantages of sharing resources, and decide to explore each other's strengths rather than exploit any weaknesses, often to achieve domination over a third party.

Processes influencing outcomes

Simmel was also first to note that the 'triad' is the simplest structure in which a dyad can achieve domination over another member. He identified three processes by which a third member can enter a dyadic relationship to influence outcomes. These are by playing the roles of either Mediator, Tertius Gaudius, or Divida et Impera, as follows:

The relevance of triads in understanding staff and customer relationships in hotels

Triadic relationships occur so often in hotels that they are easily taken for granted. For example, the 'mediator' type of triad occurs whenever an employee intervenes in an argument between two other members of staff with the aim of resolving the dispute.

A Tertius Gaudius (or 'the third who rejoices') occurs when a waiter acts as a 'go-between' by taking a guest's order, which is then passed on to a chef in the kitchen. The chef prepares the meal which the waiter then serves to the guest, who later expresses satisfaction with the meal to the waiter. When the compliment is passed on, it may be a cause of satisfaction to the chef, even though the chef never sees the guest.

Triadic relationships in which 'divida et impera' (divide and rule) behaviour takes place are more difficult to observe, because details of these tactics are not always discussed or apparent to others. As an example, a hotel manager employed two supervisors on opposite shifts, who rarely saw each other, but both left after discovering that each had been told by the manager that (s)he was due for promotion when only one vacancy was available in the hotel.

Henderson recognises the importance of triadic relationships in his study of hotel waiters when he draws attention to their instrumental behaviour, noting that 'A worker who receives 75 per cent of his income from tips is not an employee in the usual sense.' In short, the relationship with an employer counts for far less with a waiter than 'negotiations' with each guest.[53]

PRESCRIBED AND EMERGENT COMMUNICATION NETWORKS

Open systems theory has already been discussed in Chapter 1 and, as noted above, this perspective is easier to reconcile with the relational approach to communication than linear or interactional viewpoints. This is because organisations are viewed as comprising interrelated sub-systems which have to adapt to fresh inputs from 'known' and 'unknown' environments so that agreed goals can be accomplished.

The relational approach to communication allows any organisation, or its sub-units, to be viewed as responding to this tendency for new inputs to modify outputs through the creation, or maintenance, of various interweaving, criss-crossing communication networks in which individuals are linked by patterned flows of information.

A useful analogy here would be to compare the organisation to a rope which, when unravelled, consists of interwoven strands that are made up, in turn, of single weak fibres. Just as it is the strong rope that ties a ship to a wharf, so also it is through 'organisation' that individuals decide how best to cope with a turbulent environment. Yet the strength of the rope, as we have noted, is not derived from any individual fibre, since none of these extends along the entire length, but it comes about because these are interwoven into strands which do extend along the full length of the rope.[54]

Similarly, it is through the communication network that individuals relate to each other in reciprocated dyads, triads or larger cliques. Following Tichy *et al.*[55] and Weick,[56] communication networks may be classified as either 'Prescribed' or 'Emergent'. Prescribed networks are normally introduced by senior management to transfer information between members using the linear approach to communication described above.

Prescribed communication networks

Prescribed communication networks mainly consist of 'formal' flows of information and possess the basic characteristics of the mechanistic organisation, described in Chapter 3. These flows may occur at any level in an organisation but normally have the 'top-down' approval of senior management. They result in the following transactions between managers, supervisors, other employees, and people who are not employed in the focal organisation but are in contact with its members by belonging to a 'known' or 'unknown' environment:

- the exchange of information (e.g. about future hotel reservations);
- the exchange of goods (e.g. such as door keys, cash, or equipment);

- involvement in decision-making (e.g. whether to accept a credit card as payment from a customer).

It follows that employees with more status and responsibilities in an organisation, rather than those without, will tend to figure more prominently in prescribed communication networks.

Emergent communication networks

The characteristics of emergent communication networks are not elucidated by Tichy *et al.* or Weick, but the author argues that these occur when prescribed networks are modified as a result of the continuous re-definition of individual, dyadic, triadic, group and organisational tasks through ongoing interrelations.

These adaptations occur as the members are drawn together, first by the task itself but also through affiliation, friendship and effect, until they come to rely on ad hoc decision-making arrangements as the most effective way of coping with unpredictable changes in the inputs from a turbulent environment. In short, emergent communication networks mainly consist of a blend of 'formal' and 'informal' information flows and possess the basic characteristics of organic organisations, as described in Chapter 3.

The continuing impact of these 'informal' adjustments on the prescribed network results in an emergent network which will contain both mechanistic and organic characteristics. As Burns and Stalker note,

> . . . the two forms of system represent a polarity not a dichotomy; there are, as we have tried to show, intermediate stages between the two extremities empirically known to us . . . the relation of one form to another is elastic, so that a relative change may also oscillate between the two forms.[57]

An organisation may (and frequently does) operate with a management system which includes both types.

A comparison of the emergent communication networks recorded in two British hotels is shown in Figure 11.9. The two diagrams show staff who interacted daily in both the formal and informal networks. These were employed in three departments in the coastal hotel but were spread across six departments in London. The liaison roles played by respondents 107 and 111 (who were not members of management) and number 5 at the coastal hotel, in linking their own with other departments, should be noted. Similarly, the pivotal roles played by respondents 73, 75, 81, 84, 96, 97, 98, 112 and 113 (none of whom was a manager, although five were supervisors) in linking the six departments was an important characteristic of the 'daily emergent communication network' recorded in the London hotel.

An example of how individual managers manipulate prescribed and emergent networks with regard to security measures in hotels is described in the next section.

COMMUNICATION NETWORK ANALYSIS

The vocabulary and research methods of communication network analysis are virtually unknown in the literature on organisational behaviour. As mentioned earlier, the latter subject and most communication theory were regarded as incompatible. Researchers

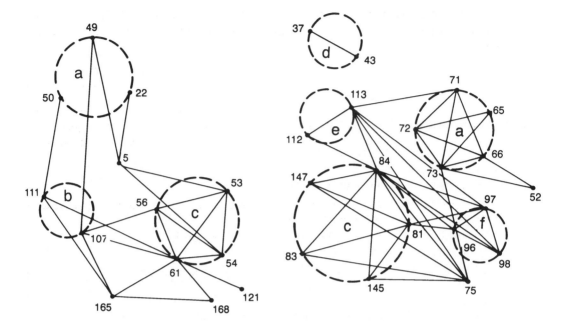

Fig 11.9 Opinion leaders in the Time 1 (1982/3) emergent networks who interacted daily in two hotels
Key: a, reception; b, banqueting; c, kitchen; d, maintenance; e, room service; f, coffee shop
Source: McEwan T, Unpublished doctoral thesis, Cranfield Institute of Technology, UK (1988)

have since developed their own agendas and forums for debate in subjects like organisational communication and communication network analysis, especially in the United States. For example, the International Communication Association has held over 40 annual conferences and these attract over 2500 academic members.

Unawareness of developments in communication theory and research present a serious drawback for anyone interested in studying behaviour in organisations. The methodology of communication network analysis is relatively simple and a number of discrete survey techniques have been developed. Many writers in the field have also sought to avoid the major shortcoming in Moreno's early contribution to sociometry which, as Rogers and Kincaid note, failed to address the problem:

. . . that the sociogram may be wrong. An infinite number of sociograms can be drawn from one set of network data, each of which can be used to convey a different picture of the communication structure. There is no objective, standard procedure for drawing sociograms.[58]

What is agreed, however, is that there is the possibility of using communication relationships, such as dyads and triads, as units of analysis, providing that reliable rule-based computational techniques are available to eliminate bias on the part of the researcher. Such techniques for analysing survey findings using network analysis exist and computing packages are widely used, mainly in the United States.

The principal dimensions and properties of communication networks have also been described by Tichy *et al.* and Rogers and Kincaid, and an amended compilation appears in Figure 11.10.

Property	Definition
Transactional content	Type of exchange in network: expression of effect, influence, exchange of information, exchange of resources or goods and services.
Nature of the links	
1. Intensity	Strength of relation.
2. Reciprocity	Degree to which relation is commonly perceived by all parties to the relation.
3. Clarity of expectations	Degree of clearly defined expectations.
4. Multiplexity	Degree to which individuals are linked by multiple relations.
Structural dimensions	
1. Size	Number of people in network.
2. Density or connectedness	Number of actual links in network as a proportion of total possible links.
3. Clique	Sub-systems in network whose members interact with each other more frequently than with others.
4. Clustering	Number of dense regions or groupings in network.
5. Centrality	Degree of hierarchy and restriction on communication in network.
6. Stability	Degree to which network pattern changes over time.
7. Reachability	Average number of links between any two individuals in network.
8. Openness	Number of actual external links as a proportion of total possible external links.
9. Opinion leader	Individual with highest number of nominations.
10. Bridge	Individual who is a member of multiple clusters in a network.
11. Liaison	A star who also links the network to external networks.
12. Isolate	An individual with few (or no) links to others in the network.
13. Dominant coalition	A clique consisting of a coalition of two or more opinion leaders.
14. Pluralistic ignorance	The degree to which individuals are unaware of the communication activities of other individuals in the network.

Fig 11.10 Dimensions and properties of networks

CASE EXAMPLE NO. 3

The formal and informal roles of hotel security staff

Security staff are normally responsible to the hotel general manager for ensuring that company property and the personal belongings of guests and staff are protected. They are also required to intervene when problems arise with guests who do not pay their accounts and, if any disorder occurs, they are expected to apprehend the troublesome guest(s) or visitor(s) and escort them quietly off the hotel premises, if need be with police assistance. Additional duties include responsibility for the health and safety of all persons in the hotel, especially guests and hotel employees. Most security staff are retired male police officers, or have gained experience in the military police service, and they normally work shifts to ensure that continuous surveillance is maintained.

As might be expected, security staff tend to keep a low profile and the typical guest would not normally be able to distinguish them from other departmental managers, since they usually wear the same company dress, and their section is normally regarded as an administrative department in the hotel's organisational structure. They have an office of their own, however, for occasions when guests and staff have to be interviewed in private. Otherwise, many of their activities are carried out in the reception area, where the hotel safe is often located along with other automatic security and safety monitoring equipment.

Other more discreet tasks undertaken by security staff, rarely discussed with other managers at departmental meetings, depend on the location of the hotel.

For example, some of the major concerns of security teams in London hotels include the prevention of fraudulent activities or drug trafficking by guests, car thefts, and ensuring that prostitutes, known as 'Toms', do not loiter in the public areas and solicit guests before they retire for the night. Electronic locks are fitted on the bedroom doors in most London hotels and movements in and out of rooms can be monitored on a control panel located in the reception area. Whenever soliciting is observed, security staff inform the guest by telephone that the room-charge will be raised from a single- to a double-room rate unless an immediate inspection is allowed, and the interloper is almost always intercepted on leaving and 'warned off' from entering the hotel again under threat of police action.

These problems rarely occur in suburban hotels where the chief security officer usually acts as a duty manager and often interviews all new employees at the start of their induction period. It is also common for security officers to 'clear' any new employee confidentially through contacts with former police colleagues. Housekeeping and laundry staff are also encouraged to report unusual guest behaviour directly to the security officer and employees who co-operate are usually nominated for an 'Employee of the Month' cash award. Despite their lack of technical skills in the running of hotels, security staff enjoy considerable informal power which is not always used impartially. For example, the dismissals or resignations of several managers were provoked by 'whispering campaigns' instigated by security staff and members of their informal cliques in two different hotels.

Source: McEwan T, *A Replicated Study of Communication Networks, Job Retention and Labour Turnover in Two British Hotels*, Unpublished doctoral thesis, Cranfield Institute of Technology, Cranfield, 1988.

PRACTICAL APPLICATIONS FOR MANAGERS, SUPERVISORS AND OTHER STAFF

Various books are available which attempt to treat communication in organisations as a separate commodity with 'purposes' that may include 'sharing the compelling vision . . . integrating effort . . . making intelligent decisions . . . and . . . sustaining a healthy community'.[59]

The problem with these texts is not their good intentions, but that more emphasis is placed on exhortation (i.e. describing what should be the case) than on citing empirical evidence which supports the practical advice provided. We are therefore entitled to ask: How do we know that this advice works? Are there any carefully monitored 'before and after' examples of firms that became more successful as a result of introducing these methods?

Scepticism is not out of place here because it has been argued in this chapter that all human behaviour involving others includes communication, but behaviour is not only communication. Therefore, effective organisational behaviour is unlikely to be achieved merely by urging people to implement various practical remedies, unless empirical evidence exists to show that these prescriptions have actually changed people's behaviour elsewhere.

What do we know, then, that is of practical benefit to managers, supervisors and other staff working in organisations?

Openness in communication

Managers and supervisors need to be aware that subordinates' perceptions of openness in communication and supervisory 'receptivity' are a powerful predictor of the latter's job satisfaction.[60]

Upward distortion of information

People in lower positions tend to distort messages transmitted to persons in higher organisational roles. This can be overcome by managers and supervisors developing an effective communication style which includes enjoying communicating with others, being approachable and open as a listener, tending to ask and persuade rather than demanding or telling people what to do, being sensitive to the needs and feelings of subordinates, and being willing to explain why policies have been enacted.[61]

Personal characteristics

Personal characteristics of superiors and subordinates probably affect the outcome of their communication relationships. For example, Wheeless and Berryman-Fink reported that, regardless of their experiences in working for a female manager, women perceive female managers to be more competent communicators than do males.[62] Infante and Gordon found that subordinates' satisfaction with supervisors was positively related to whether the latter were argumentative (i.e. they took or refuted others' positions) as opposed to being verbally aggressive (i.e. they tended to attack the self-concept of others).[63]

Feedback

Feedback is generally taken as more credible, accurate and perceptive, and giving greater personal satisfaction to subordinates, if its source is high rather than low in the organisation. This may explain why supervisors with limited authority tend not to use confrontational tactics (verbal warnings) when disciplining subordinates.[64] Subordinates soon display the 'Pelz' effect whereby they tend to bypass reticent supervisors and approach those who are perceived to be more effective.[65] When managers intervene, they tend to ask attribution-seeking ('why') questions of poor performers and 'what-do-you-think' or 'how' questions of high performers.[66]

Conflict

The particular communication strategies used by superiors and subordinates to manage conflict are to some degree reciprocally related to the behaviours exhibited by the other party.[67] In other words, aggression on one side is more likely to provoke a negative response, whereas empathy is more likely to yield a positive attitude in the other party.

Systemic variables

Insufficient studies have been carried out which confirm whether or not organisational structure, environment and technology affect the dynamics of superior–subordinate communication. (However, see Case example no. 1 above on the impact of new technology on working processes in hotels.) Jablin tentatively concluded that the communication and perceptions of managers and supervisors are dependent on their hierarchical positions and roles. Neither organisational nor group size appear to affect the quality of the communication in superior–subordinate relationships.[68] This provides empirical support for the views of those who stress the importance of analysing communication in organisations progressively, in terms of dyadic and triadic relationships.

Job retention and turnover

Both Jablin and McEwan[69] have compiled models which address the multivariate relationship between communication behaviour and job retention and labour turnover. McEwan's replicated studies in the UK hotel industry, where labour turnover is at least several times higher than the national average, confirm that employees who belong to communication cliques and, in some cases, act as opinion leaders in the dominant coalitions, are more likely to remain, for over 10 years in some cases, than those who have lower status and remain isolated; in many cases the latter left any time after a few days' to less than three months' employment in the hotels.

Membership of communication networks

McEwan observed that general managers were not members of the dominant coalitions in replicated studies carried out in two British hotels. In both cases, the hotels were said 'to run themselves' because of head office's policy of transferring senior managers after about two years in post, because it was feared that fraudulent behaviour was otherwise more likely to be perpetrated. This meant that strategy was generally implemented and most operational decisions were taken by middle management and supervisory staff who had no responsibility for the overall performance of either hotel.

CONCLUSION

To conclude, it is only when available empirical evidence about the communication behaviour of managers, supervisors and other employees in organisations has been evaluated that far-reaching changes should be implemented in the following activities:

- the preparation and composition of business documents;
- interviews, oral presentations, telephone and reception procedures and meetings;
- public relations techniques and customer after-sales service;
- the introduction of more complex management information systems.

SUMMARY

- Communication is an essential concept which affects every aspects of our lives. Because of the all-pervasive, complex nature of communication, until recently writers on organisational behaviour have ignored the concept until problems arise. There are many different theories of human communication but it is possible to gain a broad understanding through three main approaches.
- Linear cause–effect models of communication were preferred in the past, but two major problems undermined this approach. The 'receivers' of information tended to be overlooked, and the linear approach also neglected the five modes of communication which affect all organisational activity. Other communication models have been devised which support the human relations approach.
- However, these advances often fail to integrate the social aspects of communications with the legitimate goals of, for example, the owners and managers of organisations. The open systems perspective addresses this difficulty. It also allows the five modes of communication to be studied in organisations which have to be adaptive to a turbulent environment.
- Dyadic models can be expanded progressively to depict triadic, large group, organisation-wide or network relationships. Increasing numbers of empirical studies, making use of advances in computing technology, indicate that analysing communication networks is likely to provide clearer insights into the formal and informal behaviour of people at work.
- Research also confirms that those employees who belong to communication cliques are more likely to remain in organisations like hotels, which traditionally have a high turnover of staff. Other employees who remain outside these powerful elites, and may display isolated behaviour as a consequence, are less likely to stay in the organisation.

REVIEW AND DISCUSSION QUESTIONS

1 What problems could arise in departments such as front desk/reception as a result of new technology providing junior staff with information which exceeds their authority in the hotel? What can be done about this problem?

2 What action should be taken to deal with the dissatisfaction of staff such as the Scottish chef who complained about de-skilling due to the introduction of new technology in the hotel kitchens (Case example no. 1)?

3 What are the benefits and drawbacks of allowing staff like chambermaids to work in pairs rather than on their own?

4 What action could be taken to reduce the high labour turnover among hotel 'production' staff in the food and beverage and housekeeping departments?

5 Do you agree that the vaguely defined formal and informal roles of security officers are an unavoidable price management has to pay to safeguard the reputation of a hotel? How would you monitor the performance of security officers?

6 What action, if any, should have been taken against the security staff monitored in Case example no. 3?

CASE STUDY

When the last guest has gone to bed

Up-market hotels, especially in London, take pride in offering round-the-clock service to guests who may arrive from overseas on international flights at all hours, so a skeleton staff of up to 12 people is employed on the night shift from 11 p.m. to 7 a.m. They work in reception, telephone, room-service and security sections and there are also several night cleaners and kitchen stewards. All staff are responsible to a night manager. After the last of the guests has gone to bed, his main task is to supervise the 'night audit'. This entails checking the bar, restaurant and room-service receipts against actual payments, and allocating the balances to guest accounts, which are prepared in advance of the rush to 'check out' which starts at about 7.30 a.m. the next day.

Depending on the room occupancy and day of the week, this audit once took 5–6 hours when it was done manually, but it is completed nowadays in less than half that time using a computer/laser printer.

From about 2 a.m. onwards, a deep hush descends on the hotel as the taped music is turned off, the lifts no longer descend to the basement car park, the sliding front doors are locked, even the water stops rippling in the swimming pool, and the lights are dimmed in the foyer. Shortly after this, the night staff begin to gather in ones and twos and settle themselves on sofas and armchairs in the main lounge. What follows comes as a complete surprise when witnessed for the first time. A transistor radio appears from nowhere and music is turned on at low volume. Coffee, sandwiches, cold meats, pastries, and beer, crockery and glasses, are brought in on trays by two beaming night porters. Soon everyone has arrived for a late-night meal. No one discusses the work that has been completed. Porters' jackets and receptionists blazers are removed as the night shift relaxes and the talk is about sport and TV programmes.

With one exception, they are all males and the one woman is also the only English person present. She is a night-telephonist, middle-aged, fluent in four languages, and a retired Foreign Office civil servant, who reads Proust while she waits for international calls. She has taken the job 'because I am middle-aged, a spinster with a limp, and sometimes get fed up with my own company.' The remaining 11 male employees are from eight different countries and include an Indian–Jewish security officer who works permanent nights 'because I love driving in the opposite direction to the heavy traffic at rush hours', and a Sri Lankan night manager who describes how he enjoys 'the authority of being in charge, because nobody will let me run a hotel in Britain during the daytime, will they?' All 12 of them have worked in the hotel for two to eight years and none wishes to work on days again.

Not only is it clear that job status and authority are acknowledged, but never stated, but it also emerges that these after-midnight 'feasts' occur every night after their work has been completed. The informal gatherings last until about 5 a.m., when the daytime doorman and the morning papers arrive and the hotel gradually returns to its more familiar, bustling, formal routines and procedures.

Source McEwan, T, *A Replicated Study of Communication Networks, Job Retention and Labour Turnover in Two British Hotels*, Unpublished doctoral thesis, Cranfield Institute of Technology, Cranfield (1988), pp. 175–176.

(i)   Do you think the night manager was exaggerating when saying that 'nobody will let me run a hotel in Britain during the daytime, will they'?

(ii) If you were a senior manager would you stop the after-midnight 'feasts' taking place in the hotel? If so why? If not, why not?

NOTES AND REFERENCES

1. Crick W F, *Report of the National Advisory Council on Education for Industry and Commerce: A Higher Award in Business Studies*, HMSO (1964).
2. Dance F E X and Larsen C E, *The Functions of Human Communication: A Theoretical Approach*, Holt Rinehart and Winston (1976).
3. Guetzkow H, 'Communication in Organisations', in March J (ed), *Handbook of Organizations*, Rand–McNally (1965).
4. Porter L W and Roberts K H, *Communication in Organizations*, Penguin (1977).
5. Jablin F M, 'Organisational Entry, Assimilation and Exit', in *Handbook of Organizational Communication*, Sage (1987).
6. Porter L W and Roberts K H, *Communication in Organizations*, Penguin (1977), p. 95.
7. Bavelas A, 'Communication Patterns in Task Oriented Groups', *Journal of the Acoustical Society of America*, vol. 22, 1950, pp. 725–730.
8. Guetzkow H and Simon H A, 'The Impact of Certain Communication Nets upon Organisation and Performance in Task-Oriented Groups', *Management Science*, vol. 1, 1955, pp. 233–250.
9. Leavitt H J, 'Some Effects of Certain Communication Patterns on Group Performance', *Journal of Abnormal and Social Psychology*, vol. 46, 1951, pp. 38–50.
10. Shaw M C, 'Group Structure and the Behaviour of Individuals in Small Groups', *Journal of Psychology*, vol. 38, 1954, pp. 139–149.
11. Becker M H, 'Sociometric Location and Innovativeness: Reformulation and Extension of the Diffusion Model', *American Sociological Review*, vol. 35, 1970, pp. 267–282.
12. Rogers E M and Kincaid D L, *Communication Networks: Towards a New Paradigm for Research*, The Free Press (1981), p. 94.

13. McGregor D, *The Human Side of Enterprise*, McGraw-Hill (1960).
14. Roberts K H and O'Reilly C, 'Measuring Organisational Communication', *Journal of Applied Psychology*, vol. 59, 1974, pp. 321–326.
15. Likert R, *The Human Organization*, McGraw-Hill (1967), p. 147.
16. Simon H, *Administrative Behavior*, Macmillan (1945).
17. March J and Simon H, *Organizations*, Wiley (1958).
18. Cyert R and March J, *A Behavioural Theory of the Firm*, Prentice-Hall (1963).
19. Woodward J, *Industrial Organization: Theory and Practice*, Second edition, Oxford University Press (1980).
20. Pugh D, 'A Conceptual Scheme for Organisational Analysis', *Administrative Science Quarterly*, vol. 8, 1963, pp. 289–315.
21. Perrow C, *Organizational Analysis: A Sociological View*, Wadsworth (1970).
22. Porter L W and Roberts K H, *Communication in Organizations*, Penguin (1977), p. 97.
23. McEwan T, *A Replicated Study of Communication Networks, Job Retention and Labour Turnover in Two British Hotels*, Unpublished Doctoral Thesis, Cranfield Institute of Technology, Cranfield, UK (1988).
24. Orwell G, *Down and Out in Paris and London*, Penguin (1933), p. 69.
25. Katz D and Kahn R, *The Social Psychology of Organization*, Wiley (1966).
26. Weick K E, *The Social Psychology of Organizing*, Second edition, Addison-Wesley (1979).
27. Dance F E X and Larsen C E, *The Functions of Human Communication: A Theoretical Approach*, Holt Rinehart and Winston (1976).
28. Krone K 1, 'Communication Theory and Organisational Communication: Multiple Perspectives', in Jablin F M (ed), *Handbook of Organizational Communication*, Sage (1987).
29. Harré R and Lamb R, *The Encyclopedic Dictionary of Psychology*, Blackwell (1983).
30. Shannon C E and Weaver W, *The Mathematical Theory of Communication*, University of Illinois Press (1949).
31. Newcomb T M, 'An Approach to the Study of Communicative Acts', *Psychological Review*, vol. 60, 1953, p. 393.
32. Berlo D K, *The Process of Communication: An Introduction to Theory and Practice*, Holt Rinehart and Winston (1960).
33. Berlo D K, 'Communication as Process: Review and Commentary', in Rubin B (ed), *Communication Yearbook 1* (1977).
34. Smith D H, 'Communication Research and the Idea of Process', *Speech Monographs*, vol. 39, 1972, pp. 174–182.
35. Harré R and Secord P F, *The Explanation of Social Behaviour*, Blackwell (1972).
36. Penman R, *Communication Processes and Relationships*, Academic Press (1980), p. 5.
37. Berlo D K, 'Communication as Process: Review and Commentary', in Rubin B (ed), *Communication Yearbook 1* (1977), p. 12.
38. McEwan T, *A Replicated Study of Communication Networks, Job Retention and Labour Turnover in Two British Hotels*, Unpublished Doctoral Thesis, Cranfield Institute of Technology, Cranfield, UK (1988).
39. *Manpower Flows in the Hotel and Catering Industry*, HCITB Research Report (August 1984).
40. Jablin F M, 'Organisational Entry, Assimilation and Exit', in Jablin F M (ed), *Handbook of Organisational Communication*, Sage (1987), p. 679.
41. Kincaid D L, *The Convergence Model of Communication*, East-West Communication Institute, Honolulu (1979).
42. Rogers E M and Kincaid D L, *Communication Networks: Towards a New Paradigm for Research*, The Free Press (1981), pp. 37–43.
43. Goffman E, *Strategic Interaction*, University of Pennsylvania (1969).
44. Harré R and Lamb R, *The Encyclopedic Dictionary of Psychology*, Blackwell (1983), p. 103.
45. Frazer C, 'Communication in Interaction', in *Introducing Social Psychology*, Penguin (1978).
46. Ruesch J and Bateson G, *Communication: The Social Matrix of Psychology*, Norton (1951).
47. Birdwhistell R L, 'Contribution of Linguistic-Kinesic Studies to the Understanding of Schizophrenia' in Auerback A (ed), *Schizophrenia: An Integrated Approach*, Ronald Press (1959).
48. Watzlawick P, *Pragmatics of Human Communication*, Faber (1968).
49. Bateson G, *Steps to an Ecology of the Mind*, Paladin (1973).
50. Hawes L, 'Elements of a Model for Communication Processes', *Quarterly Journal of Speech Monographs*, vol. 40, pp. 208–219.
51. Trans. in Woolff K A, *The Sociology of Georg Simmel*, McGraw-Hill (1950).
52. Rogers L E and Farace R V, 'Analysis of Relational Communication in Dyads: New Measurement Procedures', *Human Communication Research*, vol. 1, no. 3, 1975, pp. 222–239.
53. Henderson J B, *Labour Market Institutions and Wages in the Lodging Industry*, Michigan State University,

Bureau of Business and Economic Research, East Lansing, Michigan (1965).

54. Wittgenstein L, *Philosophical Investigations*, Basil Blackwell (1953).

55. Tichy N, 'Social Network Analysis for Organisations', *Academy of Management Review*, vol. 4, 1979, pp. 507–519.

56. Weick K E, 'Prescribed and Emergent Networks', in Jablin F (ed), *Handbook of Organizational Communication*, Sage (1987).

57. Burns T and Stalker G M, *The Management of Innovation*, Tavistock (1966), p. 122.

58. Rogers E M and Kincaid D L, *Communication Networks: Towards a New Paradigm for Research*, The Free Press (1981), p. 92.

59. See, for example, Francis D, *Unblocking Organizational Communication*, Gower (1987).

60. Pincus J D, 'Communication Satisfaction, Job Satisfaction, and Job Performance', *Human Communication Research*, vol. 12, 1986, pp. 395–419.

61. Redding W C, *Communication Within the Organization: An Interpretive Review of Theory and Research*, Industrial Communications Council, 1972.

62. Wheeless V E and Berryman-Fink C, 'Perceptions of Women Managers and Their Communicator Competencies', *Communication Quarterly*, vol. 33, 1985, pp. 137–148.

63. Infante D A and Gordon W I, 'Superiors' Argumentativeness and Verbal Aggressiveness'. Paper presented at the annual meeting of the International Communication Association, Chicago, 1986.

64. Beyer J M and Trice H M, 'A Field Study of the Use and Perceived Effects of Discipline in Controlling Work Performance', *Academy of Management Journal*, vol. 27, 1984, pp. 743–764.

65. Pelz D C, 'Influence: A Key to Effective Leadership in the First-Line Supervisor', *Personnel*, vol. 29, 1952, pp. 3–11.

66. Gioia D A and Sims H P, 'Cognition–Behavior Connections: Attribution and Verbal Behavior in Leader-Subordinate Interactions', *Organizational Behavior and Human Decision Process*, vol. 37, 1986, pp. 197–229.

67. Goering E M, 'The Validity of a Self-Reported Conflict Management Scale in Measuring Conflict Management Behaviors'. Paper presented at the annual meeting of the International Communication Association, Chicago, 1986.

68. Jablin F M, 'Superior–Subordinate Communication: The State of the Art', *Psychological Bulletin*, vol. 86, (1979), pp. 1201–1222.

69. McEwan T, *A Replicated Study of Communication Networks, Job Retention and Labour Turnover in Two British Hotels*, Unpublished Doctoral Thesis, Cranfield Institute of Technology, Cranfield, UK (1988).

12

IMPROVING ORGANISATIONAL PERFORMANCE

INTRODUCTION

The hospitality organisation is not only a work organisation, it is also a complex social system and the sum of many interrelated variables. In order to achieve improved performance it is necessary to understand the nature of organisational effectiveness and those factors which influence the successful management of human resources.

This chapter looks at:

- Dimensions of organisational effectiveness
- Total quality management
- The role of top management
- Organisational culture
- The management of change

- The successful implementation of change
- The measurement of productivity
- Organisational climate
- Organisational conflict
- Contrasting perspectives on organisations

DIMENSIONS OF ORGANISATIONAL EFFECTIVENESS

This book has been concerned with interactions among the structure and operation of hospitality organisations, the role of management and the behaviour of people at work. The central theme has been improved organisational performance through the effective management of people (human resources).

Organisational performance is affected by a multiplicity of individual, group, task, technological, structural, managerial and environmental variables. Handy, for example, identifies over 60 factors that impinge on any one organisational situation and which illustrate the complicated nature of the study of organisational effectiveness.[1]

Attributes for successful performance

In their study of 62 American companies (including service companies) with outstandingly successful performance, Peters and Waterman identify eight basic attributes of excellence which appear to account for success.[2]

- **A bias for action** – action-oriented and a bias for getting things done.
- **Close to the customer** – listening and learning from the people they serve, and providing quality, service and reliability.
- **Autonomy and entrepreneurship** – innovation and risk-taking as an expected way of doing things .
- **Productivity through people** – treating members of staff as the source of quality and productivity.
- **Hands-on, value driven** – having well-defined, basic philosophies and top management keeping in touch with the 'front lines'.
- **Stick to the knitting** – in most cases, staying close to what you know and can do well.
- **Simple form, lean staff** – simple structural forms and systems, and few top-level staff.
- **Simultaneous loose-tight properties** – operational decentralisation but strong centralised control over the few, important core values.

The 7-S framework

From their research, Peters and Waterman suggest that any intelligent approach to organising needs to encompass at least seven, interdependent variables (the McKinsey 7-S Framework):

- Strategy;
- Structure;
- Staff;
- (management) Style;
- Systems (and procedures);
- (corporate) Strengths or skills;
- Shared values (i.e. culture).

TOTAL QUALITY MANAGEMENT (TQM)

One particular feature of organisational performance and effectiveness is attention to quality, and this is especially important in a service industry. As we discussed in Chapter 7, the successful hospitality organisation should as a matter of policy be constantly seeking opportunities to improve the quality of its products, services and processes. The organisation must also couple quality with a required level of productivity. Such a philosophy is increasingly encompassed as part of a total quality management (TQM) culture.

Quality assurance and human resource management

There are numerous definitions of TQM which are generally expressed in terms of: a way of life for an organisation as a whole, commitment to total customer satisfaction through a continuous process of improvement, and the contribution and involvement of people. TQM emphasises the importance of people as the key to quality and the satisfaction of customers' needs.[3] Staff should be properly trained and in a position to take action about quality defects as they notice them. This involves the convergence of quality assurance and human resource management.

TQM therefore requires the creation of a corporate identity, a total organisational approach, and the participation and commitment of staff at all levels, starting with the active support and involvement of top management. It also involves a strategic focus on training for total quality. As an example, Scott's Hotels training programme for quality was based on the managing director's conceptual model of TQM[4] (see Figure 12.1).

TQM involves an increased level of empowerment and providing staff with greater authority and responsibility for self-checking, decision-making and problem-solving. (Recall, for example the discussion on quality circles in Chapter 8.) The introduction of TQM can therefore add to the pressures for a restructuring of the organisation and the move towards flatter hierarchies with the removal of a layer of managers/supervisors.

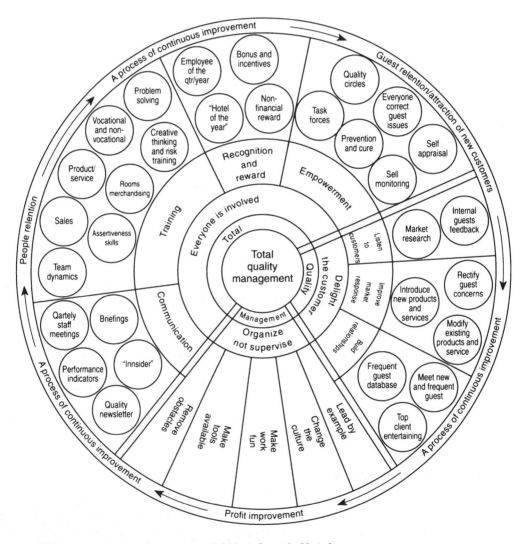

Fig 12.1 Conceptual model of TQM at Scott's Hotels
Source: Hubrecht J and Teare R, 'A Strategy for Partnership in Total Quality Service', *International Journal of Contemporary Hospitality Management*, vol. 5, no. 3, 1993, p. iii. Reproduced by kind permission of Scott's Hotels Ltd, UK.

THE ROLE OF TOP MANAGEMENT

Effective management is at the heart of organisation development and improved performance, and the contribution to economic and social needs of society. This applies as much to service organisations and the hospitality industry as to any other industry. The role of management is one of the most important factors in the success of any hospitality organisation. At the corporate level top management have a responsibility for determining the direction of the organisation as a whole and for its survival, development and profitability.

Attention to key features

Top management clearly have an essential part to play in improving organisational performance and the effective management of human resources. They need to give attention to such features as the following.

- Clarification and communication of corporate aims and objectives. The identification of key areas of performance and results including social responsibilities.
- Interactions with and responsiveness to external environmental influences, and the effective management of change.
- Pursuing corporate goals in accordance with an ethical and operational foundation, and recognition of the psychological contract.
- Design of organisation structure which takes account of the socio-technical system and is most suited to organisational processes and the execution of work.
- Organisational strategies and practices, for example relating to manpower planning and the management of staff turnover.
- Welding a coherent and co-ordinated pattern of work activities, and harnessing the efforts of staff.
- Clear, consistent and equitable policies and procedures, for example relating to the personnel function including training and development.
- A style of managerial behaviour which adopts a positive policy of investment in people.
- Recognition of the needs and expectations of people at work and systems of motivation, job satisfaction and rewards.
- Effective control of those critical activities important to the overall success of the organisation.
- Creating an organisational climate which encourages members of staff to work willingly and effectively.

The process of management

Top management have a particular concern for the community or institutional level and for the work of the organisation as a whole. But it is the role of management **throughout all levels of the organisation** to act as an integrating activity and to co-ordinate, direct and guide the efforts of members towards the achievement of goals and objectives. The process of management, however, takes place not in a vacuum but within the context of the organisational setting (discussed in Chapter 1). Applications of organisational behaviour and the effective management of human resources are dependent, therefore, not only upon the nature of the hospitality industry, but also upon the characteristic features of the individual organisation – and its organisational culture and climate.

ORGANISATIONAL CULTURE

Although most of us will understand in our own minds what is meant by organisational culture it is a general concept which is difficult to define or explain precisely. The concept of culture has developed from anthropology. There is no consensus on its meaning or its applications to the analysis of work organisations.[5] Also, there is sometimes confusion over the difference between the interpretation of organisational culture and organisational climate, which is discussed below.

A popular and simple way of defining culture is: 'how things are done around here'. A more detailed definition is:

> ... the collection of traditions, values, policies, beliefs, and attitudes that constitute a pervasive context for everything we do and think in an organisation.[6]

Culture is reinforced through the system of rites and rituals, patterns of communication, the informal organisation, expected patterns of behaviour and perceptions of the psychological contract.

Influences on the development of culture

The culture and structure of an organisation develop over time and in response to a complex set of factors. We can, however, identify a number of key influences that are likely to play an important role in the development of any organisational culture. These include: history, primary function and technology, goals and objectives, size, location, management and staffing, and the environment.[7]

History

The reason, and manner in which, the organisation was originally formed, its age, and the philosophy and values of its owners and first senior managers will affect culture. A key event in the organisation's history such as a merger or major reorganisation, or a new generation of top management, may bring about a change in culture.

Primary function and technology

The nature of the organisation's 'business' and its primary function have an important influence on its culture, for example the range and quality of products and services provided, the importance of reputation and the type of customers. The primary function of the organisation will determine the nature of the technological processes and methods of undertaking work, which in turn also affect structure and culture. Compare, for example, a traditional, high-class hotel, particularly noted for its cuisine, with a popular mass-production fast-food chain store.

Goals and objectives

Although a business organisation may pursue profitability, this is not by itself a very clear or sufficient criterion for its effective management. For example, to what extent is emphasis placed on long-term survival or growth and development? How much attention is given to avoiding risk and uncertainties? Or how much concern is shown for broader social responsibilities? The organisation must give attention to objectives in all key areas of its operations. The combination of objectives and resultant strategies will influence culture, and may themselves be influenced by changes in culture.

Size

Usually, larger organisations have more formalised structures and cultures. Increased size is likely to result in separate departments and possibly split-site operations. This may cause difficulties in communication and interdepartmental rivalries with the need for effective co-ordination. A rapid expansion, or decline, in size and rate of growth, and resultant changes in staffing, will influence structure and culture.

Location

Geographical location and the physical characteristics will have a major influence on culture, for example whether the organisation is located in a quiet rural location or a busy city centre. This will influence the types of customers and the staff employed. It can also can affect the nature of services provided, the sense of 'boundary' and distinctive identity, and opportunities for development.

Management and staffing

Top executives can have considerable influence on the nature of culture; consider, for example, the key role played by Lord Forte when Chief Executive of Trusthouse Forte. But all members of staff help to shape the dominant culture of an organisation, irrespective of what senior management feel it should be.

Culture is also determined by the nature of staff employed and the extent to which they accept management philosophy and policies or pay only 'lip service'. Another important influence is the match between corporate culture and employees' perception of the psychological contract.

The environment

In order to be effective, the organisation must be responsive to external environmental influences. For example, if it operates within a dynamic environment, it requires a structure and culture that are sensitive and readily adaptable to change. An organic structure is more likely to respond effectively to new opportunities and challenges, and risks and limitations, presented by the external environment.

The importance of culture

In the study referred to above, Peters and Waterman draw attention to the importance of corporate culture.

> Without exception, the dominance and coherence of culture proved to be an essential quality of the excellent companies. Moreover, the stronger the culture and the more it was directed to the marketplace, the less need was there for policy manuals, organisation charts, or detailed procedures and rules. In these companies, people way down the line know what they are supposed to do in most situations because the handful of guiding values is crystal clear.[8]

Organisation culture will influence the pride that people have in their jobs and the appropriateness of the manager's methods of motivation.[9] Culture is also a major determinant of organisational performance and effectiveness. In the hospitality industry culture is a vital component in the standards of delivery of service to the customer. It is important therefore to recognise the essential characteristics of service organisations and to develop a culture which encourages group motivation, harmonious working relationships and good teamwork.

Culture and ineffectiveness

According to Glover, for example, a properly developed corporate culture can be a management tool for building product quality and staff productivity. If management misunderstands the effects of corporate culture, the quality of products and services in hospitality operations may suffer through a 'cult of ineffectiveness'.[10]

Glover identifies a number of organisational characteristics that commonly give rise to a cult of ineffectiveness.

- **Missing standards** – through lack of agreement on expectations, inconsistent delivery of products and services, lack of measuring and managing quality, and evaluation based on activity not results.
- **Unbalanced accountability** – although financial accounting is highly developed, effective controls over the people area, and accounting procedures for measuring the effectiveness of managers and supervisors, are less precise.
- **Ineffective communications** – ideas and responses from employees are seldom sought, and comments from guests not appreciated. Neither group is considered in management decision-making. Top-down communication, as well as broken or misunderstood communication, engenders a cult of ineffectiveness.
- **Symptoms, not causes** – emphasis is placed on remedies for symptoms, rather than delving for the underlying cause of problems. For example, the rudeness of a waiter may have less to do with the waiter, and more to do with inappropriate selection and training or poor management practices.
- **Lack of recognition** – most managers admit that they rarely let employees know when a job has been done well. Many employees only hear from their manager when there is a problem.
- **Absence of team-work** – many corporate cultures reward competition among employees and may encourage conflict. If employees are rewarded on the basis of individual action, this can thwart the development of teams. Yet the nature of hospitality operations demands effective teamwork.

- **Inadequate training** – a common means of training new members of staff is by 'trailing' an experienced employee. This transfers the most important managerial responsibility to a line employee who may not have a clear view of the company's objectives. Also, managers and supervisors are often expected to sink or swim as they are introduced to new responsibilities .
- **Recriminations** – complaints or other problems are often an occasion for blame, finger-pointing and defensiveness rather than being taken as an opportunity to improve operations. Management has a responsibility to limit problems in the first place.
- **The need for effectiveness** – many hospitality managers fail to recognise the difference between effectiveness and efficiency. 'Getting the job done' should include effective delivery of the product or service and result in achieving established standards.
- **Actions of top management** – an organisation is more than the sum of all its operations and departments. It also includes a culture that is shaped by the actions of top management. The informal social organisation affects all levels of the company, and influences its ability to deliver products and services to the customer.

Culture in 'short-life' hospitality organisations

The need to achieve a high level of performance and avoid a cult of ineffectiveness raises interesting questions relating to the nature and influence of culture in 'short-life' hospitality organisations. These are organisations which are created to run for only a short period of time, such as an arts festival or national garden festivals. For example, how important and influential is a strong organisational culture? How does culture develop when the organisation has little or no prior history, has short-term goals and objectives, and there is only limited time for top management to exercise their influence? How do managers in such organisations attempt to inculcate culture?[11]

THE MANAGEMENT OF CHANGE

Whatever the nature of its culture, the organisation can only perform effectively through interactions with the broader external environment of which it is part. Factors such as uncertain economic conditions, fierce world competition, the level of governmental intervention, scarcity of natural resources, changing social attitudes and rapid developments in new technology combine to create an increasingly volatile environment.

As the hospitality industry is concerned with both production and service it is particularly susceptible to environmental influences.[12] In order to ensure its survival and future success, the organisation must be readily adaptable, therefore, to the demands placed upon it. A key factor in performance and effectiveness is the successful management of change.

The forces of change

Change is a pervasive influence. We are all subject to continual change in one form or another. It is an inescapable part of both social and organisational life. Change also originates within the organisation itself, for example as part of the natural process of ageing of buildings and equipment, or as skills and abilities become outdated. There are a wide range of forces acting upon organisations which make the need for change inevitable. These forces of change can be summarised under five broad headings: changing technology, the knowledge explosion, rapid product obsolescence, the changing nature of the workforce, and the quality of working life.[13]

- **Changing technology** – for example, advances in computing systems and information technology, and the increasing use of microwave ovens and cook/chill systems. These changes can result in the de-skilling of jobs, especially in the kitchen.
- **Knowledge explosion** – for example the number of people in some form of education, new ideas and methods of working, the number of scientific journals and new books, the increasing number of hospitality management students.
- **Rapid product obsolescence** – changes in consumer preferences together with changing technology have influenced the delivery of many products and services, for example the popularity of convenience foods, an increasing trend away from silver service and towards self-service, reduced personal contact between receptionists and customers.
- **Changing nature of the workforce** – for example, demographic influences and changes in the composition of the workforce, broader educational opportunities, part-time working, changes in family life-cycles, and equal opportunities.
- **Quality of working life** – for example, increased attention to the satisfaction of people's needs and expectations at work, human resource management, job design and work organisation, and styles of managerial behaviour.

Managerial resistance to change

Although the organisation has to adapt to its environment, there is often resistance at the managerial level against change.

- Major change often requires large resources which may already be committed to investments in other areas or strategies. Assets such as buildings and furnishings, technology, equipment and people cannot be altered easily.
- Attention is often focused on maintaining stability and predictability, especially in large-scale organisations. The need for formal structures, the division of work and established rules, procedures and methods of work can result in resistance to change.
- Management may feel comfortable operating within the structure, policies and procedures which have been formulated to deal with a range of past or present situations. Managers may set up defences against change and prefer to concentrate on the routine things they perform well.
- Change may also be seen as a threat to the power or influence of management, such as their control over decisions, resources or information. As an example, middle management may be resistant to the introduction of quality circles because the increased empowerment of members is seen as an encroachment on their traditional areas of authority and responsibility.

Individual resistance to change

People are naturally wary of change, and resistance to change – or the thought of the implications of change – appears to be a common phenomenon. Some common reasons for individual resistance to change include the following.

Fear of the unknown

Many major changes present a degree of uncertainty, for example the possible effects of new technology or methods of working. A person may resist promotion because of uncertainty over changes in responsibilities or the increased social demands of the higher position. Changes which confront people with the unknown tend to cause anxiety or fear. A proposed change which is likely to break up a cohesive working group or to move an individual to a new work group may be resisted.

Habit

People tend to respond to situations in an established and accustomed manner. Habit may serve as a means of comfort and security, and as a guide for decision-making. Proposed changes to habits, especially if well established and requiring little effort, may well be resisted. If there is a clearly perceived advantage, for example a reduction in working hours without loss of pay, there is likely to be less resistance to the change. However, because of habit, some people may still find it difficult to adjust to the reduced hours of work.

Inconvenience or loss of freedom

If the change is seen as likely to prove inconvenient, make life more difficult, reduce freedom of action or result in increased control, there is likely to be resistance. For example, a manager may resist being moved to another establishment or location, especially if this involves greater travelling or moving house. Staff are likely to resist new working practices which require learning new skills or result in closer management control.

Economic implications

People are likely to resist change which is perceived as reducing either directly or indirectly their pay or other rewards, or requiring an increase in work for the same level of pay. Staff may resist a move to another job, even at the same level of basic pay, if they fear they may receive less overtime payments, gratuities or other perks.

Security in the past

Some people tend to find a sense of security in the past. In times of frustration or difficulty, or when faced with new or unfamiliar ideas or methods, people may reflect on the past and wish to retain old and comfortable ways. There may be a tendency to cling to well-established and well-known procedures as giving a feeling of security.

Threat to status or symbols

Any perceived threat to the status or symbol attached to a job or position is likely to be resisted, for example proposals to remove a private office, reserved car parking space, special uniforms or a private locker.

Selective perception

People tend to have their own, biased view of a particular situation, which fits most comfortably their own perception of reality. This can cause almost a 'built-in' resistance to change. For example, strong trade unionists may have a stereotyped view of management as untrustworthy and therefore oppose any management change, however well-founded might be the intention. Managers may have a particular bias towards a particular theory or practice of organisational behaviour and discard new ideas which they feel to be of no concern or value to them.

THE SUCCESSFUL IMPLEMENTATION OF CHANGE

Continual change is inevitable and the effective implementation of change is an increasingly important managerial responsibility. New ideas and innovations should not be perceived as threats by members of staff. One of the most important factors in the successful management of change is the style of managerial behaviour.

In certain situations it may be necessary for management to use compulsion and the hierarchical authority to impose change. This *may* be appropriate, for example, if change is clearly going to be detrimental to staff. It should also be recognised that some people may prefer, and respond better to, an autocratic, directed and controlled style of management. In most cases, however, the introduction of change is more likely to be effective with a participative style of management. If staff are kept fully informed of proposals, are encouraged to adopt a positive attitude and have personal involvement in the implementation of the change, there is a greater likelihood of their acceptance of the change.

Human and social factors of change

Managers must be responsive to change. But activities managed on the basis of technical or economic efficiency alone are unlikely to lead to optimum improvement in performance. The efforts made by management to maintain the balance of the socio-technical system will influence people's attitudes, the behaviour of individuals and groups, and thereby organisational performance and effectiveness. Management must therefore take proper account of the importance of human and social factors of change. This demands that management:

- create an environment of trust and shared commitment, and involve staff fully in decisions and actions which affect them;
- maintain full and open communications, and the genuine participation of all staff concerned, preferably well before the actual introduction of the change;
- emphasise benefits of, and potential opportunities presented by, the change;
- encourage team management and a co-operative spirit among staff;

- give attention to job design, methods of work organisation and the development of cohesive groups;
- provide suitable economic incentive schemes to safeguard potential loss of earnings or job security, and to ensure an equitable allocation of any financial savings resulting from the change;
- design a personnel management action programme directed to a review of recruitment and selection, natural wastage of staff, training and re-training, provisions for early retirements, and other strategies to reduce the possible level of redundancies or other harmful effects on staff.[14]

THE MEASUREMENT OF PRODUCTIVITY

Recent reports from the HCTC[15] and from the NEDC[16] have drawn attention to the need for and importance of increasing productivity in the hotel and catering industry. The characteristic features of service industries (discussed in Chapter 1) include the intangible nature of service delivery and the associated difficulty in the monitoring and measurement of performance. However, despite such difficulties, it is important to attempt some objective measures of productivity.

McLaughlin and Coffey, for example, suggest a classification of available productivity measures including output/input ratios, work measurement, quality and outcome performance, statistical comparisons and mathematical programming techniques.[17] In order to tackle the issue of productivity in service operations, McLaughlin and Coffey suggest that management should:

- specify the reason for investigating productivity;
- analyse the present or proposed service delivery including key specific operational areas;
- be absolutely clear about the service package it wishes to deliver, and specify the characteristics of strategic importance at each process stage and the key decision areas;
- select and investigate the methods of productivity measurement;
- be prepared for all kinds of objections to productivity measures on the basis of quality;
- involve fully the members of staff concerned and secure their acceptance to proposed measures of productivity.

Productivity in the hotel industry

As part of a collaborative research project the HCTC and the Birmingham College of Food are investigating the nature of, and influences on, productivity in hotels, including the importance of training. One of the main aims of the project is to create a comprehensive model which takes into account the factors that impact on productivity in the hotel industry[18] (see Figure 12.2).

Differences in customisation and service mix of operations make it difficult to draw meaningful comparisons between levels of productivity between different units, for example a two-star hotel and a five-star hotel. In attempting to create a productivity model it is also necessary to consider the problems of:

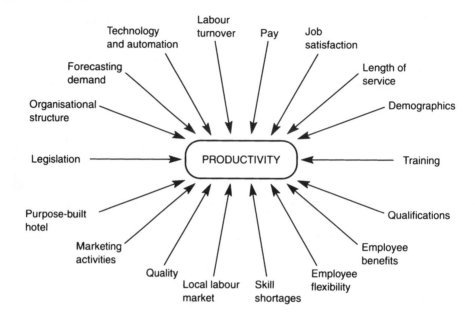

Fig 12.2 A productivity model for the hospitality industry
Reprinted with permission of the Hotel and Catering Training Company from Lane P, Ingold T and Yeoman I,
'Productivity in Hotels', *Proceedings of CHME Research Conference*, Manchester Metropolitan University, April 1993

- the interrelationships between variables, for example the cause–effect relationship between job satisfaction and productivity;
- dealing with a large list of factors and investigating the impact of individual factors, such as training, on productivity within a dynamic and constantly changing environment.

Despite these problems the model provides a helpful basis from which to consider the factors which impact upon productivity in the hotel industry.

ORGANISATIONAL CLIMATE

In addition to arrangements for carrying out organisational processes, management has a responsibility for creating a climate in which people are motivated to work willingly and effectively.

Climate can be said to relate to the prevailing atmosphere surrounding the hospitality organisation, to the level of morale, and to the strength of feelings of belonging, care and goodwill among members.

Organisational climate, however, is another general concept and difficult to define precisely. It is more something which is felt. Climate arises from a combination of forces, some of which are better understood than others.

The perception of employees

Whereas organisational culture describes what the organisation is about, organisational climate is an indication of the employees' feelings and beliefs of what the organisation is about. Climate is based on the **perceptions** of employees towards the quality of the internal working environment.[19] The extent to which employees accept the culture of the organisation will have a significant effect on climate.

Climate also relates to the recognition of the organisation as a social system and the extent to which membership is perceived as a psychologically rewarding experience. It can be seen as the state of mutual trust and understanding among members of the organisation.

Characteristics of organisational climate

Organisational climate is characterised, therefore, by the nature of the people–organisation relationship and the superior–subordinate relationship. These relationships are determined by interactions among goals and objectives, formal structure, the process of management, styles of leadership and the behaviour of people. A healthy organisational climate might therefore be expected to exhibit such characteristic features as:

- the integration of organisational goals and personal goals;
- the most appropriate organisation structure based on the demands of the socio-technical system;
- democratic functioning of the organisation with full opportunities for participation;
- justice in treatment with equitable personnel and employee relations policies and practices;
- mutual trust, consideration and support among different levels of the organisation;
- the open discussion of conflict with an attempt to avoid confrontation;
- managerial behaviour and styles of leadership appropriate to the particular work situations;
- acceptance of the psychological contract between the individual and the organisation;
- recognition of people's needs and expectations at work, and individual differences and attributes;
- equitable systems of rewards based on positive recognition;
- concern for the quality of working life and job design;
- opportunities for personal development and career progression;
- a sense of identity with, and loyalty to, the organisation and a feeling of being a valued and important member.

The management of organisational climate

If organisational climate is to be improved, then attention should be given to the above features. The climate created by managers will have a significant influence on the motivation and behaviour of employees.

> Creating the right climate involves a realisation that all management activity, from the design of systems and procedures to the way the manager handles interpersonal interactions with customers and staff, will contribute to the overall atmosphere of the workplace. The manager is a role model that staff will follow.[20]

The management of organisational climate is therefore an important means of improving productivity and standards of work performance.

In hospitality operations, customer satisfaction relies heavily on group-based activities and the need for different departments to work closely together. It is particularly important, therefore, to develop an organisational climate which encourages good teamwork. However, although similar types of organisations may share certain common features, each will have its own distinctive characteristics. Every organisation has its own climate, or internal environment or 'personality'.

Main dimensions of climate

Climate will influence the level of morale and attitudes which members of the organisation bring to bear on their work performance and personal relationships. Although morale is difficult to measure objectively, a carefully designed and conducted description questionnaire (or attitude survey) will help to establish the true feelings of members on factors contributing to organisational climate.

There are many possible survey instruments with which to gauge climate. Different questionnaires vary greatly in the number of items and in the number of categories. Mill, for example, suggests that climate can be described in terms of six main dimensions: clarity, commitment, standards, responsibility, recognition and teamwork (Figure 12.3).[21]

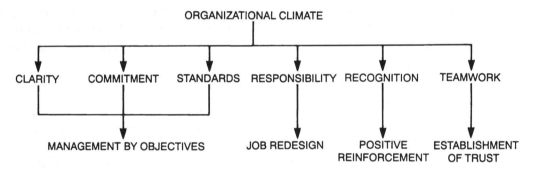

Fig 12.3 Organisational climate and management action
Reprinted, with permission, from Mill R C, *Managing for Productivity in the Hospitality Industry*, Van Nostrand Reinhold (1989), p. 125

If clarity, commitment or standards are low, this suggests the need for a system of management by objectives. This involves the setting of clearly stated objectives and targets, and developing commitment among employees by participation in agreeing standards of performance .

Where responsibility is low, this suggests the need for attention to job re-design and passing on to employees increased autonomy for the planning, organising and control of their jobs.

When recognition is lacking, management should provide positive reinforcement by giving employees rewards and encouragement when they do something right.

If teamwork is lacking, then management should attempt to develop a feeling of trust and supportive relationships with employees and among groups of employees.

Mill suggests that management by objectives, job design, positive reinforcement and the establishment of trust form a basis for management action to improve organisational climate.

ORGANISATIONAL CONFLICT

Conflict is an inevitable feature of organisational life, and a reality of management and the behaviour of people at work. Within the hospitality industry conflict situations are a common occurrence and manifested largely at the individual, group or unit level rather than on a collective bargaining basis. Organisational conflict is a common theme in discussions on the general nature of working in the industry such as interdepartmental competition,[22] or related to specific features, for example high staff turnover.[23]

Common definitions of conflict are usually associated with negative features and situations which give rise to inefficiency. Conflict is the harmful side of differences within organisations.[24] The traditional view of conflict is that it is potentially dysfunctional and represents forms of deviant organisational behaviour which should be controlled and changed.

Clearly, conflict situations can give rise to emotional and physical stress and in extreme cases can have very upsetting consequences for some people.

Conflict can have adverse affects on organisational performance and effectiveness. However, it is also arguable that, properly managed, conflict can, at least to a point, have potentially positive outcomes.[25] It can have an energising and vitalising effect within an organisation. Conflict may be seen as a 'constructive force' and in certain circumstances it can be welcomed or even encouraged.

The radical (Marxist) approach

The radical approach, which is associated with the ideas of writers such as Karl Marx, challenges the traditional view of conflict. The radical approach views organisations in terms of the disparity in power and control. Organisational conflict is a feature of the unequal nature of organisational life and is a means of bringing about change.[26] Collective bargaining was not seen as particularly helpful in a system stacked against the workers. Organisational conflict is a natural part of the class struggle between owners and controllers of economic resources and means of production and the workers and wage earners.

According to the radical approach the design of organisation structure, management systems and the choice and use of technology all form part of the struggle for power and control within the work organisation. Greater attention should be given to relationships between the formal and informal aspects of the organisation and the study of conflict between the needs of the individual and those of the organisation, and between workers and management.

CONTRASTING PERSPECTIVES OF WORK ORGANISATIONS

An appreciation of the nature of conflict can help an understanding of social and organisational behaviour, the nature of employee relations and applications of human resource management. Differing views on the explanation and outcomes of conflict can be related to contrasting unitary or pluralistic perspectives of work organisations.

For example, it might be expected that a healthy climate would be reflected by complete harmony in working relationships, and loyalty and common commitment to the goals and objectives of the organisation. This view of work organisations as 'happy families' is a worthwhile and creditable ideal, and as such is implied by many leading management writers.[27] Such a view suggests a unitary perspective of the organisation.

The unitary perspective

With the unitary perspective, the organisation is viewed as a team with a common source of loyalty, one focus of effort and one common leader. There is an image of the organisation as an integrated whole, and with supportive and co-operative structures. Management and workers are viewed as sharing a common interest. Trade unions are seen as an unnecessary evil and restrictive practices are outmoded or caused by troublemakers.

The unitary perspective views authority as vested in management. Where conflict exists it represents a malfunction within the organisation and is attributed to poor communications, personality clashes or the work of agitators. Personnel policies and managerial development can be seen as reflecting a unitary ideology. Developments in human resource management can also arguably be seen as imposing new forms of control and a managerial approach to facilitating organisational goals and the involvement of employees which furthers a unitarist perspective.[28]

The pluralistic perspective

The pluralistic perspective presents an alternative view in which the organisation is viewed in terms of competing sub-groups with their own loyalties, goals and leaders.[29] These competing sub-groups are almost certain to come into conflict. From the pluralistic perspective conflict is seen as an inherent and accepted feature of work organisations and induced in part by the very structure of the organisation. Conflict can be an agent for evolution, and internal and external change.

Restrictive practices may be seen as a rational response from a group which regards itself as being threatened. Conflict is generated through individuals and groups pursing their own diverse goals. It is the job of the manager to bring about compromise, and to manage and accommodate the competing interests of different parties. Belief in the principles of a pluralistic perspective can therefore restrict the implementation of a unitary approach to employee relations.

Understanding the views of other people

While neither the unitary or pluralist perspective can be seen as 'right' or 'wrong', these contrasting views will influence the nature of employee relations and the management of human resources. The following observation from a Hotel and Catering Training Company publication serves as a salutary comment on which to conclude this book.

> Whatever their judgement about these differing views, managers, staff and union representatives need to be aware, in order to operate effectively, that:

- people's actions are determined partly by their ideals and aspirations
- such ideals vary greatly
- we need to understand other people's views as well as our own in forming judgements and making decisions.[30]

SUMMARY

- Organisational effectiveness is influenced by a multiplicity of variables. One particular feature of special importance for successful performance in the hospitality industry is concern for quality. This must be coupled with a required level of productivity. The adoption of a total quality management culture involves the convergence of quality assurance and human resource management.
- Effective management is at the heart of organisation development and improved performance. At the corporate level top management have an essential part to play in determining the direction of the organisation as a whole. Top management should also give attention to key features in the effective management of human resources.
- Applications of human resource management are influenced by the nature of organisational culture and organisational climate. The culture and structure of an organisation develop over time and in response to a complex set of factors. A key feature in organisational behaviour is the management of change including proper attention to human and social factors.
- It is important for the hospitality industry to give attention to increasing productivity. This involves the study of many interrelated variables including the impact of training. In addition to arrangements for carrying out organisational processes, management has a responsibility for creating a climate in which people work willingly and effectively.
- Conflict is a reality of organisational behaviour and management. It is a common theme at the individual, group and unit level within the hospitality industry. There are alternative views on the negative and potentially positive features of conflict. An explanation of the nature and outcome of conflict can be related to contrasting perspectives of work organisations.

REVIEW AND DISCUSSION QUESTIONS

1 Identify clearly examples of main factors which influence the performance and effectiveness of a hospitality organisation of your choice.

2 Critically review the role of top management in your own organisation and the extent to which attention is given to key features of effective human resource management.

3 Explain what is meant by organisational culture. How might corporate culture influence the effectiveness of hospitality operations?

4 Why do people in organisations tend to resist change? As manager, explain what actions you would take to help overcome the social and human problems associated with the introduction of technological change.

5 As a senior manager, explain fully the actions you would propose in order to increase the level of productivity in your organisation.

6 What do you understand by organisational climate? Discuss with practical examples the main areas in which action could be taken to help improve organisational climate in the hospitality industry.

7 Discuss the extent to which you believe conflict is an inherent feature of work organisations. Explain your understanding of the radical approach to organisational conflict.

8 Contrast the unitary and pluralistic perspectives of organisations giving specific examples of their influence on employee relations and human resource management within the hospitality industry.

ASSIGNMENT

You are the newly appointed personnel manager of a large hospitality organisation. The general manager asks you to address a group of sceptical line managers and supervisors on the practical value of behavioural science, and the study of human resource management. Outline clearly the content and manner of presentation of your address.

INTEGRATIVE CASE STUDY 1

The Southsea Castle Hotel

From humble beginnings, Jack Davidson had, by most standards, succeeded in business. He had amassed a considerable personal fortune as a result of his bookmaking exploits, which had generated sizeable cash profits. Davidson was by this time coming to the conclusion that he should be moving his funds into property and six years ago paid £1.5 million for the freehold of a hotel on the south coast sea front – the Southsea Castle Hotel. The purchase was made primarily as a capital investment in property, but Davidson also felt that he would be able to generate worthwhile profits from the business. He has no previous experience in the hotel field, but has supreme confidence in his instinctive feel for a profitable deal and his past record seemed to indicate that he had the 'Midas touch'! As a teenager Davidson had started work as a bookmakers' runner, then moved into trading in used cars and various other entrepreneurial pursuits before returning to his first love of the turf. He had passed rapidly through a tempestuous marriage after which he had become something of a workaholic.

The only positive effect of the marriage was a friendship which developed between him and his wife's sister June. Davidson had first met June on his wedding day and they instantly liked each other. After his divorce Davidson regularly travelled to south Wales to stay at the free-house which June and her husband Gareth Walker owned. The Walkers were an effective partnership both in private and in commercial life. The fact that their hostelry, the Red Dragon in Tenby, was one of the most popular in Pembrokeshire could be attributed mainly to the extrovert warmth and gaiety of Gareth Walker, whilst June's eye for control guaranteed the pub's profitability. Tragically, eight years ago, Gareth was drowned when his fishing launch capsized. Much shaken, June Walker persevered at the Red Dragon, but never with her previous enthusiasm.

Following the bereavement Davidson drove frequently to Tenby from his Southampton home, especially immediately after the event. As soon as he had exchanged the contract on the hotel, Davidson telephoned Mrs Walker to tell her the news. She was aware that he had been working on a major project, so was not totally surprised. However, she was much taken aback when he went on to offer her the post of manager. 'You have never been happy at the Red Dragon since Gareth died,' Davidson said, 'and you were never able to show your true potential there. This will be a fresh start for you.' Mrs Walker was not convinced. She said to Davidson 'At 48 I am not sure I want that sort of responsibility, especially not 250 miles away from all my friends – except you, of course!'

However, two weeks later, Mrs Walker was shown through the front door of the Southsea Castle Hotel by Jack Davidson and within two days she had decided – or been persuaded – to accept the job. The Victorian property had been bought as a going concern and most staff were staying on, but the general manager Karl Brucke, a 62-year-old Austrian with increasing asthma problems, had wished to retire soon anyway, so had offered to work on until a replacement could be found. This arrangement seemed fortuitous all round; certainly Mr Brucke's charming gentlemanly ways would have been at odds with Davidson's brash, aggressive style.

Davidson and Mrs Walker discussed at length the terms of reference of her position at the hotel. Eventually, it was decided that Mrs Walker would have full control of the day-to-day running of the hotel, but matters of major policy would be discussed and/or ratified by Jack Davidson prior to implementation. They also decided that Mrs Walker would purchase a 20 per cent share of the business, using most of the proceeds of the sale of the Red Dragon. Davidson suggested that Mrs Walker should spend a while with Mr Brucke 'learning the tricks of the trade', as he put it. A month later, Karl Brucke departed for Vienna and, with some trepidation, June Walker found herself manager of the Southsea Castle Hotel.

June Walker sat on her favourite stool at the end of the Forecastle Bar, and reflected that exactly six years had elapsed since she had 'taken the helm' of the hotel, and she was all too aware that events had not taken a totally satisfactory course. Over the years, the two bars had both been successful. The smaller bar, the Forecastle, was popular with local businesspeople and guests. The Poop Deck Bar which had introduced a rapid bar snack menu to capitalise on the opening of the D-Day museum was regularly busy dealing with holiday-makers, shoppers and local workers at lunch-time, and equally busy with a fairly young clientele in the evening. The bar staff were all part-time, mostly students and young married women, and she had retained personal control of this area in all respects.

By contrast, the restaurant was a nightmare for Mrs Walker. Seating 130 covers, the capacity was never fully utilised and on Monday nights in January it could be virtually deserted. The kitchen brigade was lead by Edward Mason, who had joined the hotel as sous chef from the Royal Navy 11 years ago. Mason was the longest-serving member of the kitchen brigade when, seven years later, the then head chef left. Mrs Walker immediately appointed Mason as head chef without advertising the post or soliciting any internal applications. Mason was pleased with his enhanced salary but within a month Mrs Walker began to have serious doubts about the wisdom of her decision.

The doubts began when a regular customer complained to the restaurant manager, Alfredo Riva, about the repetitive menu. Riva was a young Italian who had been recruited to the hotel five years ago when he was only 22 as a result of an impulsive offer of employment made by Jack Davidson. Davidson had been dining with friends in a very chic Italian restaurant in Mayfair where he was much impressed by young Riva's flair and expertise. Aware that Mrs Walker needed a new restaurant manager, and slightly the worse for drink, Davidson offered him the job, which shortly afterwards was accepted. Mrs Walker was not at all pleased with the way this matter had been handled, but she had no choice but to accept the situation. Now 27, Riva had married a local woman and had started a family, but considered himself – as he often said – 'too good for this place'. Riva had little respect for Mason and chose to communicate the customer's comment about the menu to Mason at a busy moment.

A major altercation ensued. Since then their relationship had been variable but never cordial. Mrs Walker at first attempted to improve the atmosphere across the hotplate, but soon gave up. Mason had a reputation with his staff for being dictatorial and inclined to brief obsessions. All food purchasing and receiving was the chef's responsibility, and wastage appeared to be increasing. He had two full-time assistant chefs (ex-RN colleagues) who had worked for him for some years. However, kitchen porters came and went with accelerating frequency, and Mason was constantly pleading lack of staff as a justification for any shortcomings in his department, especially the standard of cleanliness, which had given rise to a recent warning by an Environmental Health Officer.

Mason was constantly comparing his departmental staffing position with Riva's restaurant brigade. The restaurant brigade was largely made up of full-time staff. Few were locals and a large Victorian house which had been included in the hotel purchase provided staff accommodation. Some part-timers were used to bolster the staffing on Friday and Saturday evenings. Riva accepted that his team was not always fully utilised but he always insisted that he needed adequate cover to meet any demand, and with a little more advertising and better menus he thought the restaurant occupancy could be much improved. Riva had proposed that if it was necessary to reduce staffing he would have to move away from silver service and use family or plate service for lunch and dinner, and buffet service for breakfast. Predictably, Mason strongly opposed this view.

The relationship between Mason and Riva was, Mrs Walker thought, instrumental in the general low level of morale in food and beverage departments, especially the restaurant. Mrs Walker had heard from Vera Woodall, the head receptionist, that talk in the staff canteen frequently criticised the facilities provided for staff. The changing rooms, the staff accommodation, staff meals, the uniforms, the lack of any incentive bonuses and the amount of split-shift working were among a long list of topics that Miss Woodall reported.

Vera Woodall had joined the hotel as a school-leaver almost 30 years ago and had been head receptionist for the past 16 years. With an invalid mother to nurse, she had never married, and since her mother's death she had lived in a small terraced house within a short distance of the hotel. Mrs Walker and Miss Woodall had developed a mutual respect and Mrs Walker went to Miss Woodall's home increasingly frequently. As she once said, 'when you "live over the shop" you need to get away now and again'. Miss Woodall was a totally loyal member of staff – the hotel had become her whole life. She welcomed Mrs Walker's visits as she felt the loneliness of her home life and was flattered that Mrs Walker confided in her. Often Mrs Walker would bring a bottle of vodka with her and they would talk long into the night. Occasionally Mrs Emery, the housekeeper, would join them, but as she had two teenage children these visits were rare.

Miss Woodall's reception team consisted of three full-time receptionists and a cashier. All of them were trained to NVQ Level 2 Hotel Reception standard and Miss Woodall was very conscientious about their further development. However, reception had been the only bright spot in a gloomy report by a local training adviser, Chris Williams, on the current state of training in the hotel. The report had identified a lack of systematic training in most departments and had criticised specifically the arrangements for induction training. Williams had singled out Miss Woodall as a laudable 'natural' trainer, and suggested her skills might be developed by a programme of 'off-the-job' trainer skills courses. Mrs Walker saw the whole training issue as a problem of awe-inspiring proportions and decided that she would have to set aside a day to address the problem soon.

Vera Woodall had enjoyed her discussions with Chris Williams. She thought of herself as a lonely voice in the wilderness where staff training was concerned, and found Williams to be a kindred spirit. She had told Chris with total frankness that little was being done generally in the hotel regarding training and development because there was no one person responsible for personnel. She illustrated this by recalling an incident when a fire had broken out in the stillroom causing a major emergency because no staff on hand had any idea of how to handle the fire promptly and effectively.

Miss Woodall operated an advance reservation system using a conventional letting chart and hotel diary. Guest accounts were prepared on an ageing Sweda mechanical billing machine, and room status recorded on a bedsheet system. All room rates were on a bed-and-breakfast basis. Sometimes Miss Woodall wondered if the system could be considered adequate for a hotel with more than 100 rooms. At busy checkout times the pressure on front office staff could build to the point where tempers became frayed, and occasionally guests complained about the receptionists' attitude.

In the housekeeping department Mrs Emery had a team of 12 part-time room attendants who worked a variety of shifts. Most of the attendants were middle-aged married women and Mrs Emery attempted to cover the hotel's needs by a complex system of rostering geared to the domestic responsibilities of 'her ladies'. From time to time this arrangement broke down and levels of absenteeism were high. The attendants frequently complained to Mrs Emery that distribution of the workload was inequitable as each was expected to service a certain number of rooms regardless of whether they were single, double or family rooms, or suites. This was hardly fair when family rooms and suites were much larger and had, on average, three people using them. There were a total of 15 singles, 25 doubles, 65 family rooms and six suites so that the most common unit for an attendant to service was a family room.

Mrs Emery set her staff high standards, and frequently checked every let room herself. The standards of decor and furnishing were a constant worry to Mrs Emery. Guest complaints about the wear and tear became more frequent and she suspected than many more guests did not bother to complain but just did not return. The maintenance crew of two (an electrician and a general handyman), although nominally under her control, were kept constantly busy in the kitchen areas where the ageing equipment had become very unreliable. Since the warning from the Environmental Health Officer both maintenance staff had been working exclusively either in the kitchen areas or attending to the increasingly troublesome central heating boiler. Consequently they had been unable to devote any attention to the exterior of the building, which had begun to show signs of neglect, especially on the seaward side.

One of the issues troubling Mrs Walker had stemmed from a conversation with Jack Davidson which had occurred a few weeks previously. It had been a particularly busy morning and Mrs Walker had been searching for the P45 for a departing kitchen porter when Davidson entered her office. It seemed to her that every time he burst in unannounced like that he caught her at a disadvantage. This time she could conceal the fact that she had lost an important document, but there was no hiding the littered desk with today's mail dumped unopened on top.

As usual, Davidson came straight to the point. 'I don't care what you are doing,' he had said, 'sit down a minute and let's talk. What was the occupancy like last week?' Mrs Walker had replied, rather defensively, that she did not know exactly but that it had been a little disappointing. 'Disappointing!' Davidson retorted, 'it was awful! I've just got some figures from Vera and we're way down on last year. No wonder the bottom line has been a bad joke lately. We've got to do something about it and, much as it goes against the grain, this might just be it.' Davidson opened his briefcase and brandished a large envelope. He extracted an impressive dossier of information headed 'Celebrity Hotels Consortium', the first page of which read as follows:

The Celebrity Hotels Consortium
The Celebrity Hotels Consortium has been successful in establishing a group of well-known hotels throughout Britain. To realise its full potential, however, it needs a fuller range of accommodation in a number of gateway major cities and strategic touring areas and is seeking a mixture of the best in newly built hotels and older style traditional hotels.

The consortium has 165 member hotels in the United Kingdom with a total of 8300 bedrooms. In addition there are 2800 hotels in affiliated groups in 23 countries world-wide. 25 reservation offices in 16 countries handle the group sales.

The consortium offers its members a most comprehensive package of services in respect of Marketing and Sales, Purchasing and Training.

Regional structure
Every hotel within the Celebrity Hotels Consortium is a member of a region. There are eight in all and they meet on a regular basis to discuss, amongst other things, ways of promoting business

within the region, central office activities, local and national purchasing and training matters. Each region elects a member to Celebrity Hotels' four sub-committees – Marketing, Purchasing, Training and Finance and Administration – which meet regularly to discuss the day-to-day running of Celebrity Hotels affairs. The chairperson and vice chairperson of these four committees form the policy-making executive of Celebrity Hotels.

Cost of membership
The Consortium is financed by a combination of subscription and commission income. Subscriptions are based on the size of a hotel (i.e. the number of bedrooms) whilst commission is levied at a variable rate on business placed directly with a Member hotel. There is a once-only joining fee ranging from £450, dependent upon the size of hotel, which covers the provision of all purchasing back data, Membership plaque and brochure rack.

'Let's face it,' said Davidson, 'we have tried local and national press advertising, and we are in all the guide books that we can get in. It seems like an admission of defeat to join in with this consortium outfit, but perhaps we should give it a shot. There seem to be some good hotels tied into this already.' Mrs Walker scanned through the papers and said, 'Well, I think I will have to go through all this carefully, but my first reaction is that this is sure to cost us a lot of money and there is no guarantee we will get anything out of it. Yes, business has been poor lately, but give it time and we will recover.'

Privately, Mrs Walker had already decided that she would block this move if she possibly could. She perceived the proposal as a criticism of her management and was determined to prove that she could succeed without artificial external support. 'Look,' said Davidson, 'I don't like this consortium idea any more than you do, but I think we may not have any alternative. Don't forget, if this business folds up it's your money down the pan as well as mine.' Not for the first time, Mrs Walker saw red. 'Don't give me that old line again,' she exploded. 'You may have more money in this than me, but I'm the one who slogs away here night and day whilst you're swanning around in your Mercedes.' 'Steady, steady,' said Davidson, 'don't lose your temper. I have to go now – I am late for a meeting already – but let's talk about this again tomorrow.'

Mrs Walker, far from being pacified, was now thoroughly agitated and in a pugnacious mood. 'Tomorrow is Sunday,' she said through clenched teeth, 'and Sunday is my day off. I *always* have Sunday off, as you well know. I need a regular break from this place and if you think you can drag me in to discuss this nonsense tomorrow, you can think again.' At this point, Davidson snatched up his briefcase and left. Mrs Walker glanced at her wristwatch; she did not normally take alcohol before 1 a.m. but this was proving to be a particularly dreadful morning.

During the following week Davidson reappeared in the hotel, unannounced as always. Although they had not communicated since the consortium issue had been raised, neither Davidson nor Mrs Walker made any reference to the previous meeting.
Such events were not unusual. 'Before we start talking about the Consortium again,' said Davidson, 'there is another issue I want to talk about.'

Mrs Walker thought to herself 'Oh no! what now?' but she let Davidson continue. 'I want to talk about this wretched ornamental garden.' The ornamental garden in question was a large area of formal gardens which had originally been laid out when the hotel was built. It comprised a complex geometric pattern of gravel paths edged with low box hedges and many small lawned areas and flower-beds. The professional gardeners who maintained it were expensive and hardly any guests used it. As the garden was adjacent to the Poop Deck Bar, Davidson and Mrs Walker had thought about the possibility of extending the bar and dispensing with some part, if not all, of the garden. Pat Greensmith, a highly respected young architect, had surveyed the garden site with a view to making proposals for its development.

'This morning', said Davidson, 'I went to Greensmith's office to talk about the possibilities. We tossed a few ideas around then we hit on a real winner. We could turn the garden area into a leisure complex. We have sketched out the sort of layout that could be put together and it sounds really exciting. First of all, at basement level we would have a swimming pool, two saunas and changing facilities. On the ground floor there would be a fitness room with a "multigym", two squash courts and a reception area, on the first floor table-tennis and snooker tables and a solarium.' 'Sounds very exciting,' said Mrs Walker, 'and a lot of guests come up to me in the bar and ask if we have any of these kinds of facilities. It seems they are becoming expected, especially by our business clientele.' 'That's right,' Davidson went on. 'And we could easily make it a club and sell membership to local residents.'

Mrs Walker hesitated, 'Fine, but how do you envisage paying for all this?' 'Well,' said Davidson, 'I have enough money in gilt-edged securities to easily cover this sort of thing. Pat Greensmith says it would certainly cost less than a million, and that's no problem – I reckon I would easily see my money back. Pat is going to work flat out on an accurate costing and get back to me.'

In due course, Greensmith presented Davidson with an accurate breakdown of costs. The building would cost £600 000 and equipment and internal decor a further £250 000.

'This all appeals to me a good deal more than your Celebrity Hotels Scheme,' Mrs Walker observed. Davidson lit a cigar thoughtfully. 'OK,' he said, 'let's go down to the bar and look at that once again.'

This case study has been prepared jointly with, and from original material provided by, the author's colleague Gerry Banks, Highbury College, Portsmouth.

INTEGRATIVE CASE STUDY 2

Monarch Hotels

Monarch Hotels, formed shortly after the Second World War, consists of a small chain of 11 units, ranging from 67 to 145 rooms, owned on a freehold by S.W. Monarch Ltd, with a Head Office located in Harrington Gardens, London. The company has gone public although the Williams family retain a majority shareholding. The available accommodation is fairly equally split between London and the provinces.

All the units are of a three-star standard with three units providing bed and breakfast only. The hotels were mostly built during the Victorian period and have been maintained to a high internal standard featuring traditional decor and furnishings. Externally, the London units have benefited from an external repair and redecoration programme over the last two years whereas the other hotels are overdue for similar attention and in some cases have an untidy appearance.

The Monarch group has a policy of operating unlicensed, although not temperance, hotels. Guests are free to introduce their own liquor at no charge, the company providing the glasses, ice and a good range of mixers.

There are women managers in each of the London hotels, with men in all the provincial units. It is policy to promote from within the company wherever possible.

The maintenance of the hotels is controlled by the maintenance manager whose office and workshop/stores are located near the Head Office in London.

Head office management structure and profiles

The management structure is shown in Figure 12.4.

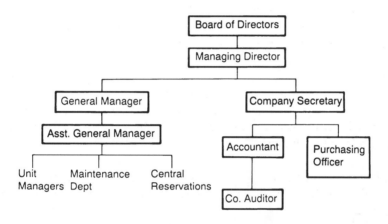

Fig 12.4 Head Office management structure, Monarch Hotels

Board of Directors
Chaired by Sir Geoffrey Albert, aged 78, who has extensive property interests and is a major shareholder in the company. There are six directors including a member of the Williams family. The Board meets monthly at the Head Office and the general manager and company secretary are invited to attend.

Managing Director
Andrew Henry, aged 70, who opted not to retire at 65. A protege of Mr Williams (the founder of the company), Mr Henry works on average three days per week and is still very much in charge of the operations. He was promoted from general manager ten years ago.

General Manager
Michael Egbert, aged 45, ex-Army Catering Corps, joined the company 12 years ago as assistant general manager, with no formal hotel training, and was promoted when Mr Henry took over as Managing Director. Responsible for day-to-day operations of the group with special responsibility for the property aspects of the units.

Assistant General Manager
Richard Noble, aged 30, responsible together with the general manager for day-to-day operations with specific responsibility for Central Reservations, Training and Sales. Mr Noble is an HND diplomate recently appointed from a large group-owned hotel in London.

Company Secretary
Lynn Walker was appointed to the post following the retirement of the previous secretary some 12 years ago, having held various posts within the company including accounts clerk and accountant. The company secretary is also responsible for Head Office clerical staff and personnel/disciplinary matters relating to all units.

Accountant
Stephen Edwards, aged 42, a chartered accountant, has been with the company for three years, having left his previous post working as an auditor for an international firm of chartered accountants. The accounts department employs five personnel covering all aspects including bought and sales ledgers, and wages and revenue control featuring mainly manual systems.

Auditor
Thomas James, aged 56, ex-CID. Mr James is authorised to make regular, sometimes unannounced, visits to any unit to establish the integrity of the various company records.

Purchasing Officer
Avril Frances, aged 52, is French by birth, and is responsible for all non-food purchasing for the group. In addition to her purchasing duties Mrs Frances organises the duty rosters for the main office.

Company management policy

It is company policy to exercise strict control over all unit activities. This is achieved by means of a very detailed and comprehensive operations manual issued to all managers, frequent visits by either Henry, Egbert or Noble, and regular returns which each manager must complete on a weekly basis. These returns are examined at the weekly executive meetings attended by the General Manager, the Assistant General Manager, the Company Secretary and the Accountant. Managers are actively encouraged to telephone the appropriate executive with any problems they may have. A very serious view is taken of any departure from company procedure as laid down in the operations manual, which also requires frequent referrals to Head Office in many day-to-day functions.

Communication – Head Office/units

There is an internal telephone system covering Head Office and the London hotels; other units rely on the normal telephone network or await the regular Head Office visit. There is a telex installed only at Head Office and which is used almost exclusively by the Central Reservations Office.

Central reservations office

Staffed by a supervisor and two clerks, the Central Reservations Office takes bookings from the various agents and operators with whom the company conducts business. Hotels are notified of bookings immediately by telephone, and this is followed up in due course with a booking slip. Availability details are phoned through from each hotel in the morning and again in the evening.

Business profile

The London hotels benefit mainly from tourists, in particular from the European and American markets, with a substantial number of business guests. Small conferences are catered for in London with larger events being held at the Marina Park, located at Weybridge. The provincial hotels maintain a significant following amongst the traditional domestic holidaymakers and have had some success in attracting their share of the business and conference trade in their particular areas.

In addition Monarch Hotels accommodate some 145 permanent residents. These are evenly spread throughout the Group with the exception of the bed-and-breakfast-only units.

Current situation

Andrew Henry has now decided to retire completely and the Board of Directors have appointed Christopher Charles in his place. Mr Charles was previously managing director of a small, fast-expanding chain of hotels in the Midlands and has secured an excellent remuneration package from S.W. Monarch Ltd. He has also gained approval from the majority of the Board of Directors to license some or all of the hotels and this has resulted in the resignation of Sir Geoffrey Albert. Mr Charles is keen to expand the company's London operations as soon as possible but the company policy is to be completely self-financing. Present thinking suggests that London expansion would therefore imply the disposal of other assets.

The Windsor Hotel

The Windsor Hotel is located in a prime seafront position. The site is absolutely central so far as the tourist traffic is concerned and the area is extremely busy throughout the summer months. The area is thronged with younger people in the evening due to the presence of two very popular nightspots. Off season, the area continues to attract visitors with its fruit machines, its popular bars and its ballroom dancing. There is another large hotel next door and the two, being rather similar, have traditionally been engaged in very keen competition. There are three other substantial hotels in the general seafront area. Other large hotels compete for the business and function trades within the conurbation.

Alec George, the hotel's general manager, is a 32-year-old hotel and catering graduate who joined the company four years ago, from Hilton Hotels, as assistant manager of the Elizabethan House Hotel. He proved to be extremely effective at the Elizabethan House and gained temporary promotion after a year to replace the hotel general manager who had gone into hospital for a back operation. The general manager resumed his position after a four-month absence and Mr George was very pleased to be offered the post of general manager of the Windsor. This was particularly attractive to him as his parents had owned a hotel close to the Windsor during his childhood and he had regarded the area as his home until they retired to Spain eight years ago.

When he joined the hotel Mr George was the seventh manager to be appointed in a ten-year period and feels now that he can quite understand why his predecessors tended to move on so swiftly. In his own case, however, he is trying very hard to establish himself in the local community and is quite determined to make his return home a permanent one. He married five years ago and has two small children. He has joined the local Round Table and has become treasurer of the local wine circle despite the fact that his spare time is very much limited. He is very pleased with the way his family and social life are developing and feels that they are now beginning to get on the right lines after all the years of a rootless, though pleasurable, existence as a rather nomadic hotel junior manager.

Life in the hotel, however, is not quite so satisfying, although there have been one or two brighter patches. George arrives at work from his new flat by 8.30 every morning and spends at least an hour checking yesterday's tabular ledger and the in-house guest accounts which have been updated and left ready by the night auditor. Usually by 9.30 or 10 o'clock he has completed the daily guest return for Head Office and this becomes the first item in the day's mail, which tends to occupy most of the rest of the morning.

The hotel secretary, Pat Norman, arrives for work at 9.00 each weekday morning and opens the mail. Each item is taken from its envelope and is put ready for Mr George's attention. When the daily guest return is finished Pat takes the mail and remains in the manager's office to take dictation. Almost invariably Pat also takes in the first of the day's 'open door' calls.

Mr George is convinced that one of his prime duties as general manager of the hotel is to be available to staff to help with their problems and so his 'open door' policy is given priority at all times. The aim is to demonstrate to the staff that the manager is supportive of their efforts and that any troubles are given due attention. It does seem, however, that some staff tend to over-use the open door and it certainly makes it difficult to get mail dealt with!

Processing of the day's mail is always completed before lunch is taken and George has been known to order sandwiches in his office so as to complete this task without leaving any matters outstanding. He feels very strongly that action should be initiated immediately to avoid piling up routine work and to ensure an image of efficiency with the hotel's outside contact. Incoming cheques are passed to reception for banking and invoices are cleared and dated for payment. Letters are dictated to prospective customers who may have sent a deposit or a request for a room.

Other mail is dealt with immediately if possible and out-going cheques are signed for despatch. The work is often interrupted by open door calls and incoming telephone enquiries but George makes it a golden rule never to leave his office before going to lunch at his table in the restaurant punctually at 1.30 p.m. unless he has sandwiches in the office. He believes that he should be available during the morning and that staff should be able to rely on him being at his desk if they need him.

George's afternoons are mainly devoted to keeping a very close eye on the hotel's day-to-day business. On Monday afternoon the weekend figures are co-ordinated, floats and cash drawers are checked and a banking is prepared in accordance with Head Office instructions. Tuesday afternoon and most Wednesday afternoons are spent in checking food stocks, and preparing the weekly Food and Beverage sales and costs report for Head Office.

On Thursday the hotel payroll is calculated and checked, and the midweek banking is put up. Mr George always goes to the bank just before 3.30 on Thursday afternoon to deposit midweek revenue and to draw out currency for making up the Friday pay packets. Friday and Saturday afternoons (Mr George tries to take Sunday off each week, although he is almost invariably called out) are devoted to making up the weekly summary for Head Office, to paying out wages and to catching up with the various unscheduled administrative tasks which have arisen during the week.

Evenings are Mr George's favourite times in the hotel. At this time the administrative staff have gone home and he is free to mingle with the guests in the restaurant and the lounge. George loves to play the part of host of the hotel for the evening business and makes a point of bringing his wife in to dine in the restaurant at least three times a week. His main regret is that the hotel, being part of the Monarch group, has no bar. He feels that this is a most severe limitation on the potential of the business.

The hotel's accommodation
The hotel has 96 letting bedrooms of which 28 are single and the remainder are rather large double or family rooms. All the rooms have private bathrooms. The hotel was once a four-star rating but five years ago was reduced to three-star. The bedrooms occupy the upper two floors of the four-storey building together with the front part of the first floor. The first-floor back is given up to storerooms and offices. The hotel's public rooms are all on the ground floor and there is a large, dry, full-width basement which is presently empty except for ladies' and gents' cloakrooms and a new sauna.

The interior condition of the hotel is quite good although some further redecoration is needed. There are no structural defects and rooms on the upper two floors have been repainted over the last two years. The public rooms on the ground floor are next in line for attention but Head Office has refused to authorise the work until the present round of company changes has settled down. The hotel's external condition is beginning to give cause for concern. The building is totally exposed to sea breezes and salt spray and Mr George had recommended exterior painting as urgent in his first report to Head Office, shortly after his appointment. External decoration, however, requires the written approval of the Board of Directors. This has not been forthcoming because, it was said, of the hotel's poor recent profit performance and the company's policy that all units must be self-financing.

The large car park behind the hotel is also in need of some repair. About half the area is now unusable in that the unpaved surface is rutted and often very muddy. There have been thefts from guests' cars during the evenings and overnight. Mr George did put forward a plan by which lighting would be provided, aggregate laid and the area fenced, but this was rejected. Sir Geoffrey Albert had pointed out that levels of business, though improving, were not yet such that the whole car park would normally be required and that thefts from cars could best be discouraged by the obvious presence of the police. The thefts were not, in any event, the responsibility of the company and so there was no reason why money should be spent on their prevention.

Food and Beverage operations
About half of the ground floor of the hotel is devoted to the food and beverage facilities. Both kitchen and restaurant had been run on a very traditional English resort pattern prior to the arrival of Mr George. As an immediate reaction Mr George began to plan the introduction of a Coffee Shop and opened negotiations with the head chef and the head waiter about fundamental changes to the dinner menus. Both these aspects of the business were cited in Mr George's first written report to Head Office as being in need of urgent attention if the decline of the hotel's occupancy (which had been a feature of the previous three years) was to be halted.

The Coffee Shop
The plan for the Coffee Shop was to take half of the restaurant space, put in generally bright furniture and decor and an exhibition kitchen, and fit large windows so that the whole scene would be attractively visible from outside. There would be an internal door to the hotel via the main restaurant and a street door for non-residents. The Coffee Shop was to be open from 7.30 a.m. until 5.00 p.m. and would cater for the service of breakfast both to guests and to passing trade, followed by morning coffee, light lunches and afternoon teas. The normal breakfast staff would run the Coffee Shop until 9.30 a.m., when a newly appointed manager and staff would take over for the rest of the day. Mr George's projections indicated that the initial investment would be recouped by increased business over a three-year period.

The reaction of the Board of Directors was only partly encouraging. They commended Mr George for his analysis of the situation and agreed that his recommendations would be likely to work out exactly as planned. They pointed out, however, that it had always been the policy of Monarch Hotels that each hotel should be self-sufficient and that all funds for investment should be generated internally. The general pattern of business at the Windsor had shown a decline over the past three years and the hotel simply did not have the funds for the proposal. What funds were available in the hotel had already been earmarked for redecoration of rooms on the upper two floors and this really had to go ahead since the first-floor rooms had already been done last year and the remainder must now be brought up to the same standard.

Having said all this, however, the Board did agree that their new manager deserved some encouragement and that the recent decline in business was hardly his fault. In a quite unprecedented move the Board agreed to release £30 000 from group reserve to fund a pilot project. The exhibition kitchen would have to be withdrawn and the size of the proposed Coffee Shop must be much reduced but a partition could be erected, some refurnishing could take place and decor and lighting could be provided. George duly set about replanning the facility along the lines specified and the Coffee Shop finally opened two years ago. It could not, of course, cope with the service of breakfast because of its smaller size and it did not look so attractive as the original scheme had envisaged, but it was open to both hotel and street, and business prospects seemed good.

The main restaurant

In the matter of the main restaurant, George found himself totally unable to initiate change. The restaurant and kitchen staff had been serving the same menus in the same way for a number of years. Apart from admitting that the room needed redecorating they could see no reason to modify their approach. They had a staunch ally in the Group general manager, whose influence at Head Office was entirely applied to the conservation of hotel standards and the maintenance of established practice in the provincial hotels.

George actually supported the inclusion of a full English breakfast in the guests' half board terms. He took the view that many holidaymakers really enjoyed a large and leisurely breakfast and that even for business people an unstinted service at this time of day was a major attraction. The dinner menus were, however, another matter. George felt that the traditional English dinner was no longer the unvarying attraction it may have once been (and privately doubted whether it had ever been really enjoyed). He had a very strong urge to change completely the menus, the timing and the service methods for the evening meal.

George felt he could do much better by changing the evening structure. He particularly pointed out the almost complete absence of chance guests in the evenings, despite the fact that the restaurant was open to the public and regular advertisements were placed in the local press. In fact, it was known that an increasing proportion of hotel guests chose to go elsewhere for their dinner even though they knew it had been included in their tariff. George argued that this could not possibly be good practice but he was told that there would always be a percentage of dissatisfied guests and that he should really be pleased because they were saving the hotel money by eating out.

Banqueting

The hotel had in the past been well known locally for its banqueting service even though there were no specific function rooms. The size of the main restaurant made partitioning quite possible and this was frequently employed. On occasions the residents' lounge could be used for functions, although lack of direct access to the kitchen made lounge operations a little more difficult .

Mr George sought to reverse a decline in the hotel's function trade. There seemed to him to be good potential in the area for this type of business although the hotel staff – in the form of the head chef and the head waiter – expressed the view that banqueting represented an unwarranted imposition on staff where the facilities were not really adequate. The Group general manager thought the current level of banqueting was high enough and so refused to approve the purchase of additional cutlery and crockery which would have been necessary to facilitate any expansion.

The situation therefore remained blocked until the local Round Table found themselves in dispute with the Sundrome Hotel, at which their monthly dinners were normally held. Mr George, a relatively new member of the Round Table, was asked whether the Windsor could take on the business and he duly passed the request to Head Office for approval. Somewhat to his surprise, the request was agreed on condition that the functions could be held in part of the main restaurant and that no purchases of equipment would be required beyond the necessary tableware.

The first function was held nine months ago. George personally designed the menu for the event and earned the sincere congratulations of his fellow Tablers for what they said was their best evening function for many years. The dinners have continued to be very well received each month with Mr George trying to offer something a little different each time, and undertaking personal supervision of the preparation and service of each meal. A number of Round Table members have asked Mr George about the possibility of holding other functions at the hotel. He remains convinced that a viable market opportunity exists in this field although Head Office will not allow him to pursue the matter at the present time.

Alcoholic beverages
Whilst the policy of Monarch Hotels has been to eschew the sale of liquor, the Windsor has an arrangement with a local publican who provides wine for sale in the restaurant and brings in a mobile bar for the various functions. Guests may take advantage of this provision or may, indeed, buy their own drinks outside and have the use of the hotel's glassware and other equipment. Similar arrangements to these are to be found in most of the hotels in the Group.

The new Group managing director has, however, persuaded the Board to revise the policy in respect of alcoholic beverages and it is expected that some hotels will be permitted to apply for liquor licences in the near future. Mr George is convinced that the Windsor could benefit in a number of ways by becoming licensed. He is very much hoping that it will be one of the hotels selected by Head Office for this development of the company's business.

The hotel staff

One of Mr George's principal objectives during his tenure as general manager of the Windsor has been to get staff costs down to an acceptable level. He believes that he has now done this and is very pleased that the reduction was managed completely without redundancies. In fact the main source of savings has been the non-replacement of part-time staff rather than any displacement of full-timers.

Mr George has total authority over his staff so long as he does not countermand the dictates of Head Office and he has always found this position of authority something of a problem. He has two general assistant managers, Jane Thomas and Christopher Deacon, who are both in their mid-twenties and who earn identical salaries with full live-in facilities. Both completed B/TEC National Diploma courses at the local college and Jane went on to take her HCIMA membership examinations. George finds the services of these two enthusiastic people quite invaluable in that they can both take over duties in any part of the hotel on either a supervisory or an operational basis.

The staffing of the hotel analysed by department is shown in Figure 12.5.

Mr George feels that the staff turnover at operative level is unacceptably high and that productivity in many areas is comparatively low because of poor training. He has strong views that although the company prominently displays a copy of the training policy on each staff notice board, this is not put into effect because of the lack of laid-down system. The company, he feels, pays only lip service to training. Mr George has made his views known to Mr Charles during a regular Head Office management visit.

	Full-time	Part-time	Full-time equivalent
Front Office/Porters	12	5	14
Admin.Offices	6	–	6
Housekeeping	2	9	6
Restaurant	4	6	7
Coffee Shop	2	–	2
Kitchen/Stores	10	–	10
Maintenance	1	–	1
			46

Fig 12.5 Staffing at the Windsor Hotel

There had been no formal employee relations policy within the Windsor Hotel to date. However, an incident had recently occurred following the appointment of Mr Dave Redman as a hall porter.

Early one Friday morning, Mr George's secretary informed him that Dave Redman wished to speak to him. An articulate man in his early twenties, Redman had joined the Windsor Hotel from a local competitor which is part of the Park Hotels (UK) Ltd, a nationwide chain of business hotels. Park Hotels recognises the HCWU (a section of the General, Municipal and Boilermakers' Union) and about 25 per cent of their staff are card-carrying members. Whilst he was with Park Hotels, Redman had joined the union and continued to subscribe to it after joining the Windsor. His interview at the Windsor had been a sketchy affair during which he had not been asked whether he had any union affiliations. It had not occurred to him to volunteer this information, nor to ask if any other staff were union members.

However, after he had settled into his new job, Redman began to enquire whether there were any other union members on the staff. Having asked the majority of the operative staff he had discovered that an elderly electrician on the Maintenance staff was the only one apart from himself. Consequently, Redman began to recruit members. He distributed leaflets printed by the HCWU which explained their policy, subscription rates, etc., in the staff restaurant, and spent a good deal of his time both on and off duty recommending that his colleagues should join .

His success had been limited to two chefs, two kitchen porters, one receptionist and one of his fellow porters. Some others had expressed interest, but failed to follow it up. Redman felt that he had recruited enough members to call himself a 'shop steward', and presented himself to Mr George as such when he called into the manager's office. George was astonished by this – he knew nothing of any trade union activity in the hotel, not even the electrician who had joined the EETPU at 15!

The main thrust of Redman's discussion with Mr George was to request approval to call a Union Meeting at 3.00 p.m. on the following Wednesday. Redman said that he felt it necessary to deal with various matters and presented a rough draft of an agenda as follows:

1. Formal inauguration of the Windsor Branch of the HCWU.
2. Introduction of Mr Percy Billington, District Officer HCWU.
3. Election of Shop Steward (nominated so far: D. Redman).
4. Wage negotiations.
5. Staff canteen facilities.
6. Overtime and rostering.
7. A.O.B.

Redman commented that items 4, 5 and 6 were included because there was much dis-satisfaction within the staff on these matters and he felt that industrial action 'was by no means out of the question'. The 'request' for the meeting was expressed in the tone of a demand, and Redman stated that he expected the democratically elected shop steward to be consulted in future about any decision which would materially affect union mem-bers. Mr George, considerably bewildered, invented a pressing engagement, and excused himself after assuring Redman that he would notify him of his decision.

Future prospects

Despite improvements in performance over the past three years, the future of the Windsor Hotel is uncertain.

There are significant changes taking place in the Monarch Group and the advent of Mr Charles, the new Group Managing Director, gives particular cause for concern. Mr Charles has already said that the Group seems to be rather widely dispersed and he is known to favour the development of the London hotels at the expense of those outside the capital. He may even, it is rumoured, support the disposal of some or all of the provincial hotels as a means of financing the refurbishment of the London units and there is believed to be substantial support on the Board for the adoption of this strategy.

Mr George, on the other hand, feels that his work at the Windsor is beginning to pay dividends and that the hotel is now being operated efficiently within the constraints imposed by Head Office. Last year's profit represented an adequate, if not generous, return on capital. Profit figures could be much improved, he believed, if opportunities to increase sales were firmly and courageously grasped and if some funds, though not an excessive amount, were available for investment in the business.

The local authority has recently taken a new initiative in marketing the area as a tourist resort and in developing industrial and commercial activities. All parties involved fully realise that the Windsor would benefit greatly from any resultant increase in visi-tor traffic. Mr George, who makes a point of keeping very much in touch with local events, believes that a substantial increase may indeed arise in the very near future.

This case study has been prepared jointly with, and from original material provided by, the author's colleague Martin Brunner, Highbury College, Portsmouth.

NOTES AND REFERENCES

1. Handy C B, *Understanding Organisations*, Fourth edition, Penguin (1993).
2. Peters T J and Waterman R H, *In Search of Excellence*, Harper & Row (1982).
3. See, for example, Lammermeyr H U, 'Human Relationships – The Key to Total Quality Management', *Total Quality Management*, vol. 12, no. 2, 1991, pp. 175–180.
4. For an account of the application of total quality management in Scott's Hotels Ltd, see Hubrecht J and Teare R, 'A Strategy for partnership in Total Quality Service', *International Journal of Contemporary Hospitality Management*, vol. 5, no. 3, pp. i–v.
5. See, for example, Smircich L, 'Concepts of Culture and Organisational Analysis', *Administrative Science Quarterly*, vol. 28, 1963, pp. 339–58.
6. Mclean A and Marshall J, *Intervening in Cultures*, Working Paper, University of Bath (1983).
7. See, for example, Handy C B, *Understanding Organisations*, Fourth edition, Penguin (1993); and Mclean A and Marshall J, *Cultures at Work*, Local Government Training Board (October 1988).
8. Peters T J and Waterman R H, *In Search of Excellence*, Harper & Row (1982) pp. 75–76.
9. See, for example, Venison P, *Managing Hotels*, Heinemann (1983).
10. Glover W G, 'The Cult of Ineffectiveness', *Cornell HRA Quarterly*, February 1987, reprinted in Rutherford D G (ed), *Hotel Management and Operations*, Van Nostrand Reinhold (1990) pp. 29–33.
11. Mullins L J, Meudell K and Scott H, 'Developing Culture in Short-Life organisations', *International Journal of Contemporary Hospitality Management*, vol. 5, no. 4, 1993, pp. 15–19.
12. See, for example, Hornsey T and Dann D, Manpower *Management in the Hotel and Catering Industry*, Batsford (1984). Also Mullins L J, 'The Hotel and the Open Systems Model of Organisational Analysis,' *The Service Industries Journal*, vol. 13, no. 1, 1993, pp. 1–16.
13. Hellriegel D, Slocum J W and Woodman R W, *Organizational Behavior*, Sixth edition, West Publishing (1992).
14. For a more detailed account, see Mullins L J, 'Information Technology – The Human Factor', *Administrator*, vol. 5, no. 8, September 1985, pp. 6–9.
15. *Meeting Competence Needs in the Hotel and Catering Industry: Now and in the Future*, HCTC Research Report, September 1992.
16. *Costs and Manpower Productivity in UK Hotels*, National Economic Development Council, 1992.
17. McLaughlin C P and Coffey S, 'Measuring Productivity in Services', *International Journal of Service Industry Management*, vol. 1, no. 1, 1990, pp. 46–64.
18. Lane P, Ingold T and Yeoman I, 'Productivity in Hotels', *proceedings of CHME Research Conference*, Manchester Metropolitan University, April 1993.
19. Tagiuri R and Litwin G H (eds), *Organizational Climate*, Graduate School of Business Administration, Harvard University (1968).
20. Jones P and Lockwood A, *The Management of Hotel Operations*, Cassell (1989), p. 59.
21. Mill R C, *Managing for Productivity in the Hospitality Industry*, Van Nostrand Reinhold (1989).
22. Wood R C, *Working in Hotels and Catering*, Routledge (1992).
23. Riley M, *Human Resource management: A guide to personnel practice in the hotel and catering industry*, Butterworth-Heinemann (1991).
24. Handy C B, *Understanding Organizations*, Fourth edition, Penguin (1993).
25. See, for example, Townsend R, *Further Up the Organisation*, Coronet Books (1985).
26. Salaman G, *Class and Corporation*, Fontana (1981).
27. For example, see Drucker P F, *The Practice of Management*, Pan Books (1968).
28. See, for example, Horwitz F M, 'HRM: An Ideological Perspective', *International Journal of Manpower*, vol. 12, no. 6, 1991, pp. 4–9.
29. Fox A, *Industrial Society and Industrial Relations*, HMSO (1966).
30. *Employee Relations for the Hotel and Catering Industry*, Seventh edition, HCTC (1990), p. 21.

ASSIGNMENT ANALYSIS SHEETS

Management teams: A self-perception inventory (Assignment 3)

Interpretation of total scores and further notes

The highest score on team role will indicate how best the respondent can make his or her mark in a management team. The next highest scores can denote back-up team roles towards which the individual should shift if for some reason there is less group need for a primary team role.

The two lowest scores in team role imply possible areas of weakness. But rather than attempting to reform in this area the manager may be better advised to seek a colleague with complementary strengths.

Self-perception inventory analysis sheet

Transpose the scores taken from the table in Figure 9.11, entering them section by section in Figure 9.11A. Then add up the points in each column to give a total team role distribution score.

Section		CW		CH		SH		PL		RI		ME		TW		CF
I	g		d		f		c		a		h		b		e	
II	a		b		e		g		c		d		f		h	
III	h		a		c		d		f		g		e		b	
IV	d		h		b		e		g		c		a		f	
V	b		f		d		h		e		a		c		g	
VI	f		c		g		a		h		e		b		d	
VII	e		g		a		f		d		b		h		c	
TOTAL																

Fig 9.11A Self-perception inventory analysis sheet
Source: Belbin R M, *Management Teams: Why They Succeed or Fail*, Butterworth-Heineman (1981), pp. 156–7.

CHAPTER 10: MANAGERIAL LEADERSHIP

Leadership questionnaire (Assignment 3)

Interpretation: T-P leadership style profile sheet

To determine your style of leadership, mark your score on the **concern for task dimension** (T) on the left-hand arrow in Figure 10.10A.

Next, move to the right-hand arrow and mark your score on the **concern for people dimension**(P).

Draw a straight line that intersects the P and T scores. The point at which that line crosses the **shared leadership** arrow indicates your score on that dimension.

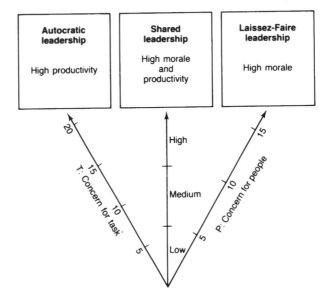

Fig 10.10A Shared leadership results from balancing concern for task and concern for people
Source: Pfeiffer J W and Jones J E (eds), *A Handbook of Structured Experiences for Human Relations Training*, vol. 1, San Diego, CA, Pfeiffer & Co (1974), p. 12. Reprinted with permission of American Educational Research Association.

INDEX

HOSPITALITY MANAGEMENT
A human resources approach